Origin of Mime and Dance

Mikhail Berkut

Origin of Mime and Dance

The phylogenetic transformation of natural everyday movements, gestures and mimicry into the motions of body language and the performing arts.

Part I

NATURAL MOTION

The Genesis of Communication

Origins of Mimetic Culture

Part II:

ARTIFICIAL MOTION

Sacred Ceremonies and Secular Events

Ritual Dance as a Key Social Activity

Vanguard Press

VANGUARD PRESS

A CIP catalogue record for this title is
available from the British Library.

ISBN 978-1-784656-11-9

*Vanguard Press is an imprint of
Pegasus Elliot MacKenzie Publishers Ltd.*

www.pegasuspublishers.com

First Published in 2019

**Vanguard Press
Sheraton House Castle Park
Cambridge England**

Printed & Bound in Great Britain

DEDICATION

To my unforgettable teachers,
who passed to me, so generously,
the baton of research and creativity.

Contents

Chapter IV: RITUAL DANCE AS A KEY SOCIAL ACTIVITY 317

LIST OF CHARTS/ILLUSTRATIONS

Preface

A vast body of literature has accumulated on the subject of motion in its many forms, from the movement of inanimate elements like water and fire to the motions of animals and plants or movement within the universe itself. The nature and function of movement is studied in fields as diverse as mechanics, mathematics, particle physics and astronomy.

Here, we restrict ourselves to exploring the motion of the human body, and its gradual evolution from instinct to artifice – the long journey from *unconscious* reflex to *self-conscious* performance.

Any musculo-skeletal movement is generally the result of some physiological signal - a neural response to a particular circumstance, irritant or stimulation. In nonverbal communication, this mechanism can be triggered either by reflex or a conscious mental decision.

Although there are many theories about spoken language and human plasticity, many fundamental questions remain unanswered:

- What were the anthropological origins of human communication, and when?
- What were the earliest systems of plastic motion communication?
- What are the essential differences between the ways in which the communication systems of hominids, apes and other primates evolved?
- What impels plastic motion in the human body, and how does it function in everyday life?
- How do humans control these everyday motions in artistic performance?
- How are *natural* actions transmuted into *artificial* ones – and what are the differences between the two?
- What inspires people to perform often dangerous tricks in sport, dance, circus and other entertainments?
- Why do the same motions in dance or sport, with identical choreography and conditions, look so different when performed on stage?
- What sets a competition winner apart from other competitors of basically identical age, weight, physical structure, and sometimes even instruction?
- From where do choreographers get the new steps and tricks they devise for their compositions, and how are these applied artistically for the stage?
- What determines the best visual and expressive effect of performed motion sequences?
- How do great artists manage to depict movements and gestures more expressively than others? What technical and artistic criteria apply, and how subjective are they?

Naively, it used to be thought that sporting or performing stars were born with special attributes. We now know that this is not the case – excellence, even in somebody with average physical and mental abilities, depends much more on individual character, along with methods of tuition and the calibre of the instructor.

The instructor therefore has to know the personal characteristics of each pupil, and to be competent not only in the required professional skills, but also in anatomy, biology and medical treatment as well as the principles of self-control, balance, coordination, artistry and so on.

When trainers and teachers prepare their own choreography, they deepen their knowledge of the nature of motion and gesture and their understanding of the plastic harmony of kinetics, amplitude, dynamics, extension and other ways of achieving highly technical feats of artistic expression. They also have to study the aesthetics of transforming everyday *movements* into performed *motions*, along with the methods and technologies of stage composition, and the constant search for new *steps*, *sequences* and *tricks*. Without this knowledge, the result is invariably discord and disappointment. Competitors or performers risk losing their opportunity to excel, or worse still, injury.

This study is not intended to give complete answers to every question on the subject, but to clarify some basic principles regarding the anthropology and evolution of **natural** motion and its transformation into **performed** compositions. In the process, we hope to open up new ways of looking at these issues for others to explore further.

Prologue

In this study, the term **movement** is used in the general sense to describe the musculo-skeletal act of shifting the body, or part of it, in space and time. By contrast, **motion** is *movement* that is *consciously* motivated by certain objectives, thoughts or feelings. The difference between the two is discussed in more detail later.

Developmentally, the earliest manifestation of *movement* in humans and other mammals occurs as a foetus in the womb, when the parental genes combine to build the foundation for future patterns of motion. The genetic mix decides which parent's potential eventually dominates in respect of the new-born's plastic and emotional functions.

The fundamental characteristics of an individual's *movement* remain essentially the same throughout life. It is of course possible to develop the body's physical capabilities – but its basic structure and the individual's emotional temperament cannot be changed without artificial intervention. People's motion characteristics are therefore as individual as their personalities, which accounts for the rich diversity of human *movement*, both in everyday life and in performance.

Thanks to their intellectual abilities, hominids are the only species who learn from other animals – hunting techniques from wolves or big cats, defensive strategies from zebras, elephants or bison, fishing skills from bears and birds. This, together with their increased range of plastic motion facilities, has helped to secure the species' dominance of the planet.

Hominids identified themselves with the natural world by assuming the names of living creatures or the elements of their environment. The totem after which a youngster was named during ritual initiations was chosen to reflect the individual's personality, temperament and motion characteristics.

The living environment provided our ancestors with a vast amount of visual and practical information. As they gradually formed social structures and belief systems, the plastic style and character of their movements evolved in parallel with their social and cultural activities. Throughout the long progression from primitive communal groupings to the nation states of today, humans, like every other species, have constantly competed and fought for their place in the life on the planet.

Through the exertions of hunting, fishing, gathering food, building shelters and enclosures, hominids gradually improved the physical apparatus of their body and extended its repertoire of instinctive motions. In the harsh world where only the strongest could overcome the countless challenges of daily survival, these improvements in dexterity, reaction times, motor coordination and bravery could make the difference between life and death. The merciless process of natural selection thus impinged directly on the evolution of plastic abilities.

As sentient creatures, early hominids no doubt tried to understand why hunting or fishing went well one day and not the next. Why did they conquer one enemy, but suffer defeat at the hands of another? What guiding force determined these victories or defeats?

Our ancestors' inability to analyse such phenomena in their own terms left a void of incomprehension that was filled by creating deities to whom responsibility for life events could be ascribed. Reassuringly omnipotent, a higher being (or beings) could also be called upon to intercede in the solution of virtually any problem.

However, a direct link with these unknowable supernatural forces was required. This link took the form of the magic shaman, endowed with mystical powers to mediate between the worshippers and the deity. By combining the secret lexicon of special symbolic motions used for communicating with the gods with the plastic vocabulary of familiar *movements* imitating animals, shamans wielded complete emotional and spiritual control over their audiences. As a true show, this was the genesis of artificial modes of plastic communication.

Whether the 'dialogue' with the deity consisted of appeals for blessing or prohibition, forgiveness or punishment, support or revenge, the shaman was a potent figure within the community – simultaneously a psychologist, doctor, choreographer, producer, artist and performer. The shaman was custodian of all the secret routines of the mystic show which, from generation to generation, developed into a complete system for controlling all the tribe's vital activities as well as the power of the chief.

As the shaman's plastic lexicon gradually became richer and broader, the magic cult evolved into a mass ritual. In addition to the motion repertoire, participants began *singing* and making *rhythmic sounds* using shells, horns, bones and hooves as instruments. Others danced the shaman's choreographic routines clad in animal pelts. Children, older people and remaining members of the tribe watched these well-prepared and highly effective rituals in awe of the unknown, or in anticipation of divine judgement. In a primitive form, these were genuine 'theatrical' performances.

Traditional rituals of the Hunt, Battle, Harvest and Fertility, together with rites of passage such as Birth, Puberty and Death were central to the social and cultural life of the tribe, and during the matriarchal period, gave rise to separate dance compositions for women. They also developed plastic abilities and engendered respect for those who could *move* gracefully in their everyday functions, or could dance well in shows. Although the *steps* and *gestures* used in these dances were of course very simple, they were technically clear and emotionally powerful.

Ancient rock paintings depict dances by women *holding* hands and *moving* in a circle with synchronised *steps*, as some communities still do today. These dances cannot however be described as artistic performances. Although both dances by women and male pantomimes in Palaeolithic times played an important role in traditional magic shows and performances that mythologised the story of the tribe, they were essentially just enacting parts of the ritual.

Many archaeologists suggest that these primitive performances predate Homo Sapiens by 200,000 years, to the era when man was first beginning to communicate through spoken sounds. Neanderthal man started making images on rock – all the way back to the origins of Homo Erectus, which the latest estimates place at around 2.5 million years ago. All the evidence points to the fact that systems of bodily communication have been in use for a very long time to bind together tribal groups through the social and cultural activities that were intrinsic to the everyday fight for survival. The language of plastic body motions, accompanied by rudimentary vocalisations, was the only available means of social intercourse for much of our early history.

But where did this language come from? How was it learned? What kind of a system was it? Who controlled the vocabulary? Did different tribes use different motion 'dictionaries'? What part was played by the voice and rhythmic noises?

For the answers, we must turn to archaeological findings, current research and the rich heritage of illustrative material in the form of rock drawings and paintings, votive figurines, vessels, sculptures and other artefacts. For the purposes of analysis, it is useful to divide the evolution of human plastic abilities into two major areas:

1. Natural motion – natural body motion communications including mimicry and the *grimaces, gestures, postures* and *steps* of everyday domestic life.

2. Artificial motion – the same motions when stylised for the purposes of sacred ceremonies and secular performance.

There are basically five categories of motion response:

1. *Instinctive/reflex* motion in response to external irritants
2. *Volitional* motion in response to external stimulus
3. Motion motivated by *subconscious* impulses
4. *Volitional* motion for *communication*
5. *Conscious* imitation of *instinctive* motion

Each of these categories encompasses only a small part of the otherwise unlimited body motion vocabulary, and the following short-hand notation is used to describe each motion element:

Abbreviations:

R – right, L – left, C – communication, B – body, M – male, F – female
Symbols:

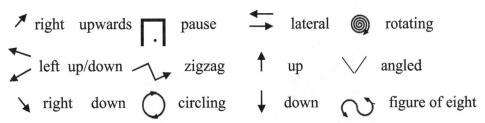

Generally speaking, any plastic motion of animals to some extent combines both **Functional** and **Performance** behaviours. By Functional, we mean everyday Instinctive/Unconscious vital activities such as *eating, drinking, mating, nursing, walking, running, burrowing, climbing, descending, hanging, gliding, swimming, diving, washing, preening* and so on. When the same repertoire involves the Conscious use of tools, they are described as **Semi-Functional**.

Performance involves Conscious, artificial, stylised actions mimicking images and occurrences in ritual pantomimes; **Semi-Performance** refers to a subconscious motion repertoire of natural *poses* and *gestures* for communication, courtship and ceremonial rites, secular contests and social dancing events. Hominids used this plastic language specifically for and about themselves.

PART ONE

NATURAL MOTION

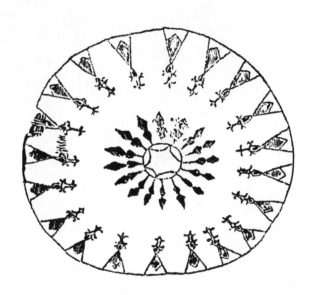

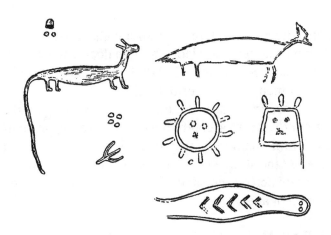

Chapter 1: The Genesis of Communication

Anthropology and evolution

THE PHYLOGENESIS OF HOMINID SPECIES

Six or seven million years ago, the ape **Australopithecus Afarensis** underwent a radical change in posture, from quadruped to biped. Gradually, a hitherto essential part of its physique – the tail – lost its utility, and consequently atrophied away over thousands of generations.

The approximately twenty-million-year transition from the Great Apes to hominid species is thought to have begun in the Miocene period and been completed in the Pleiocene with the arrival of **Australopithecus Africanus**, the next rung on the human evolutionary ladder.

In the millions of years that followed, the anatomy, constitution and plastic capabilities of the Pleistocene hominid advanced enormously. Differing from their quadruped forebears not only physiologically but also mentally and socially, they could *run* and *walk* on two legs, leaving the arms free to acquire new functions in the daily struggle for survival.

This was **Homo Habilis**, the most intelligent member of the ape family. Apart from having more highly developed upper extremities, they fought, hunted and bred much like the other animals around them between three and five million years ago.

Around 2–3 million years ago, a new species emerged: **Homo Erectus**. *Walking* upright as the name suggests, this ancestor learned how to use sticks and stones for attack or defence. They built shelters and learned how to make and safeguard fire. Between 900,000 and 400,000 years ago, more advanced tool-using hominids like **Homo Heidelbergensis** had evolved.

Nevertheless, the problem of inter-tribal communication remained. Although their relatively high intelligence gave them a unique advantage in the animal kingdom, these ancestors of ours had to muster all their intellectual resources in pursuit of sufficient food and shelter and the protection of their families and communities. Seeing what happened to their weaker and slower peers, they realised that they had to *run* faster to catch animals or escape attackers. They knew that the stronger the arm and the more accurate the eye, the greater the chance of killing prey with a spear.

Right from the start, the need for these qualities was informed by the animal instinct for survival. Then, by memorising the lessons of experience, the new man-like creature gradually began to apply this information on different occasions and in different circumstances. Little by little (and to a certain extent, collectively), individuals made the abstract connection between cause and effect, and used this knowledge to help decide the next course of action.

Neanderthals appeared between 200,000–400,000 years ago, a true human species able to think and act on the basis of memorised information.

In a limited Pavlovian sense, practically all animals can do this - but the difference is that all other species do so *instinctively*, as a conditioned reflex response (partly genetic, partly acquired by copying adults) to a positive or negative stimulus. A gazelle calf, for example, will *stand* unaided and *seek out* the source of its mother's milk within minutes of birth. Turtle hatchlings can immediately *run* across the sand to the ocean. Most living creatures are pre-programmed in this way – except apes.

INFANT DEVELOPMENT AS AN EVOLUTIONARY ANALOGY

Hominid infants are incapable of independent action at birth because their physiological structure and neurological systems are so much more advanced and complex that the nine-month gestation period cannot accommodate the degree of development required.

The human foetus has been filmed in all stages of its development, from fertilisation to parturition. Astonishingly, it develops through stages that are closely analogous to the evolution of life on this planet from the aquatic stage onwards, as if millions of years were condensed into nine months.

As far as the evolution of plastic motion abilities is concerned, the same principle can be applied to the development of human infants from birth to three years old, by which time the essentials are in place.

A new-born child lies helplessly on its back, convulsively *twitching* its head, arms and legs as it squeals helplessly for milk until its open mouth is physically guided to the mother's breast. The baby immediately stops *moving* its head, but continues *moving* its arms and legs in a different motion, gently *touching* the mother's body to confirm that the milk is still there. Its limited capabilities are in stark contrast to those of the turtle.

During the first week or so, the baby's vision is still very poor, but it already recognises the voice and smell of its mother, towards whom it constantly tries to *turn*. When vision improves and the baby can see a colourful world around, the attraction is so strong that its scope for plastic motion increases tremendously. Curious, it *turns* it head from side to side as it learns the colours of its surroundings. The baby still *moves* both upper and lower extremities involuntarily in a chaotic motion as well as occasionally *stretching* them to reach an object or *sucking* its fingers or toes in the expectation of milk.

By the time the baby can sit unaided, it is able to play with objects, consciously *moving* its arms from the fingers to the shoulders in a much more intensive way. It can use its feet to *manipulate* objects, or to *squeeze* the mother's finger with its toes as infant apes do when *hauling* themselves onto their mother's back.

At the *crawling* stage, the human infant tries to work out its balance and coordination, and can *raise* its head at will to see the world around. Its whole body is now developing rapidly. Though it cannot yet talk, it can *point* to objects of interest and in the direction it wants to take – a similar gestural language to that used by Mesolithic hominids thousands of years ago.

Complete mental control is still a long way off. Around one year of age, the infant changes its spatial orientation from horizontal to vertical when it starts *walking* instead of *crawling* on all fours. Like our first bipedal ancestors, it now sees the world from a different angle, and can reach many things it could not before. The infant quickly learns how to *climb*, *jump* and *move* things around, how to extend its reach by *standing* on tiptoe, how to *bend* both knees quickly to cushion a fall. It learns how to open and shut doors and to interact physically with its domestic environment.

In this way, many of the characteristic skills of each phase of hominid evolution can be recognised in the three years of development from a helpless baby to a self-sufficient toddler. By this stage, most of the infant's physiological and neuro-plastic development is complete.

From now on, the child's future depends mainly on personal qualities resulting from its genetic inheritance and those acquired during its short life. Thereafter, it learns most of its plastic vocabulary by natural instinct and by mechanically *copying* the *movements* of those around it. A toddler seeing a sibling eat an apple will immediately try and do the same thing with a ball if there's one within reach.

Similar actions are observed in the routine family communications of apes. Although selected, adapted and improved over the generations, these remain merely natural motions, strictly Instinctive by nature and unrelated to the intellect.

Intellect only starts playing a part with the acquisition of speech. This is the real turning point in the psycho-physical evolution of the species, just as it is in the development of the child. It is analogous to the Neanderthal era from which the first cave paintings date.

But what drove them to produce these graphic representations? And is it art? For an answer, we must turn to our direct ancestor, **Homo Sapiens**, who appeared some 350,000 years ago and subsequently evolved into modern man, **Homo Sapiens Sapiens**.

SOCIOCULTURAL SIMILARITIES AND DIFFERENCES

At first glance, it seems strange that different peoples of the later Palaeolithic times, with different histories, living far apart from each other, should use the same subject matter, but portray different action and styles.

Many theories of the social and cultural evolution of early communities have been advanced over the centuries, some based on the cosmological or religious factors that can be deduced from the archaeological record, others preferring the methods of dialectical materialism. Despite these profound differences of approach, most come to the same conclusion: that plastic language was the prime form of communication before the spoken word.

Although we are not talking in this instance about the everyday bodily motions, physical movements and vocalisations used while hunting, fishing, making fire, cooking, eating or the many other natural actions that we ourselves perform in the same way today, these must be kept in mind when interpreting the visual archaeological information on which our analysis is based.

The prelude to hominid evolution

THE THREE EVOLUTIONARY STIMULI: SOCIALISATION, WORK AND INTELLIGENCE

Prehistoric man needed the combined strength of the tribal or extended family group in order to survive in a hostile environment. Over time, this instinct to **socialise** in communities, however small, became a psychological necessity.

Work, fighting, celebration and commiseration became essentially communal activities. Unlike the Great Apes, the primitive human societies of the Mesolithic and post-Palaeolithic periods after the Ice Age nevertheless developed effective methods of inter-tribal communication and a comparatively high standard of cultural activities.

Hominids were forced to work for most daylight hours, day in day out, in order to survive – and it can be argued that work is a quintessentially human activity. But what about animals, who also work hard to find food and water, to raise their young, and so on?

These impulses are among the many standard behaviours genetically pre-programmes before birth, and are not 'work' in the modern sense. By **work**, we mean a pre-planned, organised process of regular actions necessary for survival, and which are acquired in life by each new generation rather than naturally instinctive. Kangaroos eat plants, but can't grow them. Bears fish, but can't cook. Big cats look after their offspring (sometimes more diligently than their human counterparts), but are hopeless at making clothes. By contrast, our precursors the Great Apes knew how to use primitive tools.

The third and most important characteristic of humans was their unique ability to **think analytically**. These three major characteristics – socialisation, work and intelligence – are at the root of human physiological and psychological evolution.

Both archaeology and the study of the few remaining primitive societies confirm profound socio-cultural similarities between peoples all over the world. The fact that body language evolved in almost identical ways on all five continents testifies to the common humanity of the communities in question, and the central role of plastic motion in what it is to be human.

ENVIRONMENTAL EFFECTS ON HOMINID EVOLUTION

Geographical and environment factors vary, but the laws of nature are the same everywhere, so it is unsurprising that ancient peoples should develop so many characteristic traits in common. Though local circumstances no doubt influenced specific adaptations of hominids along with all living creatures, their physical and psychological make-up was essentially very similar, as were their behaviours. Naturally, they communicated in similar ways, at least as far as vital daily functions were concerned.

Take the indigenous peoples of North America, for example. Those living in the northern climate of what is now Canada, looked different from those in the warmth of what is now Mexico. Although little remains of their respective original traditions, these two peoples differ clearly in their anatomy and plastic motion characteristics.

The former are generally taller and slimmer, with longer extremities. They *move* gracefully – almost in slow motion – and seem temperamentally placid. By contrast, the southern tribes tend to have shorter and heavier bodies, with sharper *movements* and more volatile temperaments. The spiritual customs and traditions of both peoples, however, have identical roots.

The Northern Inuit and Southern Buryat peoples I studied in Siberia, demonstrate how geographical factors can also affect styles of work and cultural activity. Although the ancient customs and practices of both groups were better preserved than those of their Amerindian counterparts, different climatic and environmental conditions had left their mark on the plastic vocabularies and social activities of these similar looking peoples.

All aspects of Inuit life are connected to, and depend on, the Arctic ocean – hunting polar bears and seals for their food, clothing, shelter, weapons and tools. Very heavy clothes made from bear or reindeer skins hamper the movements of arms and legs; although excellent hunters, their plastic dictionary for social and communication purposes was therefore relatively limited.

The Buryats of southern Siberia had a culturally richer evolutionary history in that their exceptionally religious community preserved a belief in spiritual interaction with the mountains around them. Traditional social and cultural activities were well preserved, as if in a living museum. Though not particularly advanced, their plastic abilities were more highly developed than those of their northern counterparts. Since the deer, boar and goats that Buryats hunt require considerable skill, strength and co-operation to catch and subdue, their arms and legs tend to be stronger and better developed.

There is anthropological evidence for similar disparities in plastic anatomy between the early European Scythian and the Asian Mongol peoples, for example, or between African Bushmen and Australian Aborigines. However, the petroglyphic record points to far more similarities between these disparate societies than differences; their common humanity massively outweighs local environmental variations.

The physiology of Homo Sapiens was partly conditioned by geographical factors: survival in snow-capped mountains requires different capabilities than making a living from the sea or inhabiting a jungle or desert environment. These local factors influenced perceptions of the relationship between hominid communities and the elements, the living world and each other.

PRIMORDIAL PLASTIC MOTION VOCABULARIES

Tribal groupings formed at different times in different parts of the planet.

Although the original hominids are often assumed to have migrated out of Africa across Europe, then to Australia and later to the Americas that during the Palaeolithic era, they all passed through the same process of physiological and plastic evolution. The language of body motion was then the only way for any group to unite all its members, communicate and survive, until Homo Sapiens developed new forms of communication with paintings on cave walls.

In the interim, the prehistoric plastic language dictionary was based primarily on *grimaces, gestures, postural signals* and *movements* of the entire body. Over time, these musculoskeletal media became impressively flexible, allowing hominids to learn and communicate new information about their tribe, environment, and inner thoughts and feelings.

A language has to be learned before it can be used, and it was no different for our ancestors. They were obliged for reasons of survival to hunt in groups, which involved learning how to *imitate* the motions of the animals around them and communicating with their fellow hunters, presenting young hominids with the challenging task of passing the 'first grade' of a lifelong learning process.

Early social customs

LIVING AND WORKING IN GROUPS

Our subject is the motion capabilities of primitive peoples, and how these developed through every day social and cultural activities to their eventual transformation into Art in the modern sense.

Consider the three main drivers of hominid evolution: socialisation, work and intelligence. Many animal species function in groups, and early hominids were no different. They lived in small tribes isolated from the outside world, in circumstances where effective communication was essential to survival. The Neanderthals of the Mesolithic period knew how to make tools: axes from sharpened flints lashed to sticks and knives from bone. They carved wooden vessels and made liana ropes.

But hunting and fighting as a group was complicated by the fact that a single mistake by one member could mean losing the prey or defeat in battle, with consequent loss of life. Because individuals had become interdependent in this way, community members had to rehearse their hunting and fighting tactics before each encounter — and on their return, these same routines were repeated as a visual report to the other tribe members.

As our ancestors depended on the natural world for their survival, they continually observed the animals, birds and reptiles around them from childhood onwards, memorising their every *move* in great detail, their eating habits and sleep patterns. Each and every nuance of their motion was meticulously studied.

These observations were translated into perfect *plastic imitations* of animal behaviour under various circumstances, and this was the motion vocabulary which all primitive peoples gradually enlarged and improved for their publicly performed nightly rituals.

SPIRITUALITY AND RITUALISATION

However, it still wasn't art, any more than singing psalms in church or processing behind a funeral cortege is art. It was simply participating with others in a socio-religious activity.

These ancient peoples believed strongly that destiny, desire and ability were controlled by divine powers. At first, there was only one god: the sun, which created and controlled everything. Rock paintings show women *lifting* their heads and arms in supplication, and then *dropping* down on their knees to ask for a successful hunt or harvest. They followed the direction of the sun as they circled around the fire.

These votive rituals did not of course yield the same results every time, leading our forefathers to the conclusion that one god was not enough for such a big world. They multiplied their deities, so that eventually there were gods for each activity, element, domestic function and situation.

STIMULI FOR NATURAL MIMICRY

A conscious philosophy to become stronger, cleverer and more proficient than enemies and prey was developing throughout human prehistory. When our ancestors observed animal *movements*, they tried to *imitate* them again and again. Some, like the flight of a bird, were of course physically impossible to imitate; in such cases, ancient depictions confirm that the motion and character traits of the creature in question were transmuted into sophisticated pantomime demonstrations, much as some ethnic groups still do today.

Australian aborigines use a special trick when hunting antelope. Dressed in real ostrich skin and feathers, with the bird's head mounted on a stick inside the long neck, the hunter cautiously approaches the antelope herd in a perfectly rehearsed *imitation* of every nuance of an ostrich's behaviour and plastic motion characteristics. Slowly and carefully, he circles nearer and nearer to the middle of the grazing herd until he is close enough to *grab* one. After momentary panic, the herd once again relaxes, reassured by the non-threatening smell of the ostrich skin.

Although this is a modern example of the functional use of mimesis, there are undeniable parallels with the ancient rock drawings depicting men wearing animal heads 300,000 years ago.

The point is that early hominids were developing their plastic potential through the *imitation* of living creatures in addition to their domestic vocabulary of *gestures* and *mimicry*. This **first** stage of plastic motion was passed down from generation to generation, and later reinforced through the **second** stage through regular practice in hunting or worship. In the **third** (much later) stage, the human intellect became involved when men set down this plastic information for posterity by creating images on rock.

MOTION AS A COMMUNICATION TOOL

Postural body language is a very primitive form of human communication. Although wildlife films on TV sometimes reveal surprising similarities between the postural gestures and mimicry of apes and our own, our Miocene ancestors had a far greater plastic vocabulary than any modern ape. Their rapidly expanding social and cultural activities forced them constantly to seek new additions to their plastic vocabulary in order to improve their increasingly inadequate system of communication within the group.

An analogy today might be trying to introduce yourself to a stranger who does not speak your language, having to rely on hand gestures and facial expressions to communicate your intentions or needs. Increasingly, our ancestors must have felt a similar frustration as an everyday occurrence. These were the realities of hominid existence a million years ago.

The plastic characteristics of apes and hominids were fundamentally different, as we have seen. Apes have a limited motion vocabulary that is mainly related to physiological functions: *stretching* an arm out to beg for a fruit, *covering* the eyes with the hand in the face of a threat, grooming and embracing each other, feeding infants or acting in ways designed to attract a mate.

Although apes use primitive tools (such as a rocks and branches), they remain incapable of using these tools analytically, adapting them for different purposes, or increasing their variety. Apart from being coached by human beings to do special tricks, apes' intellectual development has remained relatively static during the human evolutionary period.

By contrast, hominids – from the same primate family – were able to use their superior intelligence to improve their knowledge, adapt to different circumstances, analyse their surroundings and select new survival tools accordingly. The plastic vocabulary of hominids was at the very beginning as limited as that of modern apes, but they could change old habits to fit new conditions when necessary. Although their basic motion characteristics remained similar, these new abilities gradually separated hominids further and further from their nearest biological relatives, the Great Apes.

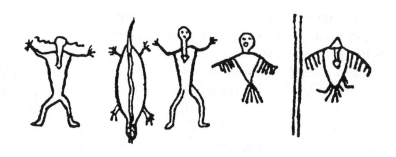

Primary communication systems

THE GROWTH OF NON-VERBAL LANGUAGE

Many theories have been advanced over the last 200 years about the relative importance of non-verbal or vocalised communication in the process of human evolution. The comparative study of new-born apes and babies can be illuminating in this respect.

The shrill, penetrating cry of an infant demands immediate attention from the moment of birth. Driven by hunger or the smell of milk, it *instinctively* demands food in this way, because body motion alone is not an effective means of communicating if the mother is at a distance, or looking elsewhere.

Once the baby is able to see its mother's face and motions clearly, it starts learning the meaning of facial expressions and the *touch* of her hands. This non-verbal dialogue between mother and child is the very beginning of communication by plastic motion. At this stage, while the baby's vocal abilities remain limited, the language of facial expressions and gestures predominates. Smell and voice confirm the mother's presence, but her smile and the *caress* of her fingers form the basis of the instinctive body language that underpins the bond between mother and child.

Body motion is the simplest and quickest means of human communication at close range – the subtle *raising* of an eyebrow, shoulder or finger can be more effective than words (*see Chapter II*).

TACTILE CONTACT IN APES AND HOMINIDS

There are no external areas of the hominid body that cannot be touched either by the individual itself or another. Touching is the most immediate and direct medium of communication between mammals, even before birth. But despite the many studies of the importance of touch in the context of treating mental and emotional disorders in humans, the history and evolution of touch has been generally neglected, apart from the occasional passing mention of the significance of tactile signals in the functional and sociocultural activities of primates.

We focus here on the everyday repertoire of tactile plastic motions, both *functional/instinctive* and artificially *performed*. The range of physiological and emotional stimuli for such motions is vast, and most apes and hominids touch themselves with various body parts up to 700 times a day – contacts that go largely unnoticed. The examples discussed in the following pages are but a representative shortlist of the main types, forms and genres of tactile motion.

Whatever the motivation, bodily contact is the aim of any tactile action, and all body touching can be characterised by three main factors: the initial stimulus, the way the intention is translated into motion and the actual physical contact.

'Touch' is used to describe many different kinds of neuro-physical expressive plastic motions of the hominid body itself, with or without accessories, under or on the skin, instinctive or volitional; tactile contact can be performed individually or with others, and in various plastic and spatial patterns. Furthermore, every type of tactile motion that has survived to the present day has its roots in the beginnings of ape evolution, and subject of tactile contact is so wide and multi-faceted that it sometimes needs to be contextualised in terms of the earliest prehistoric animal species.

Body touching has by far the largest and most versatile plastic communication vocabulary. Its origin goes all the way back to the sophisticated palp/antennae tactile motion alphabet used by ancient insect species for the last 500 million years or so. Only with the advent of the first primates did mammalian forelimbs become sufficiently liberated for their plastic facilities to significantly increase the potential for tactile motion, thereby paving the way for the advanced tactile body language capabilities of modern of apes and hominids. Primates therefore eventually acquired the secrets of forelimb communication through gestural motion and tactile contact from insects.

Body touching can be **active** or **passive**, i.e. touching and being touched. This can be further subdivided into **direct** or **indirect** touch, i.e. direct contact between body parts, or touching by means of some intermediary instrument; and three genres: **self-touching, contact between two or more bodies**, and **touching one or more inanimate objects**.

For the purposes of analysis, these three genres can be categorised into six subdivisions according to their stimuli and characteristics: **Genetic/Habitual, Chaotic/Arranged** and **Accidental/Deliberate**, each of which comprises many different binary sets, such as single or repetitive, internal and external and so on. The pyramidal representation of the nature, plastic facilities and range of tactile motion (*fig.I/1*) summarises this enormous non-verbal communication repertoire and the performing potential of its vocabulary.

As the pyramid shows, the analysis begins with **Direct** contact of a body with itself, then between two bodies, and concluding with touching inanimate objects. In exactly the same way, the second pyramid represents **Indirect** tactile connections using accessories.

Chart 1   Communication Tools and Functions

A. Emitting of outgoing Signals			
INFO TYPE	Signals	Implements	Motivations to ACT
Acoustic	Chirp, rasp, squeak,	Rubbing, Wings, Thorax, Legs.	Mate, warn, territorial claim.
	Song, cry, howl, growl.	Vocal, Cords, Larynx, Beak...	Playing, grooming, courtship.
	Whistle, hiss, puff.	Mouthparts, Thoraxbamps.	Warn, defense, attack, advertising.
	Tap, flap, clap, buzz.	Bill, Limbs, Wings, Pulps...	Exchange information, courtship.
	Stamp, Click, Rattle.	Limbs, mouthparts, tail…	Warn, keep away competitors.
	Echolocation	Vocal cords, Larynx, Mouth	Hunt, gather, test, searching.
	Ultrasonic	Body parts, Vocal cords.	Mate, warn, calling for help.
Odorous	Pheromone	Secretion spray, exocrine.	Mate, food location, searching.
	Stinky smell	Fluid glands, abdomen gas.	Territorial claim, counterattack.
Visual	Colour / ornament	Wings, body parts, skin.	Camouflage, attraction, warning.
	Body decoration	Head / facial parts, props…	Courtship, mimicry, ritual.
	Bio-luminescence	Eyes, wings, thorax, abdomen.	Attraction, hunt, confusion.
	Infrared / ultraviolet	Thorax, glands, abdomen.	Warn, defence, communication code.
	Progressive move	Limbs, wings, fins, tail.	Courtship, trance, dance, report.
	Plastic motion	Head / body parts, trunk.	Food location, threat, fight.
	Mimicry / gesture	Body shape, manner, move.	Camouflage, defense, advertisement.
	Facial expression	Head / facial parts, organs.	Attraction, mate, dominance, warn.
Tactile	Touch (Physical)	Head / facial, body parts.	Test, message, grooming, mating.
	Body contact	Closer range joint motion.	Combat, play, intercourse, nursing.
	Vibration	Wings, limbs, fin, tail, tongue.	Food sources, courtship, mating.
Psycho-neural	Alert state	Frozen motion, posturing.	Watch out, stand by, coming threat.
	Intuition	Reflex, survival instinct.	Memorable recall, defence, trust.
	Hypnosis	Eyes, voice, light, motion.	Hunt, suggestion, influence, heal.
Bio-palpable	Pressure (air, water)	Waves of moving body.	Allocation, recognition, hunt, escape.
	Temperature	Body thermostat, energy.	Oestrum, mate, hutching, anesthetics.
	Territorial marks	Mouthparts, glands, anal.	Territoriality, advertisement, warn.
	Bio-chemical	Gland's fluid, spray.	Feed, mate, defence, heal, energy.
	Magnetic	Antennae, wings, hair, pulps.	Allocation, interact, recognition.
	Electrical	Head parts, limbs, thorax.	Trace, hunt, charge, catch call.

B. Perceiving Organs of Incoming Signals		
Signals	**Implements**	**Motivations to ACT**
Chirp, rasp, squeak.	Antennae	Recognition
Song, cry, howl, growl.	Forelegs	Misreading
Whistle, hiss, puff.	Radar tail	Audial test
Tap, flap, clap, buzz.	Ears	Allocation
Stamp, click, rattle.	Mouth detector	Chasing prey
Echolocation	Sono reflective detector	Search call, audial dialogue
Ultrasonic	High frequency radar	Singing duet, mating interact
Bio-radiant wave.	Audio radiation receptor	Mutual contract along migration.
Pheromone	Antennae, whisker, nose.	Mating call, lost baby, warn.
Stinky smell	Hair, mouthparts, ovipositor.	Reading liquid marks, protection.
Colour / ornament	Eyes	Recognition, presentation, effect.
Body decoration	Optical	Subdue, attraction, confusion.
Bio-luminescence	Eyes	Intrigued, mating call, dialogue.
Infrared / ultraviolet	Optical	Intimate connection, warn, defend.
Progressive move	Eyes	Chasing, panic, escape, courtship.
Plastic motion	Optical	Silent language, food report.
Mimicry / gesture	Eyes	Alert sign, starving baby, help.
Facial expression	Optical	Surprise, demand, threat, pleasure.
Touch (Physical)	Head / facial, body parts,	Taste, message, grooming, mating
Body contact	Closer range joint motion.	Combat, hunt, nursing, play, mate
Vibration	Feathers, hair, mouth parts.	Air, water, earth, prey / predator
Taste	Tongue, proboscis, abdomen.	Chemicals, food, drink, oestrum.
Alert state	Eyes, ears, nose, limbs…	Fear, presage, stand by, watch out.
Intuition	Forbode, alert, panic.	Suspicious, expecting attack.
Hypnosis	Eyes, ears, nose, brain.	Under pressure of predator / foe.
Pressure (air, water)	Lateral line, glands.	Protection, gathering, hunt, mate.
Temperature	skin, hair, palps, heat pit	Allocation, warming up, hibernate.
Humidity / Moisture	antennae, skin, hear, abdomen	Protection from waterless / body.
Bio-chemical	Antennae, hair, tongue, palps	Pheromone, fluid venom, saliva.
Magnetic	antennae, skin, abdomen	Allocation, interact, migration.
Electrical	Ears, antennae, glands, hair.	Searching, mating, warn, hunt.
Polarized rays	Eyes, bill, feathers, tail.	Navigation, interaction, migration.
Occurrences	Thunder, lightning, floods.	Warn, escape from disaster.
Phenomenon	Earthquake, tornado, fire.	Save young's, nest, own lives

DIRECT BODY CONTACT

Self-touching is a genetically pre-programmed mode of body motion based primarily on the neuro-physical conditions of the individual and the anatomical characteristics of the species. Lemurs, for example, *scratch* their itches about three times quicker than a gorilla because their forelimbs are roughly a third of the length; by the same token, the amplitude of the *scratching* motion is three times shorter.

In addition, different members of the same species also have their own distinctive physical and emotional characteristics of course, and the resulting personalisation of touch motions is an important identifier of each individual's plastic portrait. In fact, self-touching normally accounts for some 90% of ape/hominid body *movements*. The most common are *stroking/rubbing, scratching/picking, gripping/grasping* and *pinching/ squeezing*.

These habitual self-touching motions originate in the womb. Foetal scans during the later stages of pregnancy clearly reveal the body structure in its *curled* up position, and the body parts that are *touching* each other during gestation, as well as the confines of the mother's uterus. Freed from these constraints, the new-born infant *moves* its limbs chaotically because it has lost the comforting self-touching *coiled* position as well as the all-enveloping touch of its previously warm environment.

Successful mammalian reproduction depends primarily on maintaining the constant physical connection between mother and offspring, and self-touching provides infants with a substitute for this previously continuous tactile bond. This powerful connection with the mother is common to all mammals and is the foundation of the many sophisticated nuances of tactile motion developed in adult relationships.

Like all mammals, the first prolonged post-natal body touch experience of apes and hominids is usually with the hands and lips during suckling (discussed in greater detail later). Once rested and fed, however, the infant begins to *move* its limbs, *stretching* them after their long confinement. It *rubs* its feet against each other, and sometime succeeds in *touching* its chaotically *flailing* arms. Such short tactile contacts act as subconscious reminders of the secure uterine environment in which the body was *coiled* in one piece, with no real awareness of its separate parts.

In addition to this newfound freedom of movement, infants experience the positive pleasures of being fed from the mother's warm breast, *sucking* the nipple with its lips, *nuzzling* her soft belly or underarm. In the mother's absence, the infant instinctively hunts around for a nipple substitute in the form of a thumb, finger or big toe, or adopts its previous foetal position by *nuzzling* its own knees. This process of adapting to new circumstances, involving *touching* oneself instead of another familiar body, is the genesis of all self-touch behaviour.

The extent to which self-touching motions are under *conscious* control depends partly on the –personal characteristics of the individual. Between 75–80% of these motions are in fact *unconscious*, and are therefore beyond control. They include three of the six main tactile genres: **Genetic, Habitual** and **Chaotic**. These are usually as inseparable from the body's functional repertoire as *yawning, pupil dilation,* Instinctive *facial grimaces* of disgust, *goose pimples, penile erection* and other spontaneous plastic body motions. We are of course talking here about apes and hominids in general, excluding the artificial tactile behaviours developed more recently by the civilizations of Homo Sapiens.

GENETIC self-touching motions appear at birth in a complex package of Instinctive functional actions:
I) Sucking, licking and smacking:
Instinctive touch motions with the feeding implements of the mouth and lips become habitually repeated in different forms.

II) Gripping, grasping and squeezing:
   These tactile contacts with the individual's own digits are echoes of the genetically programmed actions to stimulate milk flow in the mother's breast.
III) *Nuzzling, curling up* and *hiding* the head under the wing:
   These are rooted in the pre-natal foetal position, eventually becoming the habitual body position for resting after meals, and later for affectionate attachment to others of the same species. *Curling* up and hiding the head is also a reflex body position for defence or protection.

In their different ways, all these tactile behaviours are therefore adaptations to new environmental circumstances based on genetically programmed pre- and post-natal motions.

The HABITUAL *unconscious* tactile vocabulary is much more extensive, and includes *stroking, rubbing, scratching, picking, scraping, pulling* (hair) and *tapping*. Many also originated in genetic motions; some are virtually identical to the *functional* plastic motions on which they are based, even though the original function is itself absent (such as periodically *picking* a clean nose, *scratching* when there are no biting insects around, *tapping* the knee with the fingers or *stroking* the hair). Such self-touch motions with the hands usually accompany thought or reflection that has nothing to do with the function of the tactile behaviour concerned – they are *involuntary habitual* motions that start, stop, and change unpredictably according to mood.

In mature individuals, these sometimes develop into a tic – personal emblems of particular emotional states, such as pleasure or disgust, frustration or bravado, refusal or acceptance and so on. In combination, these Genetic and Habitual touch behaviours contribute to the individual's plastic **identity** and as such, play an important role in non-verbal communication.

Although virtually universal, only a few dozen unconscious self-touching motions feature in the functional repertoire. However, each one can be a response to a number of stimuli; *touching* the lips with the index finger, for example, could be prompted by thinking, remembering, sadness or shock. It could equally well express an invitation to speak or to remain silent, or indicate hunger or thirst. The correct reading of such *gestures* is usually facilitated by the accompaniment of appropriate facial *expressions*, body *postures* and both the individual and general plastic motion contexts. In some pathological forms of behaviour there are also of course uncontrolled *touching* motions that are totally unreadable because meaningless in themselves.

CHAOTIC *unconscious* self-touching is used to express emotion (except when symptomatic of physical or mental disorders, which are outside our present scope). A frustrated or angry gorilla will often give vent to its feelings often with violent self-touching motions such as *beating, tapping* or *flapping* various body parts, vigorous *scratching,* or *masturbating, interlocking* hands or *grasping* knees and so on. Similar reactions occur when a troop of chimpanzees panic in response to an unexpected attack.

Minor forms of Chaotic self-touching can occur when hominids are in a state of shock. The hands and arms can slowly 'walk' all over the body as if to find an explanation for whatever catastrophe has taken place, for example; *beating* the fist on the chest, or *ramming* the first into the other palm; *chewing* fingers or fingernails; *rubbing* the face with the palms; *squeezing* the head with both hands, *scratching* the skull, and so on.

Chaotic touch does not have its own motion vocabulary. As with the other major types, it is mainly based on the Genetic/Habitual self-touching repertoire of Unconscious motor *movements* of the limbs and emotional *expressions* of the head and face. Chaotic *touch sequences* are sometimes involuntarily repeated in response to waves of emotion resurfacing, and being expressed in the same plastic patterns.

Essentially the same body tools are used in **active** or **passive** touch, see fig 1.

Accidental: Unconscious and unpredictable self-touching or touch between two individuals in panic or frustration or in a casual way.

Still: maintaining motionless tactile contact as the subject of motion by another body part (such as being *scratched*).

Travelling or **on the spot**: motions such as *scratching* while sitting on a rock, or *wiping* sweat from the face while *running* or *walking.*

Jabbing: touch signal with *tapping* fingers.

Light/heavy: ranges from almost imperceptible *stroking* to a hard, almost painful, *squeeze.*

ARRANGED self-touching, although subconsciously motivated, involves some element of **volition** in its actual execution (unlike the Functional tactile routines of infants, whether genetically programmed or acquired soon after birth).

The mammalian phenomenon of nursing infants until they become independent involves a repertoire of many such touches. A mother wolf, for example, cleans the anus of her cub, *picking out* dried faecal matter stuck in the surrounding fur with her lips and teeth.

Apes and hominids *imitate* their parents' Functional self-touching repertoire for half a dozen years after birth. It includes *peeling* food items, *eating* and *drinking* with the hands, fingers and mouth, *washing, preening* and so on. The many tactile motions of the hands and fingers with other body parts have been learned in the same way for thousands of generations and are crucial subconscious behaviours that combine the **Genetic/Involuntary** and **Arranged/Volitional** genres of Functional body motion.

Hominids eventually outdistanced their ape-relatives in the use of touching motions for bodily communication and performance. At its most primitive, the touch-gesture vocabulary consists of motions such as *pointing* the index finger at the individual's own chest or at another's chest, *tapping* an object with the hand in order to direct attention to it, using *clapping* to call and *flapping* the arms.

The hominid body has seven major communicative touch units:
Face: eyelids, lips, jaws, tongue, nose, cheeks;
Arm/hand: singly, between each other, or with other body parts;
Fingers: of one hand, singly, together, between each other or with other body parts;
Both hands with sets of fingers, acting in unison or contrapuntally;
Leg/foot singly, between each other, or with other body parts;
Toes of one foot: singly, together between each other or with other body parts;
Both feet and sets of toes, acting in unison or contrapuntally.

The advent of body decoration was a gigantic leap forwards in the development of tactile motion. Painting the body or that of others by applying ochre, chalk, mud and charcoal with the fingertips, became so popular that it eventually evolved into a strong ethnic tradition, and ultimately gave birth to modern cosmetics.

Hominids *painted* the entire skin surface with incredibly complicated designs using *jabs* or light *touches* of the hands, while simultaneously exploring their own anatomy with firmer tactile contacts. These *stroking, rubbing, tapping, pressing* and other self-touch motions led on to therapeutic massaging for medical healing. These premeditated tactile routines not only combined Unconscious and Voluntary behaviour, but also encompassed both main types of body contact: **self-touching** and **touching others**.

TOUCH BETWEEN TWO BODIES

ACCIDENTAL **unconscious touching** between two or more bodies often happens as the result of uncontrolled or chaotic motion with no inherent significance, during free gnaw-play by infants for example, or when one falls from a tree onto another animal. Habit, Chaos and Accident are related to each other in various other spheres of animal activity, with similar kinds of Involuntary tactile contact, but with major differences between behaviours involving self-touching and touching others. By definition, self-touch is acted, perceived and controlled by the same body, whereas Accidental touching between two or more independent bodies is felt and perceived differently. This makes the tactile interrelation between individuals much more complex than is the case with self-touching.

In Accidental touching, the tactile effect is not delivered intentionally and therefore carries little meaning for both sides, as when individuals in group bump into each other as they flee, with no embarrassment or bad feelings involved even when substantial injury results. One of the two Unconsciously *moving* bodies in Accidental touch is nevertheless usually more dominant than the other, creating two dissimilar tactile roles: **active** and **passive**, depending on their relative speed, hardness of touching implement (hand, foot, head) and the angle of impact.

Although these three factors are of equal importance, superiority in any two by one individual could result in physical consequences for the other. Accidental touch therefore represents a bridge between individual self-touching and tactile contact with other bodies in the following plastic motion genres.

DELIBERATE touch actions performed between two or more moving individuals are Volitional, often highly advanced and dramatic, as in the genres of gesticulatory expression in bodily communication and in ritual/secular performances (*see Chapters III and IV*).

Therapeutic touch

Although deliberate body touching can hurt or even kill, it can also heal and save life. In the ancient healing repertoire, the medicine man/woman devoted much time and energy to *massaging* manipulations by the fingers and hands. Indeed, most of the shamanic therapy system is based on various touching treatments conducted in a spiritually charged atmosphere.

Communication vocabulary

Self-touching *signs* and *gestures* constitute a significant part of the bodily language of apes and hominids. There are a few non-verbal communication systems based mainly on a plastic alphabet of natural or artificial body tactile symbols. Prehistoric touch vocabularies are still used today by minority peoples whose culture has managed to survive more or less intact. Moreover, many of these self-touching habits have become incorporated in our everyday plastic expressions, passing generally unnoticed and in ignorance of their ancient origin.

Our forefathers maintained good interpersonal relations and their traditional hierarchies by means of specific touches of others, and the development of tactile communication stimulated their sociocultural evolution: the friendly sign of *placing* a hand on someone's shoulder, for example, or removing dead skin from another's body. Tenderly *scratching* another's back, or carefully *holding* an infant's hand while demonstrating how to *crack* a nut with a stone, and so on.

Reproductive context

The entire mating process is based on expressing sexual desire through touching another: *embracing, kissing, caressing* the mate's genitals, *grasping* the wrist of a female to *pull* her into the bushes and copulating either verso-dorso or verso-verso. As we have seen, the same is true of the gestation period and birth. Life itself would be impossible without Intimate *touch* between male and female.

Nursing and initiation, hunting or combat – every aspect of ancient daily life revolved around Functional tactile motion between individuals, not to mention artificial tactile performances.

Tactile skills in combat

The most dramatic tactile repertoire was used in hunting, fighting and wrestling, initially unarmed, then with weapons and combat techniques of gradually increasing sophistication and lethal potential. Initiation practices involving wrestling with a wild animal or between two hominids included highly aggressive tactile tricks.

As the contests were designed to produce a single victor/survivor at the end, both opponents would use any known *hitting* or *interlock* technique to defeat their adversary. Advanced combat motion systems involving long and arduous coaching in tactile attack and defence skills, both armed and unarmed, already existed a million years ago or more.

Tactile body memory

Blind people touch-test everything around them, recognize shapes and contours by contact. Based on tactile memory, this facility becomes intrinsic to the way their body unconsciously functions and perceives. Early blind hunters, gatherers and craftsmen did not realise how much this tactile memory helped them unseeingly to use their weapons, tools and fingers. Similarly, shamans and musicians acquired the ability to play their instruments without looking them.

All the tactile contacts between individuals summarised here are Deliberate actions. The peaceful and positive aspect of everyday domestic and sociocultural activities was balanced by the opposing principle of dramatic and negative, as in any functional system. Arranged and Deliberate touches possess both of these qualities in bodily communication. The tactile expression of *shaking* hands, for example, can reflect positive or negative signals, and be either aggressive or helpful.

In the following examples of simple and coded tactile meanings, M signifies male, F-female, S-submissive, D-dominant, L- left and R-right.

INTRODUCTORY:	M/M *interlock* complete hands motionlessly for a while, evaluating each other's personality from the steadiness, pressure and hardness of the *grip;* F *places* half of her hand loosely into the *open* palm of a M, who *covers* her fingers with his thumb, and waits until she *removes* her hand.
HIERARCHIC:	D/D of equal rank greet one another with a *stroke* of the open hand, *slapping* their palm/fingers disdainfully, looking away; D *offers* his loose hand nonchalantly to the S, who *grabs* it eagerly and *shakes* it until D *pulls* his hand away.
SEDUCTIVE:	M/F *interlock* R hands; M *strokes* F's hand repeatedly with L hand, *holding* it firmly with his R hand. After several attempts to *pull away* her R hand, F *slaps* the hand of M with her L and *pulls* her R hand away. F *grabs* R hand of M with her hands and *squeezes* it. Then she places his hand seductively on her breast.
ADMIRING:	M delicately *takes* the R hand of F into his two hands, *kneels* and *kisses* it. F *pulls* his hands up and *holds* them against her chest. F/F *interlock* one or both hands, each trying to *pull* the other to her side of a borderline.
EXPRESSIVE:	F/M face-to-face, *holding* hands with hooked fingers only as they *dance* to and fro. M/F face to face, *holding* hands tightly with interlocked wrists and *crossed* forearms as they *spin* around clockwise rapidly.
COMMUNICATIVE:	M/F or F/F use coded touch *sequences* with fingers on each other's palms to exchange secret messages in public.

As we have seen, these tactile dialogues include short arranged messages and deliberate answers, mainly communicated and understood by the fingers and hands.

The nuances of touch are huge varied, reflecting the motion capabilities of ape and hominid forelimbs, particularly the fingertips. Their abilities include talking, playing, healing, conducting, hypnotising, seducing, restraining, killing or saving lives.

Such wide-ranging capabilities are based on the extraordinary neural sensitivity of the fingertips, whose tactile dictionary is so vast that it merits further research and study.

TOUCH BETWEEN AN INDIVIDUAL AND GROUPS

Individual simultaneously touching a group of bodies is a common feature of functional relationships of many different species, as we have seen.

- Some frogs incubate forty–fifty eggs under the skin on their backs.
- A single female snake *copulates* simultaneously with a dozen males or more.
- Cats and dogs *suckle* four–six infants at the same time.
- Large groups of ants, bees, piranhas or mammalian scavengers attack a prey.
- *Pricking*/perforation when tattooing or during therapeutic treatment.

There is a great sensory difference between single and multiple touch contacts. Whereas one-to-one body touching involves only the personal characteristics of the individuals involved, group-to-one tactile contact also involves a single perceiver, but many touchers, each with their own distinct individual characteristics.

Most hominid mothers instinctively know something of the individual characteristics of the unborn infant(s) she is carrying a few weeks before delivery. They can recognise each offspring by its unique tactile behaviour even in the uterus: one may have smooth motions and a tender touch, while others could be more insistent, with hard tactile contacts.

The mother continues to study the tactile characteristics of each infant for prolonged periods during suckling and nursing. One can be shy, preferring to *nuzzle* its mother's belly, while another could be rougher, favouring the mother's neck, with its hypnotising rhythm of her breathing.

ENSEMBLE TOUCHING

Bodily touch of individuals in a group has a long history. Members of primordial terrestrial species held close to each other for safety reasons million years ago. The immense shoals of insects, colonies of penguins, bats or snakes, herds of bovines – all of them kept close together to preserve warmth and protect their young.

Large groups can confuse predators, particularly when moving – even when the group scatters. As we have seen, mammals often touch each other during gestation, suckling and nursing, and after that in the gnaw play; the same for the hoofed species while they graze, or during migration. This constant *touching* of bodies gives individuals more confidence to face the harshness and perils of their environment, and assures the reproductive continuity of the species.

Scout ants build a living bridge of bodies over some obstacle to permit the following army to cross

- Lobsters walk along the seabed *touching* each other's tail with their antennae.
- A mother shrew leads a chain of her infants, each of which firmly *holds* the rear of the sibling in front in its jaws in order to preserve the chain.
- Elephants cross a fast stream in single file, *holding* the tail of the one in front with their trunks.
- A dominant chimp leads his troop through a jungle in zigzag patterns, while the members *hold* hands to maintain the chain.

Hominids developed this tactile habit into strong clan/tribal behaviours for communal activities such as hunting, gathering, entertaining and sleeping. Hand *holding*, with or without accessories, continued with the advent of totemism, whose increasing repertoire of group ceremonies stimulated the spiritual idea of being stronger and more successful in a united tribal group.

On the night of the full moon, females *holding* hands *walked* together around a phallic object, praying for increased fertility. Males ritually rehearsed impending hunts by circling the bonfire *holding* one hand on the shoulder of the companion in front while *gripping* a weapon in the other, or jointly *grasping* the companion's weapon with the left hand when facing the centre to pray, while *stamping*, for a successful hunt the following day (see Chapter III).

TOUCHING BETWEEN TWO GROUPS

Tactile contact between two opposing Groups usually occurred in local secular competitions, ritual pantomime and/or inter-tribal combat. Until quite recently, these Double-Group activities were performed exclusively by males. Hominids religiously respected mature females as a reproductive source, and never allowed them to wear masks or to fight – at least, not officially. However, from the Palaeolithic era onwards, young women *danced* 'line-to-line' opposite men occasionally using Group tactile patterns on the ground, or partnering demi-lifts off the ground.

In traditional contests, male riders on camels, elephants or mules competed in teams to *pull down* their opponents and take them hostage. These events turned into a tactile free-for-all of animals and riders. Similar representations are seen in the Group inter-touching genres of ritual pantomime and combat events discussed later.

TACTILE MOTION WITH TOOLS

Inanimate objects

These are included because of the important role played by tools in human evolution. Certain insect, bird and primate species are known to have occasionally made use of various tools in the past, but not as a regular *functional* activity. Apes increased the range of accessories and their operating repertoire, although to very limited degree: using twigs to extract ants from their nest for a good meal, stones to crack nuts, branches to brush away bothersome insects, shells for collecting and drinking water, reeds to construct primitive shelters and the like.

Such tool use involves more than simply testing the suitability of these various materials by touch. The important task was to find the best ways to fit these inanimate objects into the anatomical shape of the hand, fingers, feet, lips or jaws.

This meant physically perfecting each potential new tool into a suitable shape for its efficient application. Each gathering tool, crafted weapon or musical instrument created by prehistoric hominids was normally used for a very specific purpose. The introduction of new tools and instruments required corresponding adjustments of the plastic motion facilities of the hand and fingers, such as *squeezing, pushing, pulling, twisting* and *hitting*. The utility of these new artefacts depended on the correct tactile relationship between the shape of the object and the abilities of the body parts by which they were operated.

The era of Homo Habilis some three million years ago saw the tool industry begin to flourish. It included the development of new tools for women, along with various domestic accessories for food gathering, making clothing, blankets and tent coverings.

It was psychologically difficult for our ancestors to adapt themselves to learn how to produce and use these primitive implements, and to adapt their old habitual tactile facilities to new ways of *gripping, grasping, pinching* or *pricking* – a daunting task. Hominids had to get used to unfamiliar shapes and handling methods, awkward ways of moving the fingers to maintain the right contact with the implement.

The **Self-touching** repertoire with accessories occurred mainly in body decorating activities, as a *conscious*, carefully prepared performance by the fingers and hands with pricking and painting instruments. Along with all other aspects of body decoration, tattooing and body painting represented one of the most important forms of prehistoric visual art, and demanded highly controlled tactile contacts with a quill or other sharp point, a bone knife or comb. Considerable delicacy of touch is required, with a strong *grip* in the zone between the fingers and the tool. The crucial touch between the instrument and the body part being decorated varied in firmness according to the technique and instrument used.

Stabbing one's own body with a fingernail is an entirely different matter from *pricking* with long, sharp needles of various shapes and thicknesses to achieve an artistic effect, requiring considerable talent, experience and skill. That Neanderthal peoples possessed such an extraordinarily refined sense of touch testifies to their tremendous contribution to our genetic family tree.

Touching others with tools

Just as self-touching with implements for body decoration was a huge step in the evolution of visual arts, the same activity applied to the body of another individual required even greater skill.

The subtle tactile connection between one body and another via an inanimate tool is a peculiar phenomenon. The operator's body must perfectly sense the substance, shape and size of the instrument through his own hand while simultaneously assessing all the characteristics of the spot being touched and what is being felt by the individual at the other end of the instrument.

Many different methods of *stroking* and *rubbing* (as opposed to *pricking* and *cutting*) were used in body painting. The major implements of this design performance were the same as in self-decoration: the tips of reeds or feathers, with dyes such as red ochre, mud, white or blue chalk and charcoal.

INDIRECT TOUCH BETWEEN AN INDIVIDUAL AND GROUPS

The main tactile conditions are essentially the same as with the same subject without accessories, differing only in the manner of their execution. The reasons for using indirect-touch methods included extending the reach to attain some object, or avoiding possible concealed dangers and the like.

A group of **hunters** armed with primitive spears surround a hibernating bear, and *stab* the animal simultaneously from all sides at an agreed signal. The enfeebled, drowsy animal cannot react fast enough to this orchestrated assault and succumbs. Each hunter *holds* his spear firmly with both hands and *presses* it deep into the prey's body with all his strength – but as each has different physical, mental and spiritual capacities, the dying bear can distinguish the different pressure points on its body and the individual tactile impact of each weapon.

The following two examples of tactile interactions between one individual and a Group of five demonstrate contrasting tactile connections, kinetic potential and sensory awareness.

A. A strong male Homo Heidelbergensis plays with five small children by *dragging* along a large branch the five youngsters are *holding* on to. He *squeezes* the thick end of the branch under his armpit and *holds* it with a firm *grasp* of both hands.

B. A team of five dogs *pulls* a sledge over a frozen lake. The dogs are controlled by reins, and urged on by a whip *held* in the hands of the driver. Each dog has an individual harness, the end of which is attached to the reins; the lead dog has an additional line *held* in the hands of the driver.

In (A), the kinetic force is concentrated in the arm and hands of the puller, and the action is conducted by one body against the friction resistance of the branch and the weight of the five children. The latter are connected by touch to each other and to the man as a Group via the intermediary of an object – the branch – which they *hold* on to with both hands for security and balance.

The kinetic energy in (B) comes from the five dogs *pulling* against the combined friction resistance and weight of the sled and driver. The operator has a double tactile contact with the dogs through the reins and through the soles of his feet on the sled. Additional tactile connections between the individual and the Group are via the whip and the harness of the lead dog.

ENSEMBLE TOUCHING WITH ACCESSORIES

The advent of paganism, as a development of the old totemic beliefs, brought with it syncretic forms of Dance/Pantomime performance. Hominids started using both natural and artificial accessories in sacred and secular public events. Females danced *holding* decorative accessories such as grasses, flowers or twigs in their hands, or fastened to various body parts. Male dancers used reeds and sticks, weapons and masks with animal attributes such as horns, tusks, bills, wings and tails. Later on, both sexes acted or danced with figurines in their hands, or with snakes, birds or flaming torches.

Females developed their moonlit ceremonies with the choreographic use of popular accessories, either *holding* them in their hands while maintaining a continuous chain with other participants in an open circle or *placing* them on their neighbour's shoulder, again without breaking the chain.

Alternatively, the decorative elements were brought to the centre as a huge posy, or the dancers *moved* close to each other in a winding spiral pattern. Whatever the subject of the ritual, females never interrupted the tactile connection to each other, either through direct bodily contact or through accessories. The tactile contact of male hunters with weapons is described later.

The next stage of group tactile entertainment was the ancient Ribbons-and-Pole dance in which each participant *holds* in one hand the free end of a long rope or liana attached to the top of a central pole. The entire group moves together in a circle, maintaining equal distance between each other – but also all connected to each other via tactile contact through the rope and pole. This touching by proxy used to have similar sexual potency as a woman today *sitting* on a man's lap, and during the dance the participants of both sexes arranged their rendezvous through coded rope-waving and self-touching signals.

The following examples of joint group action both involve individuals in moving lines, connected to each other by touch through similar chain-like accessories.

A. Captured slaves are tied to each other in a line by two long thick ropes. The upper line goes from neck to neck, while the lower one connects them by the hands tied behind their backs. This harsh double-touch security measure nevertheless allows the victims opportunities to communicate with each other. Although the men have limited motion facilities, they have two tactile sources for exchanging coded motion signals. Their necks and hands can transmit and receive information by touch-sense *movements* of the connected body parts, *pulling* the rope or *loosening* it in various rhythmic and tensile patterns.

B. A Group of females *dance* with two long flower garlands, *holding* one in each hand. They play with these accessories up and down, in succession or simultaneously, performing a serpentine display of *trembling, zigzagging* waves. Like the tied group of prisoners, the line of moving garlands also has two equal touch-motion sources through the arms and hands, but with much greater capacity for plastic motion. Despite there being no ropes involved, the tactile contact of hand with garland nonetheless guides all motions. The female body leads the garland patterns and controls the space and time of the movements.

Both are versions of the same type of group-accessory touching, displaying the same mode of successive touch from one individual in the chain to the next, and a similar linear arrangement of bodies; the only difference lies in the spatial capacity for motion and the ability to use plastic facilities freely.

GROUP-TO-GROUP TOUCHING WITH ACCESSORIES

The highest level of tactile body motion encompasses all other *functional group* genres and motivations, combining conscious and instinctive behaviour, deliberate and accidental touch, single and repetitive use of accessories, and chaotic and arranged motions. Each opposing Group requires high order ensemble touching skills and individual balance, the ability to appraise the kinetic energy of an opponent and complete physical self-control.

A. Two teams of neighbouring tribesmen compete in a tug-of-war contest, with equal numbers in each Group taking its starting position on either side of the line. The participants *hold* the rope with both hands and *kick* the soles of their feet firmly into the ground. With little or no difference in the size of each group and the ground conditions on both sides of the line, winning depends on which team has the better unity of motion, rope *gripping* technique and body angle to the opposing force. An excellent tactile sense of the feet against the ground is also required, as well as sheer body strength. The outcome therefore depends on the touch-connection qualities of each individual and their ability to work as a team, like teeth in a jaw.

B. Two prehistoric hominid tribes have outgrown the small island they inhabit, leading to serious territorial disputes. The only solution is for one of the tribes to leave permanently, although neither wants to do so, and a crucial battle ensues. The main weapons used are clubs and sharp sticks, tusks and horns, bone knives, stones and liana nets, with defence accessories in the form of shields made of pelts or bark. The life-and-death combat starts after prolonged mutual insults, after which the front ranks of warriors approach each other as unbroken lines of bodies and spears. The main objective of each side is to kill as many opponents as possible, then drive the remainder literally off the island into the sea. No prisoners are taken or opponents spared, even women and children.

Naturally, any such **close** range combat involves every personal weapon including the head, hands and feet, the use of which is effectively based on tactile contact with various body parts of the enemy – *kicking* an opponent, *lifting* him off the ground and *throwing* him over the shoulder, *hitting* with the hands and arms, *ramming* with the head and many other tactile motion skills.

All the weapons were either the combatants' own body parts, or made from natural sources and intended to disable or kill by *stabbing, slashing* or *cutting* with hard and sharp edges and points. To make sure of the kill, the warriors would repeatedly *strike* victims at the same point, or *twist* the spear several times in the wound after the first stab. The cruellest victors would then cut open the victim's body to *pull out* the heart and gorge on it, believing this to be a way of absorbing the strength and courage of the dead opponent, who was regarded as no more than any other animal prey.

Lances *clashed* in the air, *flying* towards the enemy, or *piercing* bodies; cudgels *smashed* skulls and ribs; warriors *trampled* bodies on the ground. Concerned to save their own lives, the final line of vanquished combatants retreated under the enemy onslaught in a scene of a mass butchery with innumerable touch contacts with weapons and various body parts, including those already dead. The battle continued until the very last enemy was driven into the water or killed.

The tactile characteristics of fighting accessories were very specific. In Close range, the main target was the enemy's body and outer covering – the skin. Warriors with claw-like gauntlets or knuckledusters *ripped open* their adversaries' skin to make them bleed to death. Then, using a *scraping* motion, they would *tear* at the open wound. At medium range, sharpened stones, shells and bone knives of various sizes and shapes *cut* the enemy's neck or belly with a *sliding* motion. The knife handles were locked in the warrior's palm and used at right angles to the body being touched.

Medium-range combat with lances or cudgels involved double tactile contact. Combatants would use various weapons to *strike* or *stab* each other in attack or defence. The outcome of this contest of interlocked weapons depended on the performance of two individuals with common tactile points:

- the feet flat on the ground;
- a firm hand *grip* on the weapon;
- the point at which the two weapons *clashed* against each other (*see battle motions in Chapters III and IV*).

The above examples of group-to-group touching with accessories have different acting conditions, fighting motivations and performing tools. In the tug-of-war contest (A), the action is an inter-team competition for public entertainment as a demonstration of strength and teamwork.

It involves one accessory for both teams – the rope – and a single tactile motion objective: to *pull* the opposing team over the line. Individuals in the Group have different personalities and physiques, but are united by a common desire to win.

The prehistoric battle (B), by contrast, is a contest between two large Groups, each with different circumstances and motivations. It's not a matter of entertainment, but of life or death in battle. Combatants on both sides had to be mentally prepared to accept loss of their own life, family and home base.

Such a state of mind induced them to fight to the last breath, using their combative skills and experience, plastic capacities and physical strength to the utmost. Each side acted as a cohesive unit ready to die in the common cause, but with different individual accessories, fighting techniques and modes of plastic motion.

This is the type of Group action taken by soldier ants, prides of lions or wolf packs, with two opposing Groups each united in terms of motivation, emotional power, direction of movement and often, in joint tactile motion contacts.

The result is a maelstrom of body touching, a symphony of clashing and noise, a dramatic battle for survival. The kind of accessories used is irrelevant – primitive or sophisticated, short or long, hard or soft – and their reach can always be extended and the sphere of tactile motion increased with a corresponding enhancement of the tactile manipulation techniques of arms, hands and fingers.

The large and important vocabulary of Solo and Group touching plastic motions with accessories in the dance/mime performing repertoire is described later.

TOUCHING OBJECTS WITH TOOLS

An ape or hominid unable reach the object of its desire with its arms alone would Instinctively use a tool such as a stick or a liana to artificially extend its reach, either by dislodging fruit or nuts higher in the tree with the far end of the stick or by *throwing* a liana across a high branch to *pull* it down within reach. These subconscious survival actions are similar to those of insects, birds and other primates.

Stones were the third main tool of our ancestors, and were used to knock nuts from trees and then crack them. After the transition from the arboreal habitat to life on the ground, hominids progressively developed a Functional repertoire of stick, rope and stone skills for use in everyday activities; indeed, these tools played a crucial evolutionary role.

In general, *touching* inanimate objects and using accessories was analogous to the equivalent direct contacts. The main difference was that objects do not feel touch, and are therefore easier to control and manipulate. When hominids *pulled* down a rotten tree with lianas, they knew in advance the exact height, thickness, weight and root conditions of the object being felled.

Two groups of men each *hold* one end of a **rope** thrown over the canopy of a tree, and *stick* their heels in the ground. The feel of the rope in their palms tells them the resistance of the tree to be felled, the correction needed to adjust their balance, the time to take action to avoid the falling trunk, and so on.

A similar operation might be when a group of tribesmen *move* a huge stone into their cave of worship, using a combination of wooden **levers**, small **stones** and **logs** on which to roll the object. More complex calculations are required to determine the weight, size and shape of the rock before it can be gradually levered along while others put stones under the lifted part of the rock to enable more log rollers to be put in place.

Any levering technique has three contact points: the end of the lever in the hands of the operator, the supporting fulcrum (often the ground itself) and the point of contact with the object being levered. If these three points are not correctly spaced in relation to each other, either the object will not move or the lever may break.

Finding the correct leverage points involved conducting several preliminary touch tests, with further adjustments being made after each leverage. Moving heavy objects with such triple-touch levering points is hard work, and every individual must have tactile contact with his neighbours to sense the timing of simultaneous *lifts* and *releases*, when to *squat* on the ground and to adjust body balance, sensing the ground through the soles of the feet and *placing* elbows on thighs to prevent back injuries.

These two examples involve accessories that differ in shape, length and substance. **Lianas** are strong, but soft and slippery, which makes *touch* contact unstable, especially in hands already slippery with sweat.

Although this condition required greater tactile skill when *grasping* the tool with successive pairs of hands, the flexibility of a rope gives more possibilities for manoeuvre, and has space for tying knots to increase *grip*. By contrast, the solid and unbending log, while less flexible, is much more reliable in tactile terms; it is appropriate for hand-contact in levering operations. Its manoeuvrability is however limited, and is much heavier.

TOUCH TECHNIQUES WITH IMPLEMENTS

Single-touch implements
Basically, any manual instrument transmits tactile sensations between the operator and the object. Single-action tools usually have two or three contact points, depending on its shape, size, hardness and type of operation.

- Charcoal, forks, sticks and awls have only **two** contact points: the hand on the tool, and the tool with the object.
- Rakes, pitchforks and shovels have **three** tactile points: one hand near the end of the handle, the other hand in the middle of the shaft and the third touch where the tool touches the object.
- Spades can even have **four** tactile points, when one foot is used to apply additional pressure to the top of the blade.

Double-touch implements
These are two-part implements, usually with one **active** part and one **passive**:
- Brush and paint, needle and thread. All have **three** contact points: one hand on the handle of the active tool; the contact between the active and passive parts; and the contact of the active tool with the object.
- Paddle/canoe, bow/violin, bucket/well. All have **four** contact points: two hands on the tool(s), the contact between both implements, the contact between the auxiliary tool and body parts (buttocks on canoe, violin on shoulder, hands on rope.)

Multi-touch implements

These have several separate parts involved in the same multi-touch operation: two actively engaged in tactile motion, with both hands, and passive auxiliary accessories in static touch with the object.

- Hammer, nail and wood. **Five** or more contact points are involved: one hand *gripping* the hammer, the other *holding* the nail and perhaps the foot steadying the wood; the hammer *strikes* the nail, which in turn *penetrates* the wood and forces it against the ground. A task with such complex multiple tactile connections demands knowledge and experience of the materials and tools the operator is working with, good motion coordination and a keen sense of direct or transmitted tactile resistance in the many connections being made. Our ancestors eventually learned all these skills in the university of everyday life.

SUMMARY

Unlike kinetics or mechanics, very little has been written on the subject of bodily touch. Surprisingly, most of the discoveries in the field of the body's natural tactile facilities have been made by specialists in forensics and criminality.

The diagrammatic representation of our functional touch capabilities reveals their central role in our everyday personal, professional and social lives. The distance from genetic/habitual self-touching to our post-industrial electronic age is a reminder of the immense evolutionary marathon of the last few million years – yet we hardly acknowledge the importance of body/object touching in our daily lives. There are practically no limits to what can be expressed or achieved by a simple touch with the fingertips; it can hurt and delight, make you look ugly or gorgeous, heal or make ill, play a sublime sonata or blow up a concert hall.

To recap, both the tactile action and perception in self-touching occurs in the same individual, whereas they are separate in any touch between two individuals. Direct touch provides the closest connection between two bodies, and an extensive, simple and intuitively clear plastic vocabulary for communication and cooperation. Though the principles are similar, the addition of intermediary accessories creates great tactile complexity.

The six major tactile categories are defined mainly according to their motivation (Instinctive, Subconscious or Voluntary). **Self-touching** is mainly Genetic, Habitual, Chaotic or Arranged, and **touching others**, more often Accidental or Deliberate. As illustrated by the few examples quoted, the **genre** characteristics fall into four general divisions: **Type, Spatial characteristics, Force, Emotion** – the essential elements of touch.

In the following concise encyclopaedia of self-touching behaviour and common tactile actions with accessories, particular attention is given to the subject of **touching with objects** because of their crucial role in hominid evolution. Indeed, it can be argued that these increasingly sophisticated multiple tactile interactions with objects are the foundations for all the marvellous post-industrial technologies that allow our species today to communicate instantly across the planet and reach into space and beyond.

42

A CONCISE ENCYCLOPEDIA OF TOUCH

DIRECT BODY CONTACT

Functional *Instinctive* self-touching

EYELIDS	A short *blink* – protection; Slow – falling asleep; Repetitive – neurotic tic;
TONGUE	*Scraping* the teeth, *sucking* the palate, *licking* the lips, muzzle and body parts when self-cleaning or healing own wounds; tooth *sucking*.
LIPS	*Sucking* thumb or big toe; *squeezing*, when hungry or *holding* food in mouth; *smacking* when eating; *rubbing* on hand or forearm, to clean after meal.
JAWS	*Scratching* or *gnawing* limbs; *biting* itching skin, or lips when frustrated; *biting* fingernails or corns as a habitual behaviour.
NOSE/ SNOUT	*Nuzzling* or *stroking* body parts; *rubbing* on hand or forearm to dry.
ARMS	*Hugging* self with crossed arms, or *placing* on top of the head or over the face; *covering* the chest by *putting* each hand on the opposite shoulder when feeling shy or threatened. *Flapping* arms against body parts with straight or *interlocked* arms in excitement or frustration; *holding* both knees with *interlocked* elbows in a deep *squat*.
HANDS	*Stroking* or *rubbing*, when cleaning or healing wounds. *Covering* the face with one or both hands when feeling shy or threatened; also the top of the head when shocked or surprised. *Interlocking* hands on the head when in trouble; *pressing* the forehead with the palm when in deep thought; *supporting* the head under the chin when *lying* on front; *gripping* one or both feet/ankles when *sitting* cross-legged. *Slapping* body parts and *masturbating* in frustration. *Grasping* tail; *supporting* breasts or pregnant belly from below with open hands.
FINGERS/ THUMBS	Squeezing fist; rubbing/scratching body parts; picking. or *scraping* eyes, ears, nose, teeth, toes, anus, dead skin; *stroking/pulling out* hair when *cleaning, preening* or *grooming*; *interlocking* and *twisting* when agitated or impatient; *tapping* on body parts when uncertain; *pinching* skin around a bite to *squeeze* out toxins.
LEGS	Joint contact of both when *standing, sitting, sleeping, springing, squatting, swimming; interlocking* when *sitting* on the ground; *clapping* inside of knees when excited; *holding* groin when needing to urinate.
FEET/TOES	*Rubbing/scratching* one another, or other body parts; *crossing* feet with *interlocked* ankles while *bouncing* on both legs; *sitting* on both feet *turned* in, with knees *touching* each other in front; *hooking* the toes around the ankle of the other leg when standing and watching or waiting.
TAIL	*Curling* upwards/downwards; *brushing* body sides when being bothered by insects, or as a warning signal; *covering* body to maintain warmth when asleep.

Volitional self-touching

EYELIDS	Slow *blink* when annoyed, or quick *blink* when surprised; *blinking* in coded alphabet for communication; keeping shut when ignoring or enjoying.
TONGUE	*Clucking* against palate; *flapping* or *warbling* against the upper lip, as a tremolo; *whistling* and *hissing* with the tip of the tongue against lips or teeth. *Licking* lips in anticipation of food or sex.
LIPS	*Blowing, whistling* or making plosive noises with both lips *pursed* or *vibrating*; vocal *calls* made by rhythmically covering and uncovering the *open* mouth; *sucking* poison from bites; the repertoire of silent lip expressions.
JAWS	*Grinding* and *gnashing* teeth as a warning; *opening* wide and *snapping* shut as a threat; *biting* own hands or feet, in frustration or when itching.
NOSE / SNOUT	*Pulling down* to *touch* with *turned out* upper lip, as a warning *grimace*. *Nuzzling* under own arm or between knees in a *coiled* resting position; *sniffing* own body parts.
ARMS	*Crossing* wrists on lower belly, lower back or laps when seated; *crossing* forearms on the chest when praying, or *crossing* on belly as a sign of dominance, or under the knees when sitting with legs *folded*; arms on the knees and head/cheek on arms when dreaming or thinking; various crossed *interlocks* as communication signals, such as two forearms in front of or above the head, or of one arm under the knee of one leg. Also, in ritual dance, *flapping* arms on body sides above the waist, *touching* elbow with the opposite thigh and so on.
HANDS	*Covering* face with spread fingers; *placing* open hand horizontally to the forehead to protect against glare; *covering* ears against unwanted noise; *covering* mouth with open hand when suppressing own sound; *covering* the head with two hands against rain, heat or falling objects; *stroking* head/hair with two palms when upset or uncertain; *braiding* own hair; *interlocking* two hands on the back of the neck, with elbows joined in front as a sign of distress; *grasping* own throat with one hand, as a threatening gesture. Rhythmic *clapping* with both hands, or against other body parts. In ritual dance, *holding* interlocked hands in front, behind and above the head; *placing* open hands on hips or buttocks; *holding* opposite foot with hand above supporting knee; hands *joined* vertically in front when praying. Various touch compositions of hands with the head/face, other arm, leg, foot and other body parts.
FINGERS THUMB	*Snapping*, or *tapping* body parts; *pinching* skin or *pulling, brushing* or *oiling* hair when grooming. In body decoration, *painting* the face and other body parts with thumb and fingertips. *Massaging* and *healing*. Imitating flora and fauna with thumb/fingers, representing themes such as opening/closing flowers, drinking/eating reptiles, fish *swimming*, birds *flying*, elephants *walking* and other creatures. *Crossing* fingers of the same hand, or with those of the other; the fingers and hands have a vast tactile vocabulary of signals and gestures of every type .
LEGS	*Crossing* with *interlocked* knees when *turning* around on the spot; *clapping* knees with inside thigh in a crouching position; therapeutic routines of legs *touching* other body parts when *lying* down or *sitting* with legs straight or folded. *Beating* legs rhythmically in the air when *springing* high in a dance or in conjunction with arm touches.
FEET	Soles *joined* in front when seated, with legs *folded* and feet *turned in* or *crossed* over opposite thigh. Repeatedly *slapping* the foot against the opposite thigh behind/above the calf, or *clapping* the buttock with sole or arched foot and leg *folded* behind. Rhythmical *tapping* of the feet against one another on the ground or in the air in a dance; *beating* a rhythm with the toes against the ankle of the

supporting leg. *Placing* the toes on the back of the head when performing acrobatic tricks.

Functional *Subconscious* touching another body

TONGUE	*Licking* infant clean, protecting wounds with saliva; *licking* ants off a stick.
LIPS	*Suckling*; mouth-to-mouth *feeding*; *kissing/grooming* infants or close family members. *Sucking* nutrition from fresh prey; habitual *sucking* of thumb or big toe.
JAWS	*Gnawing/holding* in infant play or during mating; *catching* prey, *biting* and *tearing* flesh, *masticating* to feed offspring. *Biting* off a new-born's umbilical cord. *Biting* the wrist, ankle or throat of an opponent.
NOSE /SNOUT	*Rubbing* noses as introduction. *Nuzzling* family members. *Ramming* one another in gnaw play. *Pushing* with the snout.
ARMS	*Holding* baby and *covering* its body; *hugging* family members, dominant individuals or friends; *embracing* the mate during courtship and copulation. *Carrying* prey or a wounded warrior. *Supporting* the old and ill during travel, *handling* domestic animals. *Locking* the arms around mother's neck. *Pulling/pushing*, *shaking/throwing* one-another in play or wrestling, *grabbing* the neck when riding, *squeezing* an enemy to death.
HANDS	Nursing an infant or wounded warrior by *stroking, washing* or *massaging* tender body parts. Salutation by *touching* or *slapping* one another's hand, shoulder, breast, belly, genitals or buttocks. *Tearing* the ear, tail or hair of an intruder when protecting an infant. *Pulling* young ones by the wrist away from danger; *smacking* to punish bad behaviour. *Grasping* parents' skin/hair when *hanging* on to their bodies.
FINGERS/ THUMB	*Gripping* small prey while skinning it, *pulling* feathers, or *scraping* the inside of a carcass. *Milking* domestic animals and *washing* udders. Grooming an infant, *picking* its nose, eyes and ears; cleaning its anus and genitals, feeding it solids. *Gripping* each other's fingers in ritual ceremonies; *touching* a female's genitals to assess her sexual receptivity.
LEGS	*Squeezing* with the thighs when riding an animal, or when an infant rides on its mother's back or neck; *kicking, interlocking, twisting, pushing, pulling, stamping* in gnaw-play, and later in real contests for dominance. *Wrapping* around the male in 'verso-verso' copulation.
FEET/TOES	Foetal *kicking* from within uterus. *Pressing* belly while *sucking* mother's breast. *Grasping* mother's thumb/fingers, as an evolutionary echo of *holding on* to branches. *Gripping* parents' skin or hair with toes when *clinging* on their back. *Grasping, squeezing, pressing, kicking*, etc. in juvenile gnaw-play or adult wrestling.
BODY PARTS	Enveloping touch of infant in the uterus, and *touching* breast, belly, neck and shoulders after birth. Chest/belly contact when *embracing* or *hugging*; when *riding* on their back or shoulders. Various full-body contact in juvenile gnaw play. Belly/buttock and genital contact in 'verso-dorso' copulation. Wrestling and hand-to-hand fighting techniques including *boxing* with fists, pressing with the extended *thumb*, *interlocking* elbows, *kicking* and *pushing* with the feet, *strangling, twisting* and *blocking* actions.

Volitional inter-body touch

TONGUE *Licking* offspring to confirm family scent; *licking* sibling's face in grooming, or submissively *licking* the chest and shoulders of the dominant individual; *licking* male genitals for sexual arousal; *licking* wounds of family members, or *interlocking* tongues during courtship.

LIPS *Picking up* termites by inhalation; mothers *kissing* infants; lip-to-lip *kissing* in courtship; oral sexual arousal.

JAWS Friendly *gnawing* as salutation; *playing* with prey for the initiation of juveniles; *biting* the snout of a predator in self-defence, and other body parts in a contest, or of smaller prey.

FOREHEAD *Nuzzling/stroking* the neck, chest, belly in courtship display. *Ramming/striking* one another during disputes or contests. *Balancing* a juvenile on the forehead, upright or head-to-head upside down, with open arms and legs vertical, as a show

ARMS The arms are used for a tremendous variety of touch communications between mother and infant, dominant and young, family members, shepherds and cattle, and so on. Patronising *touch* on the shoulder by a dominant individual to a submissive one. *Striking* the chest with a fist as a warning. *Holding* the horns while *twisting* the neck of a hunted animal, or *lifting* an attacker off its feet and *throwing* it to the ground. *Circling* an opponent's waist with both arms, *lifting* and *squeezing* him to impede respiration to the point of *breaking* ribs. *Twisting* or *squeezing* an opponent's neck until submission or strangulation. The worshipping repertoire included *holding* arms on each other's' shoulders when circling or stamping on a spot, *lifting* arms with *interlocked* elbows when praying on the knees, and *lowering* them to the thighs when *bending* body down to salute the totem; in secular dance routines, *turning* clockwise on the spot in pairs with *interlocked* elbows and anticlockwise with rigid arms. Shamans used arm motions on the leg, back, arm, neck and other body parts in physical treatments to heal the sick (including animals). Role-play to train the young in the behaviour patterns of predators and the defence skills of prey.

HANDS Infants *press* the mother's breast to get more milk, and Instinctively *grasp* and *squeeze* fingers, toes and tails. Chaotically *slapping* mother's body parts to confirm and enjoy her presence through direct tactile contact. *Shaking* and *clapping* hands and other body parts in salutation; *slapping* faces, *pulling* hair, *hitting* chest or belly with fists in disputes between females. *Grasping* the wrist of a juvenile to *pull* it up a tree, or *drag* it from branch to branch. *Joining* hands in female ritual dances when moving to or from the centre of the circle, or *turning* on the spot with a partner during nuptial rites. In mythical pantomime, males *wrestled* with hand *tricks* and acrobatic *lifts*, or mimicked animals in a hunt using many *strikes, twists* and *interlocks* of the hands and wrists. The need for effective silent communication under threatening circumstances gave rise to a complete language of coded tactile hand signals: *pressing* or *tapping* the hand on someone's shoulder, *squeezing* their wrist, *gripping* the hip of the hunter in front to prevent him from making a wrong move and so on. Apes transmit touch signals along a chain of *holding* hands.

Instinctive functional touch of inanimate objects

TONGUE	*Chewing, spitting* out pips, *licking* salt or other minerals, or nectar from flowers; *picking* food residue from the teeth.
LIPS	*Peeling* soft fruit and vegetables, *passing* masticated food to infants from mouth-to-mouth, *drinking, picking up* berries from a twig, *pulling* petals from flowers, *sucking* honey from a comb.
JAWS	Cracking nuts, biting and masticating food, breaking, holding, cutting other vegetable foods.
FOREHEAD	*Covering* face with a large leaf, bark or branch to obtain shade, enjoying cool water from falls or a rain shower.
ARMS	*Breaking* branches, *felling* trees and *carrying* logs or stones to construct a home base or pathway. *Digging* holes to find water or to store food. *Swimming* and *paddling.*
HANDS	*Rubbing, scraping, battering, cleaning, gathering* berries and tubers, *cleaning* and *storing* food. Testing water, ice, snow, salt, oil, ashes and minerals for temperature and texture. *Breaking* stalks and *pressing* out fruit and vegetable juices. *Holding* stones and tools, *digging, climbing/descending, building*
FINGERS/ THUMB	*Picking up* berries, fruit, nuts or shells; *scraping* out seeds or sap, *peeling* fruit or vegetables, *digging* out roots, *twisting* and *squeezing* plants to collect medicinal liquids, *stripping* twigs, *pulling* grasses, *walking* and *running* (on knuckles).
LEGS	*Crawling, climbing* and *swimming. Holding* heavy objects on thighs when squatting. *Squeezing* a tree trunk or branch with the thighs.
FEET	*Landing* on the ground when *walking, running* or *jumping,* and *sliding* on ice or mud. *Pushing* away from the edge of a cliff when *diving. Standing* on wet grass, unstable mud, hot sand, sharp gravel, forest floor or wet stone. *Climbing* up or down a tree trunk. *Stamping* and *hopping* in frustration; *propelling* water when *swimming.*

Volitional touch with inanimate objects

EYELIDS	Placing mollusc shells on eyelids for shamanic healing; cosmetic decoration.
TONGUE	Being pierced and decorated with metal rings or precious stones, or pinched with bamboo/wooden clips. *Vibrating* to regulate expiration when making sound signals through a reed or a bamboo stalk.
LIPS	*Holding* a pipe when smoking or *blowing* sound signals.
JAWS	*Stripping* branches to make domestic or fighting tools, *peeling* fruit or *scraping* coral for use in body decoration. *Pulling* the end of cord to tightening it. Making rhythmic signals by *tapping* the teeth against small hollow bones.
FOREHEAD	*Wearing* masks or helmets. *Pulling* a heavy sled attached by rope to a bandana above the eyebrows. *Balancing* a pole supporting an acrobatic performance. *Ramming* an enemy with a horned mask in wrestling contests. *Forming* a bridge posture with the feet and forehead on the ground.
ARMS	Contact with rope, leather, metal, feathers, bracelets and amulets in male body decoration; for females, similar adornments made of grasses, flowers, crystals, shells, metals and precious stones. Being painted. *Standing* or *walking* upside-down on the arms during entertainment and performing *cartwheels* and other acrobatic *tricks. Lifting* and *carrying* stones or logs in contests of strength.
HANDS	Building shelters from reeds, lianas, pelts, branches, leaves, ice, mud and stones. Making clothes from grasses, leaves, twigs, bark. Prepare paints from various materials. Making acoustic instruments from shells, gourds and animal skins

without special tools. In shows, juggling various objects in solo or group performance. Performing contests in stick manipulation or *catching* objects and weapons.

FINGERS/ THUMB	*Braiding* belts, decorations, baskets, trays and other domestic objects. *Knitting, binding* and *weaving* to make cloth and decorations with primitive accessories. *Playing* stringed, woodwind and percussion instruments. Painting domestic objects, ritual accessories and weapons with coloured clays or oils using stems or sponges. Acupuncture treatment with bone, shells, quills or thorns.
LEGS/FEET	*Walking, hopping* and *turning* on stilts or ladders; *skating* and *skiing.* Playing ankle bracelets or bells by *hopping* from one leg to the other. *Swinging* on a trapeze; *walking* on a rope bridge over a river. *Balancing, spinning, throwing* and *catching* objects with both feet when lying down. *Standing* bare-footed or *tapping* rhythmic sequences. *Kicking* objects for play or sport. *Pressing* for support against the bottom of a canoe when paddling; *leaping* from one branch to another.
BODY PARTS	*Crawling* on the belly and chest or *climbing* up or down a tree; *swinging/diving,* or *sitting* on a log; *rotating* a hoop up and down the body; *rolling* on the ground when playing or fighting hand-to-hand; being *covered* by animals' skins while sleeping.

In addition, there are innumerable tactile contacts between the body and inanimate objects in which the individual is merely the passive recipient of the touch: being *stabbed* with a knife, *shot* with arrow, *knocked down* by a stone or *whipped* by a whip; being rained on, and so on.

TACTILE MOTION WITH TOOLS

Voluntary touch of self or others

HEAD/HAIR	*Brushing* with a comb; *cleansing* with ash; *arranging* hair with twig or bone; *braiding* hair with grass or ribbon, *decorating* with flowers, berries, feathers, claws, etc. *Cutting* hair with blade. *Wearing* mask with spikes or horns as a weapon. *Balancing* mythical accessories on the head in ritual ceremonies, performing *headstands* or *heading* gourds as part of initiation training for combat; carrying baskets or other vessels.
TONGUE	*Picking up* prepared food from sticks. Being *stitched* or *cut* with a blade or *touched* by dental healing instruments.
LIPS	Being *painted* with lipstick or *pierced* for decoration. *Sucking* pipe burning tobacco or other narcotics. *Blowing* pigment through a straw or reed when wall painting. *Shooting* darts through blowpipe. *Breathing* through a reed while under water; *holding* bait to entice prey.
JAWS	Being cleaned by sponge or toothpick. *Scraping* flesh with teeth from bones. *Hanging* upside down in tree as a trapeze while *holding* another with a wooden jaw-to-jaw contact tool.
HANDS/ ARMS	**Body decoration**: *tattooing, piercing* with a needle, *perforating* with a comb, *cutting* with a blade, dressing the hair with sticks or bones, *painting* the body with a feather or reed. **Arts and crafts**: *painting* images on cave walls or domestic objects with a brick, blowpipe or straw, using liquid pigments. Using engraving or scraping tools to decorate wood, stone, shells, leather, gourds or coral; using implements to make vessels and other domestic objects from clay, wood, bone, stone and so on. **Food preparation** and domestic labour: making and using hatchets, ladles, graters, scrapers, scoops, plates, cooking and storage vessels. Operating a pestle to

grind food, *mixing* food with a stick or spoon, using a brushwood poker to maintain a fire, *wielding* a stick to keep intruders or pests at bay, *filling* vessels with water, *rubbing* stone or wood to wash pelts or cloth.

Hunting and fishing: making and using instruments such as sticks, clubs, blades, nets, spears, bows, axes, hatchets, lassos, stones, boomerangs, catapults, harpoons, and scrapers for skinning

Animal rearing: making and using tools such as prods, whips, leads, chokers, yokes, reins, and agricultural implements: rakes, spades, dibbers, pitchforks, scythes, sieves, machetes.

Sport: making and using accessories such as poles for vaulting, paddles, balls and discs for *throwing*; making sounds with gongs or bowed instruments.

Music: making and playing wind, stringed, plucked, and percussion instruments from wood, bone, skin, intestines, bladders, shells, baleen, bamboo and reed

Combat: making and using weapons such as slings, blades, shields, garrottes, horns, tusks, pikes whips, clubs, knuckledusters and projectiles. As all these tactile actions with accessories had their own motion requirements (*collecting, spreading, pressing, tearing, cutting, tying, whipping, hitting, throwing, catching* and so on), they each contributed to the acquisition of new plastic motion skills. Eventually, of course, these prototype accessories evolved into the vast array of manual instruments of modern times.

LEGS	*Walking* on stilts, *swimming* with artificial flippers, *climbing* with bear or cat claws, *sliding* on snow and ice with rudimentary skis.
FEET	Wearing animal hooves to disguise one's tracks, wearing bark sandals, *balancing* on a moving rock or log, and much later, operating pedal-driven machines and wearing specialised footwear for different functions, from *climbing* and *dancing* to *swimming*.

Multiple *Voluntary* contact of the body with accessories

CIRCUS ACTS:	Tightrope *walking* with balancing pole; *running, leaping, hopping* and somersaulting with ribbons; simultaneously juggling with various objects and *rotating* several rings on the neck, waist, ankles, wrists and elbows.
WORK:	*Carrying* two buckets of water with a yoke on the shoulders; *carting* building materials with a wheelbarrow. *Pulling* a barge using bandanas on the forehead and belts across the shoulders and chest. Mounted warriors wearing head and body armour *driving* their steeds with their legs and feet in the stirrups while attacking with a weapon in one hand and a shield in the other.
MUSICAL PERFOR-MANCE:	The bagpipe player *carries* the instrument on one shoulder, from where it hangs on a belt, *pressing* the air from the bladder with his elbow while *modulating* the sound with his lips on the pipe and *playing* the main tune with fingers of both hands. The accordion player *carries* the instrument with two shoulder belts, *squeezing* the bellows with the left arm while *fingering* the keyboard with his right hand. 'One-man band' entertainers take this multiple-contact dexterity to extremes, both hands *playing* a guitar hanging from one shoulder while one foot *shakes* rattles on the toes, the left foot *operates* a bass drum pedal, the elbows *clash* cymbals and the lips *play* a mouth organ fastened to a support around the neck.

fig I/1

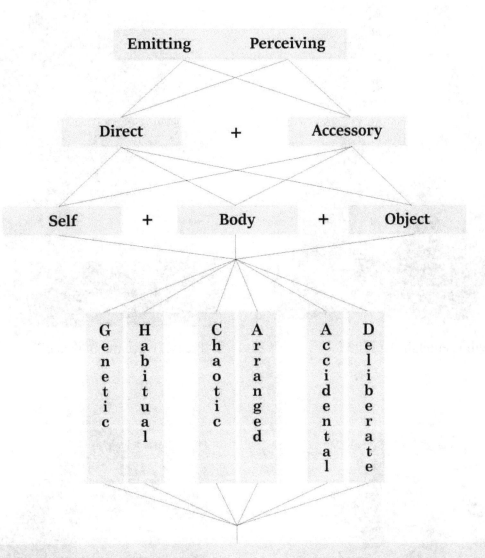

Touch - Functionary Structure

Emitting   Perceiving

Direct   +   Accessory

Self   +   Body   +   Object

| G e n e t i c | H a b i t u a l | | C h a o t i c | A r r a n g e d | | A c c i d e n t a l | D e l i b e r a t e |

Inner/Outer; Still/In Motion; On Spot/ Travelling	Space
One+One; One+Group; Group-Inside; Group+Group	Make-up
Jab/Firm; Light/Heavy; Single/Repetitive	Tense
Pleasant/Painful; Welcome/Annoy; Seduce/Assault	Emotion

"…enough is enough! Isn't it?"

"Please, leave me in peace!"

"Hey you are really hurting me!"

"…well, what are they up to now?"

Plates showing aspects of balance, from *Anatomy for Artists* by Angelo and Giovanni Morelli
1. Shift of the body relative to the line of gravity.
2. The line of gravity in walking and running.
3. The mechanism used to make the transition from an erect symmetrical position to an erect asymmetrical position.

Skeletal Facilities for Plastic Motion

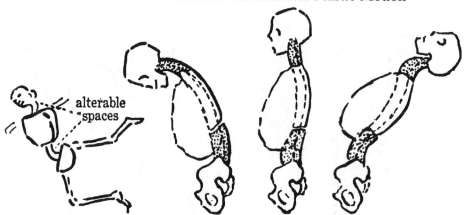

Diagrams showing alterable section and unalterable masses.
Source: B. Germain, *Anatomy of Movement* 1993

Positon of the spinal column in various dance cultures.
Selected by American dancer, Russel Meriweather Hughes (known as La Meri).

a) curious   b) puzzled   c) indifferent   d) rejecting   e) watching   f) self-satisfied
g) welcoming   h) determined i) stealthy   j) searching   k) discovering l) attentive
m) violent anger n) excited   o) stretching   p) suspicious   q) sneaking   r) shy
s) thinking   t) affected

Source: Rosemberg and Langer (1965)

Miming Sequences by male actor

Drawings from one of Meyerhold's biomechanical exercises (1922)

Drawings of Duelling sequences by various artists in the past (J. Antonio).

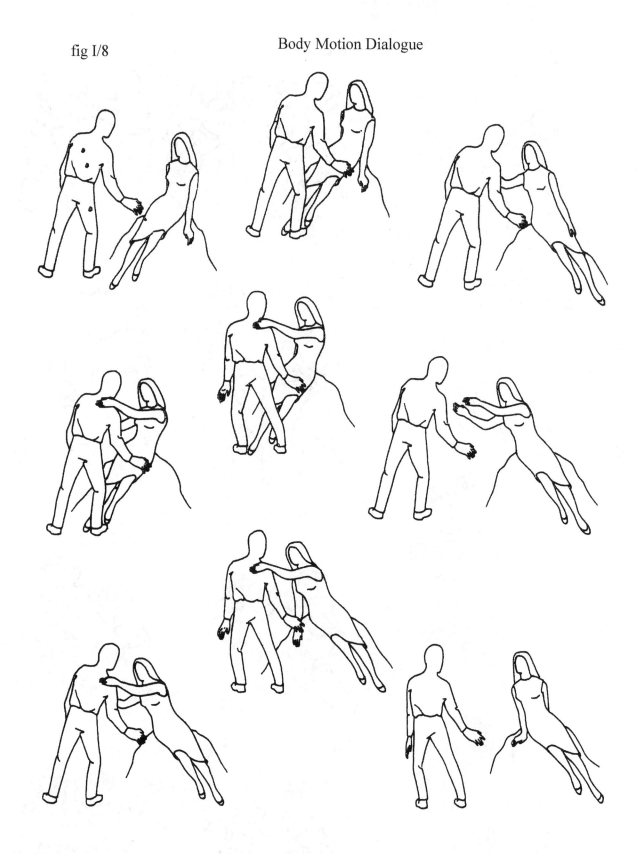

Postures in male/female encounters.
Source: Spiegel and Machotka (1974)

FUNCTIONAL POSTURING AND MORPHOLOGY

INTRODUCTION

Although the physical shape of any species evolved over a very long period to correspond with their environment, these anatomical adaptations often resulted in complicating the animal's vital functions. Major changes in local environmental conditions forced many species to live in unsuitable and arduous new circumstances, occasionally resulting in their extinction.

The survivors, like cetacean mammals, gradually changed their body shape to survive in an aquatic rather than terrestrial environment, moving around in water with virtually no gravitational limitations, mating and giving birth at sea. Flightless semi-aquatic birds like penguins modified their wings into fins for *swimming*, the short tails once used for aerial navigation becoming a fifth extremity to assist their upright body position on land. Penguins nevertheless preserved the original beak and continue breeding on terra firma. Bats, on the other hand, succeeded in adapting to the harsh environmental conditions by acquiring the ability to *dangle* upside down from precarious rock perches in caves and cliffs, and by evolving the membranes between their fore- and hind limbs into wide wings that permit sustained flight – but they lack the ability to *glide* while hunting in the air, and their terrestrial locomotion is severely compromised.

Lizards and other reptiles provide good examples of this adaptation to prevailing environmental circumstances. Some acquired body shapes with very special plastic motion facilities, allowing these ancient species to use their five extremities (four legs and a tail) for quadruped *crawling* and *climbing*, bipedal *running* and *skipping* (including over water), *burrowing* and *swimming* below the surface of sand or water, *jumping, gliding* or *parachuting* through the air, and even the extreme ability to amputate their own tail to avoid predation.

Lizards were also the greatest posturing performers before the advent of marsupials. On land, it is they who pioneered motionless body actions such as *curling/crouching, inclining, sagging* and *twisting*. They also developed an extensive vocabulary of postural gestures with the four legs and tail to communicate in their courtship repertoires. They eventually became great mimics, acquiring the ability to feign death or pose as terrifying monsters to deter predators.

Unlike lizards, giraffes failed to adapt their physical facilities as fully to similar changes in their savannah environment, as camels did. Although they developed the exceptional body height, with a very long neck and legs, required to reach the tree canopy, this adaptation presented the giraffes with problems when it came to drinking water at ground level This obliges them to *place* their forelimbs far apart in order to *lower* the head sufficiently to reach the source – an awkward body stance that inevitably made them uncomfortably vulnerable to predators.

Our close relatives the apes eventually lost their fifth extremity – the tail – along the evolutionary journey from arboreal to terrestrial living, when their original quadruped locomotion was supplemented by the option of moving around on the hind legs alone. Hominids nevertheless retained the five-toed feet once required to *grasp* branches. Practically useless as these are to shoe-shod humans, it is reasonable to assume that, over time, these superfluous digits will eventually evolve out of existence, paradoxically reverting the highly evolved species to the condition of ungulates in this respect.

MAIN POSTURAL SPHERES OF MOVEMENT

All vertebrates and species with hard exoskeletons have a well-defined three-dimensional body shape. Those without, such as worms and similar species, have more amorphous body shapes, with very limited postural possibilities (although they are instantly recognisable by their predators and prey by their plastic characteristics and motions).

Species with various extremities (fins, wings, limbs, tail, proboscis, horns, tusks and so on) have more complicated body structures that can deliberately be made visually confusing. Some change their basic body shape by *puffing out* or *shrinking* their crop or thorax, or use their extremities to *enlarge* or *reduce* their body outline - birds by *spreading* or *folding* their wings and tail, tortoises by *projecting* or *retracting* the head and legs out of and into the shell, elephants by *coiling* or *stretching* the trunk and/or tail, snakes by *curling* up or *elongating* the entire body. Other species use postural mimicking to disguise themselves as rocks, twigs, lifeless bodies, other predators or poisonous animals.

Snakes *press* their tubular bodies to the ground in order to absorb the sun's heat, and *coil* their bodies at night to preserve the warmth accumulated during the day. After *swallowing* a bigger prey, the snake's body *expands* to accommodate the bulk of the victim, and remains in a linear position to facilitate digestion. During copulation, the mates *wrap* their bodies around each other horizontally and maintain this position until fertilisation is complete. A similar mutual *wrapping* motion occurs vertically in some species between two competing males, and this contest posture is maintained until the weaker snake gives in.

The snake-necked turtle is the champion neck projector, and can *extend* its neck by some 30 cms – the approximate length of its shell. As well as being used to assert dominance among the turtle's peers, this astonishing facility comes as a great shock to predators or prey. The males *rise up* on their hind limbs when mating or confronting male competitors, *pushing* each other with their forelimbs and undershells while upright in an attempt to *throw* the opponent on their back – a disastrous eventuality for the loser. Being unable to right itself without outside help because of the restricted sphere of movement of its stubby legs, the defeated turtle is vulnerable to the risk of heatstroke from the sun as well as being easy prey for a passing predator.

The three main spheres of movement for most animals correspond to the three spatial dimensions: **horizontal, vertical** and **angular**.

The horizontal and vertical planes can also include inverted postures, as in the turtle example above, or snakes when they *suspend* themselves from branches.

Angular postures include steep and shallow angles, as with the mating position of male turtles. Although the same three spheres of movement apply equally in the air and under water, the motions are intrinsically freer and harder to separate and distinguish individually.

The three spheres of movement can be subdivided according to their relationship to ground level, the body shape of the species and its functional requirements and the gravitational factors influencing body posture on land, in the trees, in the air or under water.

STANDARD PATTERNS OF THE POSTURAL REPERTOIRE

Inclined:	*Bowing* to the chief or balancing on one leg while *bending* upper body laterally
Reclined:	*Reclining* head back on mother's shoulder or *arching* back to gaze at stars
Straightening:	Returning to a vertical position after *bowing* or *arching* the upper body
Leaning:	*Leaning* forwards, backwards or sideways with the body straight, as against wind or water
Lunging:	*Striding* forward when attacking or seizing
Twisting:	Upper body torsion before *throwing* a weapon
Protruding:	Head *butting* or *punching/kicking* with limbs in a wrestling duel

COMMON BODY STANCES

In all the following postures, each class of amphibian/reptile and bird/ mammalian species not only shares similar body placement characteristics in space, but also stances that correspond to their particular plastic structure and functions. When motionless: *lying, sitting, kneeling, squatting, crouching, standing, suspended*; when in motion: *crawling, floating, diving, leaping, gliding, clinging, riding.*

There are five main positional orientations: horizontal, angular, arched, upright and compound. As with the few basic colours and notes in painting and music, these basic orientations have unlimited variations and auxiliary stances and positions of the body, as well as additional plastic elements through the use of accessories.

Each of these body stances can accommodate various *posturing patterns* according to the physical condition of the body and its environment. *Lying, kneeling, squatting, gliding* and *clinging and standing/suspended* positions involve a minimal vocabulary of poses and gestures because of the body's limited mobility. *Sitting, crouching, crawling, floating* and *diving* positions have more postural scope because of their extra mobility and the higher level of the body. *Standing, hanging suspended, leaping* and *riding* positions allow virtually unlimited scope for plastic patterns, both static and on the move.

PLASTIC CHARACTERISTICS of BODY POSTURES

Stooping:	*Bending* head and shoulders forward, as when humiliated before a victorious enemy
Sprawling:	Loose, chaotically awkward positions after exertion or battle
Sagging:	*Drooping*, as when a wounded warrior is carried away
Curled up:	When receiving a blow to the belly
Drawing up:	Assuming the pre-fighting stance
Akimbo:	*Spreading* the arms and legs, as when leaping
Folded:	*Wrapping* one another amorously in an embrace with interlocked necks and limbs

All postures are based on the physical characteristics of the body concerned – its morphology and musculoskeletal structure, centre of gravity, kinetic power and plastic motion facilities. They also depend on the mentality and mood of the individual.

Each postural pattern evolved through millions of years into an instinctive functional repertoire for practical everyday use, communicated genetically from one generation to the next.

The diagram below (fig. I/9) illustrates the evolution of on/off-ground postural repertoires and their changing spatial orientation – notably, the gradual development and deformation of the spine in the transition from flat-to-the-ground, through semi-raised positions to the fully upright stance.

The inherent survival advantage tendency of attaining a higher body position is underlined by common behaviours of many amphibians and reptiles during their daily feeding, mating and contests. This constant pressure to appear taller (and therefore stronger) was a powerful stimulus for the spinal column's steady adaptation from its original horizontal orientation into *angular*, and later, *vertical* stances.

Hominids were of course far from being the first to discover the advantages of the upright stance, and became aware of them by observing many other species standing on their hind legs, often for extended periods, when mating, competing or feeding.

With apes, the phenomenal transition from quadruped to biped existence is often misrepresented as a by-product of superior hominid intelligence, implying some sort of a 'Eureka' moment to prompt the change. The reality is of course very different, in that even the smallest anatomical adaptation takes place over many generations. The bipedal stance of hominids was the product of intense observation and painstaking trial and error experiments, and the consequent anatomical changes gradually took place over millions of years.

BODY SHAPE AS IDENTIFIER

Body shape is determined by selective evolution in response to local environmental phenomena rather than choice. The resulting form always corresponds exactly to surrounding ecological conditions, and is superbly adapted to the animal's main functional requirements in terms of feeding, reproduction, communication and so on.

Although many animal species do not see in colour, most are able instantly to identify other creatures by their body shape. This visual recognition may be genetically programmed and used instinctively by infants from birth, and complemented thereafter by knowledge accumulated through personal experience (including the accompanying acoustic and scent characteristics).

Most animals have sophisticated visual memories of their surroundings, whether underwater, on land or in the air, because memorising, classifying and recalling thorough observation of the environment is an essential for survival. This unconscious reflexive behaviour allows instant recognition of familiar body shapes, friend or foe, to prompt the appropriate response of acceptance, indifference or rejection.

This internal archive of remembered shapes represented a vast database for non-verbal communication and mimetic culture in general, and encompassed the expression of emotion, mimicry, gestures, dance pantomime, silent language and other visual forms of expression. The growing success of these sociocultural activities depended crucially on the ability to make graphically clear bodily signs through postural patterns, and the visual ability to recognise such signs made by others. Unsatisfactorily transmitted or incorrectly understood bodily messages could involve tragic consequences for the individual or the entire tribe.

Vulnerable species therefore sought to prevent such problems by initiating their young into these skills from the very beginning, instructing them in the entire lexicon of body posture patterns, ear/tail gestures and muzzle grimaces. Although some of these performing and perceptual abilities were genetically programmed, the more complex gestural skills were acquired by the young themselves through gnaw-play or by copying adults.

This initiation programme included the posturing vocabulary of other local creatures (including predators) in addition to the pack or tribe's own plastic communication repertoire. Infants learned from an early age how to distinguish positive signals from threatening ones, and how to recognise aggressive postures in good time. The constant imperatives to assert dominance for reasons of feeding, mating, social position and territorial defence stimulated the gradual creation of an encyclopaedic dictionary of body shapes and gestural postures, to be memorised and subconsciously systematised by creatures of supposedly limited brainpower. Some species even managed to *imitate* the body shape and plastic signatures of common predators, much to the discomfiture of their vulnerable neighbours.

MORPHOLOGICAL EVOLUTION

The genesis of body posturing can be traced back to the earliest life forms, with the unicellular organisms whose micro-spherical shape changes reflexively in response to various stimuli for functional or security reasons. Motivated solely by the survival instinct, the plastic range of these unconscious behaviours grew with the advent of more advanced apodal (legless) species like worms and jellyfish. These can be seen to engage in bodily dialogue between sexually attracted individuals, by slightly *lifting* the tail-tip or head, for example, or making a tiny *sideways move* in the middle part of the amorphous jellyfish body or a worm almost imperceptibly *flattening* part of its tubular body. Such stances are used to express attraction or warning as well as for functional reasons such as the need to absorb heat.

The appearance of primitive limbed crustaceans like **lobsters** and **sea scorpions** was an important stage in the evolution of body shape, and heralded the beginning of a postural alphabet of meaningful gestures by the head, antennae, thorax, limbs, abdomen and tail. After some 600 million years of evolution, these ancient species remain to this day very efficient plastic communicators, forming complex postural patterns with various body parts. Some five million years ago, they handed over the baton of the evolutionary relay race to insects such as ants and locusts, which proceeded to develop their own posture/gestural vocabulary to the highest level of bodily communication.

As soon as morphological adaptation to the environment reaches its optimum level, the essential body shape of any species has no stimulus for evolving any further, which is why so many have remained virtually static for millions of years.

After **ants** and **locusts, lizard** species became the new pioneers of gestural evolution, massively increasing their plastic facilities using the highly developed extremities.

The next stage of morphological evolution was initiated by semi-upright mammals like **marsupials** and **bears**, which could function on their hind limbs for prolonged periods and use their liberated forelimbs for defence and signalling purposes. With their greater plasticity and more advanced performing skills, they elaborated various communicative bodily stances and gestures which for the first time began to approach the postural facilities of upright bipedal **lemurs, monkeys** and **apes** – the final stage of the gestural evolution process.

The body shape and posturing repertoire of **chimpanzees** and **gorillas** closely resembles that of **hominids**, although significant differences in plastic anatomy, stance and motion coordination remain. By contrast, **Homo Erectus** gradually lost many of the apes' structural body attributes during the adaptation process, such as the *crouched* and *squatting* stance, the disproportion in relative arm and leg length, pelvic stiffness when *carrying* the weight of a *dangling* body, a centre of gravity mainly suitable for quadruped balance and motion coordination facilities in the horizontal position.

The stance that came with **Homo Erectus** was concomitant with a new body shape based on the single-curvature upper back of the ape evolving into the double-curvature spine we have today. This serpentine backbone and its accompanying musculoskeletal changes created the new centre of gravity required for permanent bipedal existence.

Later still with the advent of **Homo Habilis** and **Neanderthalis**, the upright stance allowed the body plastic facilities of their extremities to develop the highly sophisticated gestural coordination that underpins all primal nonverbal communication.

COMPARATIVE MORPHOLOGY OF APES AND HOMINIDS

The transition from an age-old **horizontal** body position to a **vertical** stance was as formidable a functional and psychological challenge as the adaptation from one physical environment to another. Although the planet-wide environmental cataclysms that forced terrestrial creatures to revert to their original aquatic way of life involved radical metamorphoses (especially of the extremities), no species changed the fundamental horizontal orientation of its body structure.

As we have seen, lemur and monkey primates represent the link between quadruped and biped locomotion and deploy both with equal facility, *moving* easily in a horizontal body position on all four legs, but often *walking* and *hopping* on their hind limbs alone with the body upright; *climbing* vertically and *sitting* in trees, *hanging* head upwards or upside down, or *descending* head-first using four limbs.

Great Apes like the gorilla and chimpanzee take the upright body stance to a higher level. With its bulky and square body shape, the gorilla usually *moves* slowly on all four limbs, with slightly *bent* knees and *stretched* elbows. It *stands* upright on its hind limbs with an inwardly curved lower spine and stiff pelvic area, but the upper spine allows vigorous *posturing patterns* and *gestural signs* to be made by the head and arms, accompanied by expressive *facial grimaces*.

By contrast, the chimpanzee body shape is more *crouched* and floppy, but the animal is more agile and flexible. Its quadruped position on the ground is more squat, and its centre of gravity closer to the hind limbs. The spine is more outwardly curved as a result of its primarily arboreal habitat, and the pelvis more open than the gorilla's. Chimps adopt upright stances more frequently, both on the ground and in the trees. As their *movements* are generally lighter and brisker, their *postural patterns* and *gestures* seem (to human eyes at least) more chaotic and less clearly defined.

Most animal species have the potential to hold the body upright, but in order not to expose themselves unnecessarily to danger, exercise this ability sparingly and for very short periods of time, either for the purposes of sexual attraction or to increase their field of vision.

Chart 2　　　　　Form / Types in Body Shape of Animated Species

AREA: SHAPE:	Aquatic	Terrestrial	Arboreal	Aerial
Crosswise	Frog, Ray, Skate	Frog, Crab	Dragon lizard	Crane, Stilt, Heron, Flying Frog, Monkey
Flattened	Flatfish, Oarfish, Ray, Monkfish, Sawfish	Tapeworm	Vine snake	Manta Ray, Leaping snake
Compressed	Dealfish, Discus fish, Snipe-Eel, Oarfish,	Crocodile, Lizard	Tree boa, Viper	Lizard, Squirrel.
Tubular	Pipefish, Eel, Siren, Tubesnout, Salamander	Worm, Snake, Skink, Mudskipper	Tree snake	Flying snake
Cylindrical	Seal, Narwhal, Lungfish, Dolphin, Blue Shark	Skink, Wombat, Pig, Tapir, Beaver, Mole	Larvae, Lizard, Gecko Mudskipper, Civet	Dolphin, Whale.
Oval	Medusa, Regal Tang, Manatee, Dugong	Mice/Rat, Ostrich, Bear, Armadillo	Koala, Calago, Sloth, Numbat, Opossum	Bird, Salmon, Leaping Colugo
Circular	Turtle, Torpedo Ray, Angler, Electric Ray	Tortoise, Armadillo Lizard	Frilled lizard	Flying Dragon, Lizard
Spherical	Football fish, Sargassum fish, Balloon fish	Armadillo, Echidna, Hedgehog, Ostrich	Anteater, Lemur, Macaque, Gibbon	Gibbon, Sifaka
Squarish	Sperm whale, Skate, Butterfly fish, Penguin	Elephant, Buffalo, Gelada, Gorilla, Zebra,	Owl, Tufted capuchin, Loris, Sifaka, Baboon	Flying Frog, Colugo, Squirrel
Triangular	Manta, Eagle, Stingray, Angle fish, Forceps fish	Kangaroo, Giraffe, Camel, Rabbit, Frog	Bird, Tree Kangaroo	Gliding birds, Bat, Sargassum fish
Bulky	Blue Whale, Walrus, Hippo, Crocodile	Elephant, Rhino, Tapir, Komodo Dragon	Bear, Boa, Pangolin, Tamandua	Snowy Owl, Vulture, Crown pigeon, Eagle
Slender	Saw Shark, Sable fish, Skipper fish, Pearl fish	Gazelle, Dingo, Cheetah, Camel, Glass Frog	Mamba snake, Squirrel, Loris, Monkey, Lemur	Flamingo, Crane, Squirrel, Snake
Spindly	Needlefish, Tuna, Filefish, Water Dragon	Basilisk Lizard, Mongoose	Spider-Monkey, Lemur, Marmoset	Sailfish, Flying fish, Egret, Secretary bird
Stooped	Whale Shark, Sea Dragon, Frog, Turtle, Seahorse	Camel, Hyena, Bear, Tortoise, Armadillo	Chameleon, Anteater, Porcupine.	Eagle, Vulture, Ostrich, Cassowary
Arched-In	Seahorse, Swan, Flamingo, Angelfish	Horse, Cheetah, Jungle Fowl, Giraffe	Jaguar, Panther, Lyrebird	Chicken, Albatross, Pigeon
Saggitate Fin	Catfish, Codfish, Plaice fish, Duck, Cavefish	Turkey	Woodpecker, Finches, Wall creepers, Shribs	Magpie, Barbet Thrush, Toucan
Forked Tail	Perch-like fish, Seal, Whale Scup, Milkfish	Fowl, Pheasant	Goldfinch, Forktail bird, Topaz bird,	Nightjar, Swift, Whydah bird
Extravagant	Platypus, Octopus, Sawfish, Seahorse	Giraffe, Thorny Devil, Anteater, Crab, Dragon,	Owl, Bat, Tauadua, Proboscis monkey	Ostrich, Bat, Albatross, Peafowl

Chart 3   Special Body Position/Stance and Ground-Levels

Space	Level	Function / Stance	Self-Individual			Duel	
			Feeding	Sleeping	Preening	Dominance	Submission
Horizontal	Underground, water, land, perch	**LYING**					
		On the belly	T.S.C.R.W.L	T.S.C.L.R.B	C.W.R.G.M.B.S	S.L.T.B	
		On the back		A.H.C.W.P.U	C.W.R.Z.P.A.U		W.C.R.P.A.U
		On the side		C.W.P.H.A.U	C.W.U.P.A		W.C.R.P.A.U
		Kneeling	R.C.W.K.P.A.H	G.K.R.C.W.B.Z	K.B.G.Z.C.W		
		Squatting	B.L.G.U.P.A.C	L.B.K.R	M.U.R.P.A.B	T.L.R	M.G.Z.B.U
		Standing	B.M.G.C.U.P	G.B.M.Z	M.G.Z.L.B.H	M.Z.G.B.R.W.C	M.G.Z.B.U
		Clinging	R.L.B.C.U.G	B.C.U.S.P.A	B.C.U.R.P.A	U.C.W.B.R	
		Suspending	P.L.B.S.U.R	B.P.A.S.R			
		Floating	D.F.T.S.B	F.D.T.S.B	S.L.B		
Angular	Semi-Raised	**SITTING**	U.P.A.H.R	U.R.P.A.H	U.C.W.R.P.A.H	W.C.P.A.U.H	
		Lean towards	A.W.P.H.U.R	C.P.M.K.A.H.W	U.C.W.R.P.A.H		K.U.P.A.H
		KNEELING	C.W.R.P.A.H	G.K.A.P.C.W	K.C.W.R.P.A		K.H
		Slope-down	P.A.H	G.K.A.P.C.W	K.C.W.R.P.A		
		SQUATTING	P.B.A.H.U.K	B.K.A.P.H	W.C.U.R.A.P		U.P.A.H.R
		On 2 hind limbs	G.L.C.W.R.M				
Vertical	On land	**STANDING**					
		-on 2 limbs	P.A.U.B.G.W.C	B.	B.U.A.H	U.M.G.Z.A.H	
		-on 2 limbs + tail	L.K.C.R.P.A	K.	K.C.R.P.B	K.L.R.P.C.W	
		-on one limb	B.A.H.P.K	B.	B.	K.U.P.A.H	
		-on tail	S.D.K.L			S.D	
	Pendent	**CLINGING**					
		Clinging	L.B.S.R.U.R.A	U.K.R.P.A	C.K.U.R.P.A.L	S.L.B.P.A.H	
		Up-side down	L.C.U.H.P.A.R	U.K.R.P.A	C.K.U.R.P.A.L	S.L.B.P.A.H	S.L.B.A.P
		Suspending	C.U.P.A.H.F.L			P.A.H	
		Up-side down	B.P.A.L.S.F			S.L.P.L	S.L.B.A.P
		With tail	S.L.A.P.R				
Indefinite	In The Air	**GLIDING**					
		Spread limbs	B.L.R.P.S			B.L.R.P.S	B.L.R.S.P.A
		LEAPING	S.L.D.R.C.W			L.S.R.P.A.C.W	
		PICKING UP	B.			B.	
	Compound / In a water	**LYING**	F.L.S.T.D.	F.S.T.D.R.L.M	F.S.T.D.R.L.M	F.S.D.L	F.S.T.D.R.L
		SQUATTING	U.B.T.L.F.G.C		M.U.B.L.A.H		
		STANDING	U.G.B.T.L.F.M		M.U.B.L.A.H	L.T.M.U.H	
		FLOATING	F.D.T.B.S	F.D.S.T.B	F.D.S.B.T.L	F.D.S.B.U.T	
		VERTICALY	F.D.T.B.S	F.	F.D.S.B.T.L	F.D.S.L	
		DIVING	F.D.B.S.H.T			F.D.S.L.B.U	F.D.S.T.R.L
		RISING	F.D.B.S.H.T				F.D.S.T.R.L
Consonance:			**W**-Wolf, **Z**-Zebra, **F**-Fish, **T**-Turtle, **D**-Dragon, **L**-Lizard, **S**-Snake,				

/ Duet		Reproduction				
Attacking	**Defending**	**Grooming**	**Courtship**	**Mating**	**Giving Birth**	**Nursing**
C.W.L.S.R	S.L.T.R.C.W.P	S.L.B.R	S.L.T.C.W	C.W.R.B	S.L.B.T	S.B.L
	S.L.T.R.C.W.P	C.W.U.P.A			A.H.U.P	
	S.L.T.R.C.W.P	C.W.U.P.A		S.L	R.C.W	C.W.R.U
				R.C.P.A		
C.W.G.Z.P.A.T	M.G.Z.C.W.R	M.Z.G.R	M.Z.G.R.C.W	G.Z.M.U		
M.ZG.R.C.W	M.G.Z.C.W.R	M.Z.G.R	M.Z.G.R.C.W	G.Z.M.U	M.Z.G	M.Z.G
U.C.W.B.R	L.R.C.U.S.W			B.W.C.R.P.A		B.C.W.R.P.A
						C.W.R.P.A
F.D.S.T.L		F.D.S.T.L	F.T.S.D.L.B		F.D	F.D
		C.W.K.U.P.A.H				U.P.A.H.R
		C.W.K.U.P.A.H				U.P.A.H.R
	G.Z.M.C.W.R	K.C.W.U.P.A.H	K.U.P.A	K.C.W.U.P.A.H	K.	K.
	G.Z.M.C.W.R	K.C.W.U.P.A.H	K.U.P.A			
K.U.P.A.R.H	U.K.P.A.H	K.B.U.P.A.H	K.B.U.P.A	K.C.W.U.P.A.H		U.K.P.A
M.G.Z.C.T						
U.A.H.M.Z	Z.U.P.A.H.B.M	B.U.P.H	U.P.A.H.B	M.A.H.G.Z		U.P.A.H
L.K.W.P.A.T	L.K.C.W.R.P.A	K.L.C.W.R.P.A	K.L.C.W.R.P.A	K.R.CW.P.A		K.
K.C.W.P.A.H.	K.U.C.L.P.A.H		K.B.L			
S.K.	S.K		S			
S.L.B.R.P.A	S.L.R.B.C.U.W		B.L.P.A			U.K.P.A.H
S.L.B.R.P.A	S.L.R.B.C.U.W					U.K.P.A.H
P.A.H			L.B.P.A			
P.L.A.S	S.					
B.L.R.S.P.A	B.L.R.C.P.A		B.L.R.P.A	B.		
C.W.L.R.P.A	C.W.L.R.P.A.S		B.L.R.P.A			
B.	B.		B.			
F.S.L.D	F.T.S	F.T.S.L.U.R	F.T.S.L	F.D	F.	F.L
U.R.A.H	L.G.M.Z.U.F	M.U.P.B.A				M.Z.G.B.R.P.A
U.R.A.H	L.G.M.Z.U.F	M.U.P.B.A				M.Z.G.B.R.P.A
F.D.S.L.R.B	F.D.S.T.B.R	F.D.S.L.B.R.U	F.T.S.L.D.B	T.F.S.D.B	F.D	F.D.T.B.R.L
F.D.S.L.R.B	F.D.S.T.B.R	F.D.S.L.B.R.U	F.T.S.L.D.B	T.F.S.D	F.	F.D.T.B.R.L
B.D.L.F.T.H	F.S.D.B.T.R.H		F.T.S.L.D			F.D.T.B.R.L
B.D.L.F.T.H	F.S.D.B.T.R.H		F.T.S.L.D			F.D.T.B.R.L

K-Kangaroo, **G**-Goat, **M**-Mammoth, **U**-Urso, **P**-Prosimian, **A**-Ape, **H**-Human, **C**-Cat, **R**-Rat, **B**-Bird

Environmental stimuli for Homo Erectus

This major plastic metamorphosis of the body took place over at least thirty million years, rather than three million years as was formerly thought, although future archaeological discoveries may well clarify the time frame more precisely. If gorillas and chimps are indeed our nearest relatives, their skeletal structure cannot have been so dramatically transformed into that of Homo Erectus in such the relatively short space of time represented by the intermediate species of Australo-Africanopithecus. Compared to the latter, Homo Erectus has a more oval skull, flatter face, shorter arms, longer legs, the essential *double-curvature* spine, shorter fingers and toes, a longer heel, a broader chest and ileum, bulkier shoulders, more prominent shoulder blades and more flexible elbows and wrists.

If it took some thirty million years to establish the anatomical changes that accompany Homo Erectus' upright stance, it would be logical to assume that there must have been other intermediary adaptations which must have disappeared, either because of external environmental factors or because they entailed other physical disadvantages.

The main environmental stimuli for the Homo Erectus adaptation were:

a) The need to acquire additional living space and food sources by a growing population of tree dwellers, especially where forest was being replaced by savannah.

b) The richness of savannah lands in terms of food and water supply.

c) The survival imperatives of living in wide, open spaces teeming with big predators.

Having seen monkeys and apes use the upright stance defensively in the jungle, Australopithecus presumably tried to copy them in the savannah setting, with beneficial results in terms of field of vision and the ability to scare off predators by making the individual look bigger and stronger (when *standing* on two legs to wave branches at the threat, for example). Even though the upright stance inevitably exposed the individual to being seen by predators across the open savannah, bipedalism continued to evolve because its practical benefits of outweighed this disadvantage. Survival in such a harsh environment clearly required greater speed, intelligence or fighting skill than the surrounding predators, and our forebears therefore artificially magnified their body shape with tall masks of feathers and horn, tusks, long sticks, pelts and shields.

When on the ground, Great Apes had their own versions of the familiar quadruped postural repertoire of communicative signals long before hominids. This plastic vocabulary included: *leaning, squatting, twisting, bending, crouching, stretching up* and many other postural patterns to warn, defend, attract or display. However, these postures and gestures usually involved only one leg, the other three being employed to maintain the creature's balance. The gesturing limb could of course be varied without affecting the tripod support/static horizontal body configuration.

The same principles apply to the vertical equivalent of this **tripod stance**, using hind legs and tail as support. In addition to increasing the field of vision, this variation frees both forelimbs to create *postural patterns*. It is this unique upright stance that underpins the progressive intellectual, social and cultural development of humanity.

GRAVITY, MOMENTUM AND INERTIA IN BODY KINETICS

Unlike the kinetic energy involved in locomotion, maintaining the bipedal stance involves several motionless forces. *Extending* an arm sideways for a prolonged period, *leaning* the body sideways or *squatting* for a few minutes can requires more energy and strength than a twenty-minute *walk*. A short, still, silent and unblinking session on guard duty can be surprisingly stressful and uncomfortable for the entire musculo-skeletal structure, including the ligaments and joints, the back, the lungs and the mind, all of which are working hard despite the lack of actual movement.

Centre of gravity is a primary concern of any performer, and is constantly being minutely *adjusted* in order to maintain balance. All body shapes have their own unique plastic proportions, which differ from individual to individual.

Over 2,000 common types of human posture have been identified, each of which require the centre of gravity to be correctly placed in relation to where the body is being supported. A heated exchange between two jealous females, for example, might involve countless such adjustments.

A *forward-leaning* pose with the arm *lifted* to point is counterbalanced by the muscles of the calves and lower back; in contrast, a *backward-leaning* body with a leg *raised* high to the front in a defensive pose *shifts* the centre of gravity to the supporting leg, with an accompanying *contraction* of thigh and belly muscles.

The amount of kinetic force involved depends on the spatial extent and angle of the posture and the weight of the body parts in question. Maximum gravitational resistance is felt when maintaining a limb unsupported in a horizontal position or *leaning* the body at an angle in any direction while *standing* with both feet flat on the ground.

Although balance is crucial to any volitional motion and any incorrect placement of body parts in relation to the axis of weight may unbalance the subsequent posture, all the necessary adjustments to the body's centre of gravity are of course made entirely unconsciously.

Inertia, or the tendency of a body to preserve its state of rest or uniform motion, has to be overcome for any physical action to be performed.

Momentum, as the impetus of a body resulting from its motion, is fundamentally an active state that is overcome by instinctively calculated muscular counterforce.

As can be seen below, the most dynamic postures are the motion patterns involved starting and ending an action.

Countering momentum by body size and weight:

I. *Throwing* a discus involves *three* postural dynamics:

a) The upper body *twists* to the R with bent knees *lowered* deeply to the L, and sharply *contracted* waist; the L arm is *curved* in front while the R arm *opens* laterally, *holding* the discus in the hand before the throw takes place.

b) The body *spins* to the L in this stance, creating maximum momentum for the release of the discus.

c) *Lunging* forward with the L leg, and *leaning* the body towards the target, simultaneously *throwing* the discus forwards and up with the R arm and *lifted* head, the L arm *opening* laterally as counterbalance.

II. Fighting with a stick, in three postural stages

a) Defending – *crouched* pose on spread legs with both arms in front and a stick *held* horizontally, the head *lifting* aggressively towards the target in preparation for action

b) R arm *raises* the stick threateningly, while the upper body *arches* back; L arm *curved* defensively in front, the *lifted* head facing the target

c) *Lunge* on L leg, the body *leaning* forward simultaneously *extending* the R arm with the stick towards the target, into lower front position; the R arm is *half-stretched* out in front, the L arm *opens* laterally and the head *projects* aggressively towards the target.

In both examples, the so-called 'frozen motions' in fact have a strong momentum, which have to be neutralized by the resistance of the body. Each dynamic posture has its own size, shape and spatial position; these, plus the nature of any support, distance from the ground and tissue density of every *moving* body part, all determine the power and speed of the momentum involved in the entire postural composition.

The 'frozen motions' of a posturing body indicates some expression, behavioural mode or phase of action in this way. In conjunction with ground irregularities, spatial conditions and bodily characteristics, the performer has to overcome and balance the natural forces of gravity,

69

inertia and momentum. All these elements have to be harmoniously reconciled for the desired posture to be correctly composed.

ROLE OF BODY PARTS IN FUNCTIONAL POSTURE

Five major musculoskeletal units are involved in upright biped posturing: the head and neck, shoulders and upper back, arms and hands, belly and lower back, hips, pelvis and the legs and feet. Here we consider the role of each unit as it relates to postures performed for Functional communication and ritual performance.

Body parts usually function with each other to create clear, stable postures – and like a complex electronic mechanism, the malfunction of any small part cause the totality to fail. The same body with a common functional motivation and a single mind executes gestures and postures: they succeed or fail together.

The **head** and **neck** usually play the leading role. The head *turns* towards the target to assess a potential threat, sideways when hearing a noise, or *tilts* back in shock or surprise. It can be *pulled down* between the shoulders for protection, *lowered* to searching on the ground, or *raised* towards the sky in anticipation of an attack from above; it *droops* to the chest when falling asleep. In addition to their meaning, these head positions are functionally important. The head after all guides the entire performing body, minutely and continuously regulating its balance and coordination.

The neck mainly supports the constantly *moving* head, and serves to hold firm the gestural patterns described earlier, such as *turning, inclining, arching* backward, *curving* forward, *projecting* towards an object of interest, *twisting* around and so on. Without a flexible neck, the head would become hopelessly immobile and unable to perform its leading role in bodily communications. Minor as it may be in amplitude, the frozen motion of the head and neck is the plastic finishing touch of any performed posture.

The massive **shoulder/upper back** unit comprises the two fundamental posturing tools that frame the upper torso and anchor all arm *movements*. The shoulder blades that connect the upper back to the arms control shoulder motions such as *shrugging, shaking* and *rotating*, and maintain the postures of the upper back when *crouching, arching, twisting*, and so on. As the foundation of upper body motion, the shoulders and upper back are interdependent as a functional unit, but have a limited gestural vocabulary in themselves beyond *tilting* the head, *projecting* the neck or *shrugging* the shoulders. However, their contribution to all upper body motions cannot be underestimated.

In a bipedal body, the **arm/hand** units are the most active posturing instruments, responsible for most of the functional and performing repertoire:

- EATING, *holding* both hands near the mouth while *crouching*.
- DRINKING from the palm held above upraised head while squatting.
- TENDING THE HAIR, framing the head with arms and touching the hair with the fingers of both hands above the head, while sitting cross-legged.
- FIGHTING with two fists in front of the chest in a crouched position.
- HUNTING, when pulling a lasso with two arms in front, one outstretched and the other curved at the same level, while lunging towards the prey (and when the forces of the hunter and the prey are equalised, the motion freezes, creating a perfect dramatic motif for posturing compositions).

Unlike the other postural units, the upper extremities have the more intricate task of controlling the body's physical stability and the postural patterns of extended arms, away from the centre of gravity.

When the arms and hands are held above mouth level while *drinking* or above the head during *grooming*, for example, these motions do not greatly affect the individual's balance because both forelimbs are close to body's gravitational axis.

70

Folding the arms across the chest affects body balance more, and the body has to compensate for the additional weight thus brought forward of its centre of gravity. But *stretching* the arms forward, as when *lunging* towards a target when hunting, significantly displaces the centre of gravity from its original axis to a new one above the *projected* front leg.

The latter posture affects the plastic pattern to such an extent that the body's stability and balance can be lost completely. Overextension of the *forward-leaning* body is usually counteracted not by the arms, but with the shoulder and upper back muscles acting in concert with the belly and lower back muscles and the calf of the rear leg.

Although the proximity range of the arms and hands makes them highly expressive postural instruments, these last two examples underline the physical complexity of controlling *outstretched* gestures.

The **belly/lower back** and the **hips/pelvic girdle** are separate anatomical units that support and coordinate postural patterns rather being performing tools in their own right. They are however crucial in maintaining balance in any bipedal creature, whether working in unison or opposition to each other. *Carrying* the entire upper body weight as they do, the belly and lower back muscles have the strength and minute coordination to make constant *adjustments* to balance the tall three-part structure they support, especially when *outspread* upper extremity postural patterns are performed.

The lower back primarily controls the body's centre of gravity by continuous slight shifts of the vertebrae in response to variations in upper body pressure, the belly and lower back muscles minutely but sharply *contracting* and *expanding* to adjust body balance while *leaning, inclining, arching, twisting, walking* and so on.

The pelvis supports the upper body weight transmitted by the belly/lower back unit, and is where the centre of gravity axis of an upright bipedal body is located. As well as sustaining the perpetual balancing act mentioned earlier, it connects the torso with the lower extremities and anchors the legs and feet. It drives hind limb locomotion and controls the functional and performing postures of both legs. As such, the hip joints of the pelvis are under constant weight-bearing pressure, and their inevitable eventual degradation over time causes physical distortions of the body's posturing abilities.

The **legs** and **feet** are the plastic unit that plays the main role in maintaining bipedal balance, and are rarely motionless. Overcoming the forces of gravity, inertia and momentum depends largely on the position and motion of the legs and feet on the ground:

- Joined or separated legs with *straight* knees and feet *turned* in or out.
- As above with slightly or fully *bent* knees.
- *Lunging* in any direction, with one leg *bent* and one *outstretched.*
- *Kneeling* on both legs with thighs vertical or at an angle when *sitting* on heels.
- One-legged stances with foot *turned* in or out, *straight* or *squatting.*

Many balancing adjustments are performed by one or both legs and feet. On two legs, the centre of gravity can be regulated by *displacing* one foot to a new position or *bending* one leg, or *spreading* the knees, or *contracting* the calf and *pressing* down the toes of one or both feet to correct imbalance. On one leg, the centre of gravity is usually controlled by *displacing* the heel around the sole pad in the desired direction, or *bending* or *straightening* the supporting leg, or by modulating the pressure of the toes against the ground. However, the easiest way to maintain equilibrium on one leg is by using the other leg as a counterbalance in concert with other body parts.

Upraised (bipedal) Postures

1. Running Capuchin
2. Young Polar Bears at play
3. Ibex on the edge of a cliff
4. Meerkat on a watch-shift

5. Defensive posture of Monitor Lizard
6. Fighting Kangaroos on their hind limbs
7. Confused Bonobo "To be, or not to be…"

Food-Gathering Motion

1a   1b   1c

2   3   4   5   6

1. Canopy sources
   a) leaves – b) larvae – c) fruits
2. The small young is carrying a big egg
3. Carnivorous Baboon

4. Picking out termites with a twig
5. Cracking a nut with a stone
6. Washing potato before eating it
7. Hopelessly trying to catch some fish with a stick

Warning/Fighting Action

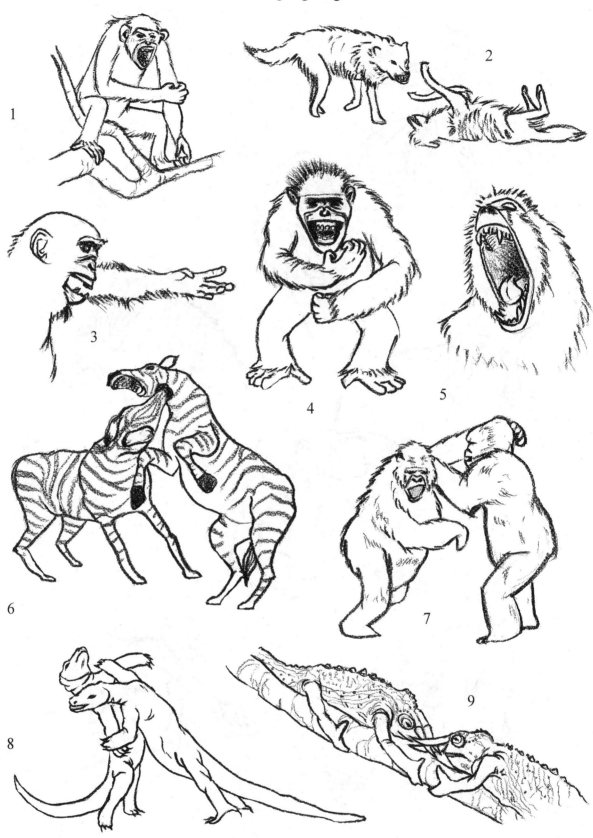

1. Alarm-screaming Chimp
2. Submissive Wolves
3. "Give me back my banana!"
4. "It's my territory!"
5. Soundless warning yawn of Baboon
6. Fourth round of Zebras
7. Fighting Gorillas
8. Monitor Lizards' Duel
9. Confrontation of Chameleons

It must be remembered that gestural precision was of the utmost importance. Each seemingly insignificant trait could deliver the wrong message, with potentially serious consequences:

1a) A **submissive** lateral pose, with R leg and upper body *twisting* to the R above *squatting* R leg, completed by *turning* the head to the R, looking embarrassed over R shoulder, *bending* the L arm in front and the R arm behind.

1b) An identical defensive pose, but with the head turned to the L and looking aggressively over the L shoulder, to imply an immediate attack.

2a) Kneeling on the R leg, then placing R elbow on the bent L knee and the R hand on the forehead, with the L arm dropped along the L side, completed by one of two contrasting motions:

- both palms open, with one *held* lightly on the forehead and the other on the L side at the waist to indicate a **negative** state such as depression, illness, frustration or recollecting a negative event.
- with fists instead of open palms against the waist, demonstrating a **positive** decision to reach a specific target, or perhaps to fight.

In the case of 1a and 1b, the different head or hand and arm positions could potentially send the wrong signal, with possibly fatal results. Even professional performers find it difficult simultaneously to control postural meanings, focus on the correct coordination of body parts, and to *hold* plastic patterns steadily in position in a harmonious way.

SUMMARY

In conclusion, the change from quadruped into bipedal body stance effected a remarkable physical and psychological transformation in ape/hominids. The transition from a stiff, bulky body with the limited plastic facilities of a *crouching* ape into the vast gestural facilities of the upright hominid was a defining evolutionary phenomenon – and the greatest challenge hominids had to face until they had to adapt these new-found facilities to the performing requirements of the Totemic ritual repertoire.

Chart 4

Peaceful Facial Plastic Motion by Functional Organs of Animals

ORGANS/TOOLS MOTIONS	Eyes	Ears radar	Trunk nose	Antenna feeler	Sponge lips	Tube tongue	Teeth jaws	Mouth beak
LOOKING FOR	S.R.N							
GAZING	M.C.R							
LISTENING		S.C.R						
SNIFFING			S.M.R.C	C.R.F.S.				
DETECTING		S.C.R	L.R.C.S.	S.C.R.F	S.C.M.R	S.C.R.M		F.C.S.R
SIGNALING	S.C.R	S.C.R.	S.F.N.C	S.C.R.F	G.M.C.P	G.M.C.P	L.C.R.	N.S.C.R
TOUCHING			F.R.S.C	S.C.R.M	F.G.M.C	F.N.S.C	N.F.G.P	F.C.N.G
SMACKING					F.N.G.C	F.N.G.C		F.N.G.S
TASTING			F.S.R.N	F.R.S.	F.S.R	F.N.G.R	F.N.R	F.N.S.C
PULLING OUT		S.R.P	F.N.P.G	S.C.R.M	F.N.G.C	F.N.G.M	F.N.G.S	F.N.G.S
PEELING OFF					F.N.M.C		F.N.M.C	F.N.M.C
PICKING UP			F.N.S		F.N.S.C	F.N	F.N.M.C	F.N.M.C
LICKING						N.G.C.M		
SQUEEZING			G.N.F.P.		F.N.G	C.F.N.	F.N.G	F.N.G.P
BITING							F.N.G.M	F.N.G.P
CRACKING							F.N.G.C	F.N.G.C
TEARING			C.F.N.P.		G.N.F.P.	G.N.F.	F.N.G.C	F.N.G.C
CHEWING						F.N.G	F.N.G.P	
SPITTING OUT			F.N.G.P		F.N.C.S	F.N.C.S		F.N.C.S
SUCKING			F.N.G.R	N.F.G.	F.N.G.P	F.N.G.P		F.N.M.G
DIGGING			F.N.G.S					F.N.C.S.P
PASSING ON			F.N.G.C	N.F.G.		F.N.S.C	F.N.C.P	F.N.C.P
PUTTING DOWN		F.G.N	F.N.S.R			C.F.N.	F.N.M.C	F.N.M.C
WASHING			N.G.M	G.N.		F.N.G		F.N.G
MIMICKING	F.R.C		C.P.R.M		C.M.P.R		C.M.F.R	P.C.R.P
PREENING			P.N.C.G	N.C.	N.G.C.E	G.C.N.	N.G.C.F	N.G.C.P
BEDECKING			C.M.R			C.R.	C.M.R	C.M.P.R
FONDLING			N.G.M.C	G.M.P.	C.M.G.N	G.N.F.		C.M.G.N
Consonance:	G-Grooming F-Feeding		C-Courting S-Searching		R-Recognizing M-Mating		N-Nursing P-Playing	

Chart 5

Plastic motions implements of Animals' Fighting

Performance \ Implements		Jaws spikes	Fangs tusks	Head-point	Forehead horns	Head	Front trunk	Sting	Forked tongue	Eyes
W A R N I N G	Glaring									PWCTA
	Baring	PWCS	PWC							
	Clacking	PWCS								
	Yawning	PWCS	PWC							
	Waving			PWCS			PWC		TAD	
	Tramping									
	Nodding	PWC				PWAD				
	Wobbling			PWC	PWDA	PWADS				
	Wagging				PWDA	PWAD				
	Jerking	PWA	PWAD	PW	PWAD	PWAD	PWA			
A L E R T N E S S	Knocking down	PA	PA	PA	PA		PA			
	Rotating			PW		PWA	PWC		PWCTA	PWCTS
	Tilting	PAK		PWTAD	PWAD	PWAD	PWCA	AD	PWCTA	
	Shuddering								PWCTA	PWCS
	Lowering		PWCDS	PWSDA	PWADS	PWADS	PSD		WCT	TS
	Raising		PWCAD		PWAD	PWAD	PWAT		WCT	CD
	Bending						PWCS		PWCTA	
	Stretching						PWC	AK	PWCTA	
	Running									
	Crouching									
	Curling									
A C T I O N	Hypnotizing									AK
	Electro-shocking			PWTAK				AK		
	Stinging/poisoning							AK		
	Picking up				PACWK				TAK	
	Ultra-sonic wave								CTAK	
	Spitting/poisoning						PWAD	AK	PCAK	
	Pushing		PADK	PAKS	PADK	PADK	PD	AK	PTAK	
	Pulling	AKP	PADK			PADK			PCAK	
	Mounting					PADK				
	Leaping at									
	Grabbing	PAK					PADK		AK	
	Hitting/slapping		PADK	PAK	PADK	ADK	PADK			
	Biting/cutting	PAK	PWADK							
	Running			PAK	PADK					
	Strangling	AK	AK				AK			
	Lifting up		PAK	PAK	PAKD	ADK	PADK			
	Throwing down		PAK	PAK	PAKD	ADK	PADK			
	"Diving" under		PADK	PAK	PAKD	PADK	PADK			
	Kicking									
	Creeping			TAK						

Consonance: **P**-Playing **W**- Warning **C**- Cautioning

Ears radar	Whisker antenna	Nose snout	Sponge proboscises	Spine beak	Palps pincers	Claws talons	Hoofs fore-limbs	Hoofs back-limbs	Torso-tube	Abdomen tail
CTDA	CTDA			PWAD	PWAD					
				PWS						
WC	CT			PWAD			PWAD	PDS	PWC	PWADS
CTDA	CTDA				PWCDA	PTAD	PWAD	PAD		PWADS
PWCTS	PWCT		TC	PWCT	PWCDA					
PWCTS	PWCT		TC	PWCTA	PWCDA					
PWCTS	PWCT		TC	PWCTA	PWCDA				PWCT	PWCT
CT	CT	PCT		PWAD	WD		PWADK		PW	PA
		TADK		AD	AK	PAD	PAD			AD
PWCTS	PWCT	CT	TC	PWCT	PWCDA				PA	PWC
PWCT	PWCTA	PWCT	CT	PA	PWCDA		PWAD	PWAD	PWCAD	DWCA
PWCTS	PWCTS	CT	CT	PA	WDS				PCDS	PWCS
PWCTS	PWCTS	PCTS	CT	PA	PWCD		PWAD	PWADC	PWCAD	PCS
PWCTA	PWCTA	PWCA		PW			PWAD	PWADC	PWCAD	PWA
PWCTS	PWCTS				PWCD		PWADS	PWADS	PWAD	PCS
PWCT	PWCTA						PWA	PWAK	PWDA	PWA
							PCTAS	PCTAS		
							PWCAD	PWCAD	PWADS	PWAD
							PCTS	PCTS	PWCDS	PWCDS
CDTAK	CDTAK	CD	CTDA	PCTAK						AK
			AK	PCTAK						AK
	CDTAK	CD	CTAK	AK	PWCADK	PCAK	PWAK			PWCAK
WCTAK	WCT		PWCT	PWCTAK						PWCA
			PWAK	PAD						
		PAD	TAK	PADK	PWTADK		PWADK	PTADK	PWAD	
			PWAK	PAK	PWTADK		PTADK	PTADK		ADK
				PAK			PAK	PAK	PWTAD	
				PAK			PTADK	PTADK	PWTAD	WTAD
				PTAK	PADK	PATK	PTADK	PTADK		AK
		AK		AK			PAK			PWAK
				PKT	ADK					
		PAK					PAD	PAD	PWADK	
			AK	PAK	AK	AK	PAK	PAK	AK	AK
		PWAD		PWAK		PTAK	PAD		PWCAD	WCADK
				PWAK			PAD		AKDS	AK
			PADK	PTDS	PADK		PWADS	PWADS	PWADK	TAK
							PWADK	PWADK		AK
				CDS	PTADS		PCADS	PCADS		WTS

T – Tracing   **A** – Attacking   **D** – Defending   **K** – Killing   **S** – Subduing

RUDIMENTARY VOCALISATIONS AND RHYTHMIC NOISE

Generally speaking, independent expression through **noise** and **voice** lies beyond our main subject. Nevertheless, sound and vocalisation did play a significant part in the plastic evolution of hominids, as demonstrated in Darwin's famous model.

As amended by his followers, Darwin's Anthropological Ladder of non-spoken communication presents three gradual stages of evolution:

I   **Body motions**: head-facial expressions, limb gestures, posturings, and symbolic hand signs.

II   **Vocalisation**: characteristic cries, tune variations, rudimentary songs, sound modulations.

III   **Illustrative symbols**: tattooing and body adornment, rock paintings, masks and hieroglyphic signs.

All these communication facilities are closely anthropologically related and often functioned together in the combined motion expressions on which we focus here.

VOICE/NOISE EXPRESSIONS

A)   When apes see something that amuses them, they *laugh* loudly, *flapping* their extremities while *jumping* and *screaming*.

B)   When under unexpected attack, these same creatures *yell* hysterically and *run* away in panic. If caught, they *fall* on their back, *wave* their extremities chaotically and make their last living sound.

     In both cases, the apes use similar combinations of plastic/vocal facilities and similar mental processes. These are natural, Involuntary reflex reactions that essentially differ only in the nature of their external impulses.

C)   The leader of a group of gorillas defends his territory by *growling* menacingly with mouth *wide open* to display big white teeth, *pounding* exaggeratedly on his chest with his huge fists, and *shaking* his head and shoulders threateningly.

D)   A female chimpanzee peacefully *playing* with her infant is suddenly interrupted by danger that threatens the entire troupe. Terrified, she *grabs* her offspring and instantly *jumps* up a tree, while *screaming* incessantly - similar to the reaction seen in example B above, but in a different manner. From high in the tree, she also *points* her free arm in the direction of the approaching threat.

Like the two first examples, C and D share the same combination of plastic/vocal facilities – and in examples, B, C and D, even the stimulus for the response is similar. The reactions, however, differ not only between B as opposed to C and D, but also between C and D. The male gorilla's reaction is an inbred, involuntary plastic/acoustic response that has evolved genetically – yet he is in full control of the dynamic modulation of his growls, the amplitude of the arm motions on the chest and the noises he makes with his jaws and *chattering* teeth while *rising* to his full height, or *jumping* towards the threat. In this performance, which is repeated again and again until the desired result is achieved, involuntary reactions are combined with voluntary ones. The instinctive response of defensive motions evolved gradually over millions of years, with small variations, into a combination of defence and warning postures. However, such plastic/vocal displays of power are essentially voluntary performances under complete emotional and physical control.

In example D, the mother chimp's first reaction is based on the natural instinct to protect her infant from danger – a mother's typical involuntary reflex. Subsequently, however, she sends vocal and gestural signals to indicate the direction of the threat. These warning signals to protect the larger family group are a Voluntary response to the same stimulus.

IMITATING NATURAL SOUNDS

Our ancestors were constantly surrounded by the many noises of the natural world. Infants learned from birth to distinguish their mother's voice, its various modulations and their association with different motions, such as *sucking, scratching, stroking, stepping* and so on.

Hominids knew from early childhood how to imitate the movements and sounds of the creatures around them. The rudimentary songs they imitated – the calls of birds, reptiles and other animals – were copied by scouts and hunters to relay information over long distances, such as the size and location of a herd, and perhaps the best direction from which to attack it. Experienced hunters knew a large vocabulary of characteristic cries and voice modulations, which could easily be read and interpreted by fellow tribe members. These rudimentary vocal dialogues are still popular in some of the indigenous societies of Africa, Australia and South America. When the hunt took place in daylight, however, scouts would pass messages from treetops or high points by postural signals, which were responded to in the same way to establish a dialogue.

RUDIMENTARY VOCALISATION

In hominids, vocal communication developed alongside the evolving body motion dictionary, but at a slower pace. The main reason for its more limited vocabulary was the constant danger of predators; a mistimed cry from a child could well be its last. The predominant code of silence was a lifesaver.

Close range
Primitive vocalisation at close range (up to 50m) included *breaths, sighs, exclamations, growls, snarls, mutters, whispers, blowing, purring, humming* and *cooing*. In pianissimo, mezzo-piano and piano dynamics, these were usually employed in threatening or intimate circumstances (mostly at night), or during hunting or fighting operations, ritual pantomime episodes, dialogues between shaman and totem, or in the course of family grooming and parents controlling their children.

Medium range
At distances of between 50 and 300 metres, a repertoire of onomatopoeic calls based on the sounds of local birds, mammals, reptiles and insects was used between family and/or tribe members both in daily life and social activities, with piano and mezzo-forte dynamics.

Long range
Emergency vocalisations were used over distances of up to 1km – loud shouts and whistles in forte or fortissimo dynamics could be heard far away from the home base to signal the sudden appearance of enemies, strangers, predators or prey, or dangers such as fire or freak weather events.

All these different types of vocal signal were created using the full range of human vocal facilities including modulations of timbre and tone, dynamic and dramatic nuances, and repeated rhythmic sequences. They allowed our forebears to maintain contact with their families and neighbouring tribes over long distances as well as within the group.

Improving vocalisation through modulation

The human voice gradually became a popular medium for socio-cultural activities. The appropriate vocal *tune* could make hominids happy or keep them in fear; it could generate veneration or revolt; it could destroy entire communities or liberate them. Shamans and witches knew how to modulate their vocal signals in order to keep the tribe under their complete control.

Both human vocalisation and instrumental noise were created through plastic motion and formed by individuals into artistic sounds, based on the personal motion characteristics of the performer while following the dynamics, tempo, rhythm, harmonies and directions given by the shaman, the conductor. The resulting sounds were perceived according to each listener's personal taste, education and experience.

- When a sleeping family hears a warning signal, they immediately *jump* up and *run* to safety; when the danger has passed, a peaceful tune signal makes the family return to their base and to sleep, once again demonstrating the strong Functional relationship between sound and progressive motions – this time, a 'sound-movement-sound' *sequence*.

The sound of voices and primitive acoustic instruments are produced independently, and could be used separately or simultaneously in synchronised combination: vocalised rudimentary tunes with rhythmic warning signals, for example. But no matter what type of song or noise, all are created under the full control of human plastic facilities; so why did our ancestors want to add the new expressive tools of voice and noise to their existing plastic vocabulary of mimes, gestures and postures?

COMMUNICATING BY COMBINING VOICE AND NOISE WITH MOTION

During the long dark nights, our forebears could not communicate clearly with each other by body motions alone, and nor could they in daytime whenever visual obstructions or long distances were involved, or while hunting.

Body language alone could no longer effectively accommodate the constantly growing amount of new information and activities, and this provided the evolutionary imperative to expand the available communication vocabularies.

To understand how these profoundly dissimilar **plastic** and **acoustic** vocabularies were combined into a coherent mixed system, we have to remember the practical realities of the era. When a chief wanted to send a life-or-death message to a scout, or vice versa, both had to be certain that the message would be correctly understood when it reached its destination; the margin for error was zero. So, erring on the side of safety, they adopted a 'belt and braces' approach in which identical messages could be communicated simultaneously in two or more media. Once learned by heart, these complicated plastic-acoustic sequences proved by far the most effective form of communication throughout millions of years of human evolution.

The shaman, as the model of spirituality, harmony and power, both venerated and feared, usually acted as the totem, *dancing, mimicking, singing* and *making noises* with **special accessories**. The desperate need of hominids to communicate effectively over long distances made them experiment with additional means of communication, and as we have seen, various mechanical sounds were later used by shamans as professional accessories.

When hunters heard the sound of *stampeding* bison, although they could not see the herd, they learned to estimate its size, composition, direction and speed from the acoustic **volume** and **intonation**. They could do the same with the awe-inspiring acoustics of approaching storms, fires or floods, the stealthy sound of a *creeping* predator or an approaching enemy force. The accurate and timely recognition of these signals was quite simply a matter of life and death.

To solve this problem, hominids turned to noise-making tools: the sound of a *blown* conch shell or a hollow tree trunk being *hit* by a club to signify approaching danger, for example. Being louder than the voice alone, this type of signal could be heard over long distances, and could potentially save many lives. Although originally used for hunting or in battle, these acoustic instruments gradually became integrated across all the tribe's socio-cultural activities (see Chapter III).

In combination with arm and leg motions, the **voice** could project powerful warning signals to stimulate the required plastic/acoustic response: to defend, escape, kill or whatever. Integrating movement-sound-movement sequences in this way represented a major step in the development of pre-linguistic communication.

These plastic/noise communication systems worked both as individual and group executions. Vocal and noise-making facilities acquired a large repertoire of acoustic messages, some for close range, others for longer distances. Rudimentary songs were constantly improved by new modulations, as were the artificial acoustic signals made by the newly discovered tools for *drumming, blowing, ringing* and so on. The expressive features of both vocal and noise signals (such as dynamics, tempo, rhythm and dramatic nuances) were controlled by body motion facilities as a seamless **synthesis** of all performing components.

ACOUSTIC INSTRUMENTS

Shamans long ago found it much easier to impress their communities by producing mysterious voice tunes and the noise of rhythmical instruments. Their centralised power helped to build strong united communities and was instrumental in maintaining social order and improving cultural standards.

This use of sound signals was after all only an extension of the ways in which individuals respond to **acoustic patterns**, like the motion responses of a hungry infant when it hears the familiar sound of its mother's approach, or of food being prepared.

Sonic communication was enhanced by the use of noise-making implements made from natural materials such as stone, wood, bamboo, shells, bone, skins and horns. Percussion and wind instruments were used to communicate over longer distances, relaying messages, carrying on conversations and announcing social and cultural activities between tribes as well as within families.

Signalling repertoire of the drum and flute

Of all acoustic communication tools, the **drum** has always been the most practical, the most sacred and the most popular. These were formed initially from hollowed-out timber with skin stretched tightly at one end; smaller tambourine-like versions are widely used by ethnic peoples to this day.

The reason why the simple drum was so very important for our ancestors all over the world is self-evident to anyone who has ever acted, danced or been healed by the magic spiritual power of rhythmic *drumming*. The importance of drums to prehistoric hominids cannot be overemphasised. Even today, whether listening to a marching band or the electronic percussion of modern dance music, the strong hypnotising effect is inescapable.

In the past, probably each group or community, each family and each individual had their own private **percussive pattern**, and **rhythmic sequences** were used for tribal interaction (for communicating messages, social meetings or emergency calls). As with the voice, drumming messages were based on the whole spectrum of rhythmic patterns, the timbre of the drum being used and the dynamics and personal sonic 'signature' of the drummer. This extensive acoustic dictionary was regularly used by every tribe member alongside their vocal and body motion vocabularies.

The other significant sound instrument in earlier days was another magic instrument, the **Flute**. Though both drum and flute were equally important as communication media for any tribe, their characteristics differed. The sharp, piercing notes of the flute warned of imminent danger or a surprise attack, bringing the entire tribe to its feet. Its **lyrical** qualities were equally suited to announcing a wedding as they were for accompanying a funeral procession.

Sound-producing motion by body parts

Clapping is an important mode of plastic expression. Clapping hands on different parts of the body created a range of different **timbres** which, together with rhythmic sequences, presented a sonic vocabulary always available for immediate use to deal with any unexpected emergency or an immediate need without special tools.

Insofar as the sound of *clapping* can resemble the *flapping* wings of a bird or ears of a mammoth, the *whip* of a tail and other natural sounds, it could be used to confuse prey whilst allowing nearby hunters to communicate with each other. As well as carrying over long distances, *clapped* messages were easily read even by children, who had to learn the meanings of these sounds from an early age.

The rhythms of the *clapping* dictionary became popular for domestic and social activities, and were also widely used in ritual pantomimes and secular events – so much so that they were eventually integrated into the performance repertoire of virtually every ethnic group on the planet. Even today, the *clapping* motion is a major form of expression in Russian, Hungarian, Spanish and many other ethnic and professional dances worldwide.

As intelligent and experienced tribal leader, the shaman or witch was naturally the first to understand the magic significance of modulating tunes created by the human voice. Having discovered the potency of sounds made by *clapping, stamping* and *slapping* various parts of the body, they soon discovered the value of making sounds with tools. The sound of a club *striking* a rock, *scratching* various objects together, *shaking* shells with dried nuts inside or the *clashing* of spears could all have a magical effect when combined with mysterious vocal modulations, the reverberating echo of a large cave, terrifying masks and appropriate decoration. Such dramatic effects allowed the shaman to work his magic, and new acoustic and visual tools were constantly being sought to enhance their performance at ritual events.

The significance of this discovery of the artistic potential of combining voice with noise cannot be over emphasised, and opened up new ways of communications for primitive societies as well as providing the stimulus for the next step in hominid evolution.

Hunt ritual example

On their return to home base, hunters would reproduce every detail of the hunt as a sacred performance for the tribe and its shaman – often several times. This elaborate show made use of every possible acoustic and optical effect to produce a colourful and exciting spectacle, synthesising *movement* and *sound* in a symphony of plasticity, symbolic design, vocalisation, and acoustic accompaniment.

While the scout and the chief exchanged postural signals in a dance duet, some hunters *sang* a rudimentary dialogue corresponding to the episode being presented. Simultaneously, other masked participants, dressed in hides, *imitated* grazing bison or other prey. At first, these 'animals' *moved slowly* from side to side, *shaking* their heads, *rumbling* quietly. Then, they started *stamping* noisily and heavily on the ground, vigorously *shaking* their big horned heads and producing warning growls. Eventually, the beasts' and hunters' voices rose in a crescendo; in the end, the 'animals' *ran* in circles around the fire trying to escape. When caught, they *jumped, turned* and counterattacked the hunters, *roaring* and *picking up* the clumsiest ones by the horns, while the rest eventually *fell* one by one to the ground in exhausted death throes. The hunters *jumped* again and again over their prey until the last beast collapsed, at which point both the performers and audience *froze* in a *pauza fermata*, waiting for the signal from the shaman.

If the shaman considered the performance a successful depiction of the hunt, the ritual would continue until the spoils were distributed between the families of the tribe, as a kind of rehearsal for the youngsters as part of their initiation rite.

OTHER HOMINID COMMUNICATION TOOLS

VISUAL MEDIA

Arm signalling with Accessories

Hominids developed systems of visual communication to supplement plastic and sonic media, being more practical over long distances and more effective in open spaces. In evolutionary terms, this was another significant step towards the modern world.

In its earliest form, visual communication between tribes and individuals was based on plastic motions such as *port-de-bras*, extended by the use of objects such as hides, ropes or sticks. Scouts would send information about the enemy or prey from the top of a hill by *holding* up a pelt with both hands and *waving* it in various ways, at different speeds and with various intervals and intermediary positions – creating what was in effect the visual equivalent of the rhythmic patterns of the drum. These coded messages were repeated several times to ensure accurate comprehension by the recipients.

In the savannah flatlands, scouts would use more advanced techniques. Grass or branches, for example, might be tied to the tip of the spear and *waved* high in the air from a covered position behind a bush or rock. The range of available signalling motions extended from simply *raising* and *lowering* the implement up and down, *waving* it from side to side, *shaking* and *jabbing*. Naturally, a greater variety of *port de bras* enlarged this vocabulary considerably, and the system progressively developed with the **simultaneous** use of spears in both arms, effectively doubling the potential speed or content of the message. This was the forerunner of the military signalling system devised by the Romans, and led eventually to the nautical alphabet of signalling flags used to this day.

Messages with fire and light

Hunters and warriors also used fire and smoke to signal visually across long distances, based on the principle of using two or three fires that are intermittently *covered* by a skin or a pelt. The interruption of the column of smoke at shorter or longer intervals was visible for miles in the daytime; at night, the same system was used by periodically *covering* the light of the fire itself.

As with the acoustic systems, very specific information could be communicated in these ways. They were used mostly in war, while hunting or when faced with an emergency, and similar systems continue to be used by aboriginal peoples in Australia, Central Africa and South America. Wooden torches made with dry grass and oil or fat were similarly employed for communication as well as for ritual performances.

The most advanced form of optical communication was based on reflecting light from polished crystals. A much later development, this system could be employed over distances of up to 500 metres. Naturally, the sender had to be in exactly the right position to redirect the sun's rays from the crystal towards the recipient. The crystal would be intermittently *covered* by the signaller's hand at varying intervals – exactly the same principle as with smoke or fire but physically easier and faster (although its use of course depended on clear skies and the sun's position in relation to the recipient).

All these ancient acoustic and visual signalling systems are based on variations, like the Morse code of today.

PERSONAL AND TERRITORIAL MARKING AND SCENT

Like most land animals, hominids knew the rules of territorial protection from the very beginning – but instead of using **scents**, they marked their territories with **objects** such as stones, large bones and pieces of timber, and other visible markings.

Coded combat/hunt information

These various marking systems were used during hunts and battles, each tribe developing its own **calligraphic** style for indicating directions where paths crossed, or to convey other information by arranging the objects in particular patterns or using objects with specific meanings, such as a piece of skin or pelt, a type of feather or a broken arrow or tool. Whether as alarms or general communications, these coded messages were clearly understood by their intended recipients – other tribe, group or family members.

Intertribal communication

This static visual communication system was eventually widely used for all inter-tribal activities like mass religious events, markets, weddings, athletic competitions and dance festivals. High posts were usually fixed in the ground at major crossroads. Like roadside bulletin board, these were either marked with a certain number of notches or by means of attaching small sticks of different thicknesses and lengths to convey information about direction and distance, warnings for travellers (of an epidemic, infestation, famine or flood, for example), emergency calls and the like. All local residents were taught to read these signs, and members of different tribes were obliged to help each other in the face of disaster on penalty of dire punishment.

Because these signalling systems were essentially abstract and symbolic, they opened up a new era in hominid communication.

THE SIGNALLING AND COMPREHENSION FACILITIES OF INSECTS

There is no doubt today that the development of human communication can be traced right back through 600 million years of animal evolution, all the way to the behaviours of the first animal species on the planet.

Modern technologies allow scientists to prove this aspect of Darwin's evolutionary hypothesis in a way that the great man could not at the time – and in any case, the application of his theory to human beings and primates met with such hostility that it would have been practically impossible for him to posit such a continuum.

The massive increase since Victorian times in the documentation of animal behaviours through film and systematic observation has provided a wealth of material with which to answers the crucial age-old questions of where, when, why and how communication began.

There is overwhelming evidence that communication has its ultimate roots in the individual and social behaviour of arthropods – especially insects. Suspend any negative feelings you may have towards these clever, highly organised, family minded and extremely adaptable creatures, and consider the few examples in the following pages.

Of all the orders of living creatures, insects come in the most astonishing variety of shapes and sizes. Some live on land, some burrow beneath; some fly, some swim, some are amphibious; there are herbivorous, insectivorous and carnivorous types; some are social, some are not. Some metamorphose in three stages, some in four; some have hard outer protection, some not, and so on.

Insects communicate a vast array of intents and fears related to territory, mating, danger and sources of food. They pass on detailed information on directions, or calls for help; some deliberately misinform. And they use an amazingly wide variety of signalling media including plastic gestures, colour, light, sound, touch, taste, dance, smell, vibration, radio waves, magnetism and temperature.

OLFACTORY SIGNALS

Pheromones are volatile compounds that generate smell. In insects, these are produced in glands on various places outside the body – on the hind tibiae in the case of female **aphids**, for example, on the backs of **cockroaches**, and with **silvery pyralis moths**, on their hind ends. Some insects produce particular pheromones to signal their location, and others (usually female) to arouse sexual partners.

Pheromones are used as communication tools by practically all social insects. **Honey bees**, for example, *release* a pheromone when injured to trigger attack behaviour in fellow bees - a pheromone which (unlike the sex attractant variety) is dispersed quickly and lasts only long enough to raise the alarm. When the **tropical stingless bee** alerts its colony to the location of a food source, it does so by *marking* the nest entrance with chemicals before leaving.

After feeding at a new location, wandering **scout-ants** *drag* their distended abdomens along the ground as they head back to their nest, thereby leaving trails of pheromones for other hungry members of the colony to retrace the route to the food using their antenna.

Similarly, mating female **butterflies** and **moths** *perch* on branches and *emit* pheromones from the tips of their abdomen. As the chemical wafts in the night air, males catch the scent and follow the trail to its source with their antennae.

Some **cockroaches** secrete an aphrodisiac pheromone on their backs to attract mates. Females *nibble* the pheromone prior to copulating, and will not permit mating before its ingestion.

Spiders have no antennae and therefore a very poor (or non-existent) awareness of smell. This may be because, as web hunters, they wait for food to come to them rather than the other way round.

Perception and emission of smell

Most of an adult insect's body is covered with sensory hairs that are connected via the neural system to the brain. In addition, the antennae (one or two pairs) can detect smell, heat, ultrasound and vibration from long distances, over or underground, in the air or through water. These segmented, flexible and highly sensitive organs are usually located between and slightly above the compound eyes, and are equipped with sensilla that respond to chemical, mechanical or thermal stimulation. In this way, antennae allow insects to *touch*, hear and detect sex pheromones and locate sources of food and water.

Desert burrowing cockroaches test the air by *extending* their antenna in order to determine the prevailing humidity and air temperature before emerging from the sand. The Indian **beetle** has fringes on its antennae that greatly enlarge their surface area, thereby increasing their sensitivity to wind-borne scents.

Butterflies and **moths** can detect minute concentrations of scent in the air, thanks to the dense coverage of receptors on their antennae, which are divided into two-branched segments to increase their sensitivity.

Cave crickets have two very long and sensitive antennae in front and two more at the back, called cerci. As well as detecting predators approaching from any direction, this arrangement allows crickets to find their way in complete darkness.

Pheromones are sometimes detected by species for which they are not intended. When **parasitic wasps** catch the scent of the sexual attractant pheromones of moths or butterflies, they follow the trail back to its source. **Water scorpions** have a breathing tube that sticks out of water at the rear, which also can detect smell, vibration and temperature.

VISUAL SIGNALS

Insects have both simple and compound eyes. Simple eyes recognise only shades of light and dark; compound eyes have multiple lenses for extended vision.

Simple eyes have a single lens lying over a layer of vision cells, some of which contain pigments that absorb light. These rudimentary structures (called ocelli in adult insects) develop at the same time as wings, and are hence absent from most wingless insects. Some insects do not require eyes at all to perceive light, relying instead photosensitive cells deep in the head, which detect light through the cuticle.

Compound eyes consist of many minuscule individual units called ommatidiae, each with its own lens, pigments and nerve cells with which to perceive a small sector of the field of vision. The information from all the ommatidiae combined in the brain to form a mosaic image of the creature's surroundings.

The ocular capabilities of each species have evolved in various ways in response to their environment and survival strategies. **Whirligig beetles** hunt on the surface of water, and their eyes are divided into two halves to allow simultaneous vision above and beneath the meniscus.

Wasps, like most insects, have both simple and compound eyes, the latter detecting the slightest movement and recognising certain colours. **Caterpillars** have tiny simple eyes and a poor vision; by contrast, **dragonflies** have huge compound eyes allowing them to observe their surroundings in great detail.

Crustaceans such as scorpions, crabs and lobsters, all have compound eyes that respond to a wide spectrum of light from infrared to ultraviolet. **Wolf** and **Nursery Web spiders** have two rows of four eyes each, the anterior row in a straight line, the posterior row arrayed in a 'U' shape. **Jumping spiders** have two of their eight eyes much larger than the others, allowing them to spot prey from a long distance.

Various bright colours and combinations of colour act as warning signals to deter predators, either as permanent features of the anatomy or produced to order in direct response to threat. Predators learn both from individual experience and the species memory evolved through millions of years that these signals relate to poison or vile taste, and avoid getting involved. Many harmless insects have evolved to resemble brightly coloured noxious species in order to take advantage of this powerful deterrent effect.

There are of course thousands of examples of colour acting as passive self-protection in another way – in the form of **camouflage** to make the creature hard to distinguish visually against its preferred environment, like a stick insect.

Although an element of mimicry is involved in both of these examples, they are species adaptations that have evolved through the long process of natural selection rather than being in any sense Volitional on the part of the individual.

Colouration for deterrence

Certain **grasshoppers** taste awful because of the toxins they accumulate from eating poisonous plants, and yellow and black stripes advertise their inedibility to predators. Similarly, the vivid colouring of the **Saddleback caterpillar** provides a visual warning of its poisonous spines.

Mimicking the colour, shape and behaviour of poisonous species (as well as inedible objects such as twigs, thorns or stones) is a well-established strategy used by many harmless insects. By confusing or misleading the predator, such mimicry helps to prevent these insects from becoming a meal.

Some **moth caterpillars** *flatten* the front sections of their body when disturbed, and *constrict* the sections just behind to form the shape of a head and a neck; false eye spots and a *waving* motion complete the disguise to disorient any predator ready to *strike*. **Monarch butterflies** taste unpleasant because they feed on milkweed as larvae. Although **Viceroy butterflies** are not as unpalatable, their orange and black wings resemble those of the Monarch, thus deterring insectivorous birds.

As the **Fulgorid bug** *spreads* its wings for flight when disturbed, it reveals large hind wing markings resembling the eyes of an owl. The **Horner moth** looks much like a hornet, and even behaves like one when in *flying*. **Hover flies** are striped yellow and black for the same reason.

Colouration for attraction

One of the most common visual signals in the insect world is the use of colour as a sexual attractant. Male dragonflies, for example, advertise their presence with their iridescent red, blue, green and purple hues that shimmer in sunlight as they *dart* through the air.

Colouration for camouflage

Treehoppers, when in danger, *raise* a spike from their backs so as to look like thorns. The body of some **mantids** resembles a dead flower or leaf, and change its colour to match the background, thereby avoiding attention from predators. Seen from the side, the head of a **planthopper** looks like a lizard's, which seems to scare off some predators.

The **golden crab spider** protects itself by changing its colour to match the flower it sits on. Hundreds of spider species copy the shape and colour of ants as a protection against the many birds that generally avoid ants because of the bitter taste of formic acid. Some *jumping* spiders even *move* like ants, *walking* on six legs while *holding up* their forelegs like antennae. **Bolas spiders**, like many others, *mimic* bird droppings as a protective measure (although when hunting, they *emit* a pheromone similar to that of a female moth in order to trap sexually expectant males of the same species).

Light signals

Bioluminescence is the ability of living organisms to generate light, and is used by a variety of insect species in addition to the **firefly** and **glow-worm**. The light is produced by means of a complex chemical reaction in an organ at the hind end of the abdomen, which converts chemical energy into light and heat. Males vary the frequency and duration of the light pulse they *emit* to signal their interest in a female, who then *flashes* her readiness in response.

In a communal courtship displays, thousands of South-Ease Asian fireflies gather on the boughs of a tree and *flash* synchronously. **Glow-worms**, the wingless females of certain beetles, attract males by flashing a distinct code using the light they *emit* near the tip of their abdomen.

Some insect attracting plants display patterns called honey-guides that are only visible in ultraviolet light to lead insects towards the nectaries. Some butterfly species have wing markings that are visible only in ultraviolet light. The legs of **melanophila beetles** are equipped with a sensory organ that detects infrared waves emitted by forest fires.

Many insects depend on detecting the angle of vibrating light waves in the sky in order to orient themselves. The atmosphere polarises light from the sun, setting most of the rays vibrating in the same plane, which insects can use as a long distance navigational tool.

ACOUSTIC SIGNALS

Calling, warning and mating

Sound is a long-range communication tool. Insects often signal with sounds produced by *rubbing* one part of their anatomy against another: wing against wing, wing against back or leg against leg. Insects that make *chirping, rasping* and *squeaking* sounds are said to *stridulate*. Each species has its characteristic call, and it is predominantly males that make sound either to attract mates, or to warn off sexual competitors. Some insects make sounds to warn others or to summon help.

The auditory organs of insects are located in various parts of the body – thorax, abdomen, mouth, antennae, wings and legs. Antennae and body hair can also help insects to detect tiny signals and ultrasonic waves from a long distance.

Some female flying insects *emit* special mating sounds produced by *vibrating* their wings. Some crickets have different songs in their repertoire – a loud belligerent song, a song advertising their presence and a courtship song.

The auditory receptors of **moths** are on their abdomen or thorax; when they detect the ultrasonic echolocation calls of a hunting bat, the moth instantly *flies* down to safety. **Crickets** have drum-shaped 'ears' below their front knees. **Katydids** have auditory organs on the foreleg. Male **chironomid midges** are equipped with what is called Johnston's organ, which senses the sound waves generated by the *vibrating* wings of the female.

The male **oak-bush cricket** *drums* its feet on leaves at night to attract females. **Grasshoppers** *move* the bumps on their hind legs against their front wings to produce a *rasping* sound like pieces of sandpaper being *rubbed* against each other. Male **cicadas** produce a very long mating song using drum-like organs called tymbals on both sides of the abdomen, amplified by an adjacent cavity. The **mole cricket** has the loudest mating call of any insect, and can be heard more than half a mile (0.8km). When male prairie mole crickets *sing* to attract mates, they do so from horn-shaped burrows that amplify the sound, and can continue *singing* for up to an hour under the right conditions.

Horned passalus beetles live in families of parents and their larvae, and communicate by *stridulating* almost constantly, using a repertoire of fourteen different sounds. The **Madagascar hissing cockroach** produces a loud *hissing* sound by forcing air out through its spiracles. Males *hiss* to attract the larger females, deter rivals or scare away predators; females and nymphs only *hiss* when disturbed.

Wasps make their warning buzz by *beating* their wings at up to two hundred beats per second. Male **broad-winged katydids** make a *lisping* sound to attract females and demarcate their territory. Both males and females also conduct dialogues using a ticking sound – the male usually begins, and when the female responds, he moves closer. This occurs repeatedly and so fast that it sounds like a continuous song. Some **leafcutter ants** emit high-pitched *squeaks* when underground.

Male **spiders** sometimes lure females by *drumming* on their webs, the frequency and amplitude of vibration differing for each species. The males of some species of **wolf spider** *scrape* the rough surfaces of their mouths to produce sounds to which only females respond. Male orb weaver spiders *attach* a mating thread to the chosen female's web and *pluck* it in a special rhythm.

TACTILE SIGNALS

Insects and spiders can detect very small *vibrations* in the air, through the ground and under water, as well as minute variations in temperature, electrical and magnetic fields. According to species, their highly sensitive touch receptors include the antennae, hair, mouth parts, limbs, palps, the tip of the abdomen and the exoskeleton itself.

The sophisticated tactile communication systems of insects and spiders vary considerably from species to species, according to their anatomical capabilities. Some insects are more sensitive to the vibrations of inanimate objects, while others are more attuned to those of the living world. Both are nevertheless closely related in that the same neurological receptors are involved – mainly the antennae for insects, and palps for spiders. These are also sensitive to winds, rain, fire and seismic disturbance.

When **honeybees** *dance* to communicate with other colony members, the latter *touch* the dancers with their antennae to 'hear' the information being imparted

Long horn beetles compensate for their poor vision by the exceptional sensitivity of their very long antennae

Ants converse by *touching* antennae, thereby passing chemical messages about food or potential threats

Tactile information is especially crucial to dweller insects like **cockroaches** and **crickets**, which rely on their sense of touch to get around

When an **orb-weaver spider** finds a web woven by a female of the species, it *touches* a thread to detect both the gender and the sexual maturity of the weaver, as well as the degree of her readiness to mate. The potential mates *move* gradually to the mating thread and begin a courtship ritual that involves repeated *touching* with their front legs, testing and reassuring each other before copulating.

Dolomedes and **brownish-grey fishing spiders** use their legs to detect *vibrations* on the surface of the water created by the insects that form their main diet.

BODY MOTION FACILITIES

Strange as it may seem, plastic body motion is undoubtedly the most advanced, effective and dynamic communication system that insects use. Insect species have been successful on this planet for some 4–500 million years. As arthropods, they may be near the bottom of the evolutionary ladder, but their highly developed anatomical structure remains perfectly adapted for survival.

Insects use most of their body parts for plastic communication in one way or another – the head, antennae, horns/spines, jaws/pincers, mouth/beak, thorax, elytra/wings, legs/claws/palps, abdomen, ovipositor/spines.

Obviously, these also perform vital functions in the processes of metamorphosis, feeding, hunting, defending, nursing, courtship, mating and cleaning, as well as nest building, digging, food storage, web spinning and so on. The body motions involved in these vital functions are described in more detail in the next chapter.

It makes sense to begin by examining the characteristic behaviour of insects in social activities and when working in groups, and what principles and patterns underlie their plastic communication.

Compared to ours, the life of an insect is short – a year of human life can equate to a matter of minutes in an insect's. As the pace of their existence is many hundreds of times faster than ours, they seem to us to be perpetually moving, their vital functions apparently ceaseless.

Because of their small size, the speed and modulation of all insect *movements* are much faster than our own, and therefore often hard for the human eye to discern in real time. The main motion facilities for insects include *moving* antennae, leg *gestures*, *tapping* feet/palps, *shaking* the abdomen, *vibrating* wings and *plucking* webs. In terms of progression, insects *walk, jump, run, crawl, fly, drop, turn, dive, swim* and perform *acrobatics* – all in different rhythms, dynamics and spatial patterns.

Antennae manipulations

Studies of insect antennae prove beyond doubt that these highly sensitive organs are complex communication tools as well as sensory receptors, with a plastic vocabulary of hundreds, if not thousands, of independent spatial positions – even more when both antennae are used in combination. Though this ultra-sophisticated plastic lexicon has not yet been deciphered, it remains a very extensive motion dictionary for each species.

Antennae have three basic segments: the scape, or basal stalk; the pedicel, a middle segment which usually has a sensory organ that relates antennae *movement* to that of the body; and the flagellum, a filamentous end piece that is adapted to suit the insect's vital requirements.

- Competing **beetles** use their antennae to learn about their opponent, then use them to threaten each other before actually fighting.
- Most male **flies** use adhesive discs on the inner surface of their antennae to *hold* the female in place during copulation.
- Aquatic **mosquito** larvae use their antennae for hunting to detect and *hold* their prey.
- **Soldier ants** are blind, and use their antennae to search for food; when they locate it, they use their antennae to inform others. All communications within the group are conducted in this way.
- **Queen butterfly** males *dust* the females' antennae with pheromones from their abdomen during courtship flights.
- **Crickets** have very long antennae helps them find their way in the dark and alert others to danger.
- **Bees** are the most communicative insects, and antennae are their main signalling tools. On their return from food gathering expeditions, bees share information with the rest of the colony by motions of the antennae. A queen bee relies mainly on her antennae to communicate with other members of the colony and control the functioning of the hive.

Wing signals

Insects were the first species to overcome the pull of gravity and fly by *flapping* their wings. The anatomical mechanisms for insect flight developed over hundreds of million years to highly advanced systems using single or double pairs of wings not only for aerial propulsion, but also for camouflage, for increasing body temperature by absorbing solar radiation and for attracting mates during courtship. More surprisingly – and as yet, still only partially understood - wings also play a role in detecting communication signals using sensors hidden in the veins and sending messages by *vibrating* motions. These communications mainly involve warning of nearby predators or form part of aerial courtship rituals.

As the sonic communication signals are less effective and more dangerous in flight than on the ground, flying insects communicate with each other during long-distance flights via ultrasonic or electromagnetic signals produced by the wings. Transmitted and received by means of biochemical reactions in the sensors in the wings, it is thought that these messages may help in adjusting various flight parameters such as course, level and velocity. These corrections involve corresponding changes in the frequency and amplitude of wing beats as well as *gliding* and *steering* motions.

In addition to these wing communication systems, signals are produced mechanically by *rubbing* motions: *rubbing* two upper wings against each other, or upper wings against the lower pair; *rubbing* the wings against the thorax or legs; causing wing cases to make sounds against each other, and so on.

By far the most effective wing signalling technique is *vibrating* the membranes to create airwaves. Not only can atmospheric conditions such as pressure, temperature and humidity be indicated in this way, but the resulting *buzzing* sound is highly audible and provides an extensive signalling vocabulary of sound sequences in various *rhythmic patterns, dynamic nuances, tone modulations* and other sonic characteristics. **Wasps, bees**, and **mosquitoes** have particularly well developed capabilities for communicating with wing motion in this way.

All flying insects have to warm up their wing muscles before a long flight. After spending time on the ground, they repeatedly *open* and *close* their wing cases and wings, *stretching* and *flexing* the exoskeleton joints of the thorax in preparation for flight. Over time, this warm up procedure in itself became a warning to others (including other species) of imminent take-off.

Generally speaking, making yourself look as big as possible is a good survival strategy, both in terms of protection and reproduction. Any insect trying to intimidate a potential opponent will *open* its wings and wing cases wide in order to appear more threatening; with a potential mate, the objective of this same behaviour is simply to appear bigger and stronger.

The hind wings of **ribbontail lacewing butterflies** have long graceful streamers whose evolutionary function remains unclear. Observations however confirm that these streamers constantly *shiver* and *vibrate* during feeding, each one independently, in a different timing and amplitude, suggesting some kind of motion signal for other members of the same species.

Chironomidae *beat* their wings at certain frequencies to locate other midges within swarms containing hundreds of different species

The halteres of **flies** *vibrate* along with the fore wings, which are packed with sense organs that help the insect to monitor flight conditions and to react swiftly to any changes. The *buzzing* sounds of their wings in various modulations act as communication signals during flight.

The hind wings of the **io moth** bear intimidating eye spots that are covered by the fore wings in the resting position. When disturbed, the moth *flashes* its wings to reveal the false eyes as a warning signal.

Butterfly courtship involves *dancing* flights that usually start by circling around each other and exchanging sexual information by scent, sound and touch signals. The couple display the attractively bright colours and graceful motions of their wings, which remain in close touch with the mate during the ensuing aerial copulation

When defending its territory, the **Purple Emperor** first *emits* warning signals by *vibrating* its wings before attacking. The combatants *beat* their wings until one surrenders

Abdominal gestures

The most flexible part of an insect's body is the abdomen, which bears certain sensory and/or signalling organs depending on the species and can *move* independently from thorax in any direction. These organs often have both physiological and communication functions such as perceiving or distributing fluids or pheromones, or enhancing outgoing or incoming signals.

Some water insects have a long breathing tube protruding from the tip of the abdomen; others have an extra pair of hind antennae, or mock eyes and jaws on their behind. Some have long ovipositors that double up as organs of taste; others have sensitive spines to detect vibration, so on. Certain abdominal motions of insects produce sonic signals like wind or percussion instruments. As noted earlier, the sound of *drumming* tymbala of the **Cicada** is amplified, controlled and modulated by *retracting* or *projecting* its abdomen. Similarly, the abdomen of other species is used like a bagpipe, *expanding* to pull air in and *contracting* to expel the air as sonic signals under the precise control of this body motion. Abdominal motions are involved in many more insect and spider signalling activities including laying traps, *tapping* and *vibrating* in code, *touching* and *weaving* webs.

Considered in evolutionary terms, the visual similarity between an insect *moving* its raised abdomen and, for example, a dog *wagging* its tail, is more than coincidental. Despite the profound anatomical differences, essentially the same mechanism is involved, modified through hundreds of million years of progressive adaptation in the tails of fish, reptiles, birds and mammals. The connection cannot have escaped Darwin when observing how his dog used its tail.

- Male **striped blue cow butterflies** have a yellow brush on the end of their abdomen, which they *vibrate* to dust scented scales on potential mates.

- Female **African cave crickets** have two sharp, sensitive spines called cerci on the tip of the abdomen, which can detect enemies approaching from behind and are also used to attack them.

- Using the breathing tube on its rear end, the **water scorpion** can *hang* upside down in the water for a long time while detecting the vibrations of potential prey both in the air and on the surface of the water.

- The male **damselfly** has a long flexible abdomen that it uses to *grip* the female's neck during copulation, thereby excluding sexual competitors.

- **Pear-shaped aphids** sport a pair of narrow tubes called cornicles that project from the tip of the abdomen to detect signals and *spray* defensive fluids when under attack

- When **darkling beetles** are disturbed, they *stand* on their heads and *emit* a foul smelling liquid from the tip of their abdomen.

- The mating call of the **eved click beetle** is made by *bending* and then *snapping* itself straight by the abdomen, making a loud *clicking* as it *launches* them up to 15 centimetres in the air.

- When a **honeybee** finds flowers rich in nectar, it informs other bees of the direction to follow by *dancing* to them. The distance to the food source is conveyed by the speed with which they *shake* their abdomen.

- **Swallowtail butterflies** exchange courtship signals by the tip of the abdomen in flight. The male then *grips* the female's abdomen with claspers to keep her in place during the aerial copulation.

- **Wolf spiders** communicate before mating by *vibrating* their abdomens in a courtship dialogue that continues in various rhythms until the female accepts the mate.

Limb motions

Insect and spider legs have adapted through the long evolutionary process into functional and communication instruments which play interdependent but separate roles as well as working in concert for the purposes of locomotion (*walking* forward, backward and sideways, *running*, *leaping, swimming, diving, skating, crawling, burrowing, tapping* and *dancing*). Forelegs are primarily occupied with feeding and mating; the middle legs with *grasping* and *digging*; the hind legs with *kicking* and *jumping*.

The highest achievement of the arthropod brain is the ability to communicate using the motion of the forelegs as they do with the antennae, but in a much more sophisticated plastic code based on more complicated spatial patterns. Fortunately, today's arthropologists seem to be on the verge of deciphering the hitherto impenetrable gestural codes of insect communication.

The legs of most land insects are slender and of even length. Being six-legged, they advance by assuming a highly stable tripod position, *raising* the foreleg and hind leg on one side and a middle leg on the other. The resulting *zigzag* gait is remarkably efficient.

Other types of locomotion mentioned earlier are usually the result of various leg adaptations that have evolved to serve other purposes than locomotion. Insects that spend their lives on or under water have feet adapted for *swimming*, while those living underground have legs modified for *digging*. Predatory insects have forelegs armed with spines with which to secure their prey. Footpads covered with fine hair and kept sticky by oily secretions allow some insects to adhere to a sheer surface and *walk* upside down. Some species have a meaothorax packed with flight muscles, giving them great speed and height as well as the ability to perform aerial *acrobatics* during courtship. The forelegs of male spiders are modified into pad palps to fertilise the female during copulation.

- The forelegs of **harlequin beetles** are so long and slender that the muscles are not strong enough to move them. The beetle therefore has to *pump* body fluids into the legs, *extending* them like hydraulic rams that apparently make it easier for them to *crawl*.

- **Desert darkling beetles** living on dunes have long spiny legs and long curved claws that provide good grip on the sand.
- Some **grasshoppers** communicate by *scratching* signals produced by their long hind legs (which are also lethal *kickers*).
- Many **butterflies** *walk* on only four legs, reserving the front pair for *holding, tasting* and communicating through *gestures* in a courtship displays.
- Some **ants** communicate by *tapping* on the side of the plant that houses their nest, thereby sharing information through the rhythmic motion of their feet.
- When disturbed, they all *tap* simultaneously. To attract a mate, the **house fly** enters room and *lands* upside down on the ceiling, a manoeuvre that involves *flying* close to the surface, *reaching* back over the head until its feet *touch* the ceiling, then *somersaulting* in front of the mate.
- **Pond skaters** *walk* on the water almost without denting the surface, detecting ripples caused by any insect struggling in the water, and *running* across for the kill
- The male **dance fly** includes an attractive *manipulation* with a silken package in his courtship choreography – a gift to the female, in effect.
- The elongated oar-shaped hind legs of the **water boatman** help it to *swim* fast and to *catch* small fish or tadpoles with its forelegs.
- Wingless insects like **fleas** can only communicate by locomotion signals such as *crawling* and *jumping.*
- When the worker **honey bee** *dances* in the hive to report the location of sources of nectar or pollen to others in the colony, its repertoire includes a round dance and a *waggling* dance. The round dance is used when supplies are within a certain distance; in the *waggling* dance, the bee executes a figure of eight, indicating the presence of food further away. The number of *waggles* account for the distance, while the angle indicates the direction to the supplies relative to the sun. Young bees watch and *mimic* the action with foreleg gestures and *touch* the *dancing* bees to learn the codes of communicating by plastic motion in this way.

The functioning of all social insect species is predicated on effective communications. Although aspects of insect communication have not yet been decoded, its existence is beyond doubt - and in some ways, is arguably as advanced as any nonverbal signalling system we ourselves have developed.

When two or more individual insects work together, their efforts will only be productive if the body tools of both operate in concert towards a common objective, whether this happens to be *attacking, cutting, dragging, storing* or whatever. The colony's communally constructed shelters are efficient architectural structures created by all the available body motion resources in a perfectly organised mass complementary effort.

- Male and female **tunible bugs** cooperate to *chew* off a piece of dung, which they *pack* into a ball and *roll* with their hind legs, one *pushing*, the other *pulling*.
- The **spider**'s main operating tools are its legs. No other species, including humans, has limbs with such excellent motion capacity, along with highly advanced working techniques, body coordination, balance and plasticity. Spiders' legs are very sensitive organs for *emitting* and receiving communication signals, as well as crucial weapons and tactile sexual implements.
- The **ogre-faced spider** *builds* a rectangular silken web the size of a postage stamp, then *hangs* from it upside down near the ground, its forelegs *holding* the corners of the web. When an insect *passes* below, the spider *throws* the web over the prey like a net, *wrapping* the insect in it with its free legs.

- The **Sydney funnel-web spider**, when disturbed, *rears up* on its hind legs, *lifts* its front legs straight over its head and *exposes* its chelicerae, tipped with forbidding fangs. When attacking, it *grips* the prey with its hind legs.

- The **giant crab spider** is known as the **dancing dune spider** because of its long and flexible legs. It often *points* its fore legs towards a hiding insect to detect its characteristics. This 'search' choreography ends with a sudden *strike, catching* the prey with its fore and middle legs.

- Male **jumping spiders** perform various body *movements* in their courtship dance, carefully *approaching* a mate in a *zigzag* pattern. Without exactly the right dance *movements,* the female will withdraw.

- The **thrice-landed crab spider** has very flexible legs that look like those of a crab which allow it to *move* quickly forwards, sideways and backwards to *grab* passing insects with its *outstretched* forelegs.

- When a male **wolf spider** encounters a female, he *crouches* low and begins *waving* his palps and *raising* and *lowering* his fore legs. He *drums* with his palps, making a clearly audible *stridulating* sound. He then *pauses* for about fifteen seconds before resuming his display. The female may respond during these pauses by *waving* her own fore legs to encourage the suitor to repeat the performance more intensively until she eventually *touches* him with her fore legs to signal her readiness for mating.

Conclusion

This brief excursion into the world of insects and spiders provides at least part of the answer to the questions posed at the beginning of this section. The behaviours of insects and spiders are fundamental to this study because they are living proof of the origins of body motion for communication throughout the animal kingdom.

The important role of plastic motion in any vital function of insect life is self-evident and unquestionable. And it is because every single tiny movement of their body parts is so exceptionally economical, specific and effective that they became ritual symbols for our earliest ancestors (Homo Erectus) – an ideal for creating the beauty and harmony of motion.

Obviously, animal evolution right up to humans has developed these basic capabilities to a tremendous degree in terms of physiological, musculo-skeletal and neurological systems. We nevertheless have to recognise that as humans, the price we have paid is the irretrievable loss of the unlimited self-preservation strategies and survival adaptations of humble insects and spiders.

There remain many questions to be answered about insects – their metamorphosis, their use of camouflage and mimicry, their social life and communication systems. However, what we already know about these creatures, together with the almost weekly advances in research, confirm our fundamental hypothesis about the genetic roots of animal communication in general, and the evolution of plastic motion in particular.

fig. I/12

Courtship/Mating Performance

1. Kissing introduction
2. "I love you, darling, trust me!"
3. Sexual stimulation

4. The love of Bonobos
5. Copulation arrangements
   (a,b) back to face (c,d,e) face-to-face

Nursing/Motherhood, Mammals

1. Elephant family on the move
2. Lioness changes her lair
3. Climbing lesson for a bear cub
4. "Come on … jump to mummy!"

5. Chimp mother and her twins
6. Wildebeest calf plays with its mother
7. Safe protection for a tiny cub
8. Father's greeting to a happy family

1. Fox cubs practising hunt skills
2. Jumping over the heads of adults
3. The colts at play
4. Peculiar equilibrium
5. Polar bear cubs in a pushing match

6. Young langurs dancing in the sun
7. Play of young Japanese macaques
8. Wolf cubs play fighting
9. Brown bear cubs confront in the water
10. Playing dialogue

fig. I/15

Social Interrelation

1a 1b 1c

2a 2b 2c

3a 3b 3c 3d

1. (a,b,c) Chimps
   "Let's make friends!"

2. (a,b,c) Monkey and ape couples grooming
3. (a,b,c,d) The joy of entertainment

Touching Contacts

1. Kissing/sniffing motion
   a) Bear cubs   b) Orangutans
   c) Penguins   d) Hippos
2. Fighting elephants
3. Python strangles a rat
4. Courtship of zebras
5. Self-touching motion
   a) Young seal
   b) Young grizzly bear cleaning its fur
6. Copulating salamanders

Terrestrial Locomotion

1a

1b

1c

2

3

4

5a

5b

6

7

8

9

1. (a,b,c) Leaping antelope
2. Progressively bobbing sifaka
3. Running cheetah
4. Trotting wolf
5. Lizards: a) running on water surface
   b) trotting on hot sand

6. Galloping horse
7. Fleeing wildebeest
8. Walking mother with baby shrews in a caravan
9. Wagging motion in a carriage with galloping horse

fig. I/18 Arborial Locomotion

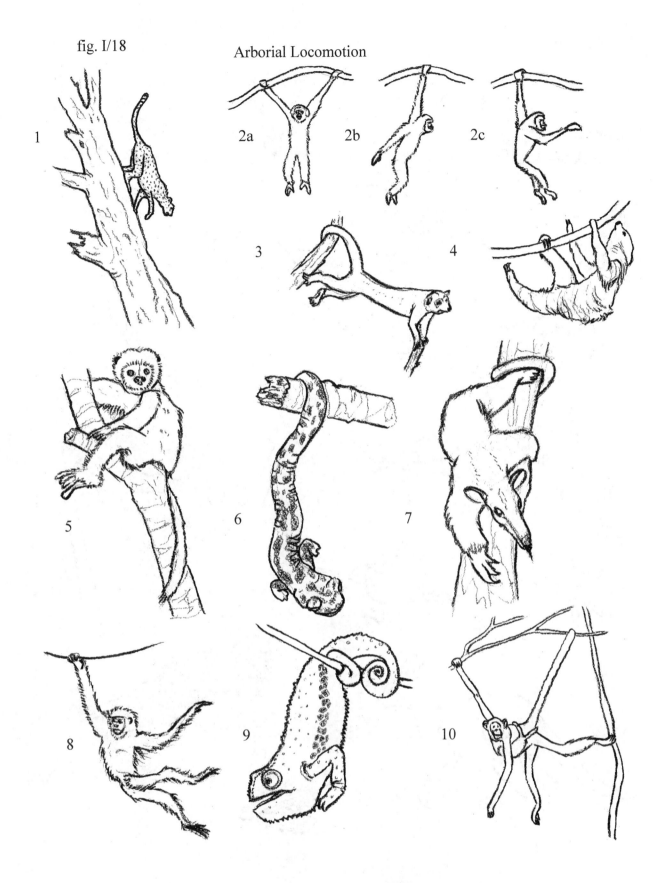

1) Cheetah climbing down tree
2. (a,b,c) Gibbon travelling
3. Stretching out squirrel
4. Sloth moving along upside down
5. Balancing capuchin

6. Hanging salamander
7. Crawling down Guiana
8. Swinging gibbon
9. Camouflaged chameleon ambushing its prey
10. Spider monkey stretching out with baby

Aerial Locomotion

1. Gliding bat
2. (a,b,c) Leaping squirrel
3. Proboscis monkey with baby jumps
   between branches
4. Gliding squirrel
5. (a,b) Gliding lizards

6. Japanese spider floating down
7. Spider-monkey leaping
8. Gliding tree frog
9. Bobbing young cat
10. Leaping kangaroo
11. Flying fish

Chapter II: The Origins of Mimetic Culture

THE MISSING LINK IN THE EVOLUTION OF SPOKEN LANGUAGE

The first hypotheses about primal human language emerged some 400 years ago, when European scholars were first able to visit other continents to study apes and other anthropoids in their native habitat. Although their controversial publications aroused worldwide interest in anthropology, the theories of human evolution and the origin of language they contained were inevitably somewhat naive. Nevertheless, despite the diversity of their academic backgrounds, most of these scholars proposed a similar underlying thesis: that body motion (in the form of **mimicry, gestures** and **posturings**) had been the earliest system of hominid communication and the probable genesis of spoken language.

THE PRIMACY OF BODY MOTION IN NON-VERBAL COMMUNICATION

"Language must have begun with manual gestures..." *(Cresol, 1620; Bulwer,1644; Dalgarno, 1661)*
"The apes are quite human-like and might be capable of learning the sign language." *(Samuel Pepys, 1661)*
"Our primal language was thought to be concrete – that is, lacking in abstract concepts – and based on facial expressions, gestures of hands and body." *(Condillac, 1746; Rousseau, 1755)*.

By 1804, the English philosopher Adam Smith was advancing a theory of the origins of language based on the laws of mimesis and associations.

As these few examples show, the belief in body motion as the primal communication system of humans was well established several centuries ago, despite the limited archaeological and anthropological knowledge and resources available. The beginning of Chapter I describes the stereotypical instinctive behaviour of human and other mammalian infants at the very early stages of nursing. Through plastic expression of its body parts, the newborn creature self-evidently makes these natural spatial movements for a specific purpose.

The entire human reproductive cycle is based on body movement and plastic motion without the need for any vocalisation from the initial body contact in copulation, through childbirth to nursing. Humans can live long and productive lives, enjoying both family and socio-cultural activities without recourse to sound. However, they cannot do so without motion. Once the heart stops beating, life ends; in the animal kingdom, while there is body motion, there is life. Just as movement is the dominant force of the universe in general, so is body motion for humans.

DARWIN ON PRE-VERBAL COMMUNICATION

In *On the Origin of Species* (1859) and *The Descent of Man* (1871), Charles Darwin wrote of the difference between "stereotyped instinct" of animals and "learned behaviour" based on their individual experiences. For Darwin, this was clear evidence of intellect. Not only did he believe that animals could have "abstract concepts", but that some of the higher mammals had a "continuity of mind" and a small degree of self-consciousness which may have been based on their culture and experience.

Darwin wrote much about social cooperation in animals, their moral capacities and communication systems. He demonstrated the existence of birdsong dialects, which he compared by analogy to those of humans. The great anthropologist also noted that human beings use facial grimaces and gestures the same way as apes, combining them with sounds to express motions such as pain, fear, anger, surprise and joy. He concluded that the most distinctive trait of human communication must therefore consist of the more abstract cognitive features of our languages.

Darwin posited three stages in the transition from ape communication to human language:

1) **Intellectual power** – that as a precondition for linguistic development, pre-verbal hominids must have undergone some fundamental change that extended their capacity for cognition. In other words, Darwin believed that his first stage was predicated on primate intelligence acquiring the capacity to represent the world **symbolically**.

2) A **"vocal communication system"** – not some earlier version of a dictionary of signs, but direct **onomatopoeic** imitation of natural sounds, together with creative use of the voice in **rudimentary cries** and songs. Darwin argued that the suitability of the voice as an apparatus for spoken language was developed through its constant use in these ways.

3) **"Long trains of thought"** which had the effect of increasing intellectual capacity to the extent that sign languages could be conceived of and used.

This very brief summary of Darwin's initial analysis the origin of language shows some confusion about the primal stage of hominid communication. After initially categorising facial expressions and gestures as merely emotional accompaniments to vocal sounds, his later observations and analyses of ape behaviour led him to conclude that the face, gestures and postures are the plastic implements of a discrete non-verbal communication system.

If in fact most animals maintain complete silence in the presence of predators for reasons of self-preservation, yet continue at the same time to communicate plastically through appropriate facial and bodily motions, creating camouflage and the like, Darwin's theory that the evolution of language was led by the voice sounds unconvincing. The reason he did not believe that body motion could be the origin of spoken language was that he thought of the gestures and posturings of apes as merely "stereotyped instinct" – that is to say, involuntary reflex behaviours.

Though admitting that facial expressions and Gestures may have evolved somehow in early humans, Darwin rejects the notion that the elaborate alphabet of hand signs could lead to spoken language. Nowhere does he satisfactorily explain why he rejects body motion as a precursor of linguistic development. His main argument was that if the primal form of language had been a formal system of hand signs, then vestiges would remain – especially in exclusively oral cultures. In the absence of any such vestiges, he concluded that spoken language must have originated elsewhere, and be tied to progressive developments in vocalisation.

The case against Darwin's hypothesis

We agree partially with Darwin's last thesis because the human respiratory apparatus remains essentially the same, as does the vocal technique. It was, however, the final rather than the initial stage in the evolution of language, long after the establishment of body motion vocabulary.

There is an overwhelming case that the real genesis of spoken language was in fact bodily expression, in the form of facial *grimaces, gestures* and *posturings* accompanied by *rudimentary cries, vocal modulations* and *rhythmic sounds* produced by the teeth, feet and *clapping* hands against various parts of the body.

It is hard to accept that an intellectual giant of Darwin's calibre was either confused or forced to compromise his academic principles. There must have been a reason – perhaps that the publisher wanting to avoid yet another scandal in the wake of hostile press and clerical reaction to Darwin's previous study of similar body motion implements used by apes and humans.

It is also possible that Darwin's observations of the Tsiren language of deaf-mute children led him to conclude that this symbolic medium could not be the primordial human communication system he was searching for. Rightly so – the hand-sign alphabet is a modem invention, an artificial symbolic system which has nothing to do with the original plastic motion vocabulary of primates.

Darwin wrote that human facial expressions are greatly elaborated versions of those used by apes, and that the use of what he called "**gross body posture**" in humans is essentially similar to that used by apes, although somewhat more inhibited. He argues that this level of expressive communication may have preceded symbolic language in hominids, since there would have been no evolutionary reason for its development after spoken language had established itself.

The weakness of this argument lies in the fact that even after some three million years of evolution, apes still make widespread use of various "gross body postures" in their communication, and they do so without spoken language. Darwin believed hominid facial expressions to have been very effective devices for communicating emotion in small groups, and that their continued use by modem humans, despite all their sophisticated linguistic skills, is a vestige of this early adaptation.

In other words, Darwin accepted the existence of body motion in the early stages of human evolution, but only as a spur to the development of vocalisation rather than main medium of communication for our earliest ancestors. All the evidence points to the reverse being true.

Darwin also mentions the link to ritual dance as a group social experience, and the association of song, dance and music in performance. But he did not realise that these syncretic performances were in fact the repositories of the original forms of hominid language. The great man's failure to make this association may either have been due to his lack of knowledge of body language and its capacities, or an understandable reluctance to advance yet more socially and academically contentious ideas.

THE ROOTS OF MIMETIC CULTURE

Prehistoric arts all over the world were based exclusively on the body motion of animals, including their cries and sounds. The long evolution of this system of communication by analogy was slow but persistent, driven by the desperate need to extend the vocabulary of expression and requiring intensive study of the surrounding fauna.

The origins can be traced right back through the primate genetic hierarchy to the lemur. Close observation of these animals clearly reveals different expression in their eyes and faces during gathering or social activities. Indeed, they **signal** with the head, body and tail to call for attention, exchange information or send out warning messages.

With no secondary sources to rely on, our ancestors had to watch and study nature at close range – not for reasons of entertainment or research, but as essential knowledge for their very survival as part of the unending quest to get food while avoiding becoming food themselves. Only by studying the behaviour of different creatures, memorising and **copying** what they saw through endlessly repetitive practice for application in everyday social and domestic activities could hominids achieve this.

Inevitably, such a profound and prolonged psychological and physical experience gradually developed the musculo-skeletal apparatus as well as the hominids' body motion vocabulary – and most importantly of all, the brain. This enlarged cerebrum helped our forefathers to invent more advanced hunting and gathering skills and tools. It allowed them to add new, more complex and sophisticated body motion and voice signals, which in turn stimulated the linguistic function of the brain in a virtuous cycle of evolutionary development based on practicing mimicry. By widening the scope of possible socio-cultural activities, this process made an essential contribution to the hominid evolution in general.

Mimetic culture flourished in routine communication as well as in rite ceremonies. Mythical mimetic performances, and hunters performing during rituals, began to make use of heavy **make-up** and **masks**, which precluded the use of facial expressions. The main reason for this change was the introduction of a cast of mythical characters with imaginary heads. This type of performance gave the shaman opportunities to portray other creatures and the totem at a higher, more respectful and super-human level, while retaining the spiritual essence through clearly defined body motion patterns.

The mimetic, non-verbal language was still widely used, and was further extended (along with rudimentary cries) during everyday activities. The body motion language based on natural facial expressions, gestures and postures gradually established itself as the fundamental vocabulary for communication. The hunting and mythical rituals that followed created a performance alphabet of artificial body motions and vocalisations that was the first step towards art theatre as we know it today.

The multitude of head, face, hand, arm, leg and torso motions is too vast to list comprehensively. However, using representative examples of the most common motions for each body part, one can attempt to:

- analyse their individual expression facilities, amplitude, kinetics and meaning.
- demonstrate the evolutionary process in plastic anatomy and cultural spirituality.
- show how single and double motions were harmonised in psycho-physical performance.

The very first instinctive movement of any new-born creature is to search for food. A blind infant *turns* its fragile head sideways to find the mother's nipple, and impulsively begins an eager *sucking* motion. If there is any difficulty in locating the breast, the infant continues to *move* its head while persisting with the *sucking* motion until it finds the nipple. This simple body motion function has the highest priority throughout the entire mammal family.

The genesis and anatomy of body motion

THE DIFFERENCE BETWEEN MOTION, MOVEMENT AND GESTURE

To avoid confusion, it is important first to clarify exactly what we mean by these three words. According to the Oxford dictionary, **Movement** simply refers to the act of moving. **Motion** implies a particular manner of moving the body. **Gesture** means a significant movement or a rhetorical device – that is, one that signifies something – or an action designed to convey an intention or evoke a response.

In terms of behaviours as opposed to words, Movement, Motion and Gesture represent a hierarchy of increasing complexity and sophistication. As the OED says, an animal's body motion is indeed "a process ... a particular manner of moving the body". Not all body movements can therefore be described as motions – blood circulation, digestion and tripping over, for example, clearly lie outside this category. **Plastic Motion**, i.e., motions of the musculoskeletal structure – can be conscious or unconscious, premeditated or impulsive, habitual or instinctive, but in all cases it can be reproduced at will. In the same way, not all motions are gestures – only those intended to convey feeling or meaning.

As far as this study is concerned, the term **plastic motion** covers all external physical movements of the musculo-skeletal system produced as a conscious or reflex reaction to any stimulus.

Body Motions include:
- facial expressions
- gestures of the head, limbs and other body parts
- progressive movements such as *walking, running* and *jumping*
- *moving* body parts such as the hair, beak, antennae and tail
- physical actions of external organs, such as *sucking, sniffing, grazing, tasting* and *touching*
- mimicry and posturing

All Motions involve different parts of the body with their own plastic facilities, but not all of them have the characteristics of gestures. Only **intentional** body motions motivated by the creature's emotional and mental state can be described as Gestures. Gestures are plastic motions **consciously performed** using particular body implements such as the head, neck, ears, proboscis, beak, jaws, lips, tongue, eyes, antennae, wings, fins, arms, legs, tail, torso and so on.

Although body motion and gesture have the same physical range, creative potential and aesthetic qualities, operate within the same limitations of time and space and have the same evolutionary roots, gestures are conscious acts, and their exceptional diversity lies at the root of non-verbal communication and mimicry.

Traces of the ancient origins of Gestures and other plastic Motions lie buried in the deep recesses of the brain's motion memory. As we shall see, household pets under conditions of stress, for example, can revert subconsciously to motions originally acquired by the species millions of years ago.

THE METAMORPHOSIS OF ANIMAL SPECIES

In the first Chapter, we outlined how the phylogeny of body motion is clearly reflected in the development of human infants at different stages, and described how the long and tortuous evolution of limbs related to the anthropology of movement.

The gradual development of the four extremities from prosimian species such as lemurs, via monkeys to the great apes was based on constant *swinging* through trees and *grasping* branches. Living most of the time high in the tree canopy, these primates had simultaneously to *grip* a fruit in one hand, *peel* it with another, keep their balance their hind limbs and tail, while also attempting to *suckle* an infant or *scratch* themselves.

Before our ancestors became surface-dwellers and lost their tails, their forelimbs were already so strong and flexible, and their behaviour so advanced, that they were able to use various tools such as sticks, rocks, reeds or shells for gathering or hunting on the ground, building shelters, making weapons and domestic objects. However, in the open savannah, apes were forced to change their communication system from audible signals to plastic gestures. In the trees, apes had been relatively protected from land predators, but unable to see each other clearly because of the dense foliage surrounding them. They therefore communicated with *shrieks* and *screams*: techniques entirely unsuited to life in the open grasslands, as they would only serve to attract predators.

Evolution therefore did a U-turn, reverting to the silent plastic motion communication systems of earlier times, which were infinitely better suited to the dangerous new environment. The transition from tree canopy to open grassland was therefore the main stimulus for the original evolution of body language. Although the head gestures and facial grimaces of low primates had rapidly improved, they were inadequate for apes and their more sophisticated communication requirements. The combination of a fast growing population and the danger of living in surroundings where predators constantly lurked demanded a wider vocabulary of **gestural signals**. With their larger brains and capacity to learn, more highly developed musculo-skeletal structure and complex socialisation, apes were well able to perfect these new plastic facilities, especially with the gestural capacity of the arms.

It must be remembered that evolution is no more a linear, incremental process than history itself is. New species emerge, only to revert to previous forms, or to disappear forever. Advances occur in one branch of the evolutionary tree and not in others; crustaceans, insects and spiders, for example, have had highly sensitive limbs with far more sophisticated capabilities than those of apes for some 300 million years. The front flippers of whales are anatomically close to our own hand and forearm structure, with five sets of finger bones and two sets of short arm bones – but whales developed them 250 million years ago.

Amphibians and reptiles developed their extremities even more. Some have webbed feet of four or five toes, suitable not only for *running* or *swimming*, but also for *jumping* and *gliding* from one tree to another. Although birds have only two legs, with three or four-toed feet, these have the same facilities as the quadruped equivalent. The presence of vestigial wings in flightless birds, or the anatomical similarities between a bear and a sea lion testify to the influence of the environment on the evolution of animal anatomies; in the same way, the evolution of the plastic capabilities of limbs can only have been the natural result of necessary adaptations for survival in changing circumstances.

Only hominids, after taking over the phylogenetic relay race from their ape ancestors, were able fully to satisfy this crucial requirement for a new body language. The upright stance of the great apes progressively freed their forelimbs from the need to support the upper torso when *walking*, and this is what liberated our ancestors to adopt new motion characteristics that made use of their enhanced sense of balance and coordination and greater visual flexibility to exploit the vast range of body motion capabilities required to immerse themselves in the increasingly sophisticated sociocultural interactions that became intrinsic to the survival of the species.

Modern hominid anatomy has twenty-five joints, with limbs developed into multifunctional tools able to carry out an almost infinite variety of motions and gestures across a wide range of activities from hunting and gathering to feeding and fighting, nursing and grooming, courting, building and so on. The so-called primitive *grasp* developed via the precision *grip* to the dextrous finger manipulation required to play pan flutes or bowstrings.

SILENCE AS THE STIMULUS FOR BODY LANGUAGE

Although early hominids had a limited everyday gestural vocabulary inherited from apes and constantly acquired new communicative gestures from others during their endless confrontations and social activities, the main source for increasing the range and vocabulary of gestural communication was hunting and combat.

The need for **silence** in both activities imposed an imperative to develop efficient body language. Unlike the Great Apes, our ancestors mostly lived on the ground, surrounded by predators and potential enemies. Hominids therefore learned from childhood how to *move* and act noiselessly in order to avoid attracting unwelcome attention, and the constant search for new and improved gestures was a question of survival.

For all our thousands of years of study, we humans remain largely ignorant of the motion phylogeny of animals and the anatomical transitions our fellow creatures have undergone; even more so about the behaviour of insects or fish. Being based on limited data, the interpretations set out here are inevitably sometimes speculative or intuitive, although for the most part they are consistent with the latest anthropological thinking.

THE GESTURAL SIGNALS OF LOW MAMMALS

Aquatic mammals

The strong, flexible tails, fins and flippers of whales and dolphins undoubtedly follow an as yet undeciphered dictionary of gestures for visual communication. A whale's fluke often sticks out of the water and *waves* signals for a few seconds. In deep water, during their prolonged courtship displays, whales swim slowly around each other in a love duet, gently *touching t*heir pectoral fins in *curling* or *vibrating* motions in a Gestural Duet.

Like the forelimbs of their terrestrial relatives, the pectoral fins of many marine animals such as dolphins, seals and walruses have a much wider range of gestures than their tails.

A small group of **dolphins**, for example, *hangs* in a circle in shallow water, facing inward as if holding a kind of conference, *gesturing* with their pectoral fins as they *hold* themselves stationary with their tails. The motion score is of a gestural 'conversation' accompanied by the sounds of *tapping* beaks and soft *whistling*. The dolphins *move* their flippers individually in varied rhythms, periodically interrupted by long *pauses* before continuing with new motion patterns, either as solos, contrapuntal duets or canonical trios. Highly intelligent creatures, dolphins and whales deploy an exceptionally rich plastic vocabulary to conduct these body motion dialogues, whose precise dynamics deserve further research.

Terrestrial mammals

Gestures originated in early mammals as a survival response in an unforgiving world. As their limbs were occupied with other functions, the head was the first gestural implement to indicate warnings or to convey a direction. As low primates gradually developed their forelimbs, particularly the front pair, these were used more and more frequently for new motions in addition to their existing functions like *running, grasping* and *grooming*. As their flexibility and motion vocabulary increased, forelimbs became more and more important as communication tools.

Most fighting motions were, with constant practice, transformed into *gestures* for warning and protection, and for indicating dominance or submission. Over thousands of generations, young canines and felines, bears, kangaroos, prosimians and apes used their forelimbs actively in play-wrestling during thousands of generations. The frozen fighting motion of a forelimb *curved* outwards towards the enemy thus eventually became a warning of impending aggression, just as the forelimb *raised* to cover the head and face came to signal defeat or submission. Indeed, both motions universally signify these same intentions today.

The famous *curved* foreleg motion of Darwin's dog on observing some obstacle has a different meaning, and has variously been described as an **expression**, a **motion** and a **gesture**. It is in fact all three: an expression because both gesture and motion are elements of body communication; gesture is the right term for pack leader that *raises* a curved foreleg to signal the whole pack to remain quiet and motionless (as well as positioning itself for sudden attack or escape). And the signal has its origins in primitive *pawing* and *play-wrestling*. The domestication of dogs has of course robbed this forelimb gesture of its communicative significance, and it has become merely a bodily expression of curiosity or alertness.

Raising the curved forelimb is a *gesture* whose evolutionary history long predates the appearance of high mammals. On countless televised wildlife films, we see elephants attacking hippos who cross into their territory by *pawing* the forelimb, male kangaroos '*boxing*' for a mate and camels, horses and giraffes all *kick* with their forelegs as well as their hind legs.

It was and remains the archetypical fighting/dominance *gesture* of all animals, from the insect *manipulating* its pedipalp right the way to the ape *battering* its chest with its fist or *waving* its fists at an opponent's face. The near-universal use of this basic *gesture* as a signal of

111

preparedness to attack or escape is rooted in its role in survival itself – after all, many species could seriously injure or even kill an enemy with their forelimbs, which could also be used to protect vulnerable body parts.

LIMB GESTURES IN APES

The earliest indicative *gesture* of apes and hominids was to use a forelimb motion to *point* in a specific direction or to a specific object of interest.

- A hungry infant monkey consciously *points* to a particular fruit.
- A female chimp *points* her arm to a supply of water or towards a perceived threat.
- A dominant gorilla *points* its arm to summons a subordinate, whether for play, grooming or to confirm the other's submission.

There were basically six possible types of limb gesture – up and down, front and back, and left and right, pointing either to others or themselves. Then, instead of using their hands and arms merely for functional gestures, our ancestors began to use them to indicate various parts of their own bodies – head, nose, mouth, chest, belly and so on. This represented a significant step forward in the evolution of anthropoid consciousness, progressing from the primitive *signalling* of spatial direction to apes' *touching* part of their own body with a fully open hand to engage the attention of another group member.

- A crying infant *covers* a bleeding wound with its hand after falling from a tree; the mother at once *licks* the wound clean.
- A dominant male *rubs* its itching back with a curved arm, and *points* to the offending source of irritation for the attention of a subservient female.
- A dominant gorilla regularly *touches* the genitals of its females with a cupped hand to check their readiness for mating.

The gestural gap between hominids and other apes

Although hominids were initially not far removed from their closest phylogenetic relatives, the apes, their more highly developed brains helped them to broaden and improve their basic gestural vocabulary, and this progressively widened the gap between the two. Apes' intelligence, along with their use of body language, remained at the optimum level of adaptation needed to survive successfully in their environment.

But unlike apes, hominids continue to expand their plastic facilities and capacity for gestural communication. From using the same primitive gestures as apes in relatively free and uncontrolled motions of the arms and touches of the hand, their superior intellects gradually made it possible to develop more complex *gestures* connoting more than one meaning. While still rooted in natural everyday functions, in other words, new hand gestures developed that conveyed subsidiary meanings as well as being simply indicative. *Pointing* by hand to certain parts of the body, for example, acquired other connotations.

Examples of **connotative** hand gestures by *touching* body parts with index finger:
- Eyes: "Watch out/I can see it".
- Ears: "Listen/I hear it".
- Nose: "Can you smell that?/Yes, I smell it".
- Mouth: "Keep quiet!/Speak up".

This revolutionary break away from primitive *pointing* gestures to those with additional personal meanings allowed these motions to refer to the plastic attributes of the image, object or action referred to – those of an invisible predator, for example, or using imitation to identify a protagonist. The characteristics **connoted** in these ways often reflected the nature of the individual concerned – his mind-set and way of moving and behaving.

Indicative gestures include *pointing* the hand in a certain direction or to an object, *touching* body parts, as in pronominal identification. Such *gestures* could also be modified – often in abbreviated form – to connote information, such as species, sex, age or size.

Thus **indicative** and **connotative** hand gestures are the root of non-verbal communication, and spawned the imitative motion vocabulary on which the mimetic culture in the history of human communication is based.

THE EVOLUTION OF GESTURAL COMMUNICATION IN HOMINIDS

In order to make effective use of the vast gestural vocabulary that resulted from millions of years of social development, hominids had to select motion 'phrases' from the existing plastic communication repertoire and establish a new motion dictionary which could be passed on from generation to generation through **tuition, imitation** and **practice**.

To coach youngsters in this complicated body language, shamans had to teach everything from elementary rustic *grimaces* and head motions to all the advanced hand *gestures* possible with two hands and ten fingers – a formidable intellectual challenge for the shaman, and a daunting adventure for his pupils.

So why did our early ancestors choose to assume this extra burden in addition to their already harsh daily lives?

A fast growing population increased the need for living space and territory, and with it, the likelihood of territorial conflict between neighbouring groups. These two constant problems prompted the search for new accommodation within existing territory, and for better ways of exploiting the available resources – more efficient food-gathering and animal husbandry techniques, and better weapons for hunting and defence. Security had to be provided during puberty and nursing. In addition to all these functional activities, and arguably most important of all, was to deploy supernatural forces in support of all of these Functional objectives through ritual ceremonies.

Although only a brief summary of personal and social responsibilities, these imperatives clearly required an advanced body language with a large vocabulary of signs and gestures – a language that meant developing sophisticated arm and hand gestures, excellent **muscle-memory**, sharp **observation** and many other mimetic **acting** qualities along with accurate performing techniques – for even a trivial misreading of a sign could have disastrous results.

Gesturing was second only to *facial mimicry* in the evolution of hominid body language before greater intelligence and physical flexibility paved the way for more sophisticated plastic communications. The source of these *gestures* and the awareness of their dynamic potential lay partly in the animal kingdom: *shifting* the head as a sign of alertness; *signalling* with the limbs for the purposes of defence or to summon a mate; *grooming* with sensitive fingers; *waving* arms and hands to communicate over distance and so on.

Hominid adaptation to plastic motion requirements

Through millions of years' experience of making tools, building shelters and other hand crafts, hominid fingers became enormously dextrous. Most basic survival skills, from *hammering* a stone into shape or *sharpening* a spear to *skinning* an animal or *peeling* fruit, involved repetitive hand motions and the co-ordination of the opposed thumb and fingers.

The muscle memories that such activities implanted eventually became **motion archetypes**, and as such were used unconsciously in primitive communications and ritual ceremonies. This was how *gestures* evolved, the vocabulary of hand signs gradually widening in line with hominids' anatomical and sociocultural development. Each new sphere of functional or spiritual activity stimulated the emergence of a new gestural genre as plastic motion kept pace with the ever more complex meanings to be conveyed.

As we have seen, the large and varied body language vocabulary of apes and hominids depended mainly on the forelimbs as the most flexible motion tools and the most expressive gestural implements. Increasing socialisation continued to develop this facility and developed gesturing techniques to a highly sophisticated level.

The sheer abundance of ethnic and cultural variations of hand and arm gestures throughout the world makes comprehensive categorisation almost impossible, especially as the motion vocabularies of entire civilisations have not survived, and no record remains. No systematic analysis of the linguistic gestures of aboriginal societies has been published to date, and understandably, neither do the peoples concerned seem willing to entrust such ethnographical information with the outside world. These factors have necessarily restricted this study of motion anthropology to the limited number of available sources dealing with the indigenous peoples of North America, the Indian subcontinent and the northern Mediterranean. The rich heritage of mimetic gestural techniques practised by Australasian aborigines and the Bushmen of Africa unfortunately remain for the present outside the scope of this work due to lack of adequate documentation.

HEAD GESTURES

CONDUCTING THE BODY MOTION ORCHESTRA

Having the head at the apex of an upright skeleton helps hominids to observe their surroundings at a distance and from many angles – a big advantage in finding food and in allowing potential dangers to be spotted early enough to be able to warn others and protect their offspring.

The head is the sensory receptor of acoustic, optical, olfactory and taste signals. As the site of spatial and temporal awareness, the head instantly locates the source of transmission, its position and its specific characteristics, as well as recording and reacting to the signals received.

The head is also used as a weapon in combat or as an implement for carrying loads such as food, firewood or domestic objects, as well as supporting often heavy adornments. Its most important function is however to provide the creative impulse for controlling balance, coordination and the style and manner of motion.

The head is therefore the primary motion implement of all mammals, and despite millions of years of evolution, modern humans retain a similar plastic dictionary of head expressions to that of all other high order mammals (such as pets and other domestic animals). The feelings being expressed with these motions may be similar to our own; it is simply that these creatures' mental evolution remains more or less as it was in prehistoric times.

Reactions of the head
Most of our instinctive body motions are by definition unpremeditated reactions to external signals. Since our main sensory receptors – eyes, ears, nose and mouth – are in the head, it follows that the immediate response to these stimuli will be an impulsive motion of the head, *shifting* towards or away from the source of the signal. Based on an instant analysis of the incoming signal, the head directs a response with the appropriate motions, either of the head itself or any other body part.

114

INSTINCTIVE MOTION IN RESPONSE TO EXTERNAL IRRITANT

CURIOSITY
Pulling head towards unknown object and *holding still* or *sloping* head slightly sideways and *posing* in questioning motion.

SHOCK
Tilting erect head back, short *pause* face-to-face.

RECOVERY
Slowly *shaking* head sideways to stabilise balance, or *shuddering* head laterally.

PROTECTION
Pulling head down between shoulders to avoid incoming blows.

VIGILANCE
Turning head to each side, and *turning back* to keep offspring in view.

WATCHING
Raising head upwards and back, *rotating* laterally to follow movement of the object observed.

LISTENING
Shifting erect head sideways to 'read' sounds, or *placing* an ear to the ground.

SMELLING
Lifting head upwards and *turning* sideways, *pausing* periodically to *sniff* out the source of odour, either in the air or close to the ground.

BRUSHING AWAY
Moving the head in a *sweeping* lateral motion to remove an insect, branch or other irritant.

FASCINATION
Rocking erect head from side to side, facing the source, the speed depending on the degree of awe or excitement.

SWIMMING
Thrusting head front downwards under water with exhalation, *pausing* and *raising* head up front above water to inhale.

PEEPING
Shifting head sideways to *look* out from hiding position, or *thrusting* head up down to spot prey.

VOLITIONAL MOTION IN RESPONSE TO EXTERNAL STIMULUS

OBSERVATION
Rotating head slowly down-side-front-side-down, analysing new sources of food.

EXPLORATION
Turning head sideways and *thrusting* forwards when examining an object from various angles.

TRACKING
Inclining head front down and *turning* it slowly from side to side.

THREATENING
Thrusting head forward aggressively, *pushing* chin up and *pausing* with head still, with or without bared teeth.

HEARING
Wobbling head laterally in order to locate the sound source.

ATTACK
Thrusting head frontwards down to the chest to butt the opponent, or when diving into water.

DEFENCE
Shifting erect head from side to side to avoid incoming missiles or blows

PRAYER
Raising head up front and pausing, then *lowering* head front down to chest, or *kneeling, nodding* head or touching the ground.

SEARCHING
Moving head slowly and repeatedly from side to side; also *nodding* slowly.

HUNGER
Mixed head motions when *gobbling* food, *scraping* flesh from bones, *cracking* them, or *skinning* an animal.

LOOKING UP
Raising head up and *pausing* while studying stars or planets, head slowly *rotating* in the same pose.

ATTRACTION
Touching heads tenderly, cheek-to-cheek, and *pausing*; simultaneously laterally without separating.

MOTION MOTIVATED BY <u>UNCONSCIOUS</u> IMPULSE

THINKING
Head *inclined* slightly front down and held in a long pause of concentration.

DISTRESS
Erect head *shaking* sideways, *kneeling* to *knock* the head repeatedly against the deceased.

FRUSTRATION
Head *cocked* to one side and held in a *pause* while trying to contain anger then putting head slowly down towards the shoulder.

EMBARRASSMENT
Turning head away side down, putting chin on shoulder and *holding* pause with eyes *averted.*

GUILT
Head *thrust* front down to the chest and *pausing* or *shaking* head slightly in the same position.

DREAMING
Head *tilted* back and *turned* slightly to one side upwards; returning slowly after a long *pause* to the initial position.

PAIN
Head *raised* up and back and *held* in a pause; *inclining* slowly front down onto the chest, and *holding* pose.

DESPERATION
Erect head *turns* slowly sideways "en face", or *inclines* frontwards down onto the chest and *shakes* slowly from side to side.

ESCAPING
Head *twists* to the side and back to check on pursuer when *running* away, *thrust* upwards in front when begging for mercy.

SPIRITUALITY
Head *waves* in all directions, *jerking, rotating* or *shaking* in trance state to summon spirits.

BOREDOM
Head rotates slowly with pauses between each movement, while yawning with eyes shut.

PLEASURE
Head slowly *waves* sideways and *tilts* backwards, with the same head motion accelerated during ecstasy.

<u>VOLITIONAL</u> MOTION FOR COMMUNICATION

GREETING
Head slowly *inclines* respectfully front and down, or the same sequence *turning* head slightly to side and *posing.*

POINTING
Jerking head upwards to the front or sideways, *thrusting* chin up to indicate the desired location or direction.

REQUESTING
Short *jerk* with head straight up front, *thrusting* the chin up and *holding* in a long pause while awaiting an answer.

FROLICKING
Mixed head motions when *prancing* around, *teasing, pulling faces* and playing 'catch' games.

DISAPPOINTMENT
Repeatedly *shaking* erect head slowly from side to side, or repeatedly nodding head "en face" reprovingly.

UNCERTAINTY
Thrusting erect head straight down between shoulders and *inclining* slightly to the side; *holding* pose in a questioning attitude.

CALLING
Holding head to one side in an addressing pose before returning to the initial position.

DISMISSAL
Raising head up to front and *holding* pose before *waving* the head towards the desired direction of departure.

PLEADING
Thrusting head up front, *pushing* chin forward, *pause, inclining* head slightly sideways, pause; *lowering* head down to the chest.

AGREEMENT
Periodically *nodding* slowly "en face", *pausing*, then reprising the same motion at greater speed.

DISAGREEMENT	Repeatedly *shaking* head slowly from side to side – pause – reprise faster, with head *lowered* front down.
IGNORING	*Raising* head slowly up front, *holding, looking* up, *turning* slowly to the right, pause; then *shifting* to the left down, and *holding* pose.

CONSCIOUS IMITATION OF INSTINCTIVE MOTION

BISON	*Diving* head front and immediately *thrusting* up horns in an attacking motion; *twisting* head in a low front position.
ELEPHANT	Repeatedly *sweeping* head low front with lateral swings, *sniffing* ground, cooling off and simultaneously *watching* offspring.
GAZELLE	*Diving* head front to take grass, then *raising* head up, *moving* head sideways to look for danger, *ruminating.*
ZEBRA	Repeatedly *nodding* head up and down while *galloping*; *jerking* head sideways and back with *biting* motion when being pursued.
GIRAFFE	*Pulling* head straight up front, *raising, turning* head slightly sideways when *grazing*, always on the lookout for predators.
HIPPO	*Thrusting* head up front with wide open jaws, then *diving* head front down under the water to relax.
LION	*Raising* head up when awakened, *turning* head proudly to check territory, *yawning*, then slowly returning to sleep.
WOLF	*Turning* head low from side to side in a *sniffing* motion, when searching for prey; *raising* head back and high while howling, or calling the pack.
BEAR	*Diving* head into water repeatedly to catch fish; vigorously *shaking* off water, then *striking* the catch against a rock.
OSTRICH	*Balancing* head straight back and forth when *walking; inclining* head front down in lateral waving motion when searching for reptiles.
SNAKE	Head *thrusts* up/front in *zigzag* motion; position *freezes* once prey located, followed by a rapid forward *strike.*
GRASSHOPPER	Sharp *twisting* of head in any direction in angular or rotary motions *thrusting* back and forth.

THE HEAD AS THE PRIMARY MIMETIC INSTRUMENT

For thousands of years, scientific thought all over the world assumed the physical universe to be a generally stable entity, and our understanding of physics until the last century was based on the idea that fixed quantities of matter and energy transmuted from one form to another.

It followed that each stages in the evolution of the human body, mind and spirit must have had a beginning and end, however hard these may be to discern. But why and when? How did the transformation from one stage to the next occur? What historical, geographic and socioeconomic circumstances prompted these physiological and psychological transitions?

Analysis of the behaviour of the world's creatures shows many species to have head motions that are essentially similar to those of apes. As the highest species of the hominid family, human beings must have developed such universal body motions naturally, through million years of evolution, from primitive subconscious behaviours all the way to a sophisticated volitional expression of nonverbal plastic language.

Human head motions are analogous to the behaviour of other mammals, with the head held firmly in position by the surrounding neck muscles and ligaments at the top of the spine. But bipedal species with a vertical neck (including kangaroos, giraffes and many birds as well as Homo Erectus) are in a privileged position, with a unique equilibrium as well as great flexibility for expressive head *movements.*

Although the head is the main instrument for every activity from gathering, feeding, hunting and fighting to courting and grooming for all quadrupeds, the upright bipedal posture of Homo Erectus greatly increased the range of possible head movements.

Nodding as a positive gesture

Most animals use head motions mainly in a **sagittal** plane. Whether *picking up* food from the ground or *pulling* it down from a tree, quadrupeds are obliged to use a progressive up and down motion of the head. Carnivores use similar motions when *bringing down* a prey with their jaws, or *pulling* flesh from a carcass. The daily and lifelong exercise of this forceful head *nodding* motion developed the animals' neck muscles and ligaments, increasing the potential plasticity of the entire body in the process.

This primal head motion in a **vertical** plane has its origin in feeding, and is common to all quadrupedal primates. Along with other life-critical characteristics, it was passed on genetically during millions of years of evolution to the next bipedal species of great apes. Its eventual use by hominids as a body motion sign of approval, acceptance and agreement is a distant echo of this former feeding motion.

The *nod*, in the sense of confirmation or as a **positive** answer, has many variations and nuances, indeed in some parts of the world, the convoluted path of linguistic evolution has led to the *nodding* head losing its original positive connotations and conveying exactly the opposite meaning. The reasons for this apparently inexplicable reversal would make an intriguing research subject in itself.

Head shaking as a negative expression

In animals, *shaking* the head from side to side is often associated with fear of predation. Creatures that face potential danger at any moment and from any direction are obliged to be constantly vigilant. They keep a look out by repeatedly *turning* the head from one side to the other, either as a routine precaution or as an instinctive reaction to each unexpected sound or smell, in the course of all their regular functions of eating, nursing, grooming, courting and so on.

Similarly, an animal's head can react aggressively, also in self-protection, against irritation by insects. The head is *moved* violently sideways in a desperate attempt to get rid of mosquitoes, wasps, flies and unwanted parasites. It therefore comes as no surprise that this perpetual defensive motion should come to signify **negativity**, refusal and rejection for hominids.

Another hypothesis for the origin of the negative connotations of the *shaking* head is based on the subconscious behaviour of new-born apes, who in response to certain conditions, *turn* their head away from the mother's teat during feeding. Inexperienced mothers mistakenly assume that this means that the infant has received sufficient milk, whereas the real reason is that the teat was impeding its breathing by blocking its nose. It is easy to see how what initially appears to be an inexplicable reflex rejection of the food source could indeed come to signify refusal in any context.

All such theoretical explanations of the meaning of body motions are of course speculative. But by making the imaginative leap into the consciousness of the creatures involved, constantly *turning* one's head to both sides day or night to drive away insects and to keep watch for the ever-present danger of sudden death, there seems to be an intuitive truth to the association of negativity with the *shaking* head. Whatever the fundamental mechanics of this process, we can be sure that this aspect of evolution, like all others, is driven by the innate imperative for survival.

Rocking the head in uncertainty

Animals are often seen to behave in very distinctive ways when studying each other intensively or in response to unfamiliar sights, smells or sounds. Suspicious or intrigued, stare at the object with the head *inclined* sideways while they attempt to evaluate the individual or circumstance concerned. The *rocking* motion of the head and neck which expresses this emotional tension can be seen not only in the daily lives of apes, but also in the behaviour of aquatic mammals, birds, reptiles and domestic pets. As a body motion signal of uncertainty, curiosity or insecurity, it was passed on genetically via primates and apes to the new hominid species.

A similar *rocking* motion of the head and neck is still used by predators moving backwards in a zig-zag pattern when *dragging* a heavy carcass. On such occasions, the animal exerts extra physical pressure through its jaw and neck muscles to make sure of not losing its prey. After feeding, the predator executes an identical head motion when appraising the size and weight of the remains in order to save what's left of the carcass for a future feed.

The *rocking* head motion has evolved through constant hunting and killing actions between hominids and their prey, and/or combat between hominids. Using stick and stones as weapons, attacks were generally aimed at the head of the adversary or a prey; the combatants or mammals under attack learned through experience that *rocking* the head from side to side could be an effective way of avoiding these blows.

These deliberate *balancing* motions of the head are based on instinctive actions of quadrupedal mammals and transferred to apes in a more developed (and now conscious) adaptation. The *rocking* head eventually became not only a good mode of defence, but also a useful tool in the search for a way out of a frustrating hunting or a battle situation – and as such, by association, the main motion reaction to any dangerous obstacle or spiritual fear.

The deliberate head pose
'Frozen motion' does not mean complete bodily stasis, but only a pause in spatial movement. The time signature of expressive action is still pulsing in the resting body, just as it is in the visual arts with sculptures, paintings and masks. In other words, frozen motion is a *pose* that momentarily interrupts action until the next expressive *move* is activated from the same spot. It is the motion equivalent of the *pauza fermata* in a phrase of music.

As an expression of the head, such a *pose* is often aggressive in intent. All animals *project* their head out towards the object of attention when preparing to attack, when arguing with each other or when defending family members, territory, property, or other interests. They do so in order to evaluate the threat from an opponent, to show off the power of their own jaws and to hypnotise or frighten the adversary. Hominids do the same thing.

The *inclined* head pose can be an expression of courtesy or conciliation. All higher order mammals including domestic pets display this subservient motion when trying to please individuals at a higher level in the social hierarchy (including their human owners, of course). They *push* their head down in a submissive manner, looking affectionately up and *pausing*. Variations of this familiar and expressive head motion can be traced right back to the very beginning of primate evolution.

The head held *turned* away is equally expressive, but the meaning is different. Pets do this to avert their eyes from our gaze when caught in any deliberately or accidentally transgressive behaviour that the creature knows will entail disapproval by the owner. This head *pose* is an expression of the desire to escape punishment, and is frequently used as an expression of shame or embarrassment in the social lives of anthropoids.

The motionless *pose* of the head has many different meanings, many of which are also seen in modern human behaviour:

- The head is *pushed* out in front and *paused* when we are suddenly confronted with a strange or dangerous obstacle for example, or when trying to recognise unfamiliar objects, or telling off youngsters, counterattacking, or showing amazement at some unexpected occurrence.
- The head is *inclined* frontwards and downwards towards the object of attention when we are expressing gratitude, respect, grief, anxiety, deep concentration or guilt; also, when trying to hide real emotions or to re-establish self control.

- The head is *turned* away and *raising* in profile to express shame or disgust; when insulted or when rejecting a proposal; when avoiding involvement or trying to remember; or when ending a dialogue.

All of these *frozen* head motions are used equally by mammalian quadrupeds and bipeds. The main difference lies in the hominids' greater ability to manipulate their natural body motion. This was particularly evident in the exceptional mimetic skills they deployed for hunting, which derived from their superior intellect and self-consciousness.

THE FACE: THE MOST EXPRESSIVE MOTION INSTRUMENT

Facial motion is undoubtedly the richest plastic medium for expressing human thoughts and feelings. Indeed, the face instinctively reflects each moment of our inner life, even when asleep.

This enormous vocabulary of instinctive and volitional facial expressions was inherited by our ancestors from the apes, and primates before that. With their limited mental capacities, early hominids depended for communication on their elementary mimetic and body motion abilities to learn new survival techniques. In the initial stages of their evolution, this function resided mainly in the plasticity of the face and neck, as observed in the behaviour of apes.

Practically all visual, acoustic, olfactory, taste and touch signals were reflected primarily by motions of the head and facial expressions. These were later followed by plastic responses in other parts of the body, or the body as a whole, as hominid physical anatomy slowly developed to allow a wider range of body motions.

Like most mammals, anthropoids lived in groups, and shared the successes as well as problems of other group members. This involved communicating with each other in a more sophisticated manner than did the primates and apes that preceded them. Head motions alone were an inadequate medium for hominids during this first stage of evolution. As the legs supported body weight and the arms were occupied with weapons or tools, or engaged in nursing or other domestic activities, facial expressions were by far the best facility for these more advanced communications, notably using the eyes, nose, and lips.

FACIAL COMMUNICATION MEDIA

Living and working closely together as they undertook these most important everyday functions, women developed a vocabulary of head motions for communicating between each other.
- One gatherer *stopping* and appearing to *smell* smoke was sufficient for the entire group to *rush* back to home base to save their belongings.
- A brief *glance* over the shoulder by one group member would alert others around to an approaching danger, and instantly prompt readiness for defensive action.
- *Thrusting* the head upwards in a specific direction would point out to others a food source in a tree such as fruit, a beehive or eggs in a nest.
- A suddenly *frozen* posture, with only the ears moving, could signal the arrival of long awaited rain or a large herd of antelope.

When nursing or caring for elderly or disabled clan members, eye contact was the quickest and most satisfactory means of communication. Shamans could read a plea or complaint in the eyes of their patients, and vice versa. These complex motion dialogues included other senses such as hearing, smelling, taste and touch, and gradually developed into an adequately efficient system of conducting interactive relationships without requiring extensive use of other body parts.

As we have seen, silence was the main guarantee of a safe and successful hunt for hominids and other species alike. Head and facial motion signals were therefore preferable to acoustic ones.
- The hunter or a scout could easily *point* out the position and direction of a prey or adversary to a companion exclusively with eye motions.

- Facial *grimaces* could express the size, age, sex of any prey and/or enemy – even the approximate number in a pack or a group.
- Head motions and facial expressions alone were sufficient to 'discuss' which hunting or fighting strategies to adopt, by *lifting* eyebrows, *blinking, opening* and *shutting* the mouth, *vibrating* the tongue, *wrinkling* the nose and using a number of different *grimaces* or *noises* made by the teeth.

The leader of a group of hunters or warriors would normally have elaborate painted decoration all over his body (including his face), both for the purposes of camouflage and recognition. Black and white were the usual colours used, with feather decoration for the head which helped to accentuate any motion and/or rhythmic signal patterns.

Mimetic culture developed very intensively in early Neolithic era, driving forward human evolution in the process. The arms were becoming increasingly involved in hominid body language; the head and face remained the main domestic and social communication instruments, but as such they also contributed to the plastic motion of other body parts. However, this was long before our ancestors developed a modern musculo-skeletal structure which allowed the vastly more coordinated and harmonised plasticity we see evidence of in the advanced body cultures of the ancient civilisations in China, Egypt and Greece.

Mimesis was the main plastic foundation any initiation programme for young members of the tribe. Anthropoids were genetically equipped with certain body motions from birth: *sucking, blinking, yawning* and *sniffing*, together with an array of other instinctive motions and reactions. But the apes' most valuable genetic legacy to hominids was their innate ability to **copy** the motion patterns of another creature, and to reproduce the memorised plastic information **mimetically**. This is as far the ape evolution went; by contrast, the much more developed brains of hominids allowed them not only to reproduce and memorise natural motion, but also to **analyse, evaluate** and **categorise** it for use in their everyday lives.

Infants get their first lessons in mimesis from the mother, by learning and copying her facial expressions. This process continues for a lifetime, through every domestic and social function: eating, playing, gathering, hunting, fighting, worshipping, dancing, communicating, interacting sexually and so on. All of this personal information was acquired mimetically by youngsters from the behaviour of adults, based on a syllabus of face and body motions.

Functional body motion as reflected in the face

The three major motivations of facial expression reflect the main life functions of our primate ancestors: **feeding, defence** and **reproduction**. The variety of facial expressions of which they were capable was a result of the way in which the physiognomy of quadrupedal mammals had evolved, with soft fleshy tissue gradually covering the front of the head around the eyebrows, nose, mouth, jaws, cheeks and chin.

Although the organs of vision, hearing, smell and taste are located in basically the same configuration on the head in anthropoids and all other higher order mammals, the faces of prosimians, monkeys and apes are nevertheless distinctively different. All three species share very similar feelings, reactions, habits, behaviours, sexuality and social structures.

Most striking of all are the resemblances in feeding, nursing, competing, grooming, playing, courtship and mating behaviour between the three species. The following observations about the origin of facial expression are based on comparing the behaviours of these related quadrumanal primate families with the highest bipedal mammal of all: the hominids.

Face and Eyes

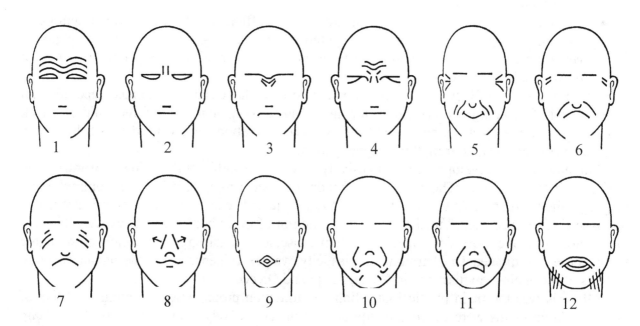

Expressions
1) attention   2) reflection   3) aggression   4) sorrow   5) laughter   6) discontent
7) crying   8) sensuality   9) pouring   10) scorn   11) disgust   12) anger

Position of Head in a Looking Direction

Direction of the Eyes and Emotions
1) attention   2) observation   3) reflection   4) meditation   5) contemplation 6) admiration
7) amazement   8) sublimity   9) enthusiasm   10) rapture   11) ecstasy   12) wonder
13) fascination 14) awe   15) transport   16) dreaming   17) delirium
Diagrams by Italian dancer and dance theorist, taken from *Physical, Intellectual and Moral Man* (Milan 1857)

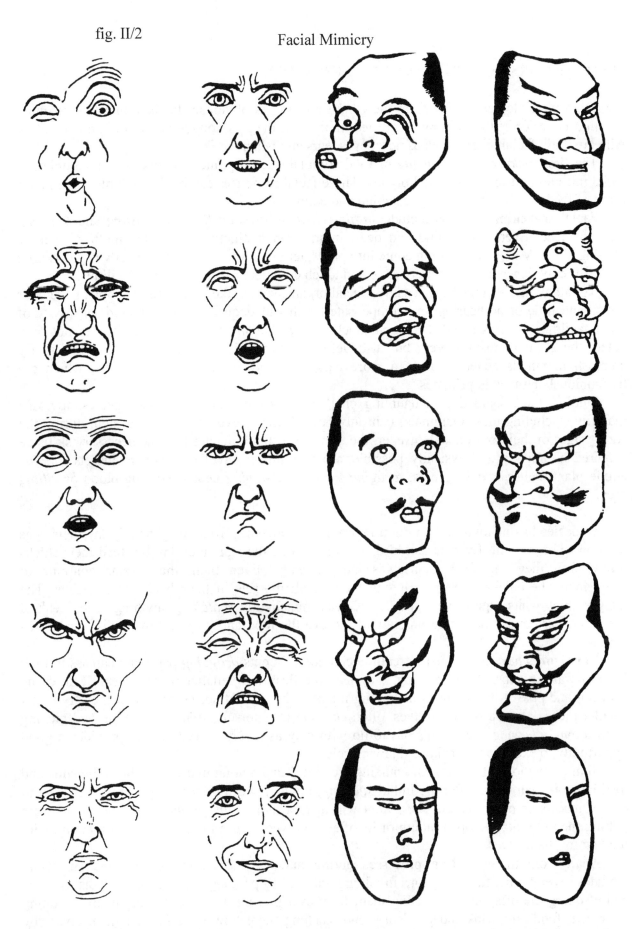

Table from Aubert's *L'art du Mime* (Paris 1901) and profile drawings of popular Japanese Noh and Kyogen masks, (the top of Fig. II/1 Source, S Gippi, *Emotion exercises Psychotechnics*, 1967.

FEEDING, NURSING AND GROOMING REPERTOIRE

The main physiological need of any new-born creature is obviously to feed, and this essential function is performed mainly by controlled motions of the lips, tongue and jaws in combination with auxiliary facial organs such as nose, eyes, ears and whiskers.

The first *sucking* or *swallowing* of food stimulates appropriate motions by this complex of facial muscles and feeding-related organs. These facial responses can be divided into three major types of feeding action: searching, catching and eating.

Facial **searching** motions include *sniffing, looking around, listening, tasting* and *touching* with the face. Even when blind and deaf, infants can instinctively find the mother's teat by sniffing alone. Vision and hearing come into play later on, until finally (after mostly negative trial and error experiences), the senses of taste and touch complete the facial search facilities.

Not all animal species have sensitive facial organs: some, like snakes for example, have poor vision and little or no hearing, but compensate for this inadequacy with increased sensitivity of other facilities such as smell, taste and touch. The *projecting* tongue of a snake can not only detect the scent of distant prey, but also define its type, size and approximate location. By contrast, mammals generally have a more balanced array of facial sense organs, which are harmoniously attuned in primates.

Finding food unaided is a daunting challenge for the infants of most species: the vast majority (including most mammals) can only nourish themselves with parental help during the early stages of their existence. However, the survival instinct dictates that the necessary skills be acquired as quickly as physically possible, whether this is involves *catching* insects, *finding* edible plant matter, *cracking* nuts, *foraging* for tubers, *sipping* nectar, *sucking* blood or *killing* prey.

Every species has its own body motion repertoire for **nursing**. Reptiles generally lay their eggs but don't brood them. By contrast, birds not only hatch the eggs they lay but feed their chicks orally until they can feed themselves independently. Even then, the parents continue to supplement the chicks' diet by bringing them small morsels in their beaks or stomachs. The hungry chick waits eagerly with wide *open* beak, impatiently *snatching* anything in the beak of the parent bird and *penetrating* its craw to retrieve the food and *gulp* it down before any of its siblings.

Carnivores have developed different techniques. Parents *dragging* parts of a carcass in their jaws to waiting cubs. While nursing, they *tear* the flesh into smaller pieces, break it down by *chewing* and *pass* it by mouth to the young infant. When the offspring are older, they try to eat smaller pieces of food by themselves, often *chewing* the morsels, *spitting* them out and picking them up and *chewing* again. This has to do with play as much as feeding, but provides a good opportunity to exercise the facial and jaw muscles.

Similar methods of feeding and nursing are also found among many other **insectivorous** and **herbivorous** mammals. After the initial *suckling*, mothers wean their young from a milk diet to one of insects or plant matter. The parent will at first thoroughly *premasticate* the food before putting the pulp into the open mouth of its offspring, who before long begin experimenting with feeding for themselves.

Apart from these **feeding** processes during nursing, the rearing of mammalian young includes several other facial motions involving the use of lips, tongue and teeth, such as *washing* and *cleaning* the offspring, protecting them from ever-present dangers, training them in getting their own food and drink independently and teaching them how to look after themselves (by memorising safety precautions, communicating with silent eye language, and so on).

The mother regularly washes her young by *licking* the face and body, just as her own mother did. A parent uses its forehead and snout to *turn* an infant from side to side on the ground, searching for fleas and other parasites, which it *crushes* with its teeth. After watching this strange operation, the siblings then start applying the same grooming technique on each other.

Mammals generally watch their offspring at play more attentively than reptiles or birds do. Whenever an infant strays from the confines of the home-base, the parent intervenes by *picking up* the offender in its mouth and brings it back. Infants are whisked to safety in the same way when a predator approaches.

The many vital facial motions which all young mammals must learn early, quickly and precisely from their parents include:
finding the shortest way to a mother's nipple, by smell

- how to *suck* milk without biting the teat.
- how to wash by *licking*.
- how to recognise the mother's voice.
- how to judge the source and direction a threatening sound.
- how to find and catch insect parasites with the teeth.
- how to find the home base by visual memory.
- when to keep the head down in silence for reasons of survival.
- how to use the large vocabulary of facial and vocal expressions for communicating with parents, siblings and other members of the pack.

Unlike the more or less universal unconscious facial expressions which are transmitted genetically, the need to pass on these vitally important acquired habits to the next generation was one of the main evolutionary drivers for the development of facial musculature and its attendant plastic motion capabilities.

Different stages of physiological and neural development can be clearly distinguished in the feeding and nursing functions and behaviour of these animals. Millions of years of progressive motion adaptations separate the python *gulping* an entire carcass in a single manoeuvre from the 'civilised' cannibalistic lunch of a chimpanzee. Crucially, these included the more complex facial musculature that permits more sophisticated expressions of the old universal emotions.

Many **insectivorous** species swallow their prey whole. In mammals, the eating process is generally more complicated than that of reptiles or birds, and involves several phases. **Herbivorous** low-order mammals *ruminate* with the tongue and jaws for a long time before *swallowing*. Even then, the partially digested cud is often *regurgitated* for further *chewing* before being *swallowed* again in a cycle that can be repeated several times. All this is carried out on a subconscious level.

Carnivorous mammals have more advanced eating procedures than their ruminant relatives. The meal is begun by attacking the belly of a carcass, *sucking* the blood and *pulling* out the soft tissue. They then *bite* off a limb or some other large chunk and drag it away from any equally hungry competitors before *biting* and *chewing* the flesh into smaller pieces which are usually *bolted* rapidly with very little *mastication* in order to ingest the food before any other creature can steal it.

This strenuous exertion of the facial and neck muscles continues later, when the sated predator brings the remains of the kill to its lair by *dragging* the heavy carcass with its powerful jaws over often considerable distances. Alternatively, some predators *tear* the remains into smaller pieces, which are then hidden away to be eaten later.

High order mammals such as kangaroos, bears, dogs, cats, rats and all primates, herbivores as well as carnivores, have refined their feeding skills through selective evolution over some two hundred million years. In this way, sophisticated physiological facilities were eventually incorporated into feeding motions for *selecting* and *cleaning* the food, rendering it soft and juicy, *ruminating* it and storing it in the mouth or crop for subsequent *regurgitation* to infants.

The **nose** *sniffs, touches, prods* and *pushes*; *darting* eyes watch and search; *twitching* ears listen to and locating the source of a sound; the **tongue** *tastes, chews* and *cleans;* the **lips** *touch,* *pick up, pull out* and *suck*; the **jaws** *bite, pull, press, crack, chew, peel* and *catch*. Used constantly over a lifetime, all these apparently basic facial motions involved in searching, catching, feeding and nursing can only have increased the plastic motion facilities of the face, as well as the corresponding functional organs of the rest of the body. All these functional facial motions gradually became the foundation for the body language vocabulary of primal communication.

The progressive development of all these mammalian feeding and nursing functions was driven by the vital necessity constantly to improve the bodily motions required for survival. Naturally, these new capabilities also had their corollaries in the sensory receptors of the brain, opening the way to more effective hunting techniques.

In every sense, **feeding** and **nursing** were the foundation for healthy generations to come, the related facial motion facilities being fundamental to virtually all activities of apes and hominids: hunting, fighting, worshipping, grooming, courting, performing and so on. These activities involved basically the same facial motions as feeding and nursing ones, but in a new mental context and with a new plastic motion code and activity-specific body gesture vocabulary.

FUNCTIONAL MOTIONS OF THE MOUTH AND TONGUE

In addition to eating, the **lips, tongue, teeth** and **jaws** have many other important functions dating back to prehistoric times.

Great Apes used their mouths not only to *pick up, chew* and *swallow* food, but also to keep part of it inside the buccal cavity or cheeks for future use, to feed pre-masticated morsels by mouth either to their offspring or a disabled family member. From the earliest times, humans have used their teeth for *cutting, peeling* and *cracking open*. During earlier stages of evolution, they also relied on using their teeth as effective fighting and hunting weapons. Hominids often *bared* their teeth or *opened* wide their jaws to enemies and predators as a warning or to scare their opponents – under threat or in extreme aggression, modern humans still do.

Jaw/teeth motions also came into play in a kind of personal 'warm-up' – a spiritual and physical preparation for combat. *Clashing* and *grinding* teeth during mock combat were common pre-fighting routines among hominids, and were also widely used in ritual pantomimes and in everyday communications. And as today, nervousness or frustration was manifest in *biting* the lips or fingers. *Biting* an inanimate object was also used to avoid screaming in pain. These are all Conscious motions, as opposed to *chattering* teeth in cold weather, which is an entirely Reflex motion.

The tongue is the most complex and versatile tactile organ in the anthropoid body, with highly flexible motion possibilities in addition to its role in Vocalisation and its unique ability to perceive taste. It is the tongue, in combination with the brain that allowed our species to evolve the sophisticated spoken language on which human civilisation rests.

The tongue:
- provides the discernment of taste that helped us to find the most nutritious food and avoid toxic ones.
- was used to *pick up* nutritious insects, fruits and vegetables as well as *licking* essential minerals.
- could wash or soothe infants and the wounds of one's own body as well as those of others.
- governs and operates the part of the feeding process that occurs in the mouth – *biting, chewing, softening, storing* and *swallowing.*
- plays an important **sexual** role in *kissing* and in *licking* body parts.
- is vital to the production of **sound** and whistles for communication, and for *imitating* the sounds of other creatures.
- allows us to speak, with all that implies in terms of complex **vocal *modulations, intonations* and *dynamics*.**

The motions of the jaws, teeth and tongue are often interconnected, socioculturally as well as physiologically. Right from the start, they produced a wide range of performing motions the plastic and sonic vocabulary of rituals.

HUNTING AND COMPETITION

Every living creature has to fight for survival from its first breath to its last. Very few creatures are exempt from the constant danger of becoming the prey of another animal.

After feeding, the most important priority is therefore to compete for sources of food and water, territory, social dominance and mating.

According to Darwinian natural selection, the better a species is adapted to its local environment, the better its chances. Similarly, strong and resourceful individuals dominate (and survive longer than) weaker members of the family. These twin imperatives of territorial protection and hierarchical dominance create intense competition for food, living space and social position, both inside and outside the group. The preference of most animal orders to live in groups is also a manifestation of Darwinian natural selection at work in that the functions of feeding, nursing, rearing young, attack and defence are usually more effectively carried out as a group rather than individually. But groups can't function without a communication system, however rudimentary.

For centuries it was thought that these communications systems were purely instinctive, creatures being considered unable to think in any real sense because of their limited brains and consciousness. But there is today overwhelming evidence that animals – even common insects such as bees, ants, mosquitoes, with their elaborately sophisticated communication systems, social hierarchies and individual behaviour patterns – are more than just machines. That is, they have the capacity to react to new stimuli in non-instinctive ways.

There is no doubt that all animal species communicate with plastic, acoustic or visual signals, though many are as yet poorly researched. The communication systems that insects and reptiles have evolved over a hundred million years are based on touch, taste, vocal and electromagnetic and ultrasonic signals, for example.

Mammals have much more highly developed facial plastic facilities than insects, fish and reptiles, and communicate clearly with outsiders of the same species as well as between group members.

The mammalian repertoire of facial fighting expressions and motions has large vocabularies for each part of the face: the eyes, eyelids and eyebrows, the lips, tongue and jaws, the nose, snout and whiskers ears, the cheeks and the chin. These elements are usually used in combination of two or three simultaneously, depending on species.

Facial fighting expressions can be divided into three pairs of opposites: **play** or **caution, warning** or **retreat**, and **attack** or **defence**. There are of course many intermediate facial motions between these extremes, Conscious or Involuntary, positive or negative, deployed operationally in an attempt to win the fight.

Non-mammalian species of course have other facial implements to express aggression such as **antennae, stings, tongues, beaks** and **probosces.**

Infant play and parenting

The offspring of all species fight for survival from their very first body motions, *pushing* their siblings aggressively away from parental food sources to secure a better chance to grow big and strong. This instinct for self-preservation is lifelong, and progressively develops during the endless play-fights of juveniles with their parents and each other. The mock-*bites* or *head-charging, pressing, pulling, knocking* each other down, *grabbing, mounting* or *diving* under, *hitting* and *strangling* are all rehearsals for real future combat.

Parents are concerned about the safety of their offspring while all this rough play takes place, constantly alert to any unexpected sound or smell, *twitching* their ears, *flaring* their nostrils to sniff, *watching* carefully all around even while feeding and *reacting* immediately even to false alarms. In a 'dog-eat-dog' world, adults err on the side of caution as far as their offspring are concerned.

Warning, attack and defence

Most animals that basically compete rather than hunt try to avoid direct combat on their first attempt at trespassing, whether the intention is to infringe on the territorial rights of others, challenge the hierarchical order, steal the food of another or penetrate the leader's harem. Challenges are met with threatening *glares, grunts* or *frowns*. Both parties *bare* their teeth and *open* their mouths wide. As soon as one protagonist realises the size and strength advantage of the opponent, it usually retreats without a fight, with downcast eyes, head and tail, casting the occasional glance of animosity to the foe as it backs away. The survival instinct comes into play to pre-empt the alternative: a real fight, possibly to the death of one or both opponents.

The main communication issue between animals is ultimately "Who eats who?" Most animals kill others for food, hierarchical dominance, mating rights or territory. Predators accomplish this mainly with facial weapons: poison glands, sticky tongues, beaks, jaws, tusks, horns, proboscis and so on. The same facial weapons are used when hunting for food as when defending against a predator to avoid becoming food. An animal that fails to escape turns these weapons on its pursuer.

All carnivores, from insects to apes, have the killer instinct in attack or defence; by contrast, herbivores are born only with a defensive instinct. They often graze in large mixed groups of species in front of watching predators, periodically feeding in the presence of their natural enemies, their attention divided between next mouthful, checking on the safety of their infants and constant vigilance against the possibility of imminent attack, while registering the best possible escape route for whenever the need arises.

Any animal that could become the prey of another at any time is obviously under continual stress, day or night. Its very survival demands that its nose, eyes and ears can never stop trying to detect any unfamiliar or threatening sound, smell or movement while it undertakes all its own life activities of feeding, nursing, courting and so on. This state of constant hyper-alertness developed over millions of years.

Herbivores, as prey, have little chance of winning in direct combat with an attacking carnivore at a close range, despite the strong defensive facial weapons with which some are equipped. Their survival therefore depends more on precautionary defence measures, such as **escaping** the threat in good time and in the right direction; when threatened, in other words, running away is the safest option, and that in turn depends on its organs of perception and instinctive reactions.

Real fights, whether in hunting or competition, are usually matters of life or death. All facial weapons are called upon to inflict maximum damage on the opponent, with the intention to kill. Here again, success depends not on the quantity or quality of individual facial weapons, but on the **speed** and **flexibility of motion**, **visual evaluation**, **physical strength**, **coordination** and **balance**.

The most effective facial weapons of mammals (jaws, tusk, forehead and horns) are under the conscious control of the brain, and projected by expressive motions. The adversaries' innate mentality, musculoskeletal structure and other individual characteristics respond equally well to instinctive behaviour in attack or defence. Darwin was right: those who are bigger and stronger, with more experience and better functioning organs survive and prosper in the evolutionary ladder.

All these motion functions have much in common, with the exception of certain aspects that relate to socio-sexual behaviour. Grooming and playing motions often lead towards, and eventually transform into, courtship rituals and the motions of sexual intercourse. Grooming, young play and mating are closely related, usually being based on a direct or indirect sexual relationship between two individuals (although some species perform these functions in a group setting, changing partners at will).

All three types of motion have to be considered in parallel to underline the similarities as well as the differences in the head and facial motions involved. Note that although some species mainly use their facial implements for grooming and courtship – antennae, beaks, tongues and snouts – other species of the same orders use their palps or forelegs for the same purpose. As we shall see later, the physiological evolution of mammals has led the emphasis away from facial implements to the limbs for these rituals.

Motherhood and nursing. The purest and most basic manifestation of grooming motion is seen in the relationship of mother and offspring. Some reptiles keep their hatchlings in their mouth for safety and warmth. Birds *preen* their chicks with their beaks, and continue to feed them mouth-to-mouth until they become independent. Mammals *lick* their newborns clean, and move them from place to place in their jaws; they *catch* fleas from their bodies with their teeth, and playfully *bite* them or *push* them with their snout. Over the generations, these parenting functions developed into a wide variety of head and facial motions which the infants respond to as the pleasant and tender touch of the mother's head implements. During adolescence, the innocently playful and emotionally charged *touching* and *fondling* by siblings or other close relatives gradually acquires an explicitly sexual context as natural corollary of physical maturity.

Playing juveniles. Shortly after birth, as soon as quadrupeds can stand, they start playing with their siblings, developing their wrestling skills and physique for future hunting and self-protection. During these endless fighting games, juveniles get used to each other's smell, bodies and genitals. All these *snapping, catching, pulling, nuzzling* and other motions increase tactile feelings in youngsters. Juveniles continue playing with parents and siblings on reaching sexual maturity, but in a different way, using more selective patterns. These mammalian social grooming activities not only help to bind together family groups, but also to develop the head and facial motion capabilities for use in other plastic forms of tactile communication.

Grooming adults. As we have seen, insects, birds and mammals developed social grooming habits more than other animal species, either with a single partner or a group setting. There are even instances of adults preening, cleaning, grooming, feeding and playing with infants belonging to a different mother.

Grooming eventually became a central social activity for all primate species, and the relationships thus formed underpinned and reflected the wider social hierarchy of each group. The bull or female leader expects to be groomed by younger or smaller competitors as a mark of deference and respect. The facial motions of grooming remain the same – *picking* fleas from the fur or skin, *licking, nuzzling* and so on – but the plastic facilities of the primate face gradually evolved into a complex and highly sophisticated instrument of communication involving the use of eyes, eyelids, eyebrows, ears, nose, nostrils, tongue, lips, teeth and jaws as well as the basic motions, gestures and postures of the head as a whole.

As part of courtship and mating, grooming involves close range body communication that expresses the **intimacy** of the relationship between the two individuals. In a world full of predators, silent communication is obviously preferable in circumstances when the attention is occupied by another individual, as in grooming and mating. This is why animals evolved such a richly expressive vocabulary of facial motions, increasing their chances of survival by avoiding the use of potentially fatal sounds.

129

The eye-language of anthropoids is so effective that they even use it to communicate at **medium** range, when calling for a mate, grooming, accepting a sexual invitation, threatening a competitor and so on. All species can easily read their own head and facial motion signals to confirm the accuracy of what has been communicated in other ways.

COURTSHIP AND MATING

Mating is the only mutual activity that guaranties the species' reproduction and continuity. It usually involves three main stages: the **mating call, courtship** and **copulation**. Some species omit the first stage during the breeding period; others avoid the second stage; some ignore both and simply copulate. Fertilisation nevertheless occurs, unsentimentally, even with partners who never meet again. This is particularly so with fish, reptiles and amphibians.

The complexity of most species' courtship and mating rituals has of course a sound evolutionary foundation, insofar as the process itself concerns selection – that is, choosing an individual with the strongest and healthiest genes to perpetuate the breed. The more demanding the female, the more elaborate the display required of the male, the greater the chances of producing healthy progeny.

Seasonal love calls

Animals employ a huge variety of mating communication signals including smell, sound, colouration, luminescence, touch and plastic motion, as we saw in Chapter I. Although most insect, fish and reptile signals (ultrasonic, infrared, radio-biological) are beyond the range of human perception, we can discern most of the other types mentioned above. But although we can recognise the motion 'emblems' of familiar species, there remain serious problems in decoding most animals' signals.

As far as head and facial motions are concerned, we know that the long-range acoustic calls of insects and fish are emitted by *moving* palps and head implements, those of amphibians and reptiles by *crying* or *hissing* vocalisations, and birds and mammals by *songs, whistling, growling, clicking* and so on. The middle-range luminescent signals of certain species are rare, but constitute a more advanced communication medium for those able to decipher and respond to the code.

Mating calls vary according to the **anatomic** structure of the species. The calls contain information about the sender's **identity**, including their species, sex, age, size, status and physical condition. The calls can only be read only by others of the same species. The oestrum female listens to the various sexual offers, studying the acoustic 'CV' of each male, and replying to those of potential interest with an invitation call containing her own shorter CV, on which basis the dialogue continues by exchanging additional information.

If it seems improbable that an individual can recognise the suitability of a mate by sound alone in this way, without even seeing them, consider the parallel with human beings. Equipped with adequate hearing and a good acoustic memory, not only will the average listener at once recognise a familiar voice on the phone, and be able to tell the gender and approximate age of the caller, but also whether the person is timid or confident, aggressive or conciliatory, weak or strong and so on. Although animals lack verbal language, there can be no doubt that they have achieved such a highly evolved sonic communication vocabulary that even we have not as yet been able to decode a great part of their signals.

The sheer extent of this almost unlimited vocal language initially seems hard to believe. But some species have numerous call-timbres, with thousands of intonations, rhythmic patterns, dynamic nuances, dramatic modulations, pitch levels, melodies, harmonies and other performing characteristics. Add to these the most common calling **genres**, such as low *grunting*, soft *buzzing*, *croaks, chirps, rasps,* guttural *moans,* musical *trilling,* shrill *twitters,* and *booming* cries.

Combine these vocal characteristics with these few common genres, and one begins to realise the incalculable number of **acoustic compositions** that are possible. Multiply this by the one and a half million species currently registered, each with its own acoustic facilities, and the scale of this dictionary of animal calling sequences in the courtship repertoire becomes apparent.

Courtship dialogues can last literally for hours before copulation takes place. Sometimes more than one suitor appears, in which case, depending on the species, there are several possible scenarios. The first male to arrive, if accepted by the oestrum female, may have priority, leaving the other suitors to look for another mate. Alternatively, all the potential suitors fight for the right to mate while the female watches and consents to accept the winner. The third possibility is that all the suitors wait to take their turn with the female on a first come/first served basis.

Courtship performance

The organs for emitting and receiving sound are mainly in the head, which is where any motion or progressive action of the body is orchestrated. The limbs also play a significant role in any courtship ritual of course, but this is discussed later; and in any case, legless reptiles and fish communicate and express themselves no less effectively by head and body motions alone.

Why do animals need to spend, and apparently waste, so much time and energy on courtship? The answer once again lies in the survival instinct. Females are only periodically fertile, and only then receptive to sexual advances; males constantly seek sexual contact, and therefore have fewer opportunities to satisfy their mating needs.

Courtship is a major factor in selective evolution, and mating is the motor of evolutionary progress. Both sexes instinctively seek the best possible reproductive outcomes. Males fight each other for mating rights, sometimes to the death; females choose the biggest and strongest suitor as their preferred mating partner. These mutual desires stimulate the search for most effective self-presentation by males in order to attract females.

Each species has its own courtship repertoire. Butterflies, for instance, have displays that involve *dancing* flights. Spiders *play* love tunes on their webs with their palps. Male scorpions *carry* tasteful morsels in their pincers to their intended mate. Some lizards perform tricks by *skating* on water with their hind legs. A snake seduces his mate by *rubbing* his cheek against her back. Dolphins 'kiss' by *touching* snouts. Birds *sing* and *dance* exuberantly. Penguins *shake* and *twist* like young clubbers. Horses *rub* each other's buttocks with their cheeks. Bats and whales *somersault*. Male baboon *wobble* their heads, *bare* their teeth and *touch* the female's genitals with their hands to check whether she is in heat.

The courtship of insects is arguably the genesis of the performing arts. Refinements of courtship rituals by later species, notably by birds and mammals, developed this primal sociosexual activity of creatures from the beginnings of their evolution into the emotionally charged multi-media performances over millions of years. These in turn became the socio-cultural foundation for all the tribal activities and communications of hominids.

Varieties of copulation

Different species mate in different ways according to their respective anatomies: **back-to-back** (camels, some butterflies); **face-to-back** (most animals); **face-to-face** (apes and humans). But irrespective of the method used, all involve ancillary motions of other body parts than the genitals, such as the head or palps. Although there are some creatures who simply copulate without preliminaries of any sort, most insects, birds and mammals ritualise the mating process into a sensitive, intimate and sometimes magnificently complex motion performance.

Most males fertilise females by a *vibrating* body motion, using head and facial expressions in the process. Each act of copulation involves two separate forces: emotional stress and physical body motion. Both are generated by the instinct to continue the species by creating new life. The head of a mammal reflects its feelings and behaviour in plastic motion before and during copulation.

Male cats reveal their sexual stimulation during copulation by sensual head motions and corresponding facial expressions, *wagging, nodding, jerking* and *rotating* the head while *snarling* exultantly. Approaching orgasm, the male '*bites*' the female's head or neck, *dilates* his nostrils, *rolls* his eyeballs in wide open eyes, and *growls* loudly upon ejaculation. The female expresses a similar range of responses while being held steady beneath the male, responding in kind to his vocal accompaniment.

Male insects and spiders *hold* the female down with their antennae, palps, mandibles or pincers when copulating. Even so, the females of some species succeed in devouring the head of their partner during sex (although the evolutionary benefit of doing so remains unclear). The decapitated male nevertheless completes the fertilisation process reflexively until all the sperm has been deposited.

Apes copulate face to back, and usually hominids face to face, looking into each other's eyes and observing the partner's facial expressions.

Group copulation

The frequency of the animal breeding season varies from once every four–five days for many insects to a four–five-year period for some mammals. However, some species copulating as often as every day, all year round. The following extracts from wildlife films were recorded during various research expeditions to Asia, Africa and Australia.

Clip 1) An entire troop of some sixty adult monkeys from Central Africa have sex with each other at regular intervals between feeding from early morning until nightfall, changing partners every ten–fifteen seconds – a kind of bacchanalia with a chorus of loud screaming instead of music. For these monkeys, as the narrator observes, having sex is like saying 'good morning'.

Clip 2) A dozen male snakes in a deep pit mate simultaneously with three females, periodically changing partners. This group breeding may go on for days without intermission, with the possible addition of some new male late arrivals.

Each species has its own predominant mating patterns, pairing for life or for a single breeding period; one dominant male with a harem of females, or vice versa; or random promiscuity. Homosexual groups of both sexes also exist in most species.

Clip 3) Hippos mate in the water, the dominant bull guarding his harem, constantly fighting off several rivals. While the bull chases his opponents in all directions, an audacious young male sneaks up to the oestrum female, and mates with her in the middle of the harem.

Clip 4) A female turtle mates with group of males on the beach for forty–fifty minutes. She carries a male 'rider' on her back underwater, until he completes the fertilisation. Then the next candidate takes his turn, and so on with the next seven–eight males. By then the female is so exhausted that she escapes into deeper waters, leaving the remaining disappointed suitors waiting on the shore.

Clip 5) After a spectacular 'pas-de-trois' courtship dance, a pair of grey whales mate in shallow waters. The second male assists the copulating couple by lying beside the female to *support* her in the required position; on completion, the two males swap positions.

Clip 6) A group of female baboons congregates away from the males, grooming each other constantly, or just playing when not feeding. From time to time, one *mounts* another female and imitates the motions of copulation until she reaches orgasm. The narrator comments that there is as yet no plausible explanation for this behaviour within the parameters of baboon social life.

Male cattle, camels, bison, yaks, goats and other species tend to remain in separate groups, away from the main part of the herd. This is mainly because the dominant bull persistently chases away any male competitor.

Clip 7) A sexually aroused adult male bison wanders among other grazing males, desperately looking for a mate. Finding no female, he mounts a young inexperienced male, and copulates anally – an action the narrator explains as the creature mistaking the sex of his chosen mating partner.

Despite all these differences in mating body motions, there are also strong underlying similarities. What they have in common includes mutual communicative contact, tactile plastic motion and often, something akin to the intimacy of a relationship.

They differ in the way these motions are performed, the vocabulary of communication signals, and expressions of emotional excitement.

The socio-sexual activities of high mammals like playing, grooming, courtship and mating are based on expressive mutuality between individuals and plastic motion duets. All influence and modify each other's functions, creating a versatile physical and emotional nexus of socio-cultural behaviour: a great achievement in the evolution of animal psycho-motor abilities which paved the way for the future civilisations of humanity.

Dictionary of mimetic facial expressions

The human face is a veritable orchestra of motion whose highly expressive plastic characteristics allows a vast range of impressions to be communicated through performance. There are basically ten motion implements: eyes, eyelids, eyebrows, nose, ears, cheeks, lips, tongue, teeth and chin. Each of these has its own plastic facilities and expressive range. Performing harmoniously as an ensemble, they play an immensely complex and sophisticated motion score.

Both physically and mentally, the head orchestrates all solo and group expressions triggered by instinctive or conscious reactions to stimuli. Any false or discordant plastic motion of the head or face would bring about a misleading communication or ritual performance, for which a heavy price would sometimes be paid.

As everyone knows, the eyes are immensely powerful communication devices, as transmitters as well as receivers. They are the most sensitive indicator of any type of emotional interaction, and can easily be read. Unconscious pupil dilation, blinks or changes in brightness reveal honesty or falsehood. Below is a selection of representative eye motions and their corresponding stimuli.

EXTERNAL STIMULI FOR <u>INSTINCTIVE</u> MOTIONS

Positive or negative feelings
- pleasant/unpleasant smell
- clean vision/unfocussed chaos
- sweet/bitter flavour
- pleasant sound/irritating noise
- tender touch/sticky contact
- sexual pleasure/forceful rape

Environmental influences
- balmy weather/freezing cold
- cosy bonfire/conflagration
- rich/bad harvest
- fertile rain/fierce storm
- tranquillity/natural catastrophe
- cattle delivering/predator attacking

Luck or misfortune:
- successful hunt/death by predator
- fertility/famine
- liberty/slavery
- victory/defeat in a battle
- totem's blessing/execution
- cohesive community/rival gangs

133

EXTERNAL PROJECTION OF INNER FEELINGS.

Positive

CHEERFUL: open *smiling* face, with *look* straight into person's eyes. Upright head *inclined* slightly laterally, pause.

ADMIRATION: *raising* head up/front, forward, gazing into person's eyes; opening mouth slightly and inclining head slowly, laterally.

TRUST: *listening* with eyes wide *pulling* head slightly forward with half-open mouth; periodically *nodding* head in agreement.

WORRY: *moving* head and eyes chaotically, diagonally and from side to side; *biting* lips, *shifting* eyebrows up and down.

FEARLESSNESS: showing off by *tilting* head back, turning head to *growling* with open jaws.

PRIDE: raising head up and slightly back; *looking* down nose; glancing up with head *turning* upwards and sideways.

Negative

SLEEPY: *shutting* eyes slowly, optimistic *inclining* head front/down; *moving* head up front when stirred by noise, *yawning;* *shutting* open mouth and then eyes.

DISGUST: *frowning, squeezing pulling* chin nose; *downturned* lips; *staring* with half-shut eyes; *turning* head away raised up in profile.

SUSPICION: *listening* with head open up front and pushed back; *squinting; smiling* slightly; *frowning.*

UNCONCERN: *rocking* head laterally, improvising rudimentary tunes; *contorting* face into funny expression; looking vacant.

FEAR: *tilting* head down into shoulders; quick sideways glances look for a fight; *looking* for help; *biting* lips, *sniffing* noisily.

MISERY: *tilting* head straight/down into shoulders; *inclining* laterally; *pulling* chin down, with head *inclining. sinking* down.

State of being (passive)

friendly, sarcastic, revealing, modest, uncomposed, thankful, admiring, sexually provocative.

vacant, set back, sheepish, easily discouraging, gloomy, honourable, jealous, angry, dishonest

suspicious, happy, intriguing, sad, disdainful, bored, uncomprehending, trustful, displaying, striking

dart/shoot, showing off, gawping, reassuring, disloyal, staring, serving, threatening, unashamed

promising, respectful, dismayed, unconfident, attractive, revering, sharp, regardful, witnessing

reliable, glance, glare, dispassionate, bearing, mannered, hateful, hopeful, severe, bashful

watchful, guarded, disbelieving, sheep's eyes of lovers, disapproving, distrait

discarding, disparaging, spurning, flirting, hypnotising, aggressive, loyal, snobbish, crazy, foolish

Expression of intent (active)

minding, paying attention, consideration, watchfulness, self-protection, mental awareness, disappointment

surprise, curiosity, ignoring, shock, disagreeable, distrustful, disturb, thanking, engagement

fixed/intended, enlightening, fearful, disillusioned, unsure, distressed, meaningless, discerning, unsound

affection, partiality, spectating, avoiding participation, guilt concentration, contemplation

agitation, aggression, caution, disarray, responsibility, relief, hope for, appearance

disgust, offence, having charge of, beholding, hoping for, aiming at, concern, lack of determination, wakefulness

deciding on action, heedfulness, looking with fascination or astonishment, eagerly awaiting

being vigilant or prepared, hidden admiration, dislike, nervousness, replacing smiling look with angry/sad look

LOOK OF ACTION

eye-contact, catching, striking;
keep one's eyes open; be on one's guard;
be in agreement

observing closely; watching intently;
inspecting or surveying; disturbing;
passing over; probing; checking; turning
one's sights on;

tasting; discovering; *searching* visually;
examining; directing or shifting the gaze;
looking: - out, - for, - around, - over, -
upon, - about, - at, - back, - on, - up,
- into, - through

expecting; turning one's thoughts to,
demanding, studying, inquiring, calling for
attention; expressing protest; following by
covert glaze; lying

watching out; disparaging;
preventing harm or danger; *raising* eyes;
indicating the presence of; keeping watch;
penetrating;

investigating; seeking opportunities for
participation or success; gazing in wonder;
ascertaining visually; sidelong glance,
disowning, watching over;

distinguishing appearance of someone's
expression; comparing two similar persons
or things, threatening, promising;
scrutinising

EYE MONOLOGUE

Look ahead. Be alert! Watch out!

Do you see it? He looks mad

Stop staring; What do you want?

You look strange. What happened?

You can rely on me, I promise

See you later. Don't go away!

Be reasonable! Go and bring her back

Where is she now? Probably gone

He looks familiar. Do I know him?

Hey, listen to me! Take care

You two, climb the tree and look out

How dare you? I am your husband!

What do you think? Can you make it?

Look who's here! Oh, not again!

May I help you? Don't be afraid

Can you help me? I'm in trouble

Stop following me! Leave me alone!

Hey you, come here! He is so slow

Be careful. Look at the future.

Captured warriors

WHAT HAPPENED? observing tied feet and hands, *glance* towards companion

WE'VE BEEN CAUGHT – *glance* at partner, closely observing own tied hands and feet

WHERE ARE WE? – *shifting* look laterally, along with simultaneous head motion

IN A PIT – *look around* from R. lower corner up/side/down to L lower corner, then to partner

HOW TO ESCAPE? – slow furtive *glance* around; return stare to his feet

THROUGH THE CEILING – *raising* head up/back, studying all the ceiling

CAN WE MAKE IT? – look to partner, and *pointing* to tied feet and arms

WE'LL TRY – *glance* to partner with appraisal of the situation, followed by a confirming look

Sexual approach

STOP STARING – *glare* at stranger, pause, *turns* away

I LIKE HER FACE – examining look; pulling loving eyes back

ALL MEN LOVE ME – *raising* eyes to the R. upper corner in a proud pose

WHAT A BEAUTY! – *shifting* gaze slowly down to breasts, hips, legs and feet

HE SEEMS TO BE OK – *shifting* gaze diagonally to lower corner

I'M TRAPPED – *glance* at her eyes, revert own eyes in shock

Mother and child

WHERE HAVE YOU BEEN? – *glare* straight down/front, with angry eyes

PLAYING IN A TREE – covered *glance* from down-up/R-down, frozen in guilty motion

LOOK AT YOURSELF! – *shifting* accusing look repeatedly up and down

SORRY – NEVER AGAIN – *darting* look up/down; covered *glance* up R. to the tree

FACIAL EXPRESSION SIGNALS FOR ACTION

Eyelid motions

Instinctive/passive

Quick *blinking* with both eyelids in strong wind, rain, hail, lightning

Winking repeatedly one or both eyelids to clean from dust or insects

Shutting both eyelids tightly when in pain or to keep self control

Protecting with both eyelids against bright fire, light or sunshine

Opening and *shutting* periodically when dreaming, enjoying music

Looking with half-shut eyelids, when bored or when drowsy

Short rapid *blinking* in pleasant surprise
Unblinking open eyes when afraid or in shock

Screwing up eyelids in disgust
Closing an eye partially when teasing, or disbelieving somebody.

Narrowing eyes in anger

Conscious/active

Looking with half shut winking eyes to conceal true thoughts or feelings

Holding eyes shut when forgiving an offence

Slowly *blinking*, when accepting reluctantly

Winking to confirm reception of message, and considering it

Winking periodically in an attractive and flattering manner

Winking to signal friendship and intimacy
Opening eyes wide when rejecting or refusing to join in an act.

Half-shutting eyes during courtship or sex
Holding eyes wide open in amazement or sexual ecstasy

Winking in greeting or warning about hidden danger

Narrowing eyes to see better over long distance

Unconscious eyebrow motions

Positive expressions

QUESTIONING (CURIOUS):
Eyebrows *raised* and out; *frowning*, eyes wide *open*.

SPIRITUALITY (ADMIRATION)
Inner ends of eyebrows *raised* slightly, upper eyelids half *closed*

SURPRISE (SHOCK)
Arched eyebrows *raised* high, revealing eyeballs

HAPPINESS (CHEERFUL)
Eyebrows periodically *shifting* slightly up/down when *smiling* fully

ANXIETY (CONCENTRATION)
Lowered eyebrows, *wrinkling* over bridge of the nose

FLIRTATION (ATTRACTING):
Raising one eyebrow periodically when observing or evaluating a person

GREETING (MANNERED):
Raising one eyebrow, addressing to the side; both if person in front

GRIMACING (PULLING FACES):
Shifting one eyebrow or *twisting* both when making an audience laugh

Negative expressions

SADNESS:
Raising inner ends of eyebrows, *contracting* temple muscles.

CONFUSION:
Lowered brows *pulled in, shifting* one eyebrow periodically up and down

BOREDOM (DREAMINESS):
Slightly *raising* eyebrows upwards and out; *drawing down/in; shifting* chaotically

THREATENING (ANGER):
Lowered brows squeezed in; *shifting* up down periodically

SUSPICION:
Shifting one eyebrow up/down, or both *lowered*; trying to understand

BEGGING (MISERY):
Raising up inner ends of eyebrows; outer ends down; screwing up face

DISGUST (ALIENATION):
Pulling both eyebrows down, *raising* outer ends up; *wrinkling* eyes

FEAR:
Raised up/pulled in eyebrows, *shaking* convulsively up/down

Combined facial motions

It is difficult to characterise motions of the various parts of the face separately, as they are all physically interconnected and operate in concert to express meaning or emotion. Although this applies to some extent to all body motions, it is most apparent than in the face.

The chin and cheeks, for example, which unlike the ears and nose, developed their motion facilities continuously over millions of years, eventually replaced them as expressive instruments. The lips are the third motion tool of the lower face, and are mentioned separately from the chin and cheeks because of their much wider range of motion.

The underlying facial musculature connects the cheeks-lips-chin with the other expressive facial instruments. The cheeks have an auxiliary function in practically all other facial actions. The upper lip is more tied to cheeks, while the lower lip is essentially the top part of the chin, with all so closely connected as to operate in a kinetic emotional expression ensemble. Here are a few examples of cheeks/lips/chin expressions, both individually and in combination:

LEADING IMPLEMENT	AUXILIARY IMPLEMENT
Cheek motions (reflex)	
Annoyance, disappointment *Raise* L cheek to the corner of L. eye	Lips *pull* up, mouth *opens* slightly; L. eye half-*shuts*; nose *twists* to L
Disgust, repulsion *Raise* cheeks inwards and up to nose	Outer corners of lips *turn down*; nose bridge *wrinkles* up to *frowning* brow
Exhaustion, boredom Cheeks inflate and exhale	Lips *pout* on exhalation, *vibrating;* chin *tilts* inwards and up to lower lip
Chin motions (reflex)	
Surprise, terror, shock Chin *drops* down and *holds* pose	Cheeks *pull* down, eyebrows *raise*, eyes *open* wide, all *held*
Threat, aggression Chin *thrusts* out in front of upper lip	Cheeks rise, nose wrinkles, frown
Entrapment, seeking escape Chin *shifts* sideways	Cheeks and lips *move* laterally, with half *open* mouth; nose motionless.
Lip motions (volitional)	
Sucking, blowing, kissing Pouting with lips pursed	Lower cheeks *pulled* in and forwards, chin *rises* and *tilts* back
Anxiety, frustration Pout, biting squeezed lips	Cheeks *move* up/down and in and out accordingly; chin *rises* and *fals*
Puzzlement, distress Closed lower lip *curls* over	Lower cheeks *fall* neck, chin *tilts* up and inwards, eyebrows *rise*

Natural Facial Expressions

agitation   attention   surprise   disgust

spite   fear   grief   joy

"…can't I make it?"   "…Who do you think you are?"   "…it is too much!"   "…what a pleasure!"

admiration   "…it is so funny!"   "…grin and bear it!"   "…I don't believe it!"

"…I must get him!"   "Stop it, at once!"

Source: Librairie Grande, *Les Singes*, 1978

fig. II/4 Artificial Facial Expressions

Heroism	Happiness	Serenity	Lunacy	Fear
Anger	Revenge	Disgust	Furious	Comic
Fatigue	Begging	Sadness	Hurting	Height
Attraction	Idiocy	Surprise	Affection	

Source: Mimic dictionary of Asia-Indian's classical dance, *Bharata Natya*, K Rao, 1988

The atrophy of motion implements

The great apes gradually lost several of their body motion tools in the tortuous path of human evolution. The communication repertoire of the head, ears and nose was massively reduced, although as we have seen, the eyes, eyebrows, eyelids and mouth (including lips, tongue and teeth), successfully compensated for these losses.

Hominids' whole musculo-skeletal structure steadily evolved, notably in the spine, pelvis, hip joints, femur, knee joint and tibia, the foot and its arch, shoulder joints, upper and lower arm bones, elbow joint, wrists and hands. These progressive changes brought with them changes in the body's plastic capabilities. Our feet and toes lost their ability to grasp. On the other hand, the limbs became more flexible, more balanced and better coordinated, acquiring in the process far richer motion facilities, with greater technical delicacy and a wider range of mimetic possibilities.

The vestigial plastic motions of the nose and ears that we see in ancient mythic rituals and professional performances of mime and drama remain as an echo of our long evolution. The art of facial expressions, now almost lost through lack of study and practice, featured a rich vocabulary whose main elements are partially described below.

EAR MOTION

Most primates have prominent, flexible ears that respond to noise in order to locate its direction and the distance of its source. Apes have comparatively smaller and less sensitive ears which are almost hidden in the head fur, but are still flexible enough to *turn* towards the sound source. Hominid ears are even less flexible and sensitive, retaining only the ability to *shift* and *twist* slightly in reaction to noise.

All primate species could hear sounds over long distances and establish their source by *moving* their ears in order to be able to react promptly to any danger. This is a conscious, volitional response to external stimulus; by contrast, the convulsive *twitching* of the ears to dislodge a troublesome insect involves an Unconscious reflex motion.

Although our ancestors lost virtually all ability to *move* their ears independently a very long time ago, the potential for doing so remains. The main reason why we can no longer control our ears is because the head itself evolved sufficient flexibility to turn fast and accurately in the direction of any incoming sound. Independent ear motion therefore became redundant, and therefore the capability was lost. Today, only a few tribal dancers, mimes and other performers can use this facility to a limited extent, and then only after much practice.

NOSE MOTION

The anthropoid nose suffered the same fate as the ears. In most primates, the powerful *sniffing* apparatus was one of the main tools for communicating within the family and group as well as for searching out food and recognising traces of predators. The olfactory faculties of apes steadily diminished over time, while hominids retained only a small fraction of their ancestors' sense of smell. This functional decline was accompanied by an equivalent reduction in the range of independent nose motions required.

However, humans still use a very limited dictionary of nose express their feelings when communicating or performing:
- the tip of the nose slightly *twitches* in response to a strong smell.
- the nostrils *move* inwards and outwards on sharp inhalation and exhalation, when **angry** or **frightened**, for example.
- the bridge of the nose *wrinkles* when frowning in **disgust, sadness, incredulity** or **criticism.**

- the nose and cheeks *rise* as the eyes *narrow* and the lips *purse* when expressing uncertainty, ambiguity or a negative opinion.
- the tip of the nose (along with one cheek and the corner of the lips when *winking*).
- In addition, there is the mimetic nose motion vocabulary used symbolically in mythical pantomime in the form of exaggerated and unrealistic *grimaces* whose meanings are only familiar to local audiences.

NATURAL AND ARTIFICIAL MOTIONS OF SMILING, CRYING AND LAUGHTER

A smile is the most confusing facial communication, whose correct interpretation depends on circumstances and the intellectual and emotional dynamic between the two people involved. The many characteristic types of smile evolved to meet the need for the increasingly subtle and complex communications needed to avoid social conflict, both within the group and outside it.

Violence was a wasteful way of resolving hierarchical, territorial and domestic conflict – one that impeded successful reproduction. It was therefore in hominids' interest to find more peaceful means of communication for this purpose. **Aggressive** tactics were gradually replaced by **diplomatic** compromises. Life experience taught tribal elders the benefit of sometimes hiding and controlling real feelings, thoughts, emotions and intentions.

Having a variety of smiles at one's disposal – and knowing which kind to use, as well as how to read the smiles of others – became an important aspect of relating to others, whether within the group or not. This involved learning to discern when a smile was 'real' from when it was being used a mask.

The human smile can be **open** or **closed**; it can vary in intensity, as a **'mini'**, **'midi'** or **'maxi'** smile; it can flash briefly or be demonstratively extended over a period; it can be transparent or conflict with a hidden meaning in the eyes. A smile can communicate, conceal, entertain and express. Like an orchestral violin, the smile is an instrument with many possible roles, which can not only lead the expression of the face, but also the motions of the entire body.

Although there are of course an infinite variety of personal expressive nuances, it is useful for the present purpose to categorise smiles by three major dualities: reflex or conscious; true or forced; and positive or negative.

PLASTIC MOTION CHARACTERISTICS OF A SMILE

Closed: mini-smile with *closed* teeth and lips, expressed mainly by *narrowed* eyes with partially *closed* lids.
Open: midi-smile with upper teeth partially revealed; maxi-smile, with lips broadly *drawn back* to show both rows of teeth and the lower jaw slightly *dropped*.
Mini: a barely perceptible smile, with the lips *closed* and slightly *stretched*, the corners of the mouth slightly *raised* and *turned out*.
Midi: the most common smile, with lips *parted* and the corners of the mouth *turned up* partially to expose the upper row of teeth.
Maxi: the broad smile, with the corners of an open mouth *raised* higher and the lips *curving* upwards. to reveal both rows of teeth.
Short: the momentary smile.
Prolonged: *covert* smile or one whose motion is frozen in shock.
Real: the *spontaneous* expression of a true feeling with honest intention.

Artificial: a smile forced in response to circumstances, social standards or other reasons.
Clear: a natural, straightforward communication of a message.
Covert: a false smile that conceals inner thoughts, feelings and intentions.
Acting: an artificial smile designed deliberately to confuse or mislead.
This represents the relationship between the various motivations for smiling to real or pretended stimuli:

fig. II/5

Performing and Perceiving Expressions of a Smile

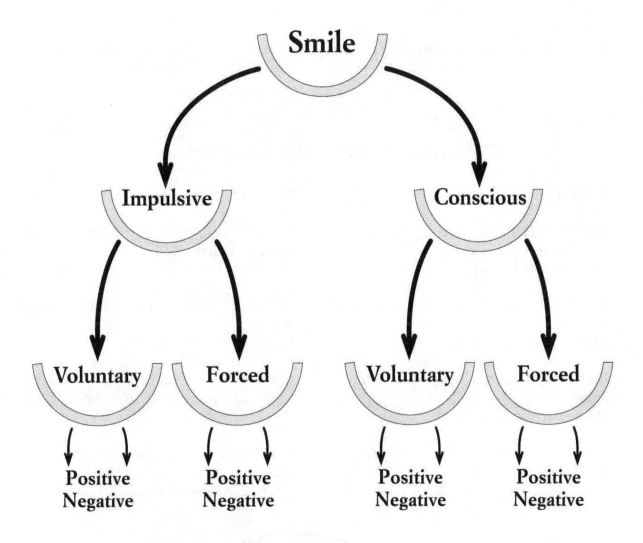

IMPULSIVE – VOLUNTARY SMILING EXPRESSIONS

POSITIVE (single meaning)

HAPPY, pleased, satisfied, natural
Open maxi-smile

IMAGINING, sleeping, dreaming, natural,
expressive, sentimental
Closed-mini or *midi* smile

PROPITIOUS, kind, natural
Closed -mini **or** *midi* smile

ADMIRING, respectful, spiritual
natural, sentimental
Closed-midi or *open-mini* smile

Negative (double meaning)

NAUGHTY, snobbish, disdainful, covert,
expressive, dramatic
Closed-mini or *midi* smile

SMIRK, silly, foolish, covert, expressive,
humorous
Open-midi or *maxi* smile

DIFFIDENT, bashful, over-modest,
covert, dramatic
Closed-mini or *midi* smile

SPITEFUL, gloating, caustic, covert.
Closed-mini or *midi* smile

IMPULSIVE – FORCED SMILING EXPRESSIONS

POSITIVE (single meaning)

SURPRISED, flabbergasted, natural, over-
reacting, dramatic
Open-midi or *maxi* smile

FRIENDLY, benevolent, natural, tender,
openly emotional
Closed-mini or *midi* smile

ENTERTAINED amused, joyful, natural,
humorous
Open-midi or *maxi* smile

GRATEFUL, thankful, natural, outwardly
expressive, emotional
Closed-midi or *open-mini* smile

NEGATIVE (double meaning)

SAD, pessimistic, depressing, covert,
expressive, dramatic
Closed-mini or *midi* smile

SUSPICIOUS, disbelieving, leery, covert,
dramatic
Closed-mini or *midi* smile

CONFUSED, embarrassed, covert,
perplexed, expressive, dramatic *Closed-
mini* or *midi* smile

SCEPTICAL, uncertain, fussy, covert,
dramatic, critical
Closed-mini or *midi* smile

CONSCIOUS – VOLUNTARY SMILING EXPRESSIONS

POSITIVE (single meaning)

PLAYFUL, childish, carefree, natural,
expressive, humorous
Open-midi or *maxi* smile

EMBOLDENED, encouraging,
supporting, covert, dramatic
Open-mini or *midi* smile

CHEERFUL, beaming, optimistic, natural,
expressive, humorous
Open-midi or *maxi* smile

TOUCHING, sweet, covert, sentimental
Open-mini or *midi* smile

NEGATIVE (double meaning)

RESTRAINED, austere, covert, dramatic
Closed-midi or *open-mini* smile

SARCASTIC, cynical, covert, dramatic
Closed-midi or *open-mini* smile

CROOKED, wily, cunning, covert,
dramatic
Closed-midi or *open-mini* smile

INTRIGUED, curious, conspiratorial,
covert, dramatic
Closed-midi or *open-mini* smile

CONSCIOUS – FORCED SMILING EXPRESSIONS

POSITIVE (single meaning)

PROFESSIONAL, polite, social, covert,
sentimental
Closed or *open-midi* smile

APPROVING, agreeable, acknowledging,
covert, sentimental
Closed-midi or *open-mini* smile

GREETING, welcoming, covert,
sentimental
Open-mini or *midi* smile

EXAGGERATED, grimacing,
entertaining, covert, humorous
Open-midi or *maxi* smile

NEGATIVE (double meaning)

GRINNING, refusing, unwilling, covert
dramatic
Closed midi or *maxi* smile

REJECTING, unwilling, covert, dramatic
Closed-mini or midi smile

AFFECTED,   paralysing   hypnotising,
covert, sentimental
Open-mini or *midi* smile

FLATTERING, covert, sentimental
Closed-midi or *open-mini* smile

The origins and evolution of smiling

Mammalian facial expressions that resemble the human smile have proved problematic to analyse. The stumbling block is where to look for the genetic roots of such an eloquent and mysterious phenomenon – in the realm of the emotions, or as strictly behavioural responses? As actions in their own right or as forms of communication?

We have already discussed the plastic motion facilities of the mammalian mouth, as the cardinal facial organ of any living creature, both functionally and expressively. **Grimaces** made by the muscles around the mouth affect the surrounding parts of the face, and in hominids, the mouth is the focus of the three main overt emotional expressions: *smiling, crying* and *laughing*.

Primates use the mouth not only for the everyday functions of feeding, playing, grooming and courting, but also for social activities and non-verbal communications, both **silent** and **vocalised**. These mouth motions are produced and controlled by facial musculature that has developed over millions of years to acquire unique plastic facilities and emotional range.

BARED TEETH EXPRESSIONS

Prompted by the need for social cohesion as well as the requirement to communicate efficiently at close range, the motion capabilities of the mouth evolved to encompass emotional expression as well as mechanical survival functions. A warning motion by *pulling* back the lips to *bare* the teeth while *vibrating* the tongue could deter predators or other opponents. In such circumstances, the facial motion accomplished a double function: to warn others to take immediate evasive action, and to demonstrate readiness to the opponent.

These **bared teeth** displays eventually developed into a complete dictionary of silent and vocal plastic signals such as *hissing, puffing* and *spitting* for medium range communications. The next stage of *open* mouth expression in all mammals (including apes and hominids) was to vocalise the bared teeth expression with *barks, shrieks* and *squeals*. There is however a long evolutionary distance between the bared teeth of the low mammals and the human smile.

The bared teeth expression was initially a response to **negative** circumstances such as a threat to the individual or its infants, physical discomfort or the need to demonstrate submission to hierarchical superiors. It was only after aeons of selective evolution that mammals developed positive emotional expressions such as greetings and reassurances, parental and sexual affection, friendly embracing and excitement or satisfaction on success at hunting, food gathering or combat.

Lemurs with full stomachs, a safe lair and healthy infants express their emotions by playing, gnaw-wrestling and baring their teeth in a plastic motion closely resembling the smiles of chimpanzees in similar circumstances (although of course facial expressions of fear are closely related to those of contentment). There can be little doubt that the bared teeth expression and the smile are related to each other not only in terms of what stimulates the response, but also in the motivation and emotional state being expressed.

The main motions of the bared teeth smile involve hard *expiration* and *drawing back* the lips and cheeks, sometimes supplemented by additional elements such as *sticking out* the tongue, *shaking* the head from side to side, oesophageal *grunts, smacking* the lips, *chattering* teeth and *moving* the eyebrows up and down. All of these undoubtedly have secondary meanings, which remain to be satisfactorily decoded.

PLASTIC MOTION PATTERNS

By the mid-20th century, much research had been devoted to the relationship between *smiling, crying* and *laughing* and the body motions these involve. Our views are these:

a) The **relaxed open mouth** expression of low mammals eventually developed into the round-mouth smile of later primates, in which the risorius muscle *drops* the chin down, and the zygomatic, triangularis and quadratus-menti muscles simultaneously *draw back* the lips and cheeks to form the mouth into a medium oval shape. Silent plastic motions project expressions of other states, such as surprise, concentration, play, observation, embracing, sexual interest and so on.

b) The **horizontal bared teeth** expression of primates gradually evolved into the silent or audible bared teeth *smile* of monkeys, with the lips and cheeks *stretched* laterally by the triangularis-oris, risorius and zygomatic muscles, with additional facial gestures of *lip-smacking* or *audibly inhaling* to express emotions such as attachment or reassurance in acts of grooming.

c) The **vertical bared teeth** expression of monkeys partially evolved into the silent relaxed open mouth expression of primates (see "a" above), with apes adding various vocalisations using the mouth, throat muscles and vocal chords. Motivated by anything from play to the defensive **vocalised** bared teeth grimace, these *shrieks, barks* and *howls* helped to develop the larynx and palate as sound instruments. This type of vocalised bared teeth expression is usually friendly, as when dominant males acknowledge deferential youngsters.

d) The **crescent smile** is the first positive expression of ape and hominid infants when feeling warm, nourished and content or recognising the familiar smell, sound, touch and face of the mother. The mouth corners are *pulled back* and upwards by zygomatic and risorius muscles, and the cheeks *drawn up* towards the eyes by levator-labii muscles so as the mouth is slightly *open* (as in mini-open smile described earlier). The hominid crescent smile can express a wide range of contrasting emotions triggered by various stimuli, and is probably the precursor of the silent bared teeth display described above.

e) The **closed mouth smile** is usually accompanied by an expressive look whose motions have already been described. A usually **positive** expression which could also harbour **negative** emotions such as scorn, it probably originated in low mammals' feelings of contentment and security, and was subsequently developed by hominids.

Unlike *crying* or *laughing*, the *smile* is a highly complex non-verbal communication device with many different functions and meanings, and involves many different parts of the face. As a projector of inner feelings, the smiling motion repertoire played a significant role in hominid evolution in terms of allowing more sophisticated interactions and relationships between individuals.

THE PHENOMENA OF CRYING AND LAUGHTER

These apparently contradictory emotional responses in fact have many basic similarities in terms of the motions involved, the effect they have and in their motivation, although *crying* preceded *laughter* in the evolutionary process.

Motivations for crying

Infant mammals *cry* when hungry, in discomfort or absent from the mother. The baby that cries the loudest gets fed first, just as a mother will protect a *crying* baby and punish an older sibling before even establishing who is the guilty party. Adults *cry* in grief over the loss of a family or group member, when defeated in combat or caught by a predator.

The many examples of *crying* behaviour in wild and domestic animals indicate the existence of emotional awareness. Elephants, wolves and apes often return to the spot where the remains of lost infants or pack leaders lie. My own young dog *cried* and *howled* non-stop for three months after losing its mate, and died soon afterwards – from grief, rather than any physical malady. Such cases suggest that other mammals have emotional feelings similar to our own.

Crying may well have initially evolved as an effective tool for defence or submission, by pleading for sympathy or forgiveness, although its role in hominid communication became infinitely more complex, to the extent of using 'false' crying as a means of emotionally manipulating others.

Motivations for and types of laughter

Laughter obviously expresses **positive** emotions, such as contentment with warmth, security, a full belly or successful copulation. Constantly preoccupied as they were with the struggle for survival, mammals experienced these feelings only rarely. Compared to the *crying* response, *laughter* was therefore only an occasional occurrence for primates and apes.

Darwin ignored laughter in his works, regarding it as a frivolous incidental behaviour that played little if any significant role in hominid evolution. Laughter was stimulated by a happy mood, an inclination to play or the enjoyment of sheer silliness: *screwing up* the face into *grimaces*, *mimicking* each other, or caricaturing the behaviour of other species. Although laughter is usually stimulated by play, *tickling* and regressively juvenile feelings, it could also be prompted by relief: escape from danger, solving a knotty problem, winning a fight and so on.

We are not concerned yet with human laughter, which is a different emotional response. Whereas the primate laugh is a more or less spontaneous and natural response to the kind of motivations listed above, humans are the only species who can in addition stimulate laughter at will, by using humour. They can even *laugh* artificially (*see Chapter II*).

Of the many motivations for, and types of laughter, we restrict ourselves here to non-human examples. When excited, primitive primates demonstrate several laughs prompted by glee and exultation. Monkeys extend the range of laugh responses to include the expression of pleasure, relief and elation. In apes, the emotional range is even greater, encompassing almost the entire spectrum from *titters* and *sniggers* to *guffaws*.

Laughter takes many physical forms – *peals, shouts, bursts, chuckles, roars* and so on – and emotional contexts: happy, morose, derisive, hysterical, silly and many more.

The common ground between smiling, crying and laughter

As we have seen, mammalian socialisation stimulated non-verbal communication through **plastic** and **sonic signals** that were produced most effectively by the mouth and vocal organs, which became the main communication tool.

The facial motion implements and accompanying musculature of primates grew progressively more sophisticated over time, able to produce an increasingly large repertoire of expressions. Indeed, only such a highly co-ordinated instrument could produce expressions of such kaleidoscopic emotional intensity as *smiling, crying* or *laughter*. In anthropoids, the development of anatomical equipment to form these complex responses has always been driven by the evolution of emotional capacities.

The motion repertoires of *laughing* and *crying* include:
- *making* tears.

- spontaneous muscular tension and facial *reddeni*.
- *pulling back* the corners of the lips and mouth.
- heavy breathing.
- intense motion of facial muscles and vocal chords.
- *shaking* the upper torso, head and shoulders.
- *stamping* feet and *clapping* hands on body parts.
- bouncing with flapping arms.
- *wandering* around and *rocking* upper trunk.
- *nodding* head and *guffawing* with vertical bared teeth.
- *howling* with raised and *wobbling* head.

The *closed* or *open* mouth and *bared*-teeth facial motions of primitive primates eventually developed into the *smile*, *cry* and *laugh*, and there are clear functional, muscular and emotional connections between former and the latter. Neither are the *smile*, *cry* and *laugh* mutually exclusive; a *cry* can imperceptibly transform into a *smile* or a *laugh*, and vice versa, depending on mood, activity, personality and circumstance.

Although most studies of *crying* and *laughter* concentrate on human beings, we are concerned here with hominid evolution before the advent of spoken language and its effect on these responses.

Most researchers single out one of three essential aspects that *crying* and *laughter* have in common insofar as their origins are concerned: **behaviour, emotion** and **action**. However, close analysis of mammalian reactions, expressions and motions does not support such a narrow categorisation of these vital functions; it is more realistic to assume that our primate ancestors developed the capability to *laugh* and to *cry* in all three of these spheres. Many other aspects of everyday mammalian life influenced the development of the *cry*, *smile* and *laugh*, including mentality, communication, spirituality, expression, sex and so on.

Another popular hypothesis is that *crying* and *laughter* originated from success or defeat in combat. The victor releases his inner tension through an emotional expression of vocalised vertical bared teeth – in effect, *roaring* with *laughter*; the loser also vents his pent-up stress in an equivalently emotional expression, a *crying howl*. This interesting theory has convincing anthropological support and a clear evolutionary logic, reflecting the formula "from motivation through action to emotional conclusion".

However, these emotional phenomena did not appear with anthropoids. If this model is correct, *crying* and *laughter* must have much longer history, going right back to low mammals, if not earlier.

The vital activity of fighting in itself would not provide sufficient emotional scope for the more sophisticated plastic expressions of crying and laughter, which could only be prompted in combination with other, more emotionally complex inner states.

Apes are too closely related to humans for these extraordinary fundamental changes in physiological and emotional systems to occur. The audio/plastic motions of *smiling, crying* and *laughter* first appeared in primitive form much earlier, probably in prosimian and rodent species, hinting at the powerful emotional capabilities that were to develop over a period of tens of millions of years.

COMMUNICATING WITH FORELIMBS

Much can be deduced by comparing the anatomy, expression and anthropology of gesture as used in communication and performance:

a) The gestural vocabulary of Indian, Amerindian and Euro-Italian peoples share many common plastic characteristics, such as single-hand **indication**, double-handed **description**, double-handed **mimesis** and so on.

151

b) Despite differences in the historical age of these three groups, the anatomy of their forelimbs is very similar and follows the same progression from *closed* fist through *cupped* hand to *open* hand with fingers and thumb either held together or fully *splayed*.

c) The range of **vernacular** mimetic signs and gestures increased all over the world by various manipulations of the fingers, involving different spatial patterns, tactile combinations and plastic shapes.

Gesturology – the study of gesture – is not recognised as an independent discipline of body linguistics; the few publications that exist are concerned with the study of psychiatry, semiotics, ritual, dance/drama or the visual arts. This virtually untouched field nevertheless has much potential to help unravel the phylogeny of the human species.

The following illustrations demonstrate a number of gestures (*figs. 6–9; 12–13*) divided into three distinctive stages:
1) **gestural syllabus**
2) **motion repertoire** of signs and signals
3) short sentences in **gestural conversations**

Each stage is illustrated by a few examples from the archaeological record and from various ethnographic materials published by researchers who wish to preserve prehistoric body language and its semantic evolution, plastic composition and motion artistry for future generations.

Comparing the stylistic motion characteristics of the three ethnic groups mentioned above reveals differences in plasticity, style and meaning that reflect different phases of cultural anthropology:

- **Realism** in the Amerindian ethnic style, with a strong background of tradition (*fig.II/10*)
- **Classicism** by Indian symbolic signs, with powerful spiritual elements (*figII/11*)
- Realism or Classicism in the **popular theatrical** Sothern European gestural vocabularies.

These stylistic variations cover all three stages illustrated.

It is logical to assume that the body language of Native American and Asian Indians have the same phylogenetic origin in the Mongol peoples of the Far East. Both have many similar, sometimes almost identical, plastic patterns of sign composition with the same meanings, although performed differently. Southern Europeans generally have a few gestures resembling both Indian vocabularies, executed in distinctively different way. Their version of gesture syllabus is based on a popular tradition of vigorous plastic motion (in strong contrast to the restrained gestures) which combines elements of the rustic Amerindian style and the Indian classical mudra filtered through generations of ancient Roman pantomime. See figs. II/6–26

Gestural syllabus

The plastic evolution of high mammals from lemurs to apes clearly indicates that the mimetic expression of forelimbs improved more intensively than that of the head. The fact that the arms and hands played such a crucial functional role for tree-dwellers contributed to evolving the forelimbs as anatomically sophisticated instruments with the strong muscles, flexible joints and plastic facilities required for gestural communication and performance.

As we have seen, hominids were the intermediaries through whom these fundamental gestural abilities were passed from apes to humans in the evolutionary relay race. The basic types of hand/arm gesture can be divided into those involving the whole arm (the original indicative gestures), the more complex indicative and descriptive signals made by using the plastic range of the forearm and hand together; and finally, gestures made by the hand alone, its far richer motion capabilities providing a fully extended motion communication vocabulary.

Like the twelve major notes in music, the ten fingers of our hands provided a virtually inexhaustible source of plastic motion patterns. The main task was not how to find the next gestural combination using anything from one to five "talking" fingers, but how to create a logical, unambiguous and clearly understandable **sequence**.

fig. II/6   Motion Characteristics of Performing Genres

A. INDICATIVE genre of gesticulation

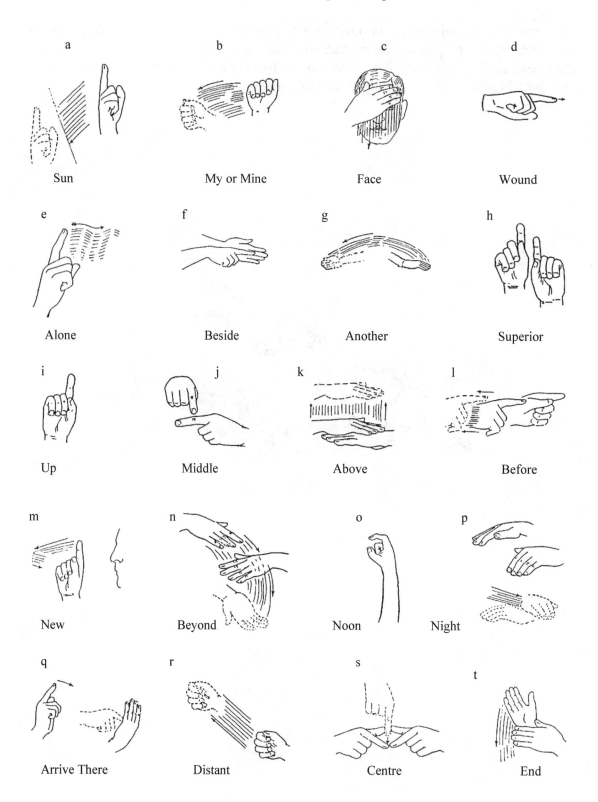

a	b	c	d
Sun	My or Mine	Face	Wound
e	f	g	h
Alone	Beside	Another	Superior
i	j	k	l
Up	Middle	Above	Before
m	n	o	p
New	Beyond	Noon	Night
q	r	s	t
Arrive There	Distant	Centre	End

fig. II/7   B. DESCRIPTIVE genre of gesticulation

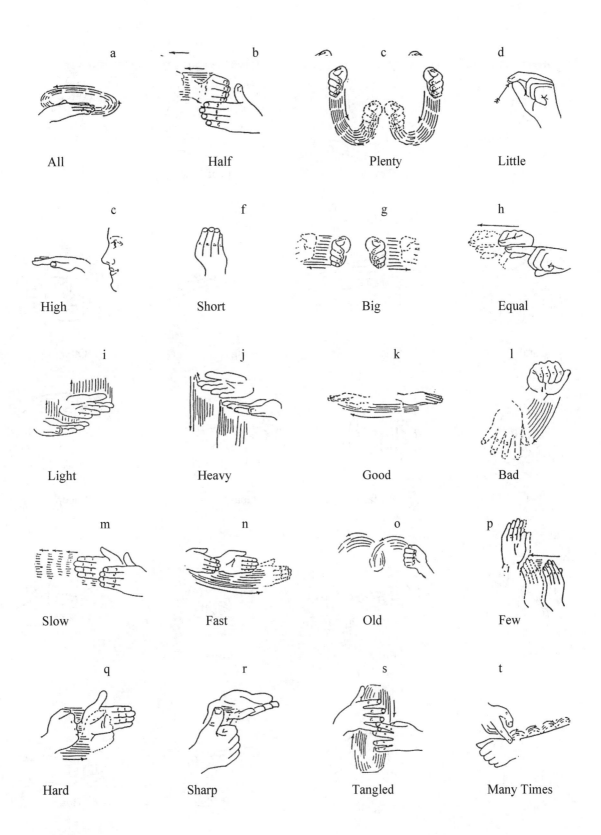

a	b	c	d
All	Half	Plenty	Little
e	f	g	h
High	Short	Big	Equal
i	j	k	l
Light	Heavy	Good	Bad
m	n	o	p
Slow	Fast	Old	Few
q	r	s	t
Hard	Sharp	Tangled	Many Times

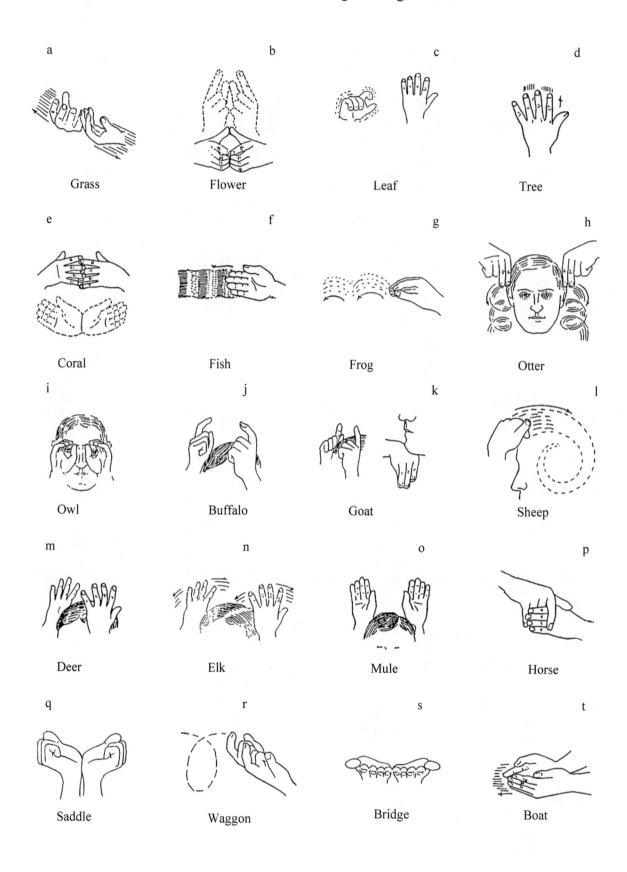

a   Grass

b   Flower

c   Leaf

d   Tree

e   Coral

f   Fish

g   Frog

h   Otter

i   Owl

j   Buffalo

k   Goat

l   Sheep

m   Deer

n   Elk

o   Mule

p   Horse

q   Saddle

r   Waggon

s   Bridge

t   Boat

D. CONNOTATIVE genre of gesticulation

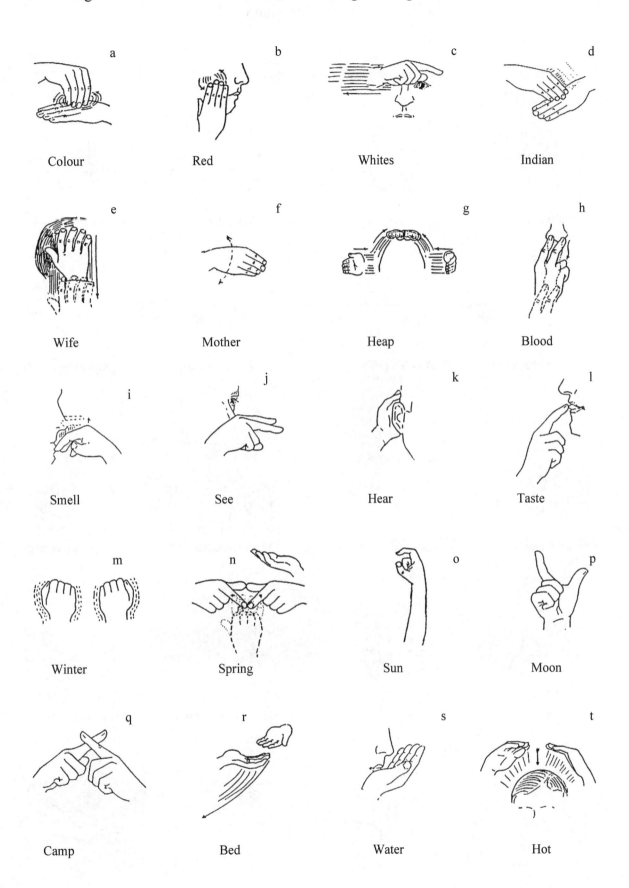

a — Colour

b — Red

c — Whites

d — Indian

e — Wife

f — Mother

g — Heap

h — Blood

i — Smell

j — See

k — Hear

l — Taste

m — Winter

n — Spring

o — Sun

p — Moon

q — Camp

r — Bed

s — Water

t — Hot

fig. II/10

E. FIGURATIVE genre of gesticulation
(Amerindian sign vocabulary)

a

Deaf (unruled)

b

Island (solitary)

c

Poor (stant)

d

Powder (unreliable)

e

Rope (commitment)

f

Awl (uniquely)

g

Wind (windbag)

h

Knife (ashamed)

i

Peak (show-off)

j

Laugh (distrust)

k

Tears (crocodile)

l

Recover (sunrise)

m

Canyon (limitation)

n

Beaver (spying)

o

Candle (uncertain)

p

Arrow (charge)

q

Cloud (darkness)

r

Bag (reticent))

s

Star (guide)

t

Tomahawk (finish)

F. SYMBOLIC genre of gesticulation
(Asian Indian sign vocabulary)

a	b	c	d	e
Supreme	Weakness	Worship	Truthfulness	Arts, Blessing

f	g	h	i	j
Tree Branches	Fruit, Egg…	Grass medicine	Village	Crocodile

k	l	m	n	o
Quarrel, Enemy	Progressive motion	Armour, Pillar	Arrow, Spear	Cleaning, Fighting

p	q	r	s	t
Breast, Beauty	Female Organ	Fertilization	Sexual Intercourse	Salutation

G. DEMONSTRATIVE genre of gesticulation

a — Grow

b — Fall (to)

c — Float

d — Fall (of water)

e — Walk

f — Miss

g — Swim

h — Dive

i — Break

j — Escape

k — Hide

l — Hang

m — Mingle

n — Paint

o — Distribute

p — Nose pierce

Q — Wrap

r — Sled

s — Strike

t — Depart

H. ILLUSTRATIVE genre of gesticulation

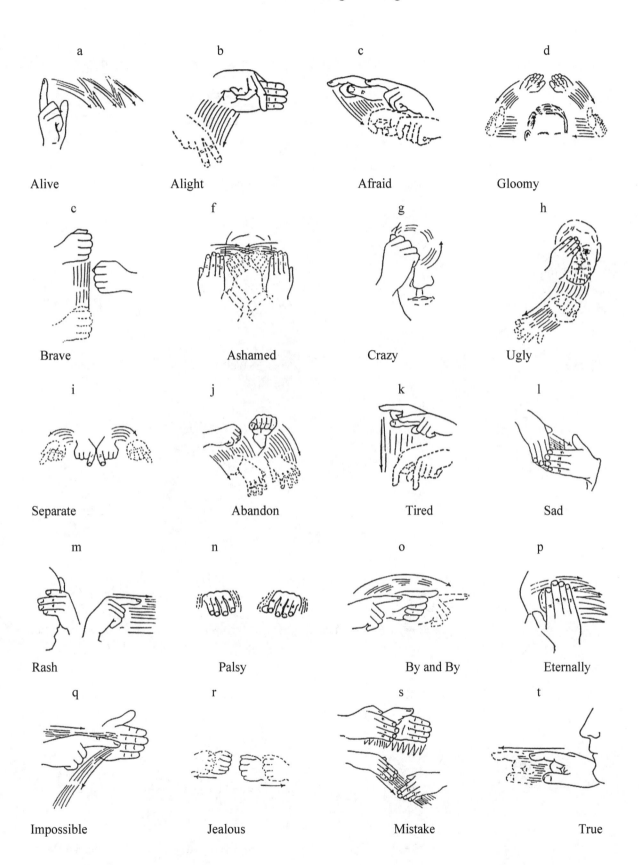

a	b	c	d
Alive	Alight	Afraid	Gloomy

c	f	g	h
Brave	Ashamed	Crazy	Ugly

i	j	k	l
Separate	Abandon	Tired	Sad

m	n	o	p
Rash	Palsy	By and By	Eternally

q	r	s	t
Impossible	Jealous	Mistake	True

I. INTRODUCTIVE genre of gesticulation

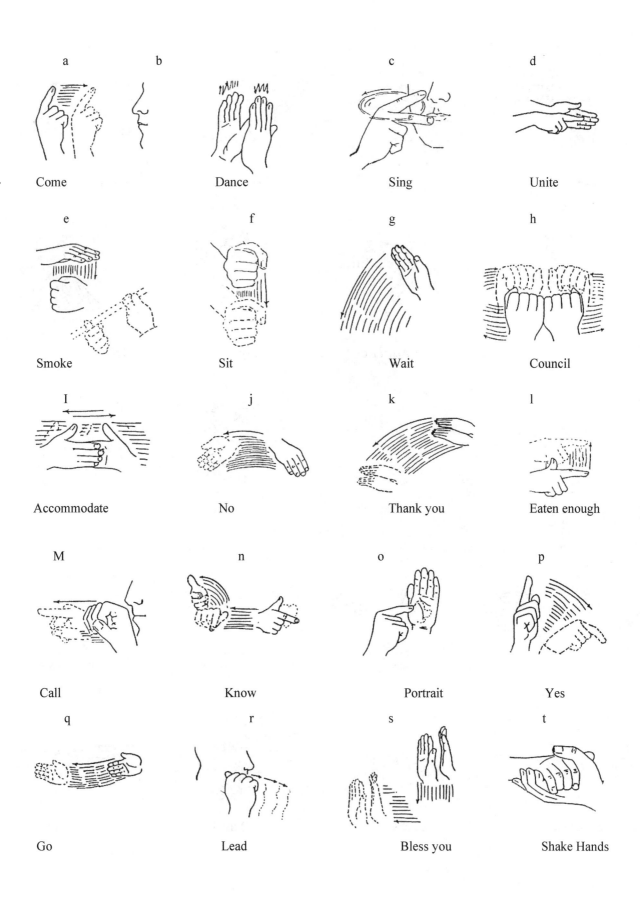

a	b	c	d
Come	Dance	Sing	Unite

e	f	g	h
Smoke	Sit	Wait	Council

I	j	k	l
Accommodate	No	Thank you	Eaten enough

M	n	o	p
Call	Know	Portrait	Yes

q	r	s	t
Go	Lead	Bless you	Shake Hands

J. INSTRUCTIVE genre of gesticulation

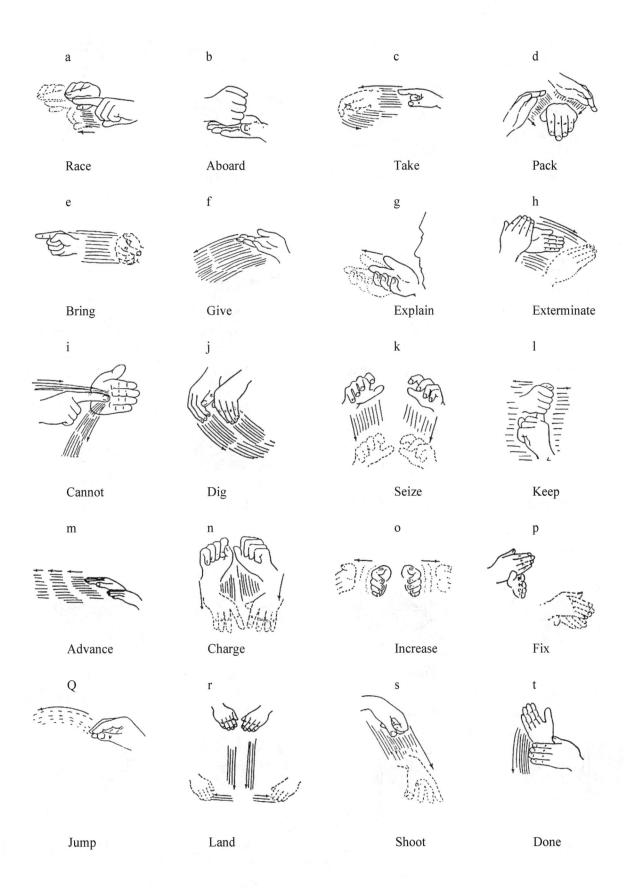

a	b	c	d
Race	Aboard	Take	Pack

e	f	g	h
Bring	Give	Explain	Exterminate

i	j	k	l
Cannot	Dig	Seize	Keep

m	n	o	p
Advance	Charge	Increase	Fix

Q	r	s	t
Jump	Land	Shoot	Done

K. INTERACTIVE genre of gesticulation

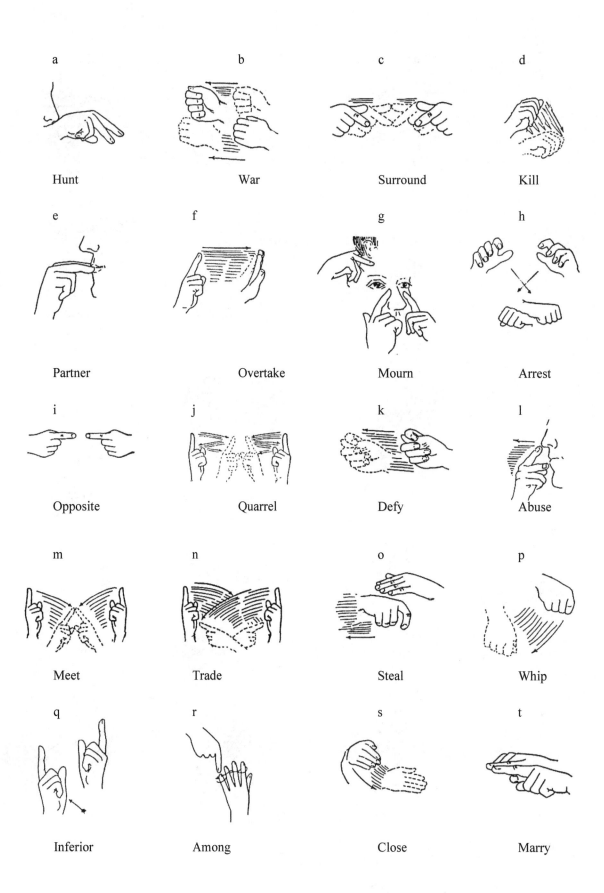

a	b	c	d
Hunt	War	Surround	Kill
e	f	g	h
Partner	Overtake	Mourn	Arrest
i	j	k	l
Opposite	Quarrel	Defy	Abuse
m	n	o	p
Meet	Trade	Steal	Whip
q	r	s	t
Inferior	Among	Close	Marry

L. TALKATIVE genre of gesticulation

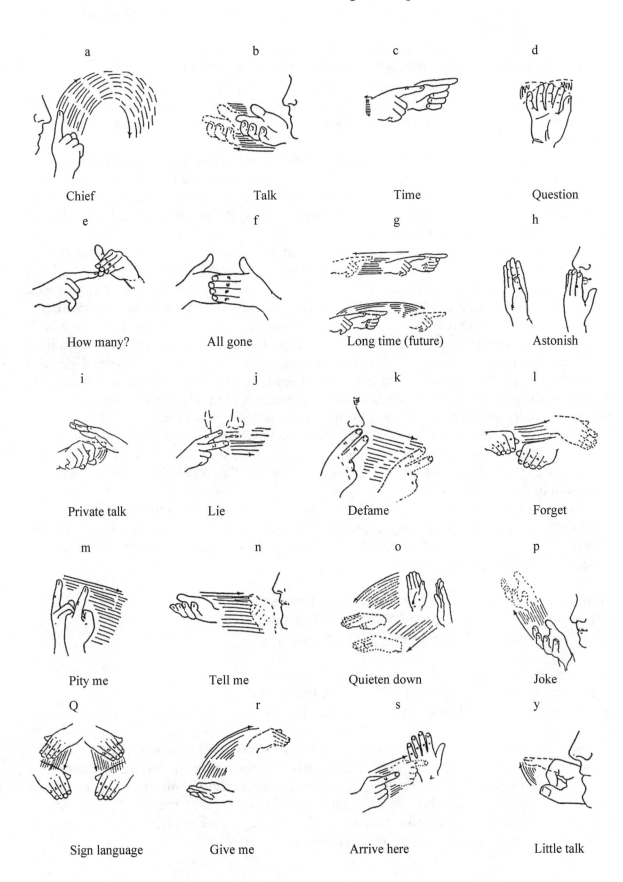

a

Chief

b

Talk

c

Time

d

Question

e

How many?

f

All gone

g

Long time (future)

h

Astonish

i

Private talk

j

Lie

k

Defame

l

Forget

m

Pity me

n

Tell me

o

Quieten down

p

Joke

Q

Sign language

r

Give me

s

Arrive here

y

Little talk

THE CLASSIFICATION OF ARM/HAND GESTURE

Systems of non-verbal communication by body language have been divided into three main categories including:

a) **Functional** gestures of mammals including apes and hominids

b) **Artificial** hand signs such as those devised for use by deaf-mutes

c) **Paralinguistic** body movements, usually accompanying speech

The first category is the main focus of this study, with *gesture* as the primal non-verbal communication tool originating at the dawn of evolution with insects and spiders (see Chapter I).

The second category involves a plastic syllabus of mainly conventional **hand signs** similar to notes in a music score, or Laban dance notations. Almost all are codified symbols unsuitable for use by primates, requiring special study and often containing many-layered or connotative readings of a single sign. Although such systems fulfil a need for artificial language, they lie outside our present scope.

The third category is concerned with involuntary personal emotional reactions rather than – gestures as such – what are termed **paralinguistic** arm and hand gestures, of the kind that we all use to accompany speech for reasons of emphasis. These subconscious motions have no specific meanings beyond the individual concerned, and can even be visually distracting

Speech often involves a mixture of functional mammalian gestures and instinctive body language in the popular sense of the term. When a speaker doubts the audience's interest in or understanding of a subject, he or she may introduce the first (Indicative) type of gestural vocabulary in his Paralanguage – but adding the third type of gesture does little or nothing to clarify meaning. A speaker who stops talking but continues to make the first type of gesture will be generally understood, but not if the third type is used in isolation.

The great pioneer anthropologists including John Bulwer, Darwin and Wilhelm Wundt left invaluable commentaries on the subject of gesture in works such as *Chirologia*, *The Expressions of Emotions* and *The Language of Gestures*. The following classification is an extension of these analyses.

Instead of Wundt's six main divisions with their potentially confusing multiplicity of subcategories, the following classification is divided into 12 categories based on the characteristics of the hominid communication function concerned, and in the chronological order of evolutionary development:

A. Mainly **static** (or involving a limited range of movement):

1. Indicative	2. Descriptive	3. Imitative
4. Connotative	5. Figurative	6. Symbolic

B. Mainly **dynamic** (or involving an extended range of movement):

7. Demonstrative	8. Illustrative	9. Introductory
10. Instructional	11. Interactive	12. Talkative

Because it can be confusing to attribute a certain gesture to a particular motion genre, each of these categories is characterised below in three ways: by the **type of questions** it responds to, by the **kind of subject** it refers to and by the plastic **motion tools** used. To classify a particular gesture, simply find the relevant type of question and subject to discover the preferred gestural vocabulary for expressing this reaction. Obviously, specifics will vary according to circumstances, culture and individuals.

Gestural execution and perception

Passive

INDICATIVE (fig. II/6)
Question: What? Who? Where? Which? When?
Subject: Place, direction, object, name, time of day
Motion: Hand pointing, touch by thumb/fingers or hand/arm

DESCRIPTIVE (fig. II/7)
Question: How big? How tall? How long? How much? How many?
How thick?
Subject: Quality, quantity, space, size, weight, colour, sex, age, race
Motion: Fixed sign, gestural motion, hand touch on body part

IMITATIVE (fig. II/8)
Question: What? Who? How?
Subject: Inanimate object, animate image, mobile substance, act, behaviour
Motion: Fixed sign, tactile hand/head sign, imagery motion archetype

CONNOTATIVE (fig. II/9)
Question: What? Who? When? Which? How? Why?
Subject: Scent, taste, sound, colour, phenomenon, relation, fauna, flora
    Sphere (aerial, aquatic, terrestrial, arboreal)
Motion: Tactile hand/head sign, imitative gesture, covert signal.

FIGURATIVE (fig. II/10)
Question: How come? In which way? What for? Why?
Subject: Metaphorical designation of characters, emotions, behaviour
Motion: Double-meaning motion signal, touch or imitative gesture.

SYMBOLIC (fig. II/11)
Question: What? Who? Where from? Why?
Subject: Animate objects, tools, conditions, feelings, spirituality, mind
Motion: Abstract imitative signs, polyvalent gestures, symbolic signals

Active

DEMONSTRATIVE (fig. II/12)
Question: Doing what? How?
Subject: Act, process, performance, function, projection,
    move, behaviour
Motion: Signalling, mime gesticulation, plastic performance

ILLUSTRATIVE (fig. II/13)
Question: What's the matter? Why? How come? What's wrong?
Are you OK?
Subject: Condition, feeling, state, characteristics, causality,
    emotion, mind
Motion: Performed gesture, mimetic sign, imitative signal

INTRODUCTORY (fig. II/14)

Question: Who are you? Where from? What brought you? Are you thirsty? Who's he?

Subject: Self presentation, acquaintance, hospitality, business, entertainment, recommendation

Motion: Mimetic dialogue, gesticulation interview, performing signal

INSTRUCTIVE (fig. II/15)

Question: What to do? Where to find? How to get? Why should I? May I help you? How to make it?

Subject: Information, coaching, testing, experimenting, helping

Motion: Signals, signs, gestural demonstration and comments

INTERACTIVE (fig. II/16)

Question: With whom? Why? Any option? Whose fault? What happens?

Subject: Conflict, opposition, stealing, fight, strategy, quarrel, trade, meet

Motion: Gesticulation duet, motion argument, insulting sign, dialogue drama, contest

TALKATIVE (fig. II/17)

Question: What? Who? Where? When? How? Why? Is it so? Which one? May I? In which way?

Subject: Introduction, information, presentation, demonstration, friendship

Motion: Gestural dialogue, conversation by motion phrases and sentences

MIMESIS REPERTOIRE OF GESTUROLOGY

Motion characteristics of performing genres

Fig. II/6–7   Indicative and descriptive genres of gesticulation.

Fig. II/8–9   Imitative and connotative genres of gesticulation.

Fig. II/10–11 Figurative and symbolic genres of gesticulation.

Fig. II/12–13 Demonstrative and illustrative genres of gesticulation.

Fig. II/14–15 Introductive and talkative genres of gesticulation.

Fig. II/16–17 Interactive and talkative = genres of gesticulation

Short gesticulatory sentences

By Amerindians in conversation phraseology of their original sign language.

Fig. II/24   Sign sentence of two–four individual gestural expressions.

Fig. II/25   Sign sentence of four–six individual gestural expressions.

Fig. II/26   Sign sentence of six–eight individual gestural expressions.

Pose/gestural alphabet of East Indian 'Bharata Natya'.

The body Karanas of postural performing repertoire.

Fig. II/20   Communicative sign/signals

Fig. II/20   Plastic mimicry – direct imitation

Fig. II/20   Plastic mimicry – connotative imitation.

Fig. II/21   Fixed motion of acting body.

Fig. II/21   Emotional expression by body parts.

Fig. II/21   Description genre of postural vocabulary.

Fig II/18   **Plastic motion articulation** of single handed gestures
Gesticulatory syllabus of Amerindians

I line: Closed hand (fist) or semi-open with tightly held and curved fingers.
II line: One or two open fingers of a partially closed hand, in motion.
III line: Tactual sign of finger-tips in semi-open and curved hand.
IV line: Open hand gestures, with semi-curved and joint fingers.
V line   Signs by fully open hand with drawn out and separate fingers.

Fig II/19   **Plastic motion articulation** of double handed gestures

I line: Closed or semi-open hands in joint identical plastic patterns.
II line: Tactile gestures by finger-tips of open hands in symmetry.
III line: Crossed sign of R. hand fingers over L. hand, firm on outside.
IV line: Synchronised motions of both hands in parallel or separate ways.
V line   Single or double gestures by R. or both hands in motion sequence.

Fig II/20   **Plastic motion articulation** of single handed gestures
Gesticulatory syllabus of Asian Indians

I-II line: Closed or semi-open hand with drawn-up fingers in combination.
III-IV line: Tactile gestures of finger-tips in semi-curved or full open hand.
V line   Imitative gestures by open or curved hand, with fingers together.

Fig II/21   **Plastic motion articulation** of double handed gestures

I-II line: Tightly joined hands in a symmetrical or contrapuntal pattern.
III line: Tactile gestures by horizontal or vertical opposite hands.
IV line: Imitative images by crossed hands in a mirror reflection design.
V line   Cross-arm position, with symbolic sign by open and curved hands.

Fig II/22   **Plastic motion articulation** of single handed gestures.
Gesticulatory syllabus of Southern Europeans.

I line: Figurative signs by closed fist of slightly opened hand.
II line: Closed or semi-open hand, with certain fingers drawn out.
III line: Open and curved hand, with separate or spread out fingers.
IV line: Tactual motion by finger-tip in semi-opened or curved hand.
V line   Tactile motion gestures with move of hand to hand in action.

Fig II/23   **Plastic motion articulation** of single handed gestures.

I line: Hand in hand join signs, with crossed and tightened fingers.
II line: Tactual signs by open hands drawn out parallel fingers.
III line: Open and curved hands in a symmetrical motion reflection.
IV line: Tactile signals by finger-tips of one acting, other hand resting.
V line   Joint motion by two hands, both acting individually.

Fig II/9   **Connotative gestures** by single handed motion.
Performing Synthesis of hand signs and facial mimicry.

I line: Figurative hand-sign with fingers held together under the face.
II line: Active hand/arm signals with open fingers in various patterns.
III line: Connotative gestural expression in vigorous manner.

Fig II/10   **Figurative signs** by single or double-handed motion.

I line: Whirling motion semi-open hand in front of face.
II line: Tactual signals by various fingers and part of the face.
III line: Gestural motions by two acting hands touching each other.
IV line: Dramatic illustrative gestures by double-handed performance.

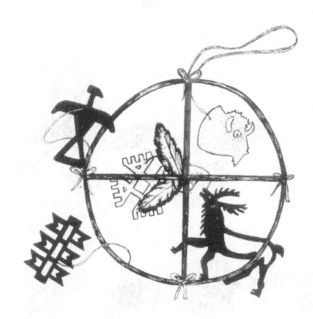

fig. II/18

Gesticulary Syllabus of Amerindians
A. Plastic motion articulation of single-handed gestures

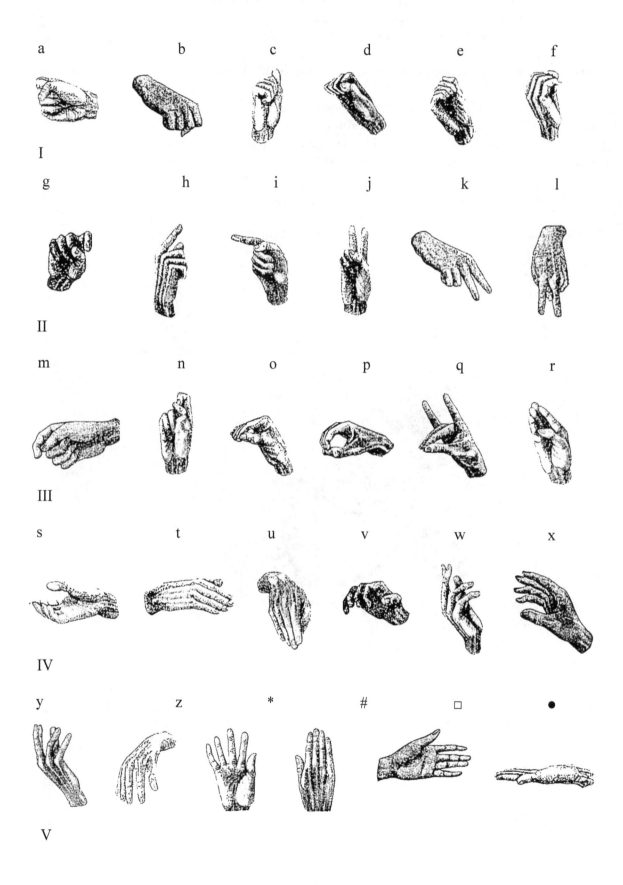

fig. II/19

B. Plastic motion articulation of double-handed gestures

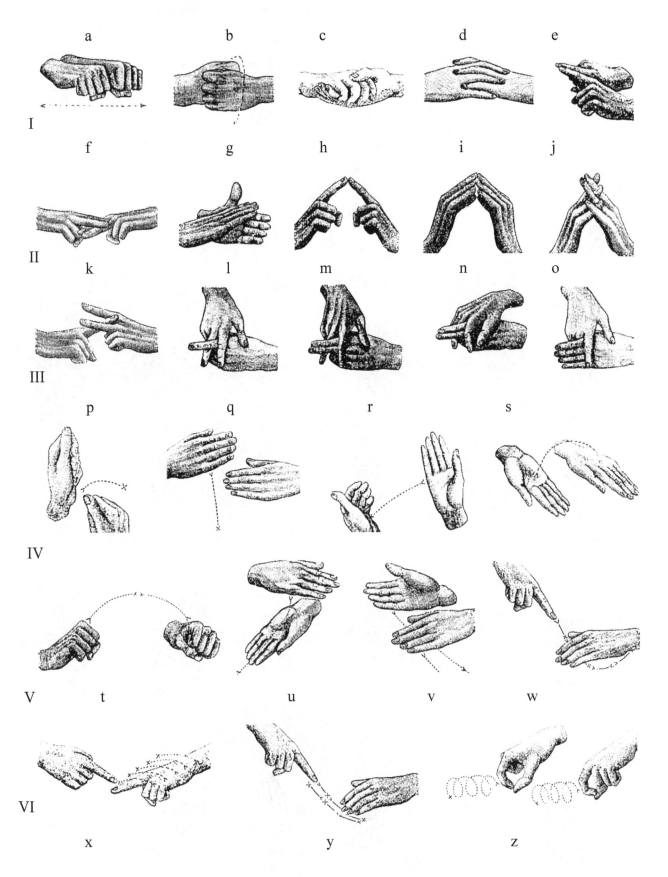

fig. II/20   Gesticulary Syllabus of Asian Indians
A. Plastic motion articulation of single-handed gestures

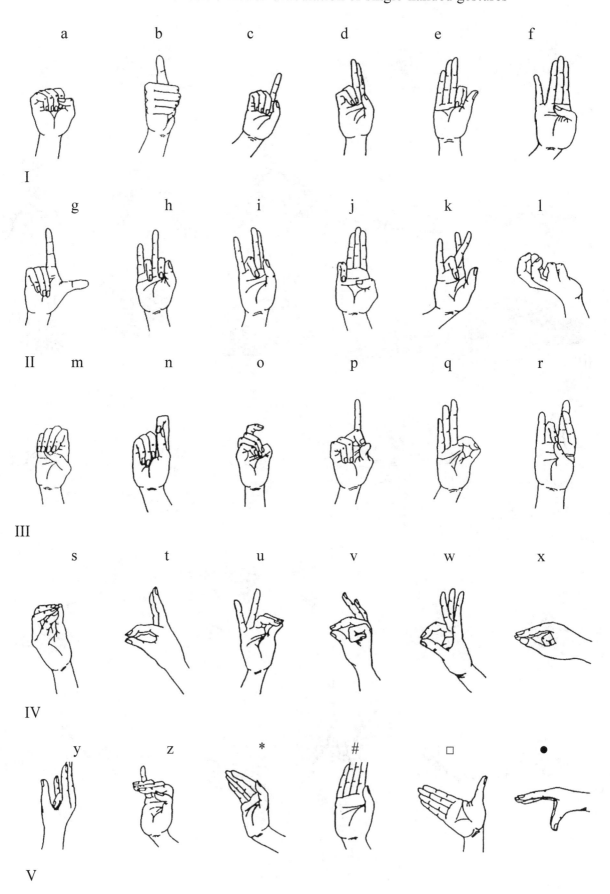

fig. II/21
B. Plastic motion articulation of double-handed gestures
Source: K Rao. *Dictionary of Bharata Natya*, 1980

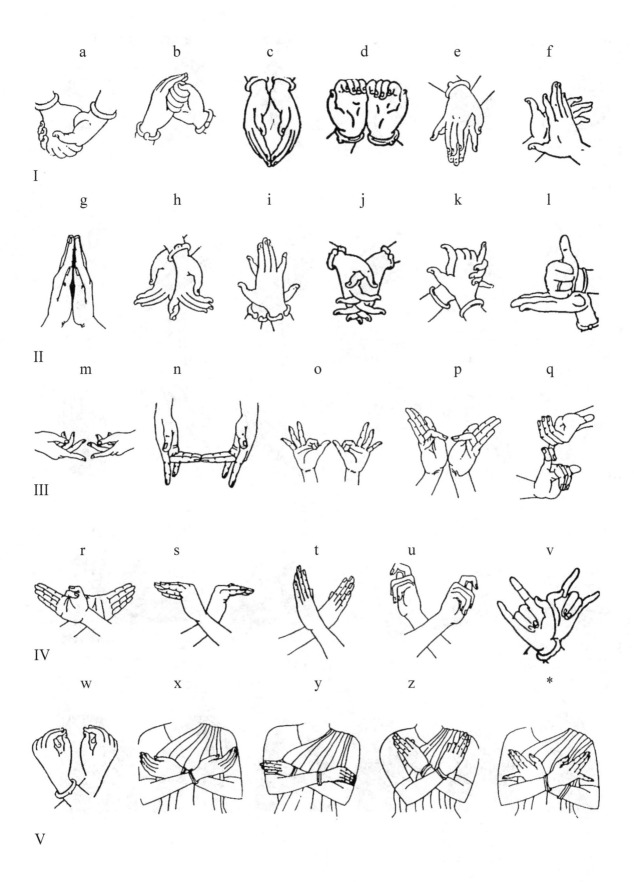

fig. II/22   Gesticulary Syllabus of Southern Europeans
A. Plastic motion articulation of single-handed gestures

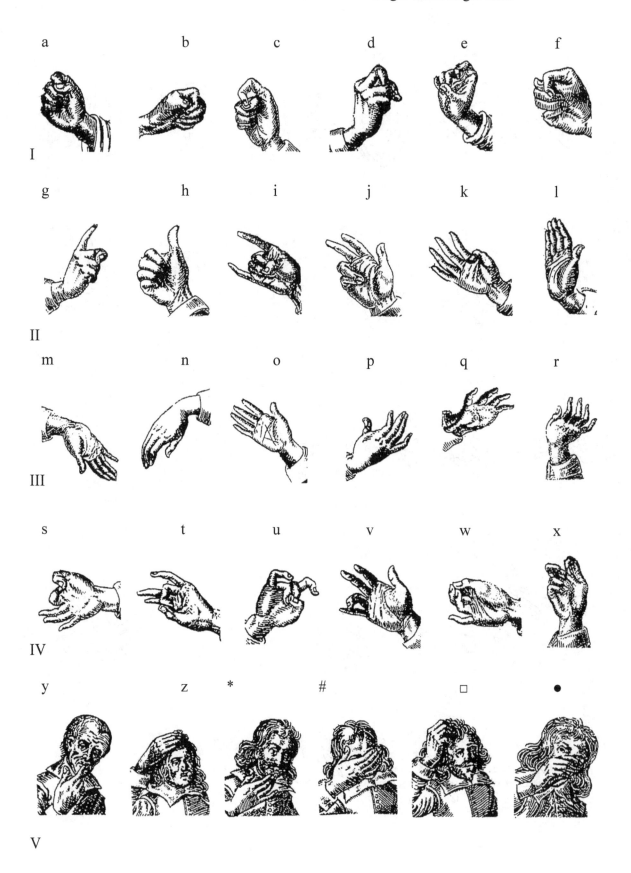

B. Plastic motion articulation of double-handed gestures

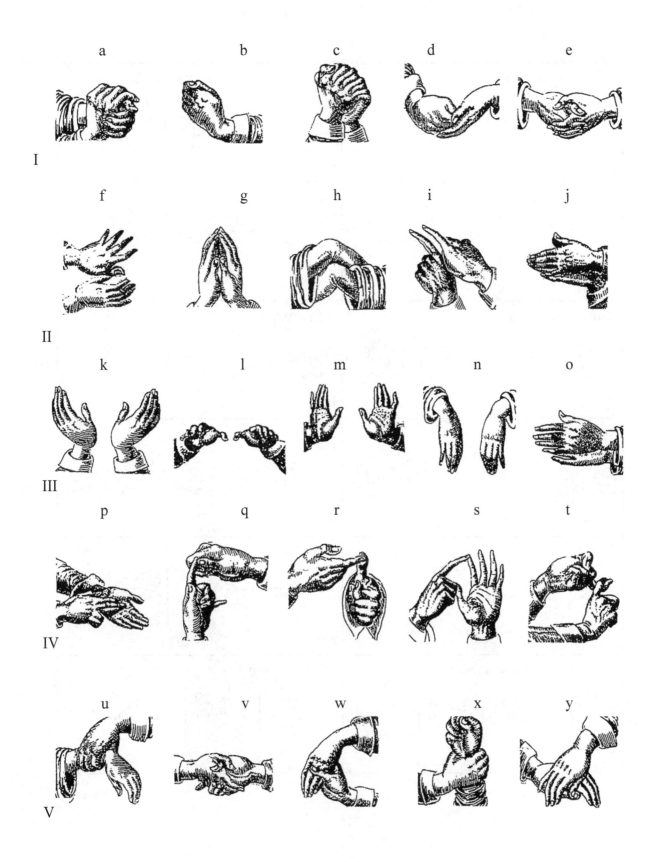

fig. II/24

Short Gesticulatory Sentences by Amerindians
A. Sign Sentence of two-four individual gesturing expressions

What is your name?	*I am hungry and want something to eat.*
a	b

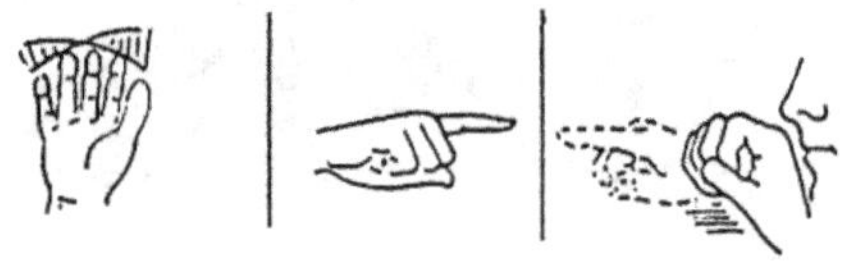

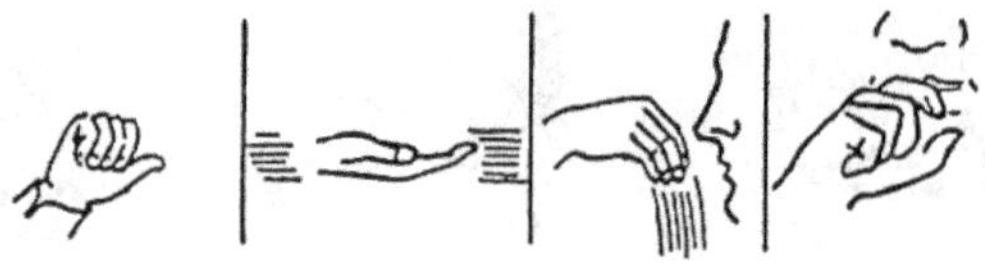

Where is your home?	*I am going home.*
c	d

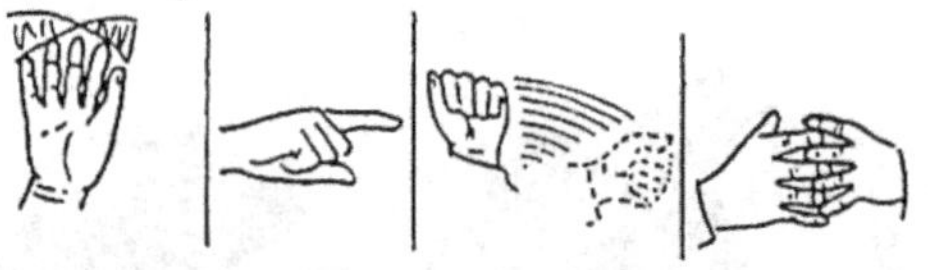

How old are you?	*I feel very sad.*
e	f

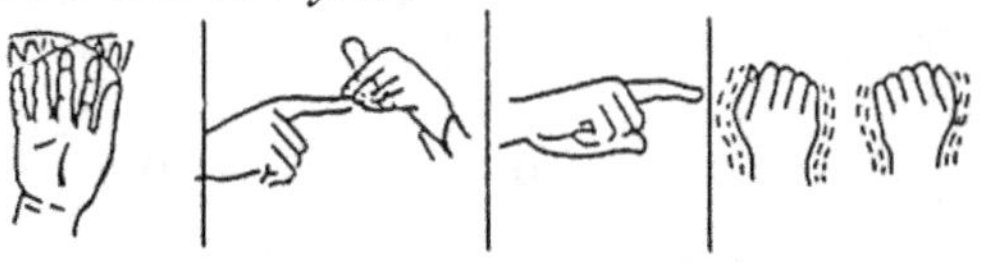

The man became very old.	*I have not seen you for a long time.*
g	h

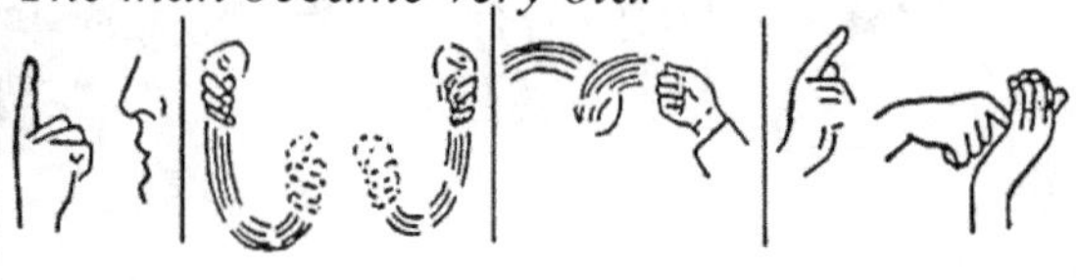

Where do you live?	*I live here.*
i	j

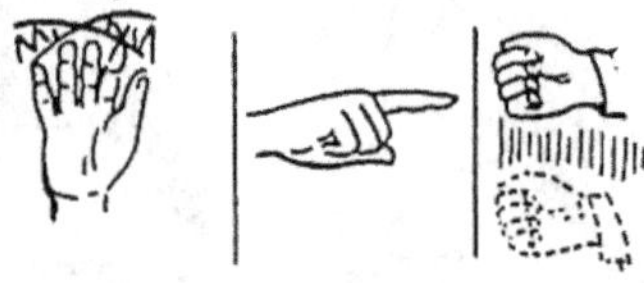

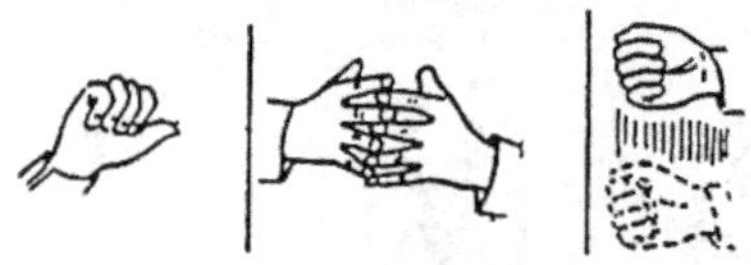

Have you had your supper? 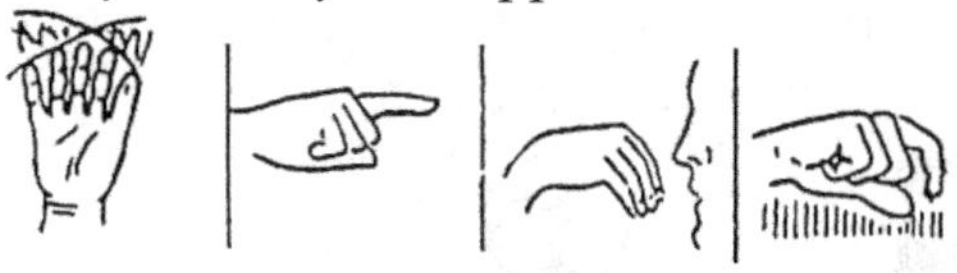	*Where is your horse?* 
k	l

B. Sign Sentence of four-six individual gesturing expressions

Where are you going today?	*I am going to make camp.*
a	b
What do you do at camp?	*I build a fire.*
c	d
I make coffee.	*I set up a tent.*
e	f
I chop wood.	*I make supper.*
g	h
I go walking.	*I catch fish.*
i	j
I go swimming.	*I go hunting.*
k	l
I see deer, bear, wolf.	*I have a good time.*
m	n

C. Sign Sentence of six-eight individual gesturing expressions

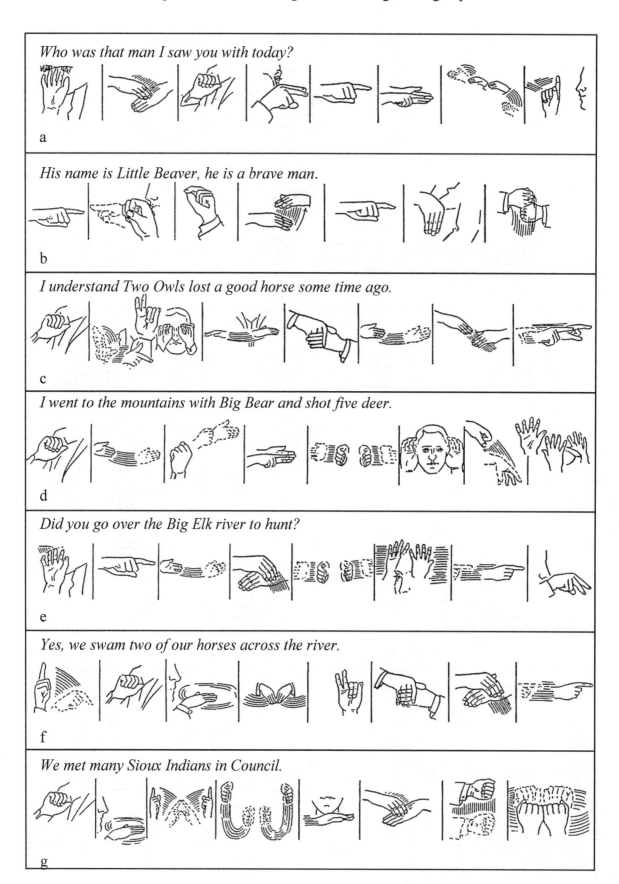

Who was that man I saw you with today?

a

His name is Little Beaver, he is a brave man.

b

I understand Two Owls lost a good horse some time ago.

c

I went to the mountains with Big Bear and shot five deer.

d

Did you go over the Big Elk river to hunt?

e

Yes, we swam two of our horses across the river.

f

We met many Sioux Indians in Council.

g

GESTURAL VOCABULARY

All the expressive gestures listed above are motivated by particular objects, circumstances, feelings or thoughts, either representationally or in an abstract/symbolic way. They can be seen as falling into four separate groups: **Defining. Designating, Performing, Interrelating**.

DEFINING gestures comprise two genres, the indicative and descriptive. As can be seen from figure II/6–7, the questions these two closely related genres answer are quite different.

Indicative gestures point to the object based on its actual or intended location, or the direction to a particular destination, or relate to the time in terms of the position of the sun or moon in the sky, and so on.

Descriptive gestures portray an object, action or substance, together with its quality and quantity and individual characteristics. As primary forms of gesture using a limited vocabulary of one or two-hand motions, both are expressed by the same type of straightforward (as opposed to connotative) signals.

DESIGNATING gestures evolved from the Indicative/Descriptive genres along with other types of PERFORMED gestures, with **Imitative, Connotative, Figurative** and **Symbolic** genres representing four successive stages of conveying meaning. These four new genres were largely based on new techniques of imitating both animate and inanimate objects.

Imitative gestures are direct mimetic reproductions of the shape, emotion, action or behaviour in question, as close as possible to the original characteristics. Although executed by motions of the whole body, we concentrate here on the upper extremities.

The advent of **Connotative** gestures was a big step forward in the evolution of body language. Instead of directly imitating a plastic motion as before, these gestures represent only the essence of a subject, in a kind of **gestural shorthand** that captures its most distinctive feature in a way that is easily understood (*see figure II/9*). As the first step towards artistic performance in the modern sense, this principle paved the way for future ritual mythic pantomime and pictographic communication.

Figurative gestures further widened the imaginative scope by introducing metaphorical representation through plastic motion – a double meaning, in other words, that alludes to the object's inner characteristics and motivation as well as its external appearance. This conceptual leap forward required highly skilled body language technique.

The **Symbolic** genre is the highest form of gesture in which hand/arm motions summarise certain characteristics or meanings into abstract plastic signs made by the fingers and thumbs, most of which would only be understood within the particular tribe. These vocabularies of Symbolic *gesture* are among the great cultural monuments of ancient and prehistoric times.

PERFORMING gestures evolved from the earlier Defining and Designating forms. The latter already showed individual characteristics when Indicative and Descriptive messages were conveyed by hand *movements*. These mimetic plastic motion characterisations were extensively developed on the basis of Imitative gestures, when hunters performed ritual images under formal conditions. The image acted out in such sacred ceremonies prompted the development of gestures for performance.

Demonstrative gestures evolved at the same time as Imitative ones, with the representation of moving images. Both were performed about a variety of subjects (real and imaginary) using similar motions to characterise the actions, emotions and behaviour concerned. Demonstrative gesture motions evolved as expressive instruments on the basis of purely Descriptive ones.

Illustrative gestures are the most technically sophisticated of all, and combined elements of every preceding genre to represent abstract emotional and physical states such as *threatening, starvation, shame, fatigue, courage, depression, urgency* and so on. The difficulties of conveying such concepts through motion posed a considerable challenge to the imagination, understanding, artistic vision and interpretative skills of those who created these gestures. As the highest form of body linguistics, this illustrative genre laid the foundation for the **gestural phraseology** which eventually opened up the possibilities of plastic motion *conversation*.

INTERRELATING gestural communication involved creating plastic motion conversations between two or more individuals, emphasising the intimate connection between motion performance and social relationships. The Introductory, Instructive, Interactive and Talkative genres represent the final stages of gestural evolution before and during the emergence of spoken language. All four genres developed alongside each other, using similar types of gesture, the differences between each category often being indistinct. However, all were attempts to develop an extended motion dialogue, rather than a simple exchange of signals.

Figure 14–17 below shows how certain gestural sentences develop from 'short' into planned, consequential 'long' trains of thoughts as per Darwin's theory.

Introductory body language gestures are the basic motion vocabulary for personal introduction and making someone's acquaintance. They include signs for salutations, interrogative and affirmative *gestures, signals* for authorising or forbidding and so on. They usually involved single arm/hand motions rather than long sentences, accompanied by facial mimicry with corresponding eye expressions. In line with one of the main principles of an animal behaviour – the less attention one draws to one's self, the less the potential for danger – this limited vocabulary was the result of having to be perpetually vigilant, as well as the imperative to avoid misreading the initial messages of others.

Instructional gestures had the widest scope of subject matter of all, and included the Descriptive, Imitative, Demonstrative and Illustrative motion vocabularies.

Gestural communication using the forelimbs was essential to the survival of many animal species from insects to hominids, so these motions had to begin being taught from very soon after birth. Some were genetically acquired; others learned from parents and elders; the final stage was to study the local gestural vocabulary from coaches. The only way our ancestors could hope to pass on their body language to future generations was through practical initiation and demonstrations that had to be copied and endlessly practised. The motion phrases involved tended to be short, reflecting the pupils' capacities. This tuition process was used for all new gestures; only much later, when the size of the motion vocabulary massively increased with the emergence of ritual pantomime did the shaman set about developing special syllabic techniques for teaching gesture.

Interactive gestures, as you would expect, involve a relationship between two individuals. The huge range of functional, social, sexual, spiritual and domestic interactions, whether positive or negative, truthful or deceptive, involved an enormous gestural vocabulary.

These meanings were often more truthfully conveyed by accompanying gestures than vocalisation. Though attempts can be made to disguise inner feeling with deliberately deceptive head/facial signals, we nearly always intuitively sense dishonest behaviour through any gestural fog.

Survival pressures taught our ancestors to be permanently alert in all such interactions. Although a fight can easily be provoked with a single **insulting gesture**, any amount of **pacifying gestures** are usually insufficient to stop one that is already taking place, and it was therefore in the interests of most animals to use plastic **warning signals** to avoid unnecessary conflict.

Many gestures were universal for hominids' everyday activities, such as collective food gathering, initiation, courtship, nursing, sacred ceremonies, entertainment and so on, but some were highly specific. Individuals learned from experience how to use these sentimental or dramatic gestures in their everyday social interactions.

Talkative gestures provided the linguistic bridge between individual motion signs and **gestural sentences**. Whereas all previous plastic motion signals involved a single gesture using one or two forelimbs to convey one or more similar meanings, Talkative gestures used a single motion sign to include several independent components whose significance was often unrelated, as in figure II/17: "all gone" = gone (disappeared) + all (not one or more but all); "Long time past"= time (period) + long (not short) + past (not present nor future).

Correctly interpreting these gestural phrases of 'short train thoughts' was essentially unproblematic, provided they accorded with the **local motion dialect**. However, the next step in gestural evolution led to the sentence consisting of three or more consecutive motions within a single plastic composition – and in the process, an even higher level of motion communication.

PERFORMING CONDITIONS and THEMATIC REPERTOIRE

- Clear, accurate articulation of the fingers and thumbs
- One or two-hand gesture performance
- Only hand/fingers syllabus or full-arm gestures
- Motionless (fixed) arm signals, or demonstrative motion
- Calligraphic clarity of gesture and correct finger spelling
- Bare-handed signs or gestures implemented by various accessories
- Free motion patterns or touching the hand on other body parts
- Placing the hand for greater clarity
- Noiseless or audible plastic signals (*clap, snap, click, bang, tap, slap*)
- Gestures in unison in a group manifestation or ceremony
- Sequential rhythm with intervals
- Plastic symbol with multiple meanings
- Natural functional or artificial forms of gesticulation
- Original plastic sign or the tribe motion dialect
- Motion phrases and sentences with syncretic sign dialogue
- Mode of gestural motion and idiomatic expression
- Synonymous choice and syntactic order of talking signs/gestures
- Motion sequential leitmotif or plastic eclecticism in a gestural sentence
- Logical gesticulatory phrase, expressing demand or proposition
- Narrative gesturing monologue, or conversational mimetic dialogue
- Interrogative or affirmative, authorising or forbidding signals
- Menacing or defensive signs; friendly or hostile gesticulation
- Imperative or supplicating signals; sympathising or insulting gestures

Conversation through gestural sentences

The evolution of body language reached its peak when the brains of our ancestors had developed sufficiently to be able to handle 'long trains of thoughts'. The primacy of facial mimicry in communications never lost its value for expressive purposes, even today.

In the beginning, the mimetic culture of hominids had developed in two distinct ways: head **motion signals** with **grimaces**, followed by **gestures** with the arms, hands and fingers.

As with all other primates, our female forebears mainly used head/facial signals because their arms and hands were usually too occupied with functional tasks. As males often donned animal masks during their hunting forays and the ritual preparations for them, they tended to use their forelimbs more extensively for everyday communications – but once the hunters stopped using the heavy masks, facial expressions tended to predominate. Women never wore masks at all (*see Chapter III*).

Over the long process involved in developing greater mental concentration, co-ordination and balance as well as anatomical adaptations, hominids eventually learned to communicate with double plastic motions using several body parts.

COMBINING FACIAL MIMICRY WITH FORELIMB GESTURES

We inherited a great cultural legacy of body language from our ancestors in the form of facial grimaces and arm/hand gestures which have been refined over the last 100,000 years or so into a complete communications system.

Surprisingly, not all ancient civilisations used both forms. Native American peoples, for example, perfected their own arm and hand gestures, but hardly ever used facial mimicry, whereas peoples of the Indian subcontinent developed facial grimaces into a fine art. Later on, the Southern Europeans synthesised both elements in the highly sophisticated mimetic culture of Classical pantomime.

EXAMPLES OF ARM/HAND GESTURAL DIALOGUE

Short, friendly conversations between Native Americans: Fig, II/24

1.) Single-hand phrase of three individual signs:

What's your name?	I haven't seen you for ages
Have you eaten?	I'm hungry and want to eat

2.) Longer two-handed conversation with four motion signs:

Where are you going today?	I'm going to make camp
What do you do at camp?	I have a good time

Southern European quarrel using single gestures: Fig II/22

1.) One-handed gestures, with free or tactile motion signal

On the other hand	He is cunning
Come down please	Shut up!
Has he changed his mind?	He's dead

2.) Two arms in free motion with tactile gestures

Among all these people	Good heavens!
Let's forget about it	He's so stubborn
They are enemies	Well, what joy!

Extended epic phrasing of Indian classical mythology
Five or more gestures, accompanied by facial mimicry and body postures: (fig. II/25)

GESTURAL SYNTAX
The syntax of ancient Amerindian gestural sentences (fig. II/24) reveals certain common linguistic components:

1. All questioning gestures (what? who? when? where? how?) have a particular plastic pattern of an *open* hand held vertically, with fully *splayed* fingers in a vibrating motion.
2. Pronouns (I, you, he/she, we, they) are expressed by *pointing* the thumb or index finger to the person concerned
3. Many functions and actions are indicated by two auxiliary verb signs meaning 'to do' and 'to go'; gestures for 'to be' and 'to have' appeared somewhat later.

SUMMARY

Although this simple system required little experience to decipher as it was based mainly on realistic plastic motion signals, it became the basic vocabulary of many types of gestural language across the northern hemisphere. Naturally, when vocalisation assumed priority in hominid communications, the use of body language in everyday life diminished – but the art of gesture continued to be enthusiastically developed for the purposes of ritual performance.

Various forms and dialects of body language can still be seen in use today by the indigenous peoples of Africa, South America, Asia and Australasia. The **gestural syllabus** was the mainstay of ancient pantomime from the rituals of Africa, via classical Greece and Rome, right up to the Baroque ballet repertoire. The rich cultures of Asia and the Far East have preserved their gestural heritage in a pure form, with highly sophisticated body motion plasticity. We can only hope that one day the ancient secrets of classical oriental gesture will be translated for wider consumption.

When a shaman and his assistants practised mimetic routines during early hunting rituals, they sought new, easily understandable plastic motion signals and gestures that would lead their audience through a mythical scenario. There was a particular need for a plastic representation of the so called 'absent personage', and this drove the shaman's team to explore the communication potential of **mimicry** and **gesture**.

The discovery of a simple body language motif that could express the essence of an animate or inanimate object marked a turning point in this search. Figures II/24–26 illustrate a few such gestures in the form of imitative hand signs touching head and shoulder to indicate the totem image of certain animals, substances or natural phenomena.

Right from the beginning of gestural evolution, these signs represented the most familiar details of an animal's appearance or behaviour – its skull shape, horn, trunk, muzzle, ears, beak, neck, tusk, teeth or tongue. Such characteristics were not only a description of the animal itself, but also the shorthand identity of a totem's image, often adapted as a family name of the clan, or sometimes even as the name of an individual.

fig. II/27   Performing Synthesis of hand sign and facial mimicry

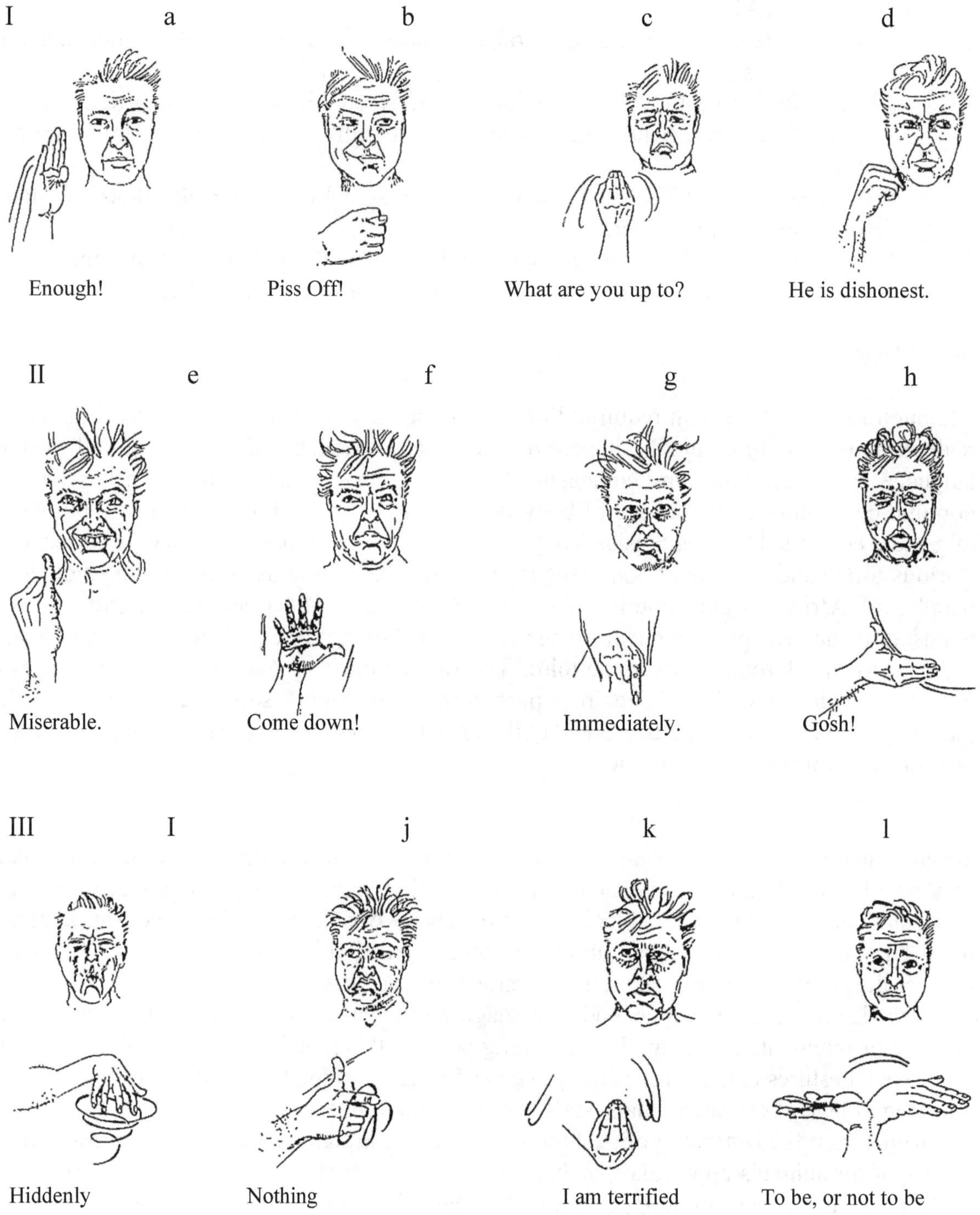

I   a   b   c   d

Enough!   Piss Off!   What are you up to?   He is dishonest.

II   e   f   g   h

Miserable.   Come down!   Immediately.   Gosh!

III   I   j   k   l

Hiddenly   Nothing   I am terrified   To be, or not to be

Source: Ethographic museum – 'Rustic Mime/Gesturing code in Napoles'.

fig. II/28

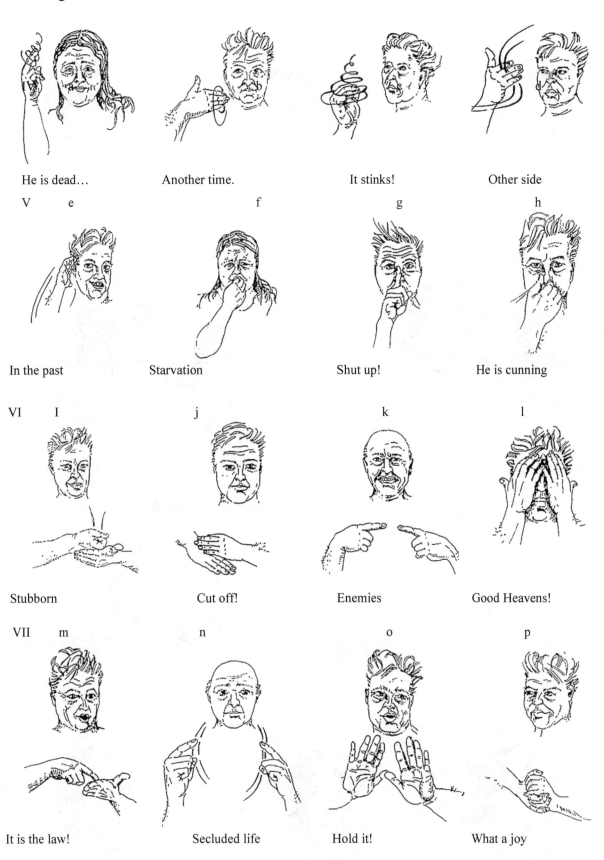

He is dead…	Another time.	It stinks!	Other side
V e	f	g	h
In the past	Starvation	Shut up!	He is cunning
VI I	j	k	l
Stubborn	Cut off!	Enemies	Good Heavens!
VII m	n	o	p
It is the law!	Secluded life	Hold it!	What a joy

fig. II/29

Tactile Motion Signs by hand with part of the head

a

Fatigue

b

Rejection

c

Silence

d

Stupid

e

Teasing

f

Deception

g

Astuteness

h

Disappointment

I

Beauty

j

Justice

COMMUNICATING WITH HIND LIMBS

No consideration of the role of the **legs** and **feet** can avoid the central issue of the evolutionary transition from four legs to two. The answers are often contradictory or confusing. Despite the many advances in the study of anthropology, kinesiology and the evolution of human anatomy, the fundamental questions remain:

What forced apes to become bipedal?

How exactly did the simian body come to be restructured?

Where, when and what were the environmental conditions that gave rise to such a phenomenon?

We simply don't know for sure – but we can make an informed guess. In this study of the anthropology of motion, we identify some of the crucial evolutionary turning points, of which the transition to bipedal stature is one of the most obvious. However, the various hypotheses advanced over the last 200 years all have weaknesses in one way or another:

a) Apes became ground-dwellers because of shortage of food in the trees'. If this is so, how come so many arboreal primates still find enough sustenance in the tree canopy 30 million years later, in a far safer environment than on the ground, where they face more predators and other potential dangers?

b) 'Standing upright, Homo Erectus could see much further to locate prey and other food sources'. Although this is self-evidently true, so is the fact that by doing so, Homo Erectus also made himself far more easily visible to predators.

c) 'Anthropoids adopted the vertical posture in order to reduce their exposure to the heat of the sun'. How then to explain the thousands of other equatorial quadruped species with even larger horizontal surface areas that have managed to survive 300 million years under these conditions?

d) 'The bipedal stance freed the arms to use tools'. Also true – but along with more productive tool use, the arms were also freed for use as lethal weapons, for religious observance, economic gain and sheer entertainment (not to mention more ignoble motives and actions).

In our view, none of these factors on its own provides sufficient motivation for the wholesale reshaping of the ape's body. On the contrary, it is more probable that most are the consequences of the transition, rather than the cause.

Look again at the twists and turns of the evolutionary path, particularly the other species with bipedal facilities: insects like the locust; amphibians like the frog; reptiles like the wonder gecko; the birds that hunt in marshlands on a single leg; mammals like the kangaroo, bear and lemur. Since all of these species were able partially or completely to balance their bodies on two hind limbs long before apes, factors like food shortage, solar radiation and brain size seem wholly inadequate explanations of this fundamental change.

The advantages of the biped stance are incontrovertible. Just as a two-wheeled vehicle is more agile than a four-wheeled one, the reduced weight and friction allows higher speeds, improved balance and greater manoeuvrability in all functional motions:

- A lizard tries vainly to catch a frog, which sails over the head of its confused predator with a single *leap* of its strong hind legs.

- A cheetah, one of the fastest animals, chases an antelope, which evades capture by *leaping* in a zigzag pattern.

- Though normally quadrupeds, bears always *rise* up on their hind limbs when threatening or fighting other bears.
- Modern dancers *turn* a dozen *pirouettes* on one foot, or some sixty-four *fouttées* on tiptoe.
- Just as cars cannot match the superior balance and agility of motorcycles, the single-wheeled barrow was chosen in ancient times for its greater manoeuvrability.
- The low friction of a single point support allows a child's top to *spin* for a long time.

These few examples illustrate a plausible reason for the evolution of the bipedal posture in apes: a survival adaptation in the face of a substantial change in the external environment. To survive it, they needed far greater **mobility** and faster **reactions**, better **balance** and coordination and **lighter**, more **stable** bodies. These and many other life-enhancing benefits of the bipedal posture resulted exclusively from the plastic reconstruction of the entire body shape at a critical stage in our ancestors' evolution.

The inability of bipedal dinosaurs and other prehistoric species to adapt in other ways to this sudden and radical environmental change resulted in their extinction. Some species nevertheless managed to adapt sufficiently to the new conditions to survive this environmental disaster, perhaps helped by favourable local circumstances.

Whatever form the cataclysm took, it proved a powerful stimulus for the selective evolution of external adaptations. It also accelerated the cerebral development of apes by bombarding their consciousness with unprecedented experiences, both positive and negative. This literally mind-expanding process of adjusting to the new realities – in effect, relearning the very nature of existence on the planet – lasted millions of years until the brain was reprogrammed to respond appropriately.

The main tools of communication during this period were of course plastic gestures of the muzzle, head and body – especially as the newly acquired upright stance now allowed unlimited gestural freedom to the arms and hands.

Leg and foot motions are mainly concerned with progression from one place to another. Like that of the arm/hand, the plastic motion repertoire can be divided into the Instinctively Functional and the Consciously Performed.

<u>Instinctive</u> Functional hind limb repertoire

This category includes five complementary dual genres: *supporting and suspending, climbing and descending, crawling and swimming, walking and running, and leaping and diving.*
- *Supporting* motions control the balance and coordination of the upright body, with one or both legs on the ground or any other object; *suspending* motions control the same functions when the body is *hanging* by *gripping* with the foot or hand, or *bending* the knee or elbow.
- *Climbing* and *descending* involve alternating motions of the fore and hind limbs and *gripping* by the feet.
- *Crawling* and *swimming* motions of limbed animals involve alternately *stretching out* and *contracting* the limbs.
- *Walking* and *running* shift the body weight from one foot to the other in rapid succession, changing the balance accordingly.
- *Leaping* and *diving* motions involve *thrusting* the body upwards or forwards by one or both hind limbs and *landing* after the trajectory on one or both feet, or *kicking* off a solid surface to project the body downwards head first.

Supporting

One of the more important aspects of boys' initiation was the physical training routine to improve *balancing* on one leg. Using branches or large stones as props, the initiate had to *hop* repeatedly on the same foot from one rock to the next or from branch to branch, increasing his speed or carrying loads of ever increasing weight, all in the guise of a competition. Such endless exercises, conducted according to the very strict rules of the initiation process, have made indigenous African and Australian men the quickest and sturdiest runners (and therefore dancers) in the world, their capabilities having been honed and passed on from generation to generation to the present day.

Balancing was so vital to motion coordination for Homo Erectus precisely because of the change of stance from horizontal to vertical. Such a major plastic transformation did not happen overnight; the age-old genetic memory of horizontality continually resisted the transition to the new upright stance, and could suddenly reawaken from some deep recess of the mind and cause momentary confusion – dangerously so, if it happened when being faced with a predator or enemy. Hominids, like any other animal, took as few risks as possible – and it was only by continual vigorous practice that the old ingrained sense of horizontality was eventually eradicated.

Suspension

A few million years ago, Homo Erectus was *swinging* from tree to tree, *grasping* branches hand and foot. After moving down to the ground, the shape of the extremities gradually changed, losing some of the *grasping* facility and confidence in *dangling* upside down. The inner self, however, never completely forgot the grasping/hanging skills that are part of hominids' essential genetic inheritance – the same heritage that accounts for the survival of intellectually inferior insect, reptile, bird and primate species through the many ecological disasters that visited our planet during the last 300 million years.

Modern aboriginal peoples still subsist mainly from tree products for their food, shelter, weapons and clothing needs. For them, the *hanging/grasping* motions of the upper and lower limbs are part of their everyday routine, despite the more sophisticated plastic facilities they have acquired. Some build complex structures up to ten stories high, using only bamboo poles and reeds. These are used for drying treated pelts and clothing, or for smoking fish.

Bushmen live in savannah/semi-desert and move around comfortably in these environments, using the arches of their *flexed* feet and *hanging* by *bent* knees. They work there and children play for long periods, apparently oblivious of the fact that they are for the most part *hanging* upside down. The free arms and hands are available for any task, or for moving from one location to another by *grasping* the nearest horizontal pole after *leaping* from the previous spot, sometimes in a half *somersault*.

In the same way, a baby will instinctively *grasp* one's finger or other small object with its feet and toes as often as with its hands and fingers. Nursing mothers feel the baby's feet *pushing* and *grasping* her breast to get more milk, just as infant mammals *cling* to the mother's back or chest by *grasping* her skin.

These *grasping* motions of the feet have their origins mainly in *clutching* at branches, or using the feet and toes to catch crabs or shellfish underwater. Later, our forebears learned how to *ride* various animals, controlling them by means of a foot *gripping* under the ears (elephant) or abdomen (zebra).

Climbing and descending

Infant arboreal primates take their first steps climbing or descending the tree in which they were born, *gripping* the trunk with the soles of their feet as well as their hands, and *raising* or *lowering* their bodies by the leg and arm muscles to reach the next position by *squeezing* with the knees. Whether going upwards or downwards, the process of locomotion is led by the legs and feet, with the arms and hands lending additional support.

With minor variations from species to species, this way of moving predominated for millions of years, in fighting, building, food gathering, play and entertainment. Modern circus pole acrobats, with their spectacular *tricks* and dexterity as they *climb* or *descend* the pole, display similar natural abilities.

Crawling and swimming

Despite the differences in resistance and friction between moving in water and on land, the plastic motion patterns of *crawling* and *swimming* are fundamentally similar in that both involve *pushing* against whatever supports the body weight. To move backwards, the motions of the limbs are simply reversed.

In both actions, the pairs of fore and hind limbs *move* in parallel patterns, either sinusoidal or by lateral *undulation*, or by each individual limb in succession. The plastic motions of amphibians like salamanders often seem to resemble those involved in *climbing* and *descending*.

The ability to *crawl* or *swim* silently, quickly and invisibly is a valuable survival asset for any animal, whether predator or prey. The initiation curriculum for boys involved learning how to *imitate* these motions, as indispensable to their future hunting and performing activities. Endlessly repeating the *swimming* motions of newts and tadpoles or the *crawling* techniques of a tortoise or crocodile may not have been much fun, but the plasticity thus acquired stood any future warrior/hunter in good stead.

Compared to *crawling*, hominids' *swimming* motion repertoire involved a much more extensive plastic vocabulary for action: on or under the water, on the ground, with the arms or legs/feet only, solo or in group performance, naturally or with artificial 'flipper' extensions, and so on.

The legacy of *crawling* and *swimming* techniques from ancient times is very varied. Continuous practice in water helped to develop greater strength and flexibility in the legs and feet unit as well as the physical harmony of the body as a whole. And as the legs and feet of all mammals tire under the constant stresses of everyday life, *swimming* also played a valuable **physiotherapeutic** role.

- Chameleon feet *grasp* with some toes facing forwards, and others backwards.
- Tree frogs have digits tipped with suction discs for rapid ascent and descent.
- Some Bornean lizards propel themselves with small forelimbs and a sideways *undulation* of the body.
- The Gopher tortoise has flattened forelimbs which serve as scoops for *digging* and *burrowing*.

Walking and running

These are closely related in terms of their motion characteristics, plastic facilities and energy sources. The principles regulating balance and coordination are similar. The only important difference between the two actions lies in their kinetic value: **speed** of movement, **amplitude** of motion, and most importantly, the **energy** committed to transferring weight from one foot to the other.

For most bipeds, *walking* involves *placing* the heel on the ground, *rolling* the flat sole of the foot towards the toes, thereby changing the centre of gravity from one leg to the other, which then repeats the same progressive motion. *Striding* is a potential *run*, with the gait prolonged by small *jumping* dynamics. *Running* starts with a small *leap* forward, *landing* first on the cushion, then *rolling* back onto the sole momentarily onto the heel, *bending* the knees to absorb the shock of *landing*, and coordinated with arm *movements* on the opposite side. The same motion pattern is then repeated by the other leg.

Simple as these motion *sequences* seem when described on paper, they are in fact highly complex and energy-consuming, given the top-heavy nature of the hominid skeleton. Long-distance *walking* or *running* marathons require a great deal of physical endurance, and even Olympic athletes sometimes lose their sense of balance and coordination (and sometimes, consciousness) towards the end of these strenuous contests.

Hominids had to overcome such weaknesses at all costs in order to get food and escape predators. The constant need to find new food sources drove our forefathers to travel. Many tribes were nomadic, sometimes *walking* as much as forty–fifty kilometres a day with their families and belongings from one overnight home base to the next. Moreover, they also had to *chase* prey, *gather* food and perform all other daily chores, mostly on their two feet.

In the process, the musculature of the lower limbs developed to a very high standard; today, regular *walking* or *running* is regarded as prolonging the human lifespan, and *walking* is acknowledged to be one of the best ways of preventing arthritis.

Leaping and diving

The kinetic energy for these two movements usually comes from the momentum generated by preceding locomotion, either *walking* or *running*. The small *leap* is actually an exaggeration of the *running sequence*, with a powerful starting *thrust* forward by the supporting hind leg/foot. Then, after travelling through the air, the body *lands* on one or both feet. Earlier hominids already copied the *hops* and high *jumps* of flying frogs, lizards, squirrels, lemurs, monkeys, and used similar motions themselves when hunting or trying to escape, *crossing* water by *leaping* from one rock to another, *jumping* gulleys, fissures and other obstacles and so on.

The *hops* and *leaps* of non-apes have certain characteristics in common. The repertoire of bipeds and species that occasionally go on two legs includes:
  a) The *hop* – a low springy *jump* on one or both feet simultaneously, upwards on the spot, with or without *turning*, alone or in groups
  b) *Bouncing hop* – the same movement, but in a sequence *travelling* forwards, backwards or sideways over a distance of a few feet
  c) *Leaps* are higher and longer *jumps* from one foot to the other over a greater distance, often in sequences of three or more with alternate legs with the body in an upright position

The *hop* and the *bouncing hop* are performed by quadrupeds in a similar way, but by synchronising the **kinetic power** of all four legs. The quadruped *leap*, however, is different in that the initial impulse is usually by both hind limbs and the body is *stretched out* in horizontal position in its trajectory through the air. The *landing* is either on forelimbs first, followed by the **spring** motion of the hind legs (hare, cat, horse) or the other way around (flying squirrel).

Diving is another technique in the hunt/fight motion repertoire – originally very similar to the *leap* in plastic terms, but *throwing* the body downwards as well as forwards. Observing the *soaring* techniques of monkeys in the tree canopy, our ancestors began using lianas to imitate them, *diving* from one high point to the next by using the momentum of powerful *leaps*. Hundreds of metres could be travelled in this way, usually involving a descent at each *leap*.

Leaping and *diving* exercises were a popular subject of boys' initiation rituals. The final graduation tests usually took place on a hilltop or plateau overlooking a lake with the tribal judges following the proceedings to select the youngster whose performance was good enough to join the adult warriors/hunters or performers.

Even today, Hamar men of Ethiopia undergo an initiation rite that involves *jumping* over the backs of some forty bulls side by side in succession, *leaping* over two or three of the unsteady animals at a time, exposing themselves to the possibility of serious injury in the process. Other such tests might involve *diving* into a pool or lagoon to retrieve a specific object placed at the bottom. The reason for these demanding tests was as much to inculcate a sense of fearlessness as it was to promote physical excellence.

- Many sand lizards have toes adapted for *running* on loose sand
- Water dragons, when disturbed while on land, *sprint* on their hind legs with phenomenal bursts of speed
- The long hind limbs of frogs are adapted to *leaping* long distances
- Iguanas have long slender legs for *jumping* onto their prey and for *stretching* from one perch to the next
- The Rana frog *skips* across the surface of the water in a series of rapid *jumps*

<u>Consciously</u> Performed hind limb repertoire

- **Domestic** routines involve one or both legs and feet interacting with other body parts in all everyday domestic activities
- Gestural **communication** by motion signals of the leg or foot in a posture or action in either natural or coded form
- **Mime/dance** motions of the legs and/or feet, separately or together, in secular or sacred events, and as part of the juvenile initiation curriculum
- **Therapeutic motions** include deliberate physical exercises, spiritual healing treatments and hypnosis

As these examples show, leg and foot motions can be conscious or subconscious, performed by one or both legs, in succession or simultaneously, independently or in concert with other body parts, *standing* or *sitting, lying down* or *hanging*, on the spot or in progressive motion, and performed as solos or duets (such as wrestling and mime/dance). Instead of describing all leg and foot motions in detail, we concentrate here on how they interact with the motions of other body parts in the various performing categories discussed earlier.

When Homo Erectus first evolved, hominids enjoyed the advantages of their bipedal stance over the quadrupeds that constituted most of the animal world. All that remained was to capitalise on this advantage as quickly as possible, not only in terms of leg motions in the domestic context, but even more intensively for the hunting, fighting and food gathering skills to guarantee their own survival. The motions involved included *creeping, kneeling, kicking, stretching* and *clasping* the legs (around the waist or neck of an adversary, for example).

Legs being much stronger than arms, our ancestors realised that they could be useful for many other functions besides *walking* and *running*. The continuing evolution of the legs' plastic facilities allowed advanced motion **techniques** and personal motion **styles** to develop; not only could individuals be recognised by their own **manner** of *running, climbing* and

194

jumping, but scouts learned to read the footprints of other tribe members, as well as other species.

These are all the conscious, premeditated motions that echo Instinctive functional motions. They are based on the same anatomical features, plastic facilities, kinetic energy, space and balance and coordination. Indeed, the *movement* itself can be the same; only the motivation is different.

Instinctive functional actions are carried out unthinkingly as a matter of habit. Although the borderline between performed and improvised motions is sometimes blurred, both are usually the result of forethought as part of a planned scenario. Both are **stylised** versions of their functional equivalents (see Chapters III and IV)

DOMESTIC ROUTINES

These everyday motion activities of the legs and feet include all labour and personal body motions: *stamping* and *pawing, holding* and *supporting* and *pushing* and *pulling*. The following examples are body motion sequences used between the first Homo Erectus to the Neanderthal period, when domestic accessories remained limited.

Stamping and pawing

These were the main plastic facilities of primates and many other species. Both have their own performing background, the feet often being used in equivalent circumstances with similar motivation, sometimes even in one joint sequence.

Stamping was originally a functional motion for getting food. Larger birds use heavy *stamping* motions in marshland to lure or scare worms and larvae out of the ground. Seeing the nutritious result of this activity, apes imitated them, though with largely negative results. Undaunted, they continued frantically *stamping* the ground until they forced out bigger creatures such as rodents from their burrows, terrified by the noise and vibration. *Stamping* then became an early expression of **emotion** – anger or fear, happiness or frustration, or the desire to show off or attract a mate's attention in a courtship display. This effective ape communication signal was eventually adopted by other species.

Hares *tap* important messages to each other by *stamping* the ground; elephants scare away intruders with heavy *stamping*; antelopes kill snakes and dangerous spiders with a *stamp* of the hoof; hippos can crush the armoured body of a crocodile by *stamping* on them like living battle tanks.

Our ancestors incorporated the various benefits of *stamping* motions into their domestic vocabulary, using it for gathering food, breeding cattle, building shelters and so on. The entire tribe would *stamp* the ground level to prepare a new site for the home base and ritual ceremonies. *Stamping* with one or both legs was used for *cracking* nuts, *stretching* pelts and skins, *mixing* dung, *breaking* reeds for shelters, extracting juice by *beating* fruit in a tortoise shell, and *smashing* large bones to make tools.

Pawing motions are used by infant mammals from birth onwards, initially during gnaw play, for communicating with their parents and eventually, in courtship display. *Pawing* is also a regular warning signal for elephants, big cats and kangaroos.

It is exciting to see the latter fighting. Two male kangaroos start out by giving warning signals with their forelimbs, a warm-up aspect. Then, in a contest for the favours of a mate, they grab at each other's head. The fighting skills of a kangaroo's hind limbs are highly developed and can deliver powerful *kick-punches*.

Pawing has non-aggressive side in the social life of mammals, too: inviting others for grooming or mating, declaring peaceful intentions or submission, begging for food or attention and so on. There are also *pawing* dialogues between mothers and infants, though these have yet to be fully decoded. The long history of hominid communication with other mammals confirms that domestic pets, horses, bovids and even elephants and bears have a reasonable understanding of *pawing* signals and respond accordingly.

Stamping and *pawing* are primal motion elements involving comparatively primitive plastic techniques. Although both have many rhythmic and spatial variations, they are all easy to learn, perform and understand. Each action requires the body balance to be adjusted when changing to the other leg or foot, in quadrupeds as well as bipeds. Fighting bipeds aim to *knock* away one or other of the opponent's legs to precipitate a fall in a way that quadrupeds do not, for obvious reasons. The acoustic timbre of *stamping* corresponds to the creature's weight, and the tone of it is dictated by its kinetic energy.

Holding and supporting

Two million years ago, Homo Habilis was the most skilful of all hominids. They could *braid* rope, *weave* baskets from reeds, *strip* a tree of its bark for poles to use in building shelters, and importantly, how to *pin down* prey with the foot unit before finishing it off and how to sever chunks of meat from the carcass.

Practically all apes use the feet and knees of their hind limbs as auxiliary *holding* tools of, and the leading function of the forelimbs always relies on the *support* of the legs and feet.

Early craft items were made by hand using primitive tools. Hominids used their laps as a workbench, usually covered by a piece of dry hide or thick bark. The legs played an important role in **securing** the object being worked on, **correcting** its balance and position by *squeezing* the knees, **adjusting** the incline of the work surface by *raising* or *lowering* the lap to facilitate the main hand and arm motions.

By the Mesolithic era, our ancestors had integrated leg and foot motions into various domestic **crafts**, and for making stone objects. Just as we make use of pedals today, the power of the legs was used to *lever, support, press* down and *hold* heavy objects; and later, for operating tools like bellows for making music or fire.

The fighting and close range hunting vocabularies incorporated the greatest range of leg/foot plastic motions. Like the gnaw play of all mammalian infants, young boys loved to practice fighting routines, of which the most complex and technically difficult were wrestling skills involving the legs and feet. These include *imitations* of the way a big cat *holds* its prey, the deadly neck *twist* by a bear's paws, *kicking, clasping, stabbing*, knocking down and many other combat techniques – all taught by a tribal trainer. The legs of the eventual winner often had to *support* two bodies at once, when *lifting* the vanquished opponent into the air to be *thrown* over the head and *slammed* down (*see Chapter III*).

Pushing and pulling

Surprisingly, the legs play a big part in these motions; the power to *move* a heavy piece of furniture, for example, comes from the legs, with the arms merely helping to *guide* the object to the desired location.

Consider the earlier hominid technique for hunting mammoth by luring or driving the animal into a large, deep pit built for the purpose. Once trapped inside, the fallen beast would be killed by *throwing* spears and stones: but how was such a vast carcass removed?

Was it devoured in situ, as other predator species or carrion might? Were chunks cut off and *thrown* or *passed* on spears to other tribe members above?

Hunters with the technology to build and camouflage such a pit had a more sophisticated solution. Once the beast was skinned with flint knives, they dismembered the carcass into several pieces weighing anything up to 300 kgs each. Only then would the meat be *raised* from the pit. Working as a team, the hunters would divide into two groups: one in the pit, the other above. Those in the pit would secure the thick ropes of braided bark, lianas or reeds thrown down to them and secure each chunk of the slaughtered animal. On the leader's signal, those above ground would start *pulling* the ropes by moving backwards from the pit while their comrades below would help by *pushing* the load upwards with their hands, chest, shoulders, arms and head.

Even for two groups working together, balancing such heavy loads on slippery surfaces was no easy task. Eventually the technique was improved, with the men above ground facing away from the pit with the rope over their shoulders, *holding* the end with both hands on the chest. Those in the pit began to use wooden poles as levers to *support* and *lift* each load out.

Things became more complicated as time went by. The people of the early Stone Age began using stone flags for building their shelters and ritual venues – but with none of the technology that we associate with heavy construction today, of course. How they managed to erect gigantic religious monuments like the great henges and menhirs of Europe, the obelisks of Mongolia, statues like those of Easter Island and the pyramids of Egypt and Mexico remains a matter of speculation. Modern attempts to repeat these achievements with the tools and technologies available at the time have met with mixed success.

This is partly because of using a workforce unfamiliar with these techniques, and partly because the researchers underestimate the role played by the legs in such undertakings. Our ancestors didn't repeat the mistake of their predecessors trying to *pull* chunks of mammoth carcass out of the pit backwards, which was both ineffective and painful for the lower back; instead, these ancient builders developed a system of transporting heavy stones using several lead ropes attached to the main rope, with wide leather loops at the end of each lead rope.

To move the load, the workers put the loop over their upper chest and arms, thereby increasing the **kinetic energy** of legs by using the full weight of the body *leaning* in the desired direction of movement. With the strain divided between the legs, lower back, upper arms and chest, the legs worked much more efficiently than when *walking* backwards and the arms remained free to adjust the loop as required. Friction resistance was minimised by rolling the object being on logs – the system our ancestors used to drag all heavy objects.

The *pushing* action is also led by arm and chest motions, but rooted in the power of the legs. Although the hands first take the weight, it passes down through the lower limbs to the ground. The procedure is similar to *walking*, except that each pace starts with a flat sole and continues with a slow *roll* onto the cushion of the other foot.

The need to *incline* the body forwards, especially to start an object moving, is simply a matter of elementary physics. The force of gravity is vertical to the earth's surface, and the desired direction of movement is horizontal. Moving the object requires its weight to be *supported* to overcome friction against the ground, and horizontal force; having the body *inclined* between the vertical and the horizontal combined both.

Beyond these few simple principles, however, many techniques of the ancient master builders remain to be discovered.

Gestural communication

The legs and feet have a more limited gestural vocabulary than the arms and hands. Little has been published on the subject as far as the prehistoric period is concerned; the main sources of information have been archaeological sites, murals, petroglyphs and decorated domestic objects. Some aboriginal peoples in Africa, Australia and the Americas retain the ability to *gesture* with the legs and feet, but mainly as performing expressions rather than as a plastic language as such. Reconstructing the prehistoric gestural vocabulary of the legs and feet would require greater research; the best data we have are from East Asia, the Far East and Central America.

LEG SIGNALS

Legs are better for communicating over long distances simply because they are bigger, and thus read more easily with the naked eye from a distance.

The primitive system of leg gestures was useful because being silent, they didn't attract the attention of enemies or predators. Like the hunter's signals with twigs and pelt described in Chapter I, they included *pawing/swinging* one leg out sideways, once or several times, alternating from one leg to the other in various combinations, changing the rhythm using *pauses*, *holding* the outstretched leg under the knee and so on. Limited as this vocabulary was, these **plastic signals** were sufficient to send urgent short messages about the location, speed, direction, quantity and type of prey, for example.

The other main leg communication system was based on small *hops* on both feet, alternating between landing with the legs together and a shoulder's breadth apart. The sequences included double and triple *hops* with the feet in varying positions, at different heights and rhythms. This apparently simple coded signalling system had a much wider vocabulary and would be used by scouts, for example, to communicate with the main hunting party.

Aboriginal Australian women used knee/thigh *clapping* in ritual dance until quite recently. These **rhythmic sequences** by the inside thighs were based on nocturnal female rituals asking the Totem or Goddess Mother for good husbands, easy pregnancy and so on. Under the full moon, the women would worship in two opposite lines, *holding* hands and with their feet together. One line *clapped* out a coded message with their legs while the other *sang* a **rudimentary vocal accompaniment**, then each line would exchange roles.

Leg gestures and poses played a significant part in the ritual repertoire. Prehistoric graphics confirm the meanings of ancient mythological illustrations and sacred rites whose gestural vocabulary contains many motion expressions and spiritual statements (totemic, pagan, Hindu and so on) as well as Indicative and Imitative signs.

Today, though, we understand only a tiny fraction of the leg/foot gestural vocabulary. Some had **multiple meanings**, learned by our ancestors from childhood onwards; familiarity with these **coded plastic signals** was of course essential in order to be able to follow the mythic narratives being enacted.

FOOT SIGNALS

Strangely, some suggest that the feet are unimportant for the study of gesture because they are incapable of expressive motions. The reverse is true; the apparent absence of published information on foot gestures should prompt us to search out this missing link in body language in order to reconstruct the ancient motion sign vocabulary of the foot.

Although the plastic facilities of the foot are of course nowhere near as rich as those of the hands, they are potentially more sophisticated than those of the other parts of the leg. Ancient Egyptian and East Asian imagery demonstrates the refined foot motions of female dancers, seated on big cushions as they *gesticulate* with their feet in time to a drum or sitar. On a visit to the Indian Embassy in Moscow during the period of Krishna Menon in the 1950s, the author learned **many gestural foot sequences** from Indian dancers of Katkhak and Bharata Natim – mainly from the plastic dialogue with the gods in the epic story of Makhabharata.

Some fifty or so universal motion signals with one or both feet can still be correctly interpreted by virtually any child of seven or older – but they are only visible with bare feet. Unsurprisingly, thirty millennia of wearing shoes have been highly detrimental to the survival of foot signs as a communication system. Modern East Indian dance groups, as well as European ballet companies still use some ancient foot *gestures* in their choreography, but as ornamental decoration rather than to convey exact meaning.

The most expressive vocabulary of foot signs involved *tapping* while wearing rattles, as described in the first functional genre. Based on the *stamping* motions of land mammals, this provided hominids with a richly communicative **sono-plastic language** that was learned from a very early age. In addition to the sound level and rhythmic pattern of the *tapping*, it involved the timbral dynamics of the rattles themselves and the personal style of each performer – an **acoustic signature** that could be recognised by other members of the tribe.

All communicative gestures of the leg and foot can be motivated by both conscious and Subconscious conditions. *Stamping* and *pawing* motions, for example, could be subconscious defensive reactions that are nevertheless consciously **modulated** so as to deliver the necessary threat without entailing a potentially lethal actual fight.

SUMMARY

This cursory overview of biped motion activities still fails to explain exactly what it was that prompted apes to change their comfortable quadrupedal existence to become bipeds, with all that entailed in terms of the long process of anatomical restructuring.

As we have seen, there is a strong case for believing that a great environmental disaster triggered the change – but why that particular change and not some other physical adaptation?

The specific stimulus is not hard to find. The history of biped locomotion reveals certain factors common to practically all terrestrial orders, from insects to mammals. Most of them rise up on their hind limbs to communicate a warning. Temporary bipedalism is used as a tactic to scare off foes by making the individual seem bigger and stronger than it actually is.

Consider how vulnerable apes must have felt when they were forced for environmental reasons to leave the comparative safety of the tree canopy to roam the savannah. Feeling at a physical disadvantage to creatures that could *stand* high, if only temporarily, on their hind limbs, they naturally copied the strategy – only to realise that by doing so, they made themselves even taller than the giants whose apparent size had previously intimidated them. Accordingly, apes – hominids included – *imitated* the hunting and fighting motions of the creatures around them, observing them closely and practising them later at the home base.

Regularly witnessing fellow tribe members being caught and killed by predators, they were acutely conscious of their own vulnerability – and they realised that the only way to stand a chance of surviving against a bear, a big cat or a pack of marauding hyenas was to make themselves look as big, strong and intimidating as possible. So they *stood up*.

The main catalyst for the transition from four legs to two was therefore the desperation to survive in the even more hostile conditions that followed changes in climate.

There were of course a number of secondary stimuli mentioned earlier: looking more presentable to potential mates, *reaching* food growing higher from the ground, being able to see longer distances while watching for predators or searching for food and water, and so on. But all these are incidental to the main driver: the **intimidation of predators**.

THE PLASTIC MOTION CHARACTERISTICS OF BODY PARTS

The main body parts involved in plastic motion act as the following interconnected units:
- neck and shoulders, upper back;
- chest and breast, torso and belly;
- hips and buttocks, pubis and phallus;
- tail and proboscis, skin and hair.

Although they are all physically interconnected and controlled (Consciously or Subconsciously) by the same neurological system, each unit has of course its own characteristic patterns of Functional motion and communicative gestures.

As gesticulatory tools, the motions of these units can be described in three ways: a) **individually**, in isolation; b) in **association** with the surrounding muscles and joints; and c), as **part of the entire body** mechanism.

Head and face motion signals have been described earlier. The NECK, linking the head and trunk, has a multifunctional role in most physical activities. Virtually all head motions rely on the strength and flexibility of the neck. As well as *supporting* the head, the neck *rotates* the head in order to see or hear better, *tilts* it back and forth, *inclines* it sideways, *pulls* the head inwards (as when trying to hide) and *projects* it forwards (to express aggression).

This unusually varied motion repertoire can be traced back over some 500 million years of the neck's evolution. Aquatic species gradually developed functional motion of the neck around 300 million years ago as part of the skull's separation from the pectoral girdle. This allowed the head to move independently of the torso, a great advantage when hunting. This anatomical evolution was arguably the precursor of what would eventually happen to land animals; compared to the movement range of a bird's neck, the plastic facilities of the hominid neck seem stiff and primitive.

As we have seen, most neck motions are driven by the muscles and ligaments of the cervical vertebrae connecting the neck to the shoulders and upper back. The plastic facilities of the neck therefore depend on the shoulder muscles and the upper vertebrae, in a soundly **triangulated** structure whose inherent strength, balance and flexibility simultaneously controls the **neck, shoulders** and **upper back**.

The rich functional repertoire of neck motions for searching, feeding, hunting, fighting, courtship and nursing progressively evolved into a gestural communication vocabulary. Expressive plastic signals by this triple unit of upper body parts can be traced all the way back to newts, salamanders, lizards, crocodiles and other amphibian and reptilian species.

Virtually all head gestures (*nodding, shaking, wagging, wobbling*) are performed and controlled by neck motions and *supported* by the upper body parts.

- **Warning** signal, with the neck *projecting* the head forwards and an *arched* upper back
- **Submission** signal, with the neck *contracting* to *lower* the head between *raised* shoulders, and *stooping* the upper back
- **Mating** call gesture, by slowly *rotating* the head.
- **Defiance** signal by *jerking* the head with an *outstretched* neck.
- **Rejection** signal by *twisting* the neck to *turn* the head away.

SHOULDERS are a heavily built element of the skeletal structure, used for both the protection of soft tissues and attack. They are essential to any strenuous manual work, such as building shelters, food gathering and nursing, as well as for gestural communication and courtship performances. Functionally as well as gesturally, the shoulders are inextricably linked to the motions of the arms, chest and upper back, forming a unit of the head and upper extremities comprising six body motion tools with a complex repertoire of plastic reactions and expressions.

This arsenal of gestural tools could of course be exploited to far greater effect in everyday life by bipedal apes than quadrupeds; indeed, the transition to bipedal posture was in itself the main stimulus for their further evolution.

Like any other body part, the shoulders of hominids have their own gestural vocabulary for social and ritual activities:

- *Shrugging* to indicate **uncertainty.**
- *Moving* the shoulder (forwards or backwards) away from an unwanted call or touch to signal **rejection.**
- *Hunching* the shoulders to express **exhaustion** or **grief,** to signify **coldness** or to keep warm.
- *Stretching* the shoulders sleepily on **waking.**
- *Shaking* the shoulders to express **sexual attraction** or extreme **excitement.**

Various additional motion signals were used in secular events or mythical rituals, and are now included in the performing vocabularies.

The UPPER BACK is often ignored as an instrument of mammalian communication – mistakenly so, as it unites and *supports* all motion tools in the top half of the body. It is also often used independently and sometimes aggressively, with potentially lethal consequences. The upper back of bovine, canine and feline species, for example, is fundamentally involved in many functional activities.

- **Fighting**: the buffalo *lifts* a predator on its horns and *throws* it to the ground using the power of its upper back and neck muscles.
- **Hunting**: big cats bring down a prey and *pull* its flesh from the carcass using the neck and upper back muscles.
- **Mating**: male mammals use the upper back to coordinate their forelimbs to *hold* the female in a convenient position for verso/dorso copulation.
- **Nursing**: mothers *carry* their offspring on the upper back, continually readjusting their balance with these muscles.

In evolutionary terms, the upper back is central to the anatomical transition from quadruped to biped posture in apes. Figure III/1 illustrates the major restructuring of the upper back vertebrae that took place over time in hominids, *stretching* upwards while maintaining the curvature of the middle spine, accommodating the forelimbs *hanging* down with shoulders *pushed* back and the head *rising*; the knees, however, remain slightly *bent*.

The natural centre of gravity of their quadruped origins nevertheless continued to pull bipeds downwards and forwards for millions of years; over time, it was gradually displaced towards the upper back to allow **equilibrium** in a near-vertical position. This tendency to be *pulled* forwards by the body's **centre of gravity** still affects the physical activity of bipeds, including the repertoire of plastic gestures.

Arching the upper back is a warning signal for many mammalian quadrupeds, giving the impression of greater size and strength to intimidate an enemy

- **Mating** signals involving *swinging* the upper body by the back muscles.
- Gestures of **invitation** by *bending* the body down and *lowering* the upper back to signify acceptance of carrying an offspring.
- Signals of **submission** in quadrupeds, *rolling* onto their back and *pawing* the air.
- *Bowing* forwards and *arching* the upper back to signify **submission** in primates.
- *Flattening* the upper back while *crawling* before an impending **strike.**

In these and many other ways, the upper back became for our ancestors a significant centre for coordinating their main plastic facilities.

The CHEST, as the largest frontal aspect of a biped's body, requires constant protection. It also offers clues to the individual's identity, with many species displaying either natural or artificial visual patterns on the chest.

Male apes often use the chest to demonstrate physical power, bravery and dominance. In combat, a strong, hard chest could be used as a weapon as well as a shield. In other circumstances, it would help *support* loads, such as carcasses; it was also a place for babies to *cling* to. In the mating season, females look for a male partner with a large chest, the implied strength of which would guarantee protection as well as healthy offspring.

Although the chest encases the main vital organs such as the heart, these only came to symbolise emotional states much later. Although the male chest seems to be an impressive tool for expressive gestures, its repertoire is in fact rather limited.

- **Self-exhibition**, by *stretching* the chest out while *pulling* the shoulders back and *turning* the proudly *raised* head sideways; the same gesture, with a repeated *twisting* motion of the chest only.
- **Negation** or **submission**, with chest *pulled in*, shoulders *hunched* and upper back *arched*; similar motions prompted by the pain of a chest wound, emotional stress or posture deformation due to old age.
- Rapid and exaggerated *breathing* in **excitement** prior to mating, feeding or fighting
- *Expanding* the chest as a **warning** signal, accompanied by repeatedly *drumming* the fists on it in staccato sequences, or *pushing* an adversary away in a chest-to-chest trial of strength before a real fight.
- **Courtship display** of touch signals, when both sexes repeatedly *nuzzle* against each other's' chest.

MAMMARIES have an entirely different repertoire of functional and performed motions. Unlike the male chest, the mammary organs are designed for feeding infants, and as such are the primary symbol of **motherhood, reproduction** and **fertility**. For young females, the enlargement of the breast signifies **puberty** and the beginning of a new phase of sexual life with all its attendant psychological, physiological and emotional changes. The expressive motions and behaviour of a future mother are established accordingly.

The Goddess Mother is always represented in prehistoric visual arts as having exaggerated breasts and buttocks to symbolise agricultural fecundity, fertile marriage and successful hunting or combat. If the response was negative, our forebears had to placate the Goddess Mother with great sacrifices, using plastic motion as the only medium of communication with the perceived supernatural forces.

Hominids believed that in order to yield the desired result, their worship had to be conducted as impressively as possible. They therefore used the best and most significant communication tool: the breast of a young female. Again and again, ancient wall paintings and petroglyphs depict the repertoire of breast motions by dancing juveniles in sufficient detail to allow us to reconstruct approximate choreographic sequences.

Decoding this vocabulary of breast gestures is inevitably speculative to some extent. The aboriginal African and Australian dancers who still practice this repertoire today aren't able fully to explain its significance or to decipher its ancient ritual secrets.

These examples of breast motions are still in use; with other reconstructed examples whose precise reading is as yet unclear.

I:

- Upright posture with feet *apart* and *open* hands on hips.
- Soft *jerks* by one or two breasts, alternating or simultaneously to various rhythms in sequences of varying length.
- Breast *swinging* side to side by *lifting* alternate shoulders, the head remaining motionless.
- *twisting* the upper body in various rhythmic patterns.
- *Vibrating* both breasts by *shaking* the chest and shoulders (small amplitude).

II:

- *Bending* upper body forward in the same stance, but with *loose* knees.
- *Swinging* breasts from side to side by *shifting* the entire body weight from one foot to the other.
- *Dropping* each breast alternately by *jerking* each shoulder and *twisting* the chest.
- *Rotating* the breasts simultaneously by *moving* the upper body and hips in a figure of eight pattern.

III:

- *Turning* the body on the spot with feet together in an upright posture and hands on hips.
- *Undulating* breast motion achieved by periodically *squatting* while *spinning* the body.

Using the breasts for these motion gestures was by no means easy, which is why naked women are often portrayed in ancient depictions *supporting* their breasts with hands during dance and rite ceremonies. It was nevertheless preferable for a young girl of the time to compromise her physical beauty than to risk being sacrificed. The cult of women's breasts, integral to the Mother Goddess mythology, was so popular that it is still practised today at sacred events by some aboriginal peoples.

The TORSO and BELLY are the least protected parts of the body, and have spiritual as well as physiological connections with motherhood in the umbilical cord. This reproductive association was the creative foundation for initiation ceremonies, the fables of totemic and funerary mythologies, shamanic healing and divination and popular compositions by ancient sculptors and painters.

The female belly has always symbolised procreation and beauty. Our prehistory is packed with positive and negative interpretations of **life** and **death** that are presumed to originate in the female belly, which is why women were usually first to be sacrificed to the gods. The belly was the external manifestation of women's greater significance in the eyes of the tribe; it symbolised how women personified **purity** and **immortality**.

Attractive to children and adults alike for its softness and warmth, the female belly has always had a powerful sexual charge, and early females understandably exploited its potential as means of attracting mates.

The belly is a highly sensitive area that reacts sharply to any unwanted touch or irritation; as such, it is a sophisticated motion instrument with exceptional plastic facilities, and capable of gestures so subtle as to be almost invisible.

The various boys' initiation rites practised in different parts of the world usually involved a demonstration of female sexuality and beauty under the aegis of the shaman or his assistants. This was often in the form of what we now call a belly dance, but for the purposes of **anatomical** and **spiritual education** rather than entertainment. The hypnotic accompaniment of drums and flutes drove the dancer into a state of spiritual trance by the end, with an equally profound emotional effect on the spectators.

The **belly dance** is fortunately a well-documented form, with detailed modern descriptions of the basic plastic techniques, vocabulary and styles of execution. Close as these may be to the ancient choreography, the only ancient dance to have survived until modern times has completely lost its original spiritual meaning and context. Its charmingly feminine plastic elements – the *trembling, jerking* skin, the rhythmic *contraction* and *expansion* of various groups of the belly muscles, the repeated forward *thrusts* of the lower torso and hips – transformed this prehistoric initiation ritual into a modern sexual performance. Today, a drunk may well shove money into the dancer's garments; in the Mesolithic era, probably no worshipper would have dared to commit the heinous sin of *touching* the dancer.

The PHALLUS was the main sacred object of women's nightly fertility rituals in Palaeolithic times. The importance of these rituals was heightened by the decline in male numbers and the increasing sexual impotence of the remaining men (*see Chapter III*).

Being more obviously three dimensional than female genitalia (depicted in their own right in the form of a triangular image of the PUBIS, symbolising fecundity and motherhood), the phallus is easy to represent in wood or stone, and such objects have been used in phallic cults from time immemorial to the present day. Like women's breasts and belly, male genitals symbolised **reproduction** as well as success in **hunting** and **combat**; a larger than life size phallic sculpture would be placed in the middle of the home base, or to decorate a sacred cave.

The functional motions of the penis go far beyond excretion and copulation, and include juvenile play, ceremonial circumcision rites, using the erection as a pre-mating display and masturbation at moments of high excitement. As with female sexual images, the original spiritual significance of prehistoric representations of the phallus has been lost; all that remains is the ethical void of modern commercial pornography.

- The annual religious festivals of **Eastern India** include contests between men *pulling* a heavily laden cart attached to their penises.
- In Africa, **Teneka** men practice a fertility rite ceremony which involves attacking and chasing each other with huge painted wooden penises attached to the lower part of the torso, to the great amusement of the spectating women and children.

The many prehistoric representations of the phallus in sculptures, wall paintings, craft objects and other decorative graphics testify to the elevated spirituality of our primitive ancestors, for whom phallic rituals played far too important a role to be the subject of amusement. Phallic images represented the growth of the family and the restoration of male sexual potency diminished by stress or injury during hunting or combat. Phallic rites were about the continuation of the species in the face of constant threats to survival, and to regard them now as mere buffoonery is to insult the memory of our ancestors.

The HIPS and BUTTOCKS are the musculoskeletal foundation of the legs and trunk. In the fundamental reshaping of the simian body that accompanied the transition from quadruped to biped, the body's centre of gravity shifted to allow the entire weight of the body to be supported by the two hind limbs. In the process, the hips and buttocks acquired an even more important role in performed plastic motions.

As can be seen in fig. III/1 and other illustrations, this apparently simple anatomical construction of a few bones, joints, muscles and ligaments is a phenomenally sophisticated mechanism capable of creating extraordinary motion patterns using the lower body and legs.

That such a top-heavy body as ours can be securely carried on the pelvic girdle with a single sacrum, a few ligaments and soft tissue is nothing less than amazing. Given the upper body weight it has to support, the hominid pelvic area has to be extremely flexible, controlling as it does the balance and motions of the trunk, its own independent functional and performance routines and those of the legs themselves.

During pregnancy, the pelvic girdle changes shape in a way that limits women's ability to perform the most physically demanding actions, although it has little effect on everyday functional motions. The male pelvic girdle is more rigid, and in most mammals, the overall physical ability of males is considerably greater from birth onwards. Apes of both sexes are nevertheless capable of executing an almost unlimited plastic repertoire with their hips and buttocks.

Male hominids of the Palaeolithic era incorporated a wide variety of advanced acrobatic tricks such as *somersaults* and *handsprings* into their ritual pantomimes. Although these tricks evolved from the gnaw-play and wrestling of primates, they could only be realised by dint of intense continuous practice from early childhood onwards, when the pelvic girdle is still soft and adaptable.

As hip and buttock motions are generally very physically demanding, they are usually more widely practised in youth than old age. This is true of all mammals. For this reason, this area of the body has been the main subject for healing and remedial therapy since time immemorial, and some of these ancient veterinary and human treatment systems are still practised today in many parts of the world.

The female buttocks, like the breasts and belly, represented **fecundity**, the sexual stability of the family unit and its spiritual protection; as such, a large and prominent derrière was an important criterion of feminine beauty for mating purposes. This of course made the study of hip and buttock motions a particularly important part of girls' initiation curriculum. From the age of eight onwards, they had to learn:

- how to *walk* gracefully by slightly swinging their hips.
- the motion techniques of *squeezing* and *protruding* the buttocks.
- how to *thrust* the hips forwards or backwards, *shaking* the buttocks laterally with *loose* knees.
- how to *rotate* one hip at a time with *outstretched* leg with toes on the ground, and both simultaneously in a 'hula-hoop' motion, standing on both feet.
- how to *vibrate* the entire pelvic area while keeping the rest of the body motionless state, with both knees slightly *loosened.*

The successful completion of this curriculum was the minimum requirement for passing the performance test prior to the girl's ritual circumcision. Once initiated into womanhood, girls were allowed to take part in the nocturnal ceremonies at full moon. They worshipped naked along with older women, using their hip/buttock motion routines in addition to their breasts to propitiate the deities. The young initiates followed the leading witch, or her assistant, in new choreographic variations of the familiar basic sequences in the middle of the sacred venue. As with the gestural motions of the belly, performers had to:

- gently *jerk* small zones of one or both buttocks, alternately or simultaneously.
- *swing* the buttocks sideways by *twisting* the hip with a *loosened* knee motion.
- *rotate* both buttocks upwards and downwards in parallel patterns, standing with feet apart and knees *loosened.*
- *slap* each buttock in turn with the foot on the same side, while *shaking* a rattle with the arms.

Women performed these and many other hip/buttock motions as solos, duets or in groups. Group performances usually followed a set choreography, with one or two parallel lines *moving* frontwards or sideways in a semicircle with a soloist in the centre, or in two or three closed circles in the case of large numbers of worshippers. In either case, the motion score was always performed in unison, the better to please the gods.

Being generally smaller and more muscular, male hips and buttocks are different in shape and capacity to the female's, and the motivation for the corresponding gestural motions also differ. The pelvic area had an even wider motion repertoire for men than for women, partly because of the physiological limitations of the female anatomy already discussed, and partly because the spiritual practices of women were necessarily adjusted to accommodate the physical realities of pregnancy. Males, by contrast had other responsibilities: hunting, fighting, building shelters, mime *dancing* in totemythical rituals, and so on.

As we have seen, boys learned how to imitate various prey – their body shape, motions, courtship procedures and so on. Hunters wore heavy masks and pelts to penetrate a herd or flock, while *mimicking* the behaviour of the animals in question. Aside from the camouflage, the hunter's bottom was the only remaining mimetic tool available for moving successfully among the prey, and could be decorated as the tail of a zebra or an ostrich. Hunters would sometimes mount horns on their bottom to confuse prey by mimicking peacefully grazing antelopes.

Hip/buttock motions also regularly formed part of totemic and funerary pantomimes, in which the male mimes played various animals or anthropomorphised creatures. This vocabulary included a rich variety of hip/buttock gestures, and secular entertainments usually contained a similar male social repertoire. Bushmen and other African and Australian aboriginal peoples are particularly adept at these dance motions, using the buttocks as a drum or ram, *hopping* while *sitting* on the ground and *travelling* or *turning* on the spot in a progressive motion of the buttocks and hips.

FORE AND HIND BODY MOTION TOOLS

Both these extremities have been functionally essential to animal species since life began. With the exception of certain primitive marine animals, food rarely finds its own way into the digestive system – it has to be sought, and that means moving around.

The propellant of the first micro-organisms was the **tail**, and the original instrument for locating and ingesting food before the mouth evolved was the **proboscis** of primitive creatures. Both the tail and the proboscis were essential for survival and the development of these early creatures' plastic anatomy.

Proboscis, muzzle and beak

EVOLUTIONARY METAMORPHOSIS

During the 500 million-year process of selective adaptation stimulated by changing geographical, climatic, genetic and other natural conditions, the proboscis metamorphosed into a vast array of different forms – **sponges, tubes, stings, spikes, trunks, muzzles, snouts and noses**. Although some species retain a modified version of the original proboscis, it generally evolved into mandibles, crushing jaws and lethal tusks, forked and extended tongues, and the mouth parts of high mammals and primates: lips, teeth, oviform tongue and palette.

Birds' **beaks** are a unique plastic descendant of the ancient proboscis, in terms of their shape, position and Functional motion repertoire. The texture and nature of a beak, whatever its shape or size, may be phylogenetically related to the protruding **horns** of insects like the stag beetle or bollant; the same can be said of marine creatures with **proboscis weapons**, like the narwhal or swordfish. Later, it evolved as a **communication tool** in mammalian species like the platypus or dolphin.

The long **bills** of birds like kiwis, curlews, storks, ibis and cranes not only *catch* and *hold* prey, but also to *tear* the flesh, and *feed* their chicks mouth-to-mouth. The beak also aids *climbing* and nest building; it is a grooming implement, and an important element in the performance of a courtship dances. It has also been suggested that the bill plays an important **navigational** role during migrations by reacting to radioactive solar emissions and polarisation effects.

The proboscis/nose shape of some creatures is so distinctive that it serves to identify their genus. We have horseshoe, flower-faced, leaf-nosed, moustached, mastiff and spear-nosed bats, for example. Likewise, the hog-nosed skunk, square-lipped rhino, plate-billed toucan, hornbill, shovel-billed kingfisher, bottle-nosed whale and so on.

Over time, this important organ developed far beyond its original sensory and eating facilities and adapted into an incredible variety of new forms, each with their own functional tools and motions:

- Primitive *sucking* tube or **sponge** (molluscs, oysters, starfish, jellyfish, octopus).
- More elaborate **sting** or **coiled pipe** of spiders and insects (aquatic, terrestrial, arboreal and flying).
- *Sucking* mouth **disc** and **projectile tongue** (amphibians, reptiles and some birds).
- The diverse **beaks** and bills of birds, with additional plastic facilities, functional and performing motion repertoire.
- The original flexible **snout** (manta ray, pipefish, elephant fish and elephant seal).
- Advanced forms of mammalian **muzzle**, often with facilities for *digging* or with **tusk** or **horn** weapons (anteater, aardvark, bear, rhino, armadillo, seal and walrus).

All these species use the frontal parts of the head and mouth for a wide range of instinctive functional and consciously performed body motion activities.

The oldest surviving proboscis tool is the trunk/nose of the mammalian order Proboscidea, which includes elephants, tapirs, dugongs and manatee. The sheer scope of plastic facilities of this incredibly sophisticated body instrument is amazing, from emotional indicator to ultrasonic analyser.

Functional capabilities

SEARCHING/DETECTING:

Sniffing and *touching* are the main functional motions of the proboscis/ muzzle and its associated sensory organs. Almost all animals emit and perceive smell signals, including blind and deaf burrowing species. The organs of smell are usually located in the muzzle/nostril or mouth/snout area – antennae, whiskers, hair, mucous membranes, tubes, tongue and saliva for detecting chemical signals as well as in some cases, the glands for producing smells, either to **attract** or **repel**.

Naturally, every individual from any species has its own specific odour that is easily recognisable by its peers. Being able to detect these scents efficiently guards against potential threats from strangers as well as being the perfect tool for searching out food, lost infants, mates or the way back to home base.

The proboscis is a highly sophisticated *touching* instrument, and the tip of the muzzle (mandibles/lips, tube/tongue and mucous secretions) is equally adept at detecting taste.

As poisoned meat does not always smell bad, it would be easy to make a fatal mistake. To avoid getting seriously hurt, scavengers always approach a carcass very carefully. After catching the scent of a dead buffalo, a starving dingo will lightly *touch* the potential meal with the tip of its snout to confirm its edibility. It *picks up* and *turns over* a piece of the carcass to make sure that there are no nasty surprises beneath before removing the chunk altogether to hide it from other hungry pack members.

Birds constantly *pick up* and discard objects with their beaks when searching for food or nest building. These upward and downward motions are practically incessant while feeding or grooming their chicks or simply when watching out for predators in every direction.

Studies of animal behaviour and communication are constantly revealing new information about the links between plastic motion signals and the roles of **sound, smell, polarisation, electricity** and **solar radiation**, the majority of which are perceived by organs located in the proboscis/muzzle area.

HUNTING AND GATHERING

Sucking and *stinging* were the first plastic motion manifestations of the hunting and gathering functions of early animal species such as molluscs, echinoderms, spiders and insects.

In its most primitive form, the *sucking* motion was through the proboscis-like movable tube (called a **tentacle**) that molluscs use to catch tiny plants and micro-organisms. This eventually developed into the proper **tubular proboscis** of the octopus, able to catch much bigger prey; this in turn was modified into the proboscidiferous **mouth disc** of the hagfish, which can *hold* the prey while simultaneously *sucking* its body tissue.

The oldest and most efficient *stinging* and *sucking* mechanism belongs to spiders, whose small proboscis-like **chelicerae** inject poison into the prey, which is then *sucked* dry by the spider's mouth immediately beneath. A small but ultra-sensitive palp on each side of the spider's mouth completes this lethal ensemble by *manipulating* the catch into the optimum position.

- Insects often use their **proboscis** (whether short and straight or long and coiled) for *sucking* nectar or blood, testing the edibility of substances, and as a *stinging* weapon to stun or kill.
- Snakes used their **forked tongue** to establish temperature and humidity, recognise an approaching prey, predator or sexually receptive potential mate.
- Chameleons and salamanders catch their prey using the poisoned saliva at the end of their long, sticky **projectile tongues.**

Netting and *gripping* motions of the proboscis or jaws are another manifestation of hunting and gathering motions. Primitive species such as sponges and anemones have always fed by *trapping* passing food particles, just as many marine creatures like whales, rays and remoras *draw* plankton-rich ocean 'soup' into their wide-open mouths, filtering out the nutrients by *expelling* the water with their facial musculature.

Most predators *grip* their prey with their beak, jaws or mandibles before killing and eating it. The modified proboscis or snout is often equipped with a poisoned projectile tongue or tube, or a weapon like a horn, tusk or spike. From saw sharks and crocodiles to pelicans, anteaters and rhinos, all such weapons have their evolutionary origin in the ancient frontal extremity of primitive unicellular organisms.

- Alligator turtles attract prey with a worm-like *wiggling* projection at the tip of the tongue. When a fish approaches to obtain what appears to be an easy meal, the turtle's wide-open mouth *snaps* shut on its prey.
- Salamanders *suck* passing insects into their mouth by inhalation.
- The tip of a chameleon's tongue is a type of a suction cup covered with a sticky mucous substance, allowing the passing prey to be *held* securely while being *transferred* to the mouth.
- As their name implies, male proboscis monkeys have big noses extending below the chin, which has to be *jerked* out of the way while feeding.

Digging and *building* by a specially **modified proboscis** is a part of the common repertoire of *burrowing* and *flying* species. Some burrowers are equipped with a hard proboscis or snout with a strong plate or spike for *digging* through impacted soil for prolonged periods without damaging themselves. The *burrowing* motion of reptiles normally begins by *pounding* the soil aside using the thick-ridged skull and neck muscles. Once inside the burrow, the head *shakes* vigorously from side to side in order to enlarge the tunnel and compact the walls. The head then *braces* against the tunnel wall to let the body *drag* itself in beside it. Although burrowing is almost always led by the snout, some animals (such as the Bushveld rain frog) *dig* backwards.

Worms and worm lizards (Amphisbaenidae) have a unique ability to burrow forwards or backwards, as both ends of their bodies are equipped with small horny scales for *digging*. They excavate each new length by repeatedly *battering* the earth with these hard, strong extremities, *moving* at will in either direction in a straight line with no bodily undulations. Their skin is attached loosely over a cylindrical body covered in scaly rings, allowing the characteristic progressive pleating locomotion based on alternately *stretching* and *contracting* the body.

- Some Caecilians use their heads as trowels when *digging* an escape route, or to poke around in mud looking for food.
- The head of a worm lizard is equipped with a number of *digging* tools, and its skull is exceptionally solid.
- Turtles have long necks and snorkel-like snouts in order to be able to breathe under water without surfacing.
- Bee-eaters hammer a cliff wall with their beaks to make metre-long tunnels.

Bird species like woodpeckers use their hard, solid beaks like carpentry tools, either for feeding or nest building. An entrance hole is first made by *hammering* the bark and the outer layer of the tree trunk with the bill tip. The *digging* continues until they reach the softer pulpy inner core, which is excavated with great skill to make a nest site that is then lined with softer materials carefully selected by texture, size, shape and colour, whether wood shavings, leaves, grasses, down or feathers. As a construction project using beak motions alone, this is a considerable physical challenge by any standards. Each nest is built to the required size in every dimension, and fully fitted for family use. In the mating season, the male often decorates the nest with colourful feathers, berries, flower petals, grasses and the like.

Mammals with elongated muzzles and snouts, such as echidnas, marsupials, dolphins and seals, all have a large repertoire of proboscidiferous plastic motions, both functional and performed. The following section describes some of these proboscis-like tools and the conscious and instinctive behaviours associated with them.

COURTSHIP, MATING AND NURSING

Waving or *rotating* motions of the proboscis can be used to express readiness to **mate**, or as a **warning** signal. They also form part of the head/muzzle gestural repertoire between mother and infant, siblings, or younger individuals with their elders. Even species whose anatomy allows them a limited range of such movements are usually able to *swing* the proboscis/head from side to side when trying to cool off on a hot day, when ridding themselves of pestering insects or when experiencing emotional stress.

The beak is the main courtship performance instrument of birds, who use it to perform *twisting, shaking* and *rotating* motion sequences or to serenade potential mates by making various rhythmic **percussive sounds**.

The elephant's trunk has exceptionally wide-ranging plastic facilities. Bulls can detect the enticing perfume of sexually receptive female at a great distance using the trunk. They signal their desire, as well as their dominant position in the herd hierarchy, with a cascade of dramatic proboscidiferous motions including *waving, rotating, coiling, striking* and *lashing* downwards. And despite the apparent clumsiness of their massive build, bull elephants use their trunks to *touch* and *caress* the female's body with great tenderness, conveying intimate messages that remain to be deciphered.

The preening activity of birds involves a spectacular range of beak motions. The male uses it to decorate the nest for its future mate and offspring. He brings to his nest various bits and pieces of different materials in bright and contrasting colours. Where nests are on the ground, these are displayed in the front, or all around the nest in special scenarios of attractive design, all of it constructed with his multi-purpose bill/proboscis.

If a visiting female is pleased with possibly new home, and is intrigued by her potential father of her future hatchings, she would confirm this by accepting the offered berry, a legally sanctioned bribe, by it from the male's beak. They often start the ensuing courtship program with a tactile introduction by bills *interlocking* them, and/or *rubbing* each other tenderly from side to side, also *biting* the other's beak tip, and so on.

Similar but even more intensely intimate *fondling* motions occur between mating partners. Male mammals *sniff* the genitals of a female to ascertain her readiness for mating; during copulation, they often fondle the female by *nuzzling, licking* and *nibbling* at the back of her head or neck.

Fondling and *nuzzling* elements of the motion vocabulary between friends or closely related individuals such as mother and infant, monogamous couples, siblings and other family members. The relationship between mother and infant is based on tactile expressions of intimacy from birth onwards, with constant *cuddling* and *licking, touching* noses, *stroking* and *nuzzling* to reassure the infant of its protection and food supply.

- Male newts exude chemicals from glands on their head, and *rub* them on the female's snout.
- Male monitor lizards continually *nuzzle* and *lick* their mates.
- Male skink *bite* the female's neck during copulation to keep her calm
- Younger and weaker members of mammalian groups demonstrate their subservience by muzzle motions, such as *licking* dominant individuals and *grooming* their fur with their teeth.
- Birds and quadruped mammals use mainly proboscidiferous motions to nurse their young. This parenthood repertoire includes mouth-to-mouth feeding, grooming, and cleaning detritus from the nest and moving the infants from one place to another.
- Tadpoles stimulate female frogs to deposit a nutritious secretion by *nuzzling.*
- Female crocodiles *move* hatchlings to safer waters in their mouths.

Grooming and preening
These are instinctive ritualised behaviours that help animals to remain free of parasitic infection and to allow individual odours from their skin glands to manifest themselves fully. Keeping the skin, fur or feathers clean is also essential to the efficient regulation of body temperature, as well as helping to avoid an unpleasant taste for suckling infants and several other survival-related reasons.

The functional significance of the proboscis cannot be over-emphasised. Insects meticulously *clean* the head/proboscis area with their palps; amphibians, reptiles and terrestrial mammals do the same with their tongues. Cats and dogs do it when anticipating a good feed. Mammals always *lick* their wounds, as well as those of their young. The first sign of a mammal's sickness is usually an increase in the temperature and dryness of the muzzle tip.

Elephants use their long, flexible, multi-functional trunks to bathe as well as to assist with eating and drinking. Pachyderms need water for more than just quenching their thirst, and will *walk* for weeks in the dry season to reach a source of water. To bathe, they *suck* water up into their trunks and *expel* it to shower themselves and their offspring. This obviously helps them to cool off and to clean their skin from parasites – but close observation of this half-hour family bathing ritual suggests that this procedure signifies much more for them than just a routine functional act. Although their exact meaning is not yet understood, the plastic motion patterns and rhythmic sequences of the trunk clearly contain repeated **gestural phrases**, often with **acoustic accompaniment** – a complete proboscidiferous language, in effect.

Elephants call each other by certain motion patterns of the trunk. They *trumpet* warning signals with it. Females *kiss* and *caress* their calves with it, or tenderly *intertwine* trunks in a *twisting* motion. They use it to *lift* a struggling new-born to its feet. The gestural vocabulary of an elephant's trunk is arguably the most extensive proboscidiferous repertoire of all, and includes *coiling/wrapping, stretching/contracting, twisting/vibrating, holding/squeezing, lifting* and *throwing* among many other plastic motion patterns.

GNAW-PLAY AND WARNING SIGNALS

The mammalian muzzle is both a powerful weapon and exceptionally sensitive. Young mammals begin playing with their siblings and/or parents soon after birth, mainly using their snout for a whole range of tactile motions including *nuzzling, nibbling, pushing, pulling, snapping* and *yawning.*

Big cats and canidae use their strong jaws and muzzle when hunting to subdue prey by *gripping* it in a painful deadlock that immediately breaks the victim's escape. The extreme physical sensitivity of the muzzle will have been discovered through experience during gnaw play.

The motion vocabulary of juveniles during wrestling and gnaw-play is based on the instinctive adult fighting repertoire. When such play becomes over-excitable, the participants *ram* each other, *stubbing* their snouts, even *biting* and *tearing* with their jaws until the screaming loser submits. Practicing these combat snout/proboscis motion techniques in this way equips youngsters well for attack and defence in real life when the time comes. Proboscidiferous warning signals include *lowering* and *raising, nodding* and *jerking,* and *bending* and *projecting.*

There are two main stages before any serious combat or contest begins, whether motivated by **territorial dispute, mating priority or hierarchical position**. The first is when the opponents attempt to avoid bloodshed by intimidating each other with visual and sonic warning signals and by increasing their apparent body size. These warning signals are mainly expressions of the muzzle: *growling, hissing* and *barking, gnashing* jaws, *baring* and *snapping* teeth, *flaring* nostrils, *waving* horns or tusks, or *yawning* widely to display the size and sharpness of the teeth.

The second stage is basically a re-enactment of the gnaw-play motions of infancy. The rivals assess each other: elephants compare the length of their tusks by cautiously *touching* the adversary's snout; hippos, their *yawning* jaws; deer, by *clashing* antlers. These pre-combat motions continue until one or other opponent walks away; if neither cedes, actual combat will take place with inevitable consequent injuries or loss of life.

Attack and defence

There are important differences between the approaches to defence and attack in combat and hunting. Whereas a hunting predator aims to kill its prey, combatants fight only to win, and usually allow the loser to escape. The target of a predator wants to save its life and escape at all costs, preferably without having to fight the predator; opponents in a contest fight to defend their personal interests and status, but can still survive to start a new existence somewhere else if they lose.

These differing motivations are reflected in the plastic motion techniques that are deployed in each case. The hunt is an instinctive act of chasing and killing (almost always another species) without preliminary warning, and with every available weapon. Combat is usually a conscious contest by two individuals of the same species. Above all, predators spend their whole lives **planning** how to kill, while a prey animal defends itself **spontaneously**.

As we have seen, the muzzle/snout is the main fighting tool for most quadrupeds, whether carnivorous or herbivorous. Depending on the individual species, the functional equipment includes the mandibles, jaws, tongue, sting, spikes, teeth, tusks, horns and long trunks or proboscis. Although not all of these tools are designed to kill, most of them are used for attack as well as defence.

- The strong mouths of ungulates can *crush* the bones of smaller predators such as cats and canidae in self-defence.
- The mongoose kills a cobra with special motion and jaw skills.
- Antelopes use their sharp horns in self-defence to *butt* an attacking lioness.
- Fish that are so equipped can deter approaching predators with proboscidiferous spikes or saws.
- Some snakes *spit* venom over great distances when attacked.

COMBAT WEAPONS AND MOTIONS

In any contest between two males of the same species equipped with the same weapons, the individual with the better courage, fighting skills and physical fitness will prevail.

- When two fighting **zebra** stallions refuse to give in, they attack each other's throats
- Two fighting male crocodiles *interlock* their huge jaws.
- Two rival buffalos *run* towards each other and *ram* their heavily plated skulls together.
- A pair of roosters *stab* each other with their sharp beaks, until severe injury ends the contest
- A female mole rat in contention for the position of the new queen kills all her rivals with her sharp teeth.

SUMMARY

As we have seen, the original proboscis metamorphosed out of all recognition during the long period of mammalian evolution, by the end of which hominids had inherited a small nose on a comparatively flat face that nevertheless boasted highly developed organs of vision, hearing, taste and touch.

Unfortunately, 'civilization' has brought with it a diminution of these facilities, thanks mainly to the advent of artificial aids to perception that effectively canged the process of Darwinian selective evolution as far as human beings are concerned. However, this is an inevitable consequence of the natural process of in itself; what we gain in advances in one field, we lose in another.

Abdomen and tail

EVOLUTIONARY BACKGROUND

The tip of the abdomen was the main locomotion tool of the earth's earliest aquatic organisms. It eventually developed into a tail, used both to **propel** and to **steer**; later it developed into an important **weapon** for many insects and reptiles, as well as a **navigational tool** for fishes and birds. For every animal species that retained a tail, it eventually it became a useful multifunctional instrument of plastic **communication**. Before the arrival of apes, abdomen/tail motion was involved in practically every functional activity: fighting and hunting, courtship and mating, building and gathering, signalling and so on.

Fish, reptiles and birds could not exist without a tail, and most grazing mammals would suffer from appalling infestations of flying insect parasites. But as the apes left the tree canopy for the lands, the tail gradually atrophied through redundancy, the main part of its role being assumed by the newly liberated forelimbs. For most other species, the abdomen/tail nevertheless remains still a significant plastic tool for both functional and performed communication.

TAIL SHAPES

The tails of fish, amphibians and reptiles come in three main shapes and sizes.

1. Vertical (i.e., higher than it is wide). Occurring in most fish, amphibians and reptiles, the vertical tail is used for the **serpentine** mode of *swimming* or locomotion, moving forward by alternating left and right **undulations** and *turning* (in water) by *bending* in the desired direction like a ship's rudder.

2. Horizontal (or flat). Present in many fish and sea mammals like whales, dolphins and manatees, the flat-shaped tail *undulates* vertically for forward **propulsion** under the water, as well as for *diving* and *rising* to the surface. It also acts as a rudder. The Australian elephant fish, with a tail rather like an aircraft's, falls between these two categories.

3. Cylindrical. Approximately round-section tails are found in many amphibians, reptiles and some fish species such as eels, lampreys, hagfish, oarfish and seahorses.

These vary from the thick tails of lungfish and ocean pouts, which are used for **propulsion** to the thin spine-like tails of rays, which are only used for **navigation**.

- The **flattened** tail of a sea snake is paddle-shaped for propulsion.
- The adept tail of **a pipid frog** allows it to *swim* by **circular** vertical motions.
- Seahorses maintain their vertical position with their tails when *swimming* or resting.
- Caecilians and salamanders *swim* like fish, with **sinusoidal** lateral tail motions.
- Crocodiles accomplish their *dives* with one powerful *stroke* of the tail.

Locomotion using the tail

Swimming and crawling

Although these involve comparatively similar motions, the tail/abdomen tip plays a very different role in each.

For limbless species, from fish and aquatic mammals to reptiles and snakes, the body and tail are the main source of forward *thrust*. Three main modes of motion are involved:

- **Undulation** of the tail (both lateral and vertical) is used on land and in water by a huge variety of species, from the zigzagging **serpentine** *crawling* motion of snakes to the *lashing* tail of *swimming* newts and crocodiles.
- **Rectilinear motion** involves the alternate *contraction* and *elongation* of sections of the body in a straight line to produce the *gliding* locomotion of worms and some snakes.
- **Helical motion** is used only for *swimming*, and involves *rotating* in a spiral around the body's horizontal axis like a drill or screw. Species such as dolphins and whales would never be able to swim as far and as fast as they do without such a powerful method of propulsion, screwing practically the whole body through the water to

maintain the forward momentum initiated by the tail. These creatures' comparatively small lateral and dorsal fins serve only to stabilise and balance the forward movement generated by the helical motions of the body and tail.

- Amphibious species with limbs often use their tails as an additional **propulsive** implement on land (where the requirement to overcome gravity is far greater), as well as for balance and direction. When *crawling*, the tail's motion vocabulary is wider and more varied.

- Amphibious and land reptiles with absent or rudimentary limbs have adapted their plastic facilities to use their tails for *crawling*, using swim-like motions for **propulsion** and **navigation**. They travel through grass, sand or mud by means of similar lateral or vertical *undulations* of the body.

Sidewinding is a *looping* style of lateral *undulation* developed by desert snakes for travelling over hot sand. They *anchor* the rear of the body to the ground with their tail and then *thrust* the head upwards and sideways, *pulling* the front of the body off the ground and *zigzagging* sideways. The head *lands* first, briefly *touching* the hot sand before *thrusting* immediately in the desired direction, even before the tail reaches the ground.

Some species can *swim* and *crawl* backwards, using specially developed **appendages** (such as spikes or scales) or modulation techniques. In these cases, tail motions are designed to *pull* rather than *push*, and the tail *leads* the way rather than following in a directional role.

Climbing and descending

These are vital **locomotion** abilities for most reptiles and mammals. Tail length generally varies from between 30% to 75% of the body. Legless creatures such as snakes and caecilians use vertical *undulations* and '**concertina**' motions to *climb* and *descend*. Whereas light creatures with short bodies can *climb* straight up and down, longer and heavier snakes often use a *coiling* variation of the same *climbing/descending* techniques, *wrapping* themselves around the support when moving up or down.

The main role of the tail in these actions is to *anchor* and *grip*. Each motion of the climber is completed by *coiling* the tail around the next highest section of what is being climbed, *gripping* it firmly by the tail muscles or adhesive discs. Once secured in this way, the tail *supports* the rest of the body for its move to the next level before being *uncoiled* and *lifted* into position for the next anchor point. Descending involves inverting essentially the same motion sequences.

The '**concertina**' motion is a common mode of *climbing* and *descending* that also differs from the *swimming* and *crawling* techniques already described. Using the tail as an anchor, the body sections *bunch up* to travel in the intended direction like a peristaltic wave until the tail can *attach* to a new hold to *anchor* the next advance. The motion is analogous to the way frogs and locusts propel themselves by alternately *contracting* and *expanding* their hind legs.

Limbless amphibians and reptiles are not particularly comfortable in *descending* in the concertina mode because of gravity problems. *Supporting* the body weight when *climbing* a vertical tree trunk by *coiling* the tail round a firm anchor is much easier than trying to do the same when suspended upside down when *descending*. Limbless creatures lack a lower anchor to *support* the body descending vertically, so they prefer a gentler, more gradual descent in which the body can *support* itself at more points to counterbalance the unsupported weight hanging down.

Some agile snakes descend by *leaping* from one branch to a lower one, thereby saving time, energy and sometimes even life. Unlike flying lizards, flying squirrels, possums and other arboreal species that use similar techniques, snakes have no limbs or any special body tools – they simply acquired the ability to *leap* considerable distances.

Jumping snakes 'fly' using the same motion principles as they do when *sidewinding* on the ground. *Gripping* a branch with their tail and rear body, they *thrust* themselves at the next branch or trunk, essentially *throwing* themselves into the air and continually *wiggling* their entire body in the classic **serpentine** motion, altering direction via sharp, convulsive motions, as cats do with their tails in free fall.

The reason for these vigorous mid-air motions is to prolong the distance of the *leap*. In this frenetic *wriggling* motion can be seen echoes of a bird's *flapping* wings – an act of primitive mimicry perhaps? Before landing, the snake chooses which branch to *grasp* with its advancing tail, which *anchors* the body again for the next *twisting leap,* and so on until it reaches terra firma.

Limbless amphibian reptiles often move on vertical rock faces. Although there are no branches to *wrap* their tails around for an anchor, they skilfully use the rear half of their body to *grip* the rough surface with their muscles or suction devices in the tail. Even from a vertically inverted position, they manage to evade predators and catch prey thanks to these tail motion facilities. Worms, caecilians and snakes also travel large distances on a daily basis to find food or mates. The tail also greatly assists the locomotion of quadruped species in terms of **coordination** and **balance**.

- Pygmy anteaters escape ground predators by *climbing* rock faces or trees upside-down.
- The muscular prehensile tail of a boa makes it an excellent climber and swimmer.
- Flying squirrels use their furry tail as a rudder when *gliding* from branch to branch, and to realign the body from its horizontal starting position to a vertical one for landing.

In addition to this passive balancing function, the tail usually plays an auxiliary role in the primary progressive movements of limbed amphibians, reptiles and mammals when *walking, running* and *jumping*. Motions of the abdomen and tail also complement the limb motion of insects, though to a lesser extent.

The role of the tail in the locomotion of limbless species and those with underdeveloped limbs raises several questions that relate to the metamorphosis of apes from quadrupeds to bipeds – the so-called 'missing link' – as much as they do to the evolution of the tail itself.

Let us begin by first summarising what tails are for. Land animals have three main type of dwelling: underground (**burrowers**), on the surface (**terrene**) and above ground (**arboreal**), of which some species use more than one type. As we have seen, the tails of marine creatures *propel* and *direct*; the rudder function also applies to the tails of birds. For terrestrial species, the tail is mainly used to *balance* the body and to protect against both predators and parasites. Tree-dwellers use the tail to *anchor* themselves in the trees. In addition, the tail is for all species also a highly expressive instrument of plastic communication for courtship, warning and so on.

As the functional motion repertoire of the tail is closely related to that of the limbs in locomotion, it is reasonable to conclude that in the initial stages of the transition from quadruped to biped stance, the long tail was used as an additional way of *supporting* the body in motion, almost as an extra limb.

The first question is why, after some 300 million years of successful survival, did limbless amphibians need limbs?

The emergence of amphibians was the evolutionary Rubicon in the transition from aquatic to land-based existence. The accompanying anatomical transformation from limbless swimmers like hagfish into species such as sirens that *crawl* with the help of two tiny forelimbs and thence to creatures capable of *walking* on four legs such as salamanders took hundreds of millions of years. Caecilians burrow into the seabed and remain in the mud after the water has receded. When the drying mud made life below the surface unbearable through lack of water and food, they sought new habitats nearer to water, using their tails as the sole means of **propulsion**.

Species that learned how to adapt efficiently to these periodic fluctuations in the availability of water survive without limbs to this day. Those for whom the environmental pressures were more intense, however, because of local climatic conditions or whatever, were obliged to seek sustenance on the surface, teeming as it was with unfamiliar predators and competitors. The evolutionary imperative to develop limbs for locomotion under these circumstances was overwhelming.

The second question is why did four-limbed aquatic species retain their tails after becoming terrestrial?

The answer is that the factors affecting the anatomical changes that accompany the transition from one habitat to another (water, underground, on land, in the trees and in the air) are many and complex, and include extreme environmental circumstances such as climate change, floods, seismic activity, meteorites and other cosmic phenomena. Some species, like penguins and seals, have probably changed habitat (and therefore anatomical structure) more than once because of such external stimuli.

The lifecycle of the frog is a microcosm of this evolutionary process, with limbless aquatic tadpoles moving around by *lashing* their tails until replaced by the limbs of the tailless amphibian adult

- Arboreal chameleons have prehensile tails and four limbs with claws.
- Though mainly land-based, the Komodo dragon also *swims* with its strong flexible tail.
- Many lizards can lose their tail when required and survive adequately until it regenerates.

As these examples confirm, semi aquatic frogs, turtles and lizards can easily exist without tails, relying exclusively on four limbs. However, crocodiles and most other amphibious reptile species nevertheless retain tails as well as legs through some deeply ingrained genetic memory of the kind of catastrophic environmental change that would make the ability to survive both on land and in water an evolutionary advantage.

The third question is why did some quadruped mammals lose their tails and not others?

The answer is partly the same as it is for reptiles and amphibians, from which lower orders of mammals inherited some anatomical, behavioural and plastic motion characteristics, but not others. Although pitilessly rigorous, evolution is not a neat process. Everything from local environmental anomalies to ecological factors affecting the whole planet alter outcomes in multitudinous different ways.

Whales and dolphins and seal and walrus species illustrate this complexity. The former evolved highly advanced tails to replace their lost terrestrial limbs a long time ago, continue to replicate themselves, and have to return regularly to the surface to breathe air. By contrast, the latter deliver their young on shore; with neither limbs nor tail at birth, the infants are incapable of *swimming* or *walking* for a considerable time, relying totally on their mothers for all their needs and protection. Their undeveloped forelimbs are genetically modified into flippers and the hind limbs are *twisted* rearwards to substitute for the missing tail, in a parallel solution for which there seems to be no logical explanation.

Although the limbs are the main device for progressive movement in most land mammals, the tail nevertheless remains a significant tool for many – but tailless species manage to survive in their particular habitats and the local environments equally well without.

Burrowing mammals use their tails mainly for *signalling* and for *supporting* their bodies when they stand on their hind legs to observe their surroundings. Others, like bears or rabbits, manage to do the same with no tails to speak of, having developed unusually sturdy hind limbs.

Marsupials like the kangaroo family have even more advanced hind legs, along with a large, strong tail that not only *supports* their erect stance, but also acts as a third hind leg while *leaping* and generally *counterbalances* other movements. This anatomical predominance of the tail was at the expense of the development of forelimbs, which effectively lost their role in *walking* and *running* are were used only for feeding, nursing, gathering, fighting and so on.

Tracing the evolution of the tail of land mammals' tails reveals a bewildering array of evolutionary stimuli for its development, atrophy, retention or loss. Some members of the family of species have tails, while others do not: armadillos, hares, rats, pigs, shrews, monkeys, primates, and so on. Most tree-dwelling mammals have proper tails to assist them in *climbing* up and down; but some, like koalas, do not. Seals have no tails, just as flying snakes have no wings; for all its relentless logic, the evolutionary process results in apparently strange anomalies.

Hominids apart, a significant minority of land mammals lost their tails - about the same proportion for whom the tail is functionally essential in everyday life. The remainder hardly use their tails at all – indeed, it can sometimes prove a hindrance when trying to escape predators, which is perhaps why so many herbivores evolved short tails.

Only tree-dwellers fully appreciate the functional value of their tails, such as anteaters and pangolins, squirrels and porcupines, shrews and lemurs, bush babies and tamarinds, monkeys and civets.

Whether predators or prey, most mammals needed to be able to *run* fast across the wide open spaces of savannah, in which the long and often bulky tails of big cats and canidae generally confer an advantage of **manoeuvrability** compared to the short appendix of their prey.

- A heavy, sated zebra or buffalo is at a serious disadvantage compared to the agile, hungry big cats or dogs that pursue it. Its attention is divided in three directions: watching its next step, looking for the best escape route, looking behind to see the predator's moves. By contrast, the predator's focus is on the running prey in front, but it needs a proper tail/rudder to serve as a balancing tool if it is to follow every sharp *twisting* movement the prey initiates. The real challenge for a savannah predator is to hunt prey that *jumps*, whether tailless like hares and springbok, or tailed like kangaroos or lemurs. A strong skilful tail helps predators to match the swift movements of these prey.

- The escaping hare *leaps* high with its hind legs and lands *touching* the ground briefly with its forelegs, which the hind legs overtake to *anchor* the next *leap*, the body *twisting* in any new direction the animal intends to take.

- The springbok flees its predator progresses in bouncing *springs* up to six feet in the air, even sometimes *jumping* over the pursuer entirely. Paradoxically, as with the hare, the absence of tail improves manoeuvrability, making the body lighter and eliminating any impediments to sharp moves and twists that a tail may cause.

- Kangaroos and lemurs use different *jumping* techniques to escape predators. The kangaroo makes high forward *leaps* by using its hind legs simultaneously with its bulky, strong tail. The latter first *anchors* the erect body, and then *propels* it upwards in an extended trajectory at the same time as the powerful hind legs. During its *glide* through the air, the tail *balances* the body, preparing it for the next intended direction. On the way down, the tail *lands* first to amortise the momentum, and *anchors* the next *leap*, together with the hind legs. It would not be possible to execute such a *jump* without the *support* of an extraordinary tail, which functions practically as a third hind limb. The forelimbs take no part in locomotion, but balance the front part of the body.

- Lemurs have a long, light, free-floating furry tails that are constantly moving. As a mainly arboreal primate, they move on their hind legs on the ground, body erect, with a *bouncing* sideways *hop*, or *turning* around on the spot with the same type of motion. This characteristic *jumping* style derives from the unusual position of the hind legs, on which the lemur *squats* while held 10–15" apart. It *hops* sideways, *crossing* its legs in the air, *straightening* them on the descent and *landing* in the *squatting* position ready for the next *hop*.

One can well imagine the confusion of a predator trying to chase a creature moving in this unpredictable way; despite their exceptional hunting skills, they find themselves outmanoeuvred because of the speed and unfamiliarity of the motions they have to try and anticipate, and because their tails cannot be effectively deployed under these conditions in the same way as they can when following the normal *turning* and *twisting* of its prey – indeed, the tail becomes a liability under these circumstances.

Although birds' tails do not generate progressive forward movement, they play a crucial role in flying – most notably as a rudder in setting direction (*see Chapter IV*); tailless birds usually cannot fly. The variety of tail shapes, sizes and colours is phenomenal, as is their functional and performing repertoire. But whatever the tail, in the air or at rest, it always serves to *balance* the bird as well as being a leading instrument of plastic communication and courtship performance. Protruding as it does from the body, the tail is also an excellent recognition device, and expresses the bird's individual behaviour, emotional and physical state.

The same is true for most mammalian predators like hyenas, dogs and big cats, but with these species the tail also plays a role in locomotion, as we have seen. Although the tail adopts many different shapes and positions for progressive movements in different species, dogs and cats, for example, generally hold their tails as follows:

Walking: the tail *hangs* down restfully, with its tip *curved* upwards
Trotting: the tail is *held* out backwards at an angle
Sprinting: the tail is *held* horizontally
Leaping: the tail *thrusts* straight up as the hind legs *jump*
Gliding: the *reverse-arched* tail acts as a parachute

- The prehensile tail of a spider monkey allows it to perform acrobatic *leaps.*
- Crocodiles *lunge* out of water by '*tail walking*' when trying to catch prey.
- Escaping basilisk lizards *run* across water on their hind legs, balancing themselves by *thrusting* the tail upwards at each step.

Functional capacity

As we have seen, the highly developed tail of legless species is the evolutionary result of desperate pressures to adapt to tough new environmental conditions, as well as a significant increase in the number of surrounding competitors and predators. The need to survive is also what drove most limbed species to enlarge the plastic scope of their tails, both in instinctive functional behaviours and consciously performed activities. Limbless amphibians and reptiles naturally developed richer plastic facilities of the tail in locomotion, but their tails are otherwise far less adept in functional/performing terms.

GATHERING AND HUNTING/PROTECTING

Gathering activities of aquatic and terrestrial species involving the tail include *cleaning* the forest floor or the surface of a pond, near their nests; *digging* into the desert sand or seabed;

218

building dams or burrows; collecting vegetation with *sweeps* of the tail or *picking up* fallen fruit with the help of a sticky discs or sharp scales on the tail; checking temperature or detecting chemical signals using the tail tip; *dragging* large prey or a branch by *coiling* the tail around the object; and *anchoring* the body on a vertical surface by tail accessories when feeding or hunting upside down.

- Rove beetles use motions of their large tails to correct their balance when feeding on unstable branches.
- A female wasp *bores* into wood with the ovipositor the rear part of the abdomen to deposit eggs.
- Beavers use the tail as a *working* tool to construct dams.
- Limbless burrowers *compress* the tunnel walls with their tails; some plug the entrance using a scale at the end of the tail.
- Penguins use their stiff tail feathers to *support* their erect body on land.
- Crocodiles use *sweeping* motions of their powerful tail to create paths to the water for their hatchlings.
- Anteaters shelter from the sun's heat by *folding* their gigantic tail over their bodies.

Hunting and **protecting** motions differ considerably according to body structure and genetic background. As a weapon for hunting, the tail is used in many different ways.

Some predators use intriguing tail motions to entice prey, or by *imitating* the movements of familiar objects such as a *shaking* leaf with the tail as a form of camouflage; others *coil* their tails around a branch and *fling* out their bodies to look like a twig while waiting for their unsuspecting prey. Some predators asphyxiate their victims with the coils of their tails; others *curve* their tails on the ground like roots, only to knock down passing prey with a sharp *blow* of the tail. Some poison their prey with a sting in the tail; others use spines or blades in the tail to *stab*.

- The *stinging* tail of a scorpion can kill prey much bigger than itself.
- The blunt-headed snake *hangs* from a branch by the *grip* of its tail to catch passing prey from the air.
- Komodo dragons can kill large bovine animals with a powerful *blow* of the tail.
- Whales kill seals with a single *blow* of their massive flukes.
- Tamandua anteaters use their hairless tails to chase termites out of their mounds.

In order to survive at all, herbivores have generally evolved a much wider range of defence skills than their predators. Their repertoire of defensive tail motions includes the use of spikes and spines at the end of an insect's abdomen, with or without stings; the vigorous *wriggling* of fishes' tails; using sharp rear-pointing tail spines; using the tail as a lever for *rising* up to increase apparent body size; *tapping* or *drumming* the tail on the ground to produce intimidating noise; *covering* the body with the armour of a wide scaly tail; and emitting foul smells from glands at the base of the tail, and *fanning* it with *sweeping* motions.

The vast number of additional defence strategies involving the tail include:

- Cave crickets use the long spines or cerci at the tip of the abdomen to detect approaching enemies.
- Some rays have sharp saw-like stings on their tails for protection.
- The self-amputated tail of a lizard continues *wriggling*, confusing the predator for long enough to give the creature time to escape.
- Gould monitors *rise up* on their tails, which look like a third leg.
- When threatened, a rattlesnake will *throw* itself up into air by *swinging* its tail.
- Armadillos *curl up* into a protective ball by *grasping* their tail with their jaws.

- The stump-tailed skink displays the head-like markings on its tail the draw the confused predator's attack for long enough to counterattack with its real head.

PLAYING, WARNING, COMPETING

These are three stages of essentially the same physical activity, using a similar motion vocabulary. A comparison of all three demonstrates the range of plastic motions involved, together with their different stimuli and motivations. As with the other spontaneous body movements we have described, these are not only interconnected with each other, but also relate to the fighting motions of other parts of the body.

Gnaw-play, as an instinctive form of social activity, is included primarily in the functional category, but also as part of the performing repertoire of young mammals, where the tail is used for balancing in coordination with the head and legs.

The individual variations of tail play in the fighting repertoire are therefore very limited:
- *Supporting* the body in an upright biped posture when *pawing* the adversary with the fore legs, or *levering* the creature's own or its rival's body weight.
- *Hitting* one another with the tail, or *drumming* it hard on the opponent's prone body as a victory signal.
- *Spinning* around on the spot, chasing the creature's own tail, or catching and vigorously *gnawing* the *swinging* tail of another, occasionally inflicting pain.

Gnaw-play practice mainly involves the young participants using the body communication system taught by their mothers from birth on, however. The tail is a major plastic language tool for tailed creatures of all orders, from insects to primates. These plastic facilities are most highly developed in cats, dogs and lemurs. Observation of these species' behaviour reveals the many emotional reactions and potential actions expressed by tail *gestures.* A tail may suddenly stop *swinging,* or an otherwise motionless tail *jerk* at the tip; it may *curve* upwards, downwards or sideways and maintain that position; it can *stretch* at various angles from horizontal to vertical, either *held* straight or in a looser, more relaxed serpentine manner.

The many emotional or physical states expressed by the tail are often communicated by changes of position so small as to be unnoticeable (and therefore incomprehensible) except to members of the same species. The stimuli for such plastic expressions of the tail include expressions of contentment, the agitation of suckling infants, juvenile curiosity or uncertainty, adult caution or alertness, mating and warning signals, intentions to hunt or assert dominance, aggression and fear.

The gestural vocabulary of gnaw play eventually became the foundation for warning signals and to prelude to contest and fighting routines. Warning messages of the tail are more spatially expansive – and therefore more visible – than *grimaces.* The early recognition of such warning signals offers an animal a survival advantage, of course.

The two main categories of warning gestures of the tail are **static** and **moving** signals. The former are plastic emblems of **passive** motion expression; although the latter are also instinctive, as active gestures, they are a spontaneous reflex response to an external stimulus.

The inter-species signalling vocabulary contains plastic signs common to most animals, and indicate positive intentions as well as negative reactions:
- **Aggression**: tail *held* upright and straight
- **Submission**: tail *curved* inwards and down
- **Neutrality**: tail lies *coiled* out on the ground

These examples of straightforward plastic messages by the tail are understood by most species, even tailless ones. Their young, with no life experience of physical danger, will instinctively cling to the ground when threatened, in a genetically acquired response.

Except for the few species of insects, fish, sea mammals and reptiles that use their tails as weapons, the motion repertoire of the tail in a contest is very limited. As with gnaw-play, adult competitors use the tail mainly as a body *support* and *balance*, or for *wrapping* and *squeezing* motions in close range combat.

Whales and dolphins use their tails as weapons during the mating season; indeed, the tail is their only weapon, and its aggressive motion capabilities are very highly developed, with the richest tail vocabulary in the aquatic world. By contrast, crocodilians and giant lizards use their tails as secondary weapons, although powerful enough to *beat* their adversaries to death.

The most spectacular use of the tail in combat is in the territorial disputes between brown and black male scorpions described earlier. No additional warning signals are necessary; when two of these rivals meet, they know exactly what to expect from one another, and no time is wasted. Unless one of them retreats immediately, the fight to the death is on. They circle each other, gradually getting closer and constantly searching for advantage and the best spot to *sting* the opponent.

The ability to transmit and receive warning signals is, as we have seen, essential to the survival of species as well as individuals. The deployment and interpretation of warning signals reduces fatalities within the same species, which is why ancient species have survived for so long.

- Rattlesnakes give warning signals by *vibrating* the rings at the end of the tail.
- Komodo dragons *lash* their tails vigorously as a warning signal.
- Lizards *stand* upright on hind legs and tail and make bodily contact in pre-wrestling positions.
- Monitors *perform* spectacular ritualised fights using their powerful tails.
- Hippos use their tails to *sweep* fresh excrement in the water into the face of a rival.

COURTING, MATING AND NURSING

Reproduction is of course the fundamental concern of all animals, and the tail of limbless species plays a major role in each of the three stages. It signals agreement to a rendezvous, and is also an attractive implement for courtship display; it is used to stimulate sexual receptivity, and as to *support* the female's body for effective copulation; it can be a warmer and protector for incubation, providing a secure perimeter for eggs and hatchlings as well as being a strong weapon of defence.

Mating calls
Most tailed species use their tails in one way or another to indicate the sexual receptivity of females and the sexual intentions of males. Although we are all familiar with such plastic motions in our domestic animals, these coded plastic tail signals as far remain largely undeciphered as far as most other species are concerned. In addition to mating signals involving sound, smell and colour, there is undoubtedly a complete vocabulary of mating signs using the eyes, ears, muzzle, skin, hair, genitals and other body parts as well as the tail.

However, the tail reacts expressively to mating signals over medium to long-range distances. Although tailed species have different reproductive processes, most consist of five main stages: mating calls, courtship play, pre-copulation contact, copulation and gestation or incubation. The tail is actively involved in each stage.

Courtship display
The males of different insect, amphibian and reptile species make impressive use of their tails in courtship performances; indeed, their chances of being accepted by a female depend on it. These displays usually consist of *vibrating, curling, stretching* and *twisting* the tail. However,

as described earlier, the most spectacular tail performances are those of birds and sea mammals. Birds introduce themselves to potential mates with their colourful tails in a kaleidoscopic display of feathers, *spreading* or *closing* them in a shimmering fan, *twisting, waving* or *flapping* and so on. The highest level of these performance skills is perhaps the aerial display of eagles, when a mating couple perform a veritable *pas de deux* using the extraordinary dexterity of their tails.

There remains much to be discovered about the tail performance repertoire of sea mammals during courtship, which is largely conducted in mid-ocean, far away from prying human eyes. Based on what we do know, however, it is reasonable to assume that these intelligent and musical creatures have highly developed plastic motion abilities of the tail. Whales and dolphins have been recorded performing complex acrobatic dance sequences of startling grace and synchronisation during the mating season, both solo and in groups, and driven mainly by the tail's propulsive and directional facilities.

Copulation modes

In some species, mating partners pay little attention to the niceties of courtship, proceeding to copulation as soon as each other's genetic credentials have been established. However, most mating couples take the time to get properly acquainted, harmonise themselves emotionally and prepare a suitably intimate area in order for the outcome of the copulation to be as propitious as possible. For obvious reasons, this is especially true of species that mate for life.

The tail repertoire at this stage mainly involves limbless species: fish, amphibians, reptiles, birds and sea mammals. It includes:

- *touching* parts of the mate's body with the end of the tail.
- the male tenderly *stroking* the genital area of the female with various body parts.
- mutual *rubbing* and delicately *intertwining* tails.
- *rotating* the tip of the male's tail in the entrance to the female's cloaca.
- *intertwining* tails to establish direct genital contact.

With certain insect, amphibian and reptile species, the mates copulate by maintaining a steady contact with both tails until the male's sperm transfers into the female's cloaca. To achieve the most effective genital-to-genital copulation, male whales and dolphins *press* their own weight down the female's body on the seabed, using their tails and pectoral fins to *hold* her firmly in position.

Limbed lizards also control the right copulation position with their strong flexible tails, using their legs to maintain balance on the ground. Indeed, the wide variety of standard patterns of *coiling* the male lizard's tail around the female's body is one of the more spectacular demonstrations of the tail's copulation motion repertoire.

Although the tail of land mammals is used extensively in mating calls and courtship display, it plays little or no part in copulation.

- A mating newt *lashes* his tail to send pleasant odours to the female.
- A red-bellied snake *throws* its body into a series of *wriggling* motions of the tail before copulation.
- A tailed male frog *transfers* sperm into female's cloaca with its tail.
- Swallowtail butterflies *copulate* in the air with the tips of their abdomens.

Incubation/nursing

Female insects, amphibians and reptiles lay their eggs (or exceptionally, deliver their young), from the rear part of the abdomen. In the process, they *shake, sweep, squeeze* and *contract* their abdomen or tail. Female marsupial frogs nurture their hatchings, *collect* the eggs and incubate them under the skin of their own backs and tails. Some male newts and salamanders incubate eggs after fertilization with their tails, which they *coil* around the eggs to protect them until they hatch, regularly *changing* the position of the tail for proper incubation.

Fish vigorously *sweep* their tails while laying eggs, strewing them in all directions over the widest area to avoid detection by predators. Some *rub* their tails on rocks in the riverbed to expel their eggs.

In some species, the mother fish *agitates* the water in a special way with her tail to ensure that her helpless hatchlings follow her. Whales and dolphins also use their tails to lead offspring away from predators, and help infants to the surface with their tails to breathe. And of course, parents teach juveniles the entire repertoire of tail motions: *sweeping, propelling, twisting, undulating, slapping, thrusting*, and so on.

SKIN and HAIR

The body's covering is usually thought of a background instrument in gestural communication rather than a plastic motion tool in its own right. The skin has a limited vocabulary in both functional behaviour and communications, and the hair even less so.

Reptiles such as snakes shed their skin; others, such as lizards, have **spikes** instead of hair; crocodiles are covered in **leathery armour** with protective **osteoderms** beneath the outer layer; some frogs have hair-like **dermal vilii** to aid cutaneous respiration when underwater; fish have **scales** and birds, **feathers**.

As the hair roots of mammals are usually sited in the pores of the skin, both are closely connected in signalling reactions to internal impulses or external irritants. These **transmitter/receptor** organs are often located on or beneath the skin.

Most species, from spiders, insects, amphibians and reptiles to mammals, regularly groom themselves. This is not cleanliness for its own sake, but to maintain these sensory organs and glands in good condition. Just as cats meticulously clean their faces and whiskers, ants repeatedly clean their palps, monkeys continually remove dead skin, parasites and other impurities from their fur, elephants bathe at every opportunity and low mammals moult each spring. After all, any deficit in the associated sensory abilities could cost the animal its life.

FUNCTIONAL SUBCONSCIOUS MOTION

Raising hackles/feathers
Raising the hair or feathers on certain body parts such as the head, chest, upper back and tail is a common emotional expression of mammals and birds alike.

These reactions can be prompted by positive factors (such as during grooming, courtship, mating, eating and gnaw-play) or negative ones (such as a sudden shock or threat, indecision, aggression or grief). Emotionally neutral factors can also induce such behaviour, such as the need to regulate body temperature, or to dry the body covering.

Even though hominids have lost most of their bodily hair along the tortuous evolutionary path, they nevertheless retain vestiges of these emotional expressions in modified form. Where follicles of body hair would once have become *erect* under conditions of **cold** or **fear**, we have the *swelling* of the pores known as goose pimples.

Birds have far greater motion expression facilities with their feathers than mammalian hair. Being able to control each part of their body covering right down to individual wing or tail feathers, they can respond to emotional stimuli in varied and complex ways, in the air, on the ground or in water.

Shivering, twitching and trembling
The skin of a new-born mammal is usually delicate, with fine downy hair. *Twitching* and *trembling* this covering is the primal skin motion, either as a compensatory *shiver* response to

any temperature drop or to repel the many parasitic insects attracted by the smell of the new-born. The sensitive nerve endings of the young skin react sharply to each bite with a brisk *twitch* of the body part concerned – a reaction that remains throughout life, and with all species including hominids.

- Low mammals *shake* their skin/hair as required to remove accumulated dust, dirt or water; or when facing a dangerous predator.
- A monkey or a rabbit will *tremble* when hypnotised by a python, transfixed as the predator slowly approaches.
- Copulating couples *shiver* when reaching orgasm.
- A mortally wounded mammal may *shudder* in agony, and the corpse may continue to *twitch* for a few moments after death.

Twitching and *trembling* are often therefore both the original and terminal body motions.

Stretching and inflating

In many species, the skin serves many more purposes beyond covering the body – to incubate eggs, for example, or to *suckle, preen, signal* and *groom*.

- Species such as **marsupials** and **seahorses** have a pouch-like **pocket** of skin on their belly to *carry* babies or food reserves.
- The female **marsupial frog** has a **pouch** on its back that can contain over one hundred eggs placed there during mating.
- The elasticity of **elephant** skin allows its trunk to accomplish an astonishing range of Functional and Performed plastic motions.
- **Snake** skin *stretches* and *contracts* enormously to accommodate large prey swallowed whole, returning to its normal state after digestion.
- Some mammals have **pleated** skin between their upper arm and chest, which they use as **wings** when *leaping* and *diving* from tree to tree.
- Male **Darwin frogs** collect eggs from the female with their mouths and keep them in their **crops** for a few weeks until a dozen or so infants eventually emerge from their massively distended crops.

The skin's main role is to **protect** the body against wind, water, impact damage and temperature extremes. Our Ice Age ancestors of course added the skins of other creatures to their own for these purposes.

Skin is also a main line of **defence** for many species, such as the scaly armour of armadillos and pangolins, the spines and quills of porcupines or the poisonous secretions of certain toads and other reptiles; and in rhinoceros horn, which consists of densely compacted hair-like cells, it can act as a weapon of aggression. Some lizard species secrete a protective coating which allow the creatures to survive the intense heat of forest fires. Birds use their multi-coloured feathers as an expressive palette to **attract** mates, to **decorate** nests in courtship displays and to perform amazing acrobatic aerial *tricks*.

But whatever type of body covering an animal has, it is always the primary means of **perceiving** external physical contact, **reacting** directly to these stimuli and passing on the appropriate sensory information to the brain. Ever since the first unicellular micro-organisms appeared on the planet, the plastic motion of the skin has therefore been a primary communication tool – *contracting* and *expanding, stretching, swelling, trembling, wrinkling, changing colour* and so on.

It remains the most sensitive interface for intimate body communications. In many species, the skin acts as a sophisticated biochemical factory, generating oils, perspiration, salt, toxins or electricity to enhance these vital receptor/ transmitter functions.

MOTION AND BODY PART EXAMPLES OF AQUATIC ANIMALS FEEDING TOOLS

- **Rays** feed on snails, *crushing* the hard shell with their **teeth** to get at the soft body within, and eliminating the shell debris.
- **Mantas** have **flipper**-like organs on both sides of the head, which are used to *guide* plankton into the mouth.
- **Sawfish** have a long flat bony **protrusion** from the snout, edged with teeth like a two-edged saw, and used to search out and kill prey.
- **Hagfish** are parasitic and use their disc-like **mouth sucker** to *hang* firmly on to their prey and *rasp* a hole in the victim's side.
- The sharp teeth of common **red-bellied piranhas** can strip an animal as large as a deer down to its skeleton within a few minutes.
- **Cookie-cutter sharks** *suck* on large fish, sinking their razor-sharp lower **teeth** into the victim and *twisting* them to cut out a chunk of flesh.
- The **remora's** dorsal fin *transforms* into a **sucker** by which it *hangs* under large predators, feeding on the leftover scraps of their prey.

Hunting skills and weapons

- **Hammerhead sharks** *batter* their prey repeatedly with the heavy and dense **protrusions** on the head before *biting.*
- The side fins of the **gurnard** are modified as sensitive '**feet**', which can detect worms or crabs in the seabed. The fish stops its '*tip-toe walking*' and uses its armoured **snout** to *dig* out the prey.
- **Unicorn fish** have three non-retractable **blades** along the snout, drawn out into a long 'unicorn' **horn.**
- **Killer whales** *dive* into a crowd of young seals, *grab* a terrified pup with their **jaws** and *toss* it into the air, *hitting* the struggling prey with their enormous **flukes** before *catching* it in their **jaws.**
- **Stonefish** are expert ambush predators, and *strike* with great speed, *sucking* unsuspecting small fish into their cavernous **mouths.**
- **Thresher sharks** hunt in twos or in a group, *swimming* around a shoal of fish to herd them with their **tails**, which they *whip* sideways to stun and kill their prey.
- **Angler fish** use their **bioluminescent bait** to mislead smaller fish, enticing them to get close enough to *grab* with their fang-like **teeth.**

DEFENCE TOOLS AND TACTICS

- Some **rays** have poison glands on the sharp saw-like **stings** of their tails, which they *lash* aggressively against enemies.
- **Surgeon fish** project a movable **spine** on each side of the tail when attacked, and *lash* the opponent laterally.
- **Lion fish** have a deadly arsenal of poisonous **fin-spines**, whose dangers are advertised by bright colouring.
- **Anemone fish** *swim* up to bigger rivals *waggling* their **fins** to signal their annoyance at territorial intrusion.
- **Grey reef sharks** lifts their **snout**, arch their **backs** and lower their pectoral **fins** to warn unwelcome visitors of an impending attack.
- Antagonistic **mudskippers** engage in a silent face-to-face duel, with each *lifting* up its head and opening its mouth wide to intimidate the opponent. The winner announces his victory by *raising* its **dorsal fins** and wagging them from side to side.
- As roommates, the **goby fish** and the **alpheid shrimp** communicate by touch signals. The goby *swishes* its **tail** laterally when it spots a predator, while the shrimp *sweeps* its long **antennae** around until it *touches* the fish so that both can safely retreat.

PROTECTIVE CAMOUFLAGE AND PLASTIC MIMICRY

- The colour and shape of the **file fish** resembles sea grass; when frightened, it lets its body *drift* around as **dead weed.**
- The sabre-toothed **mimic blenny** resembles the Blue Streak cleaner wrasse. When approaching a large predator, it imitates the services provided by the wrasse, only to *bite* a chunk from the host at the last moment and escape.
- **Frogfish** match their colour to coral dwellers and wait upside down on the seabed with their thick tail looking like an **open mouth**, with two **eye spots** – impossible to recognise for what they are.
- **Shrimpfish** *swim* head down to resemble waving sea grass and hide among the spines of black sea urchins.
- Mimic **file fish** closely *imitate* the behaviour of black-saddled puffer fish, which are poisonous.
- When **porcupine fish** are attacked, they *inflate* a **bladder** by *sucking* in large quantities of water until they resemble a prickly ball.
- The **forceps fish** has a **false eye spot** near the base of its **tail** to confuse predators for long enough to escape.

COURTSHIP AND MATING

- Male **mudskippers** use their whole body to entice females to spawn in their nesting burrows, *raising* brightly coloured dorsal **fins** and showing off by *leaping* into the air using their powerful **tails.**
- **Seahorses** perform intricate greeting and **courtship dances**, using their single back **fin** to *move* gracefully in slow motion. The female *wraps* herself around the male and deposits her eggs in a special **pouch** on its belly, which the male fertilizes and carries until they hatch.

- The **cuckoo wrasse** is unusual in its ability to change sex. When the newly transformed males take part in a group spawning in spring, they approach females in an elaborate courtship dance, dazzling them with various **colouration tricks.**
- When the **three-spined stickleback** finds a willing partner, it *dances* a zigzag pattern forwards and backwards until the female follows to the nest site.
- The mating song of the **toad fish** is very loud and goes on for hours. When a female eventually appears, the male *grabs* her in his **jaws**, and draws her into a crevice for mating.
- Male **sun fish** court females by *swimming* around her with a spectacular show of *quivering* **fins** and flashing colours, *darting* away to drive off any other males.
- Male **sharks** often *bite* females when manoeuvring them into position for mating. Being generally larger than the males, the females tend to *bite* back.

PROGRESSIVE MOTION

- The **skate's wings** make them *swim* gracefully, or *leap* into the air like whales.
- The huge **dorsal fin** of a **sailfish** is used in courtship display and *folds* down into a groove during fast swimming.
- **Tripod fish** '*stand*' on their **pelvic fin** tips and tail like a tripod, *raising* their curtain-like **side fins** head to ambush passing shrimps.
- **Frogfish** *walk* on both sets of paired **fins**, which are modified as stout little legs. These fish have lost their depth-control bladders.
- **Flying fish** have large wing-shaped **pectoral fins** that allow them to *glide*, without *flapping*. Lateral *sweeps* of part of the tail in water increases their speed through the air.
- The **pelvic fins** of a **lumpsucker** can turn into a powerful *sucking* tool that the fish uses to *hang* on rocks while guarding hatching eggs, or waiting for prey.
- Some species of **mudskipper** can *climb* trees in their mangrove home using **suckers** derived from **pelvic fins.**
- Migrating **salmon** often use spectacular **acrobatic tricks** to *swim* against the flow, manoeuvring between rocks and negotiating waterfalls with persistent high *leaps.*
- **Dolphins**, like goby fish and alpheid shrimp, also communicate by touch, *nudging, stroking* and *smacking* one another. The meaning of their vocalisations is modified by *posturing, head-wobbling, nodding* and *waggling*, along with **flipper** gestures and **tail** motions.
- **Whales** and **dolphins** have remarkable body motion facilities, being able to *roll over* gracefully in water, *leap* high into air and *somersault*, solo or in groups, in unison or in succession, in the same or different directions, using frequent changes of speed or spatial patterns.
- **Gurnards** and **sea robins** *walk* across the seabed, the first three rays of their **pectoral fins** being modified into sensitive 'feet', with sensors to *probe* the sand for the worms, crabs and sand-eels on which they feed.

The fins of sea animals in general have evolved into an astonishing variety of versatile appendages for *locomotion, feeding, courting, flying, climbing, fighting, mimicking and communicating.*

Conclusion

There are in general two main categories of motion: **active** (moving in space); and **passive** (expressed on the spot). The former can be broken down into movements in a limited space, and progressive travelling movements (locomotion) unlimited by space.

Passive motions in a fixed position can also be subdivided into two major types: with the muscles *stretched* or *contracted* in a frozen pose (such as *holding* the breath, *tightening* both knees around a trunk, *yawning* and so on; or in contact with external objects, such as trying to dislodge a rock by *pushing* or *pulling* down a tree, *twisting* a liana, or *lifting* a heavy carcass.

Analysis of each of these types will be continued in subsequent chapters.

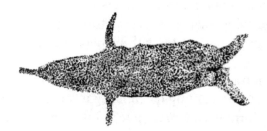

PART TWO

ARTIFICIAL MOTION

Chapter III: Sacred Events and Ceremonies

THE FUNDAMENTALS OF POSTURAL PERFORMANCE

The everyday pose/gestural vocabulary of hominids can be divided into the three modes through which it evolved: **Functional** (instinctive), **Communicative** (voluntary) and **Performed** (artificial). Although produced by the similar plastic facilities and intellect of the same body 'instrument', they differ from each other in technique and meaning:

a) FUNCTIONAL postures are usually those of a single individual, even when in a group, and reflect that individual's own body shape, behaviour and emotional state. Subconsciously, they relate to Functional activities of feeding, food gathering, hunting, courtship and so on.

b) COMMUNICATIVE postures are performed by two or more bodies interacting with each other in a **dialogue**, taking turns to exchange messages using similar body facilities and gestural patterns, with minor personal variations.

c) PERFORMED postures in ritual pantomime combine both functional and communicative modes. In **monologues**, solo performers used their own plastic facilities to describe certain personal characteristics or the actions of another. The success of such a performance depends on the knowledge, experience, emotional state and mimetic abilities of the posturer – their personal plastic 'signature'. The third element of any posturing performance is of course the audience, and their ability to read and respond to the messages they receive from ritual image being portrayed by the performer's mimetic technique and presentation.

The major types of posture therefore reflect the number of elements involved: functional, a solo monologue; communicative, a dialogue between two individuals; and performed, a three-way relationship between the performer, the sacred image and the audience.

The dictionary of postures for ritual and secular events consisted of **artificial** versions based on the functional and communicative vocabularies. Sequences of postural patterns were choreographed in advance by the shaman according to the sacred theme, compositional rules and the characteristics of the species being imitated. The choreography had to take into account: the **semantic genre** of the presentation; the **performing techniques** based on body shape, age and sex; the **number of postures** and their spatial **proximity**; the **balance** of body parts in relation to Gravity, Inertia and Momentum; and the **patterns** that would provide a clear plastic focus for the composition. Painstakingly as all these elements must have been to perform, their significance was readily understood by the audience.

Individual Posturing Patterns by Hominids

J. Antonio

Semantic gestural patterns are those that animate images or allegorical object to express meaningful actions, emotions or behaviours. By contrast, **Ornamental** posturing consists of decorative plastic compositions created for purely aesthetic reasons, with no motivation beyond artistry.

Semantic postures are a much earlier genre than ornamental ones, with a much larger repertoire of both functional and communicative postures. Ornamental performed plastic patterns nevertheless had an almost unlimited range of compositional variations, particularly in group settings of mimes, choir and musicians in totemic ritual pantomime ceremonies, or secular domestic celebrations such as births and marriages.

The semantic dictionary covers both functional and performed actions, behaviours and expressions of emotion. Indeed, the postural outline of natural instinctive functions like feeding/nursing, warming up/cooling down, or voluntary behaviours during courting/mating, attacking/defending were consciously imitated by poses and gestural patterns in ritual pantomime, with individual interpretations.

As mammalian communication evolved, the need grew for more sophisticated mimetic skills. Hominids eventually realised that merely copying the physical characteristics of their usual prey wasn't enough: to communicate effectively, they first had to penetrate the animal's mind and spirit – to become a temporary clone of the sacred creature, in total unison with its being.

It was this breakthrough that provided a strong psychological foundation for the mimetic postural repertoire at the Subconscious Functional level, opening up a new phase of emotional subjects such as: curiosity/searching, suspicion/surprise, tension/alertness, looseness/relaxation, frustration/excitement, affection/modesty, thievery/cunning, determination/snobbery, attention/observation.

Functional posturing evolved into Performed postures thanks to this dictionary of bodily communication, with its extensive vocabulary of pose-gestural expressions between two or more plastic images.

The compass of hominid emotional behaviours includes: dominance/superiority, failure/submission, welcoming/salutation, humility/deference, rejection/ignoring, aggression/sulking, appeasement/benevolence, love/admiration and hate/abuse.

How these emotions were communicated by posture depended on age, sex, social position and profile, body shape and personal characteristics. As well as individual variations, children would use different postures from adults to express the same emotion, as would males from females, warriors from herdsmen, chiefs from scouts, and so on.

POSE-GESTURAL COMMUNICATION

Semantic postures and gestures can be divided into **solo signals** and **duet** or **group interactions**, with their respective gestural genres: *indicative, descriptive, connotative, illustrative*, etc. for solo signals, and *introductory, instructional, intimate, argumentative* for the interactions (see in 'Composition Styles of Ancient Dance' section, Chapter IV). They could be performed in the three main styles described: *realistic* (natural), *artistic* (stylised) and *symbolic* (abstract).

Solo signalling postures tended to use the extremities to focus audience attention on one main plastic motif, expressed in a mixture of realistic and symbolic styles. This repertoire was used to communicate in circumstances such as:

- approaching a prey animal or predator.
- the start of a new breeding cycle.
- the discovery of a new source of food or fresh water.

- to warn of impending attack or to declare war.
- to call for help in an emergency.
- to announce the arrival of visitors or the return of warriors or hunters.
- to open secular and sacred events.
- to spread news of births, nuptials and deaths.

By contrast, **interactive** postural images attempted to 'freeze' a dynamic motion through syncretic performance involving the whole body in many different spatial conditions, with the performers either in direct physical contact with each other or far apart, on the ground or with lifts, riding animals or using accessories such as weapons, tools, acoustic instruments, decorations, and so on. This repertoire included:
- maternal behaviours.
- the elementary instruction of offspring in basic gestures.
- courtship and mating behaviours between couples.
- the initiation of youngsters.
- confrontations between hunters and prey.
- illustrations of combat by two posturers, with or without weapons.
- group pose-gestural presentations at harvest festivities.

MIMETIC IMAGES by hominids originated, as you would expect, in the Subconscious Hunting repertoire. As we have seen, this was by no means a strategy unique to apes, being adopted by many species. However, prompted by the ever-present imperative to survive, our ancestors gradually developed their mimicking and body decoration techniques to professional standards of performance far in advance of those of other mammals, who were restricted by their limitations of their intellectual facilities and quadrupedal posture.

The strong innate desire of the young to behave like their parents in order to master the natural world led them constantly to observe and **imitate** adult behaviours and motion patterns. This eventually provided the emotional plastic foundation for the convergence between man and performed images in the service of successful hunting and later, animal husbandry. Early hunters learned the basic lessons of this **realistic style** of artificial mimicry through this all-absorbing study of the body shapes and behaviour of their prey for pre- and post-hunting rituals. The range of posturing characters in Totemic pantomime had the same mimetic roots, as did the multi-faceted cast of posturing anthropomorphised creatures in funerary rites.

The next step in the evolution of mimetic culture was the **artistic creation** of animated images in these pantomimes, rather than just copying natural models to provide cover for hunting. This was a significant turning point for hominids, involving as it did an intellectual and practical shift away from stereotypic miming into performing new images of mythical animals in premeditated scenarios with pre-choreographed postural patterns. This conceptual and cultural advance engendered more **abstract thought** and **symbolic** methods of using pose-gestures to depict plants and inanimate images in seasonal ceremonies.

However, it was in totemic funerary pantomime that the pinnacle of ritual posturing was reached, with symbolic images of **anthropomorphised creatures**. These allegoric personages were a plastic synthesis of various body parts of two or three unrelated species, with the same solo performer combining the specific characteristics of the chosen insects, reptile, fish, birds or mammals in a single mythic character who usually played a pivotal positive or negative role, as a **central focus** for the sacred drama being performed. The dichotomies commonly represented by these abstract symbolic posturing images included satiety and starvation, war and peace, light and darkness, life and death, beauty and ugliness, youth and old age, mind and body, happiness and grief, love and hate, and so on.

Shamanism and witchcraft usually provided the spiritual source for the repertoire of performed postures, which had a powerful superstitious effect on tribe members. The complicated pose-gestural vocabulary, often supported by supernatural accessories, included a series of hypnotic postural patterns to concentrate the spectator's mind on their inner emotional state, manipulated as it was by the witch/shaman. Although these mystic posturing patterns were essentially similar, they nevertheless retained the plastic signature of the individual performer and his body facilities and spiritual power.

ORNAMENTAL poses and gestures for **group** presentations consisted of fixed, self-contained aesthetic images which, unlike the Semantic type, carried no narrative weight. Standard Semantic pose-gestural routines were artistically limited by the performing instrument itself, with its inherent similarities of anatomy, plastic facilities, emotional range, mentality, spiritual attitudes, local manners and so on, all of which restricted freer composition.

By contrast, no such spatial and plastic limitations inhibited the creation of ornamental pose-gesturing presentations, although far less individual personalisation was involved. Performers were all plastically united in a cohesive pose-gestural ensemble like the instruments of an orchestra, whether in unison or contrapuntally, canonical or in succession, with soloist and chorus or in separate groups. They always expressed the same specific motif in the same style, but with varying personal plastic intonations, as a harmonious postural symphony.

Earlier Ornamental pose-gestural patterns were simpler than the Semantic equivalents and played mainly an auxiliary role as plastic accompaniment to the lead performers in ritual ceremonies:

- In mythic pantomime, a postural entourage follows in harmony with the **plastic leitmotif** of the Totem soloist.
- Mythic personages are dramatically accompanied by the Ornamental gestural patterns of a standing/sitting choir.
- In sacrificial events, the shaman is given postural assistance by plastically illustrating his sacred narrative, and focusing attention on the major **compositional motifs** of his performance.
- In funerary rites, crying women perform a kaleidoscope of extravagant postures and gestures in composed dramatic sequences.
- Warriors perform aggressive/defensive postures in ritual procession prior to combat, together with warning/ threatening signals with or without weapons.
- Sexual postures are performed by females at phallic moonlight fertility rites, singing in unison, in varied plastic **formations.**
- Mass posturing is performed during Harvest celebrations, using pose-gestural patterns with fruit/ greenery and working tools.
- *Squatting, sitting, kneeling* and *prostrating* supplicants on the ground, confessing with exaggerated postural patterns, in varying succession.
- Synchronised pose-gestural sequences during official parades, with plastic salutations to the chief.

The next stage of development of ornamental posturing was prompted by the increasing popularity of secular dance/mime performance. The earliest 'round' form of ritual dance also comprised singing and miming. Primitive *steps* were often followed by various decorative plastic patterns of *posing* choristers and musicians who gradually established themselves separately from the dancers into an independent performing group, thereby considerably extending the ornamental postural vocabulary since they were now no longer subject to the same amount of choreographed movement. However, they continued occasionally to *posture* with the dance ensembles with whom they had for so long been plastically, rhythmically and spiritually linked.

Ornamental pose-gesturing was perfected over the millennia, evolving into a sophisticated and highly expressive body plastic language. Later, both semantic and ornamental forms were unified **artistically** as the model for representing animated bodies in ancient visual arts, particularly in sculptural and architectural decoration as well as for prehistoric dance/pantomime performances. Such intricate pose-gestural sequences featured strongly in the sacred and secular theatres of ancient China, India and (much later) those of Classical Greece and Rome, and reached its peak in the abstract/symbolic poses of the modern European classical ballet tradition.

PLASTICITY AS AN INSTRUMENT OF MIMESIS

Mammalian young **play** with each other from an early age, gradually building up their physical agility and strength, reaction speeds and perceptual skills. During these endless gnaw-plays they also unconsciously develop many mimetic abilities, when naturalistically feigning attraction or rejection, aggression or submission, attack or defence and so on. In hominids, all these naïve acting routines of the as yet immature body instrument prepared the way for the serious introduction to advanced mimicry, usually after the ritual initiation into adulthood.

Parents often gave practical instruction in the art of mime during everyday communications and social activities, in addition to the traditional initiation of the young by the shaman and his assistants (*see Chapter II*), who taught by means of a system based on endless repetition of fundamental plastic/spiritual routines such as:

- Pose-gestural motifs of the **head**, like aggression/passivity, dominance/ subservience, attack/defence, with or without accessories such as horns or spikes.
- **Facial** expressions of anticipation or surprise, fear or aggression, joy or despair.
- Imitating the shapes of objects such as tools, weapons or musical instruments with the **arms, hands** and **fingers**, or infants, mates or prey.
- Plastic patterns with the **legs**, such as *stretched out, squatting, kneeling, spread apart, raised, interlocked.*
- **Torso** postures: *contracted* belly or *expanded* chest, *leaning* forward or backwards, *deflected* or *swinging* sideways.

The instructor covered a more extensive version of this syllabus of plastic expressions:

- After seeing the tutor indicate a graphic image representing an animal's likeness, the youngster would be expected to demonstrate all the pose-gestural patterns of the species in question.
- The tutor would personally perform a plastic sign connoting some characteristic of a species for the apprentice to recognise. Correction through expert demonstration would follow, in a cycle endlessly repeated until the tutor was satisfied with the speed and accuracy of his pupil's responses.

Tough as this may seem as a pedagogical method, it delivered the desired result in terms of building a strong postural foundation for both bodily communication and mimetic performance.

After some 10 years of strenuous study and practice during which spiritual consciousness and trained body fused into a single performing entity, the youngster might be chosen by the shaman for the great honour of becoming a cast member for ritual events. The mime debutants then scrupulously learned the pantomime posturing repertoire, using all their performing skills to get mentally and physically into the character of a sacred totemic

236

personage. From then on until the end of their performing lives, these professional mimes would usually perform images of the same personages (naturally reflecting their own personal characteristics) in portrayals which would be memorised by fellow tribe members for generations to come.

The plastic qualities of the posturing body as a mimetic instrument depended on more than the gestural facilities of the various body parts involved; like the instruments of an orchestra, it hinged crucially on the ability to present the main narrative motif of a composition in a harmonious artistic synthesis.

Any inadequate or inappropriate execution or coordination of postures would strike a jarring note that could potentially destroy or subvert the entire performance, particularly in the case of Semantic pose-gesturing, which required each body part to focus on and reinforce the plastic motif in the correct manner. It was not enough for a posturing performer to have attractive features and a strong skilful body, any more than it would be for an average musician to own a Stradivarius; on the contrary, it was even more important to know how to use these precious facilities to have the maximum effect on spectators.

Compositional principles of pose-gestural performance

As the above overview of the instinctive functional posturing repertoire demonstrates, there was a reasonably rich pose-gestural vocabulary for the main body parts involved: the head, limbs and torso. The same pose gestural patterns were executed differently when consciously performed by a motionless posturer, in that every such static gesture was a meaningful element of a greater whole, supporting the plastic leitmotif of the entire body composition.

The biggest challenge in ancient postural composition was the creation of **multiple plastic images** to represent anthropomorphic personages from mythical pantomimes, for which the shaman/choreographer had to combine the pose-gestures, motives and expressions of different creatures into a unique new entity: the head of an eagle, for example, with the limbs of a dragon and the tail of a zebra.

Whatever the particular combination of species in question, it demanded from the performer a two or three-way split of mental focus and the simultaneous expression of mixed gestural patterns; for the audience too, it required equal concentration to be able to decode and understand these simultaneously performed multiple images correctly.

ACTING ACCESSORIES AND MASKS

Right from the earliest stages of ritual pantomime, mythical personages were portrayed using many different acting accessories such as weapons and everyday domestic objects to identify the social rank, motivation and physical ability of the mythical character. Insofar as these accessories were used to focus the spectators' attention on the main action by extending the body's postural patterns, the accuracy of their deployment was vital in order to avoid confusion – and as their various shapes, sizes and weights affected the performer's centre of gravity, coordination and sphere of movement in different ways, their correct use required great skill.

The advent of masks in performance was a key turning point that fundamentally affected the pose-gestural compositional process. As we have seen, each sacred funeral image was primarily identified by a particular mask familiar to the audience. Eventually, all ritual images and pantomime personages were identified in this way: the totem, goddess mother, chief, hunter, shepherd and so on. Although costume design varied according to the local environment and tribal custom, the characteristic accessories of each main mask/image remained structurally close to the original.

The main performance requirements for costumes and accessories were either to keep the limbs completely uncovered for the comfortable execution and clear observation of poses and gestures, or to dress them in the thinnest possible skins or pelts. Aware of the need to maintain his spiritual power over his audience, the shaman continuously had to surprise them with new posturing images, which he did largely by means of creating new and **artistically harmonious** mask decorations and accessories.

THE CONNECTION BETWEEN PERFORMER AND SPECTATOR

Although the performing arts have always been founded on non-tactile communication between performer and spectator, a defining characteristic is the powerful and mutually consenting **spiritual connection** between both parties. Without prior explanation, performer and spectator instinctively sensed the meaning of the signs and gestures identifying familiar species and describing characteristic elements of their behaviour. If the audience misunderstood a particularly intricate plastic message, the performer or choreographer would at once have to adjust and correct the depiction accordingly, in a process that led to a progressive refinement in the clarity of the postural dictionary.

What therefore is the nature of the connection between performer and spectator? How was it sustained over the distance between the two? Which plastic code was brought into play? A partial answer to these questions is discussed in the section on motion patterns of the Head and Limbs in Chapter I. But here we are dealing with **motionless performance**, which is closer to the prehistoric sculptural imagery which is also based on 'frozen' pose-gestural patterns. There are however significant differences in the creative processes involved in mime posturing and the sculptural or graphic representation of posture.

STEREOTYPIC PREDICTORS

Unicellular organisms apart, the entire animal world uses one gestural system or another, and many species prefer motionless signals because they are less conspicuous in attracting predators and their static duration makes them easier to comprehend. With their rich evolutionary background, our ancestors eventually developed silent communication over distance into a condensed system of body poses and gestures. Although this may at first sound too intricate and convoluted a structure for a body language, these **stereotypic** plastic representations of everyday functions and social and emotional behaviours became so familiar and easily understood through endless repetition that little or no effort was required to decode similar pose-gestural messages in the local Totemythic ritual pantomimes.

Like most mammals, hominids express emotions and communicate through body language mainly with the **head**. This is how the leader indicated to his followers the direction for their next move or the source of an incoming threat; head gestures would also be used to assert dominance or to invite intimacy, and so on. The same functional vocabulary of head gestures was also included in the mime posturing repertoire to lead spectators artfully through the narratives of totemythical pantomime; when a performing hunter *turned* his head to one side of the performance area, the audience knew to expect visitors or an incoming threat.

However, any one gesture, such as an *upraised* head, could signify many different things: searching the tree canopy, checking rain clouds, reading the position of the sun or stars for the purposes of orientation or estimating the time of the day, or simply expressing emotional stress or bodily exhaustion. Similarly, spatially almost identical **arm** and **leg** gestural patterns could have totally different meanings.

COMPOSITIONAL 'BEACONS'

To understand these poses correctly, spectators had to follow the narrative context. The posturer would use auxiliary patterns of other body parts and accessories to lead the observers' eyes in the desired direction towards the **compositional focus**. With their strong spiritual faith and rich imagination, Palaeolithic spectators had no need for any specific education in aesthetics; as observers, they were actually participating internally in each episode of pantomime as it unfolded.

Hominids did however receive basic information about performance during the initiation rituals of their childhood (*see Chapter II*), learning many mythical stories by heart, and passing them on to subsequent generations in vivid illustrations on rock walls, sculptures, figurines, masks and domestic objects. As the regular Totemythic and funerary rituals were thought of as life-enhancing spiritual nourishment rather than mere entertainments, it is hardly surprising that primitive Neolithic audiences could comprehend such advanced hieroglyphic postures.

When the shaman presented new anthropomorphic creatures as an entourage for the totem, our forebears soon learned how to recognise and react correctly to the seemingly **ambiguous** plastic patterns, just as the experienced listener today can discern two or three interwoven melodies in an orchestral sequence.

The advent of paganism brought with it the necessity for new sacred images in postural art. As the existing pose-gestural dictionary was already about as large as the participants' physical capacities and visual memories could accommodate, composers began to develop a shorthand symbolic vocabulary for both communication and ritual performance.

CONNOTATIVE AND FIGURATIVE DESCRIPTIONS OF COMMON IMAGES

In addition to the existing motion vocabulary, an ingenious system of **connotative** 'shorthand' for presenting animate images evolved – not based on complete bodily imitation, but by projecting one characteristic element of the species in question, such as the buffalo's horns, a kangaroo's tail, bear's paw or elephant's trunk. These were performed either with separate plastic instruments or by touching parts of the body.

Later, this developed into an even more sophisticated **figurative** posturing code based on the connotative sign of the chosen species:

- a hunter wishing to demonstrate his suspicion of another might *raise* his lower arm vertically, *forming* a spoon shape with his hand towards the object of apprehension, as a connotative sign of a cobra's neck to indicate the person's snake-like character or behaviour.
- a chieftain publicly executing a deserter might make his gesture of condemnation with the plastic sign of cowardice by *projecting* his horned L hand, with fingers vertically *spread* in a horn shape and touching his own temple with his thumb.

New generations of spectators reflected this cultural progress by gradually absorbing this new symbolic postural vocabulary until they became skilled at recognising many-layered Figurative pose-gestural signs. In this way, the original body language of natural mimetic signs developed into an **abstract** vocabulary of plastic **symbols**, whose dialect was only fully understood by locals. These postures were used in ancient rituals and represented in sacred sculptures, as prophetic messages from the gods (*see illustrations in Chapter II*).

PROXIMITY: THE SPATIAL FOUNDATION OF POSTURING

There are three degrees of postural proximity:

- **Distant** is the periphery of the extended sphere of action, or interaction with another.
- **Close** refers to the spatial positions between static bodies in communication with each other, with or without accessories.
- **Intimate** describes the spaces between an individual's own body parts in solo behaviours, or direct physical contact with another body.

All living things need space. Even when mammals occupy an area temporarily, the first thing they do is mark out their territory. The location of these outer limits depends on their functional requirements for sustenance, defence and reproduction and factor such as social rank, body size and shape and the local distribution of predators and prey. Territorial boundaries are what ultimately delineate the DISTANT proximity range. Generally speaking, the stronger and more aggressive the creature, the larger the territory it can establish – not only in terms of different species, but also between individuals within the same group.

Our present concern is with CLOSE proximity, which is delineated by the maximum sphere of movement the body parts are capable of without displacing the body itself. This sphere of potential action is limited by the length of the individual's extremities and can only be extended by the use of artificial accessories. All animals have to calculate the extent of this sphere of potential action correctly in order to function, and although the fundamentals of this spatial awareness may be genetically programmed, each individual learns from birth how to adjust this awareness to their own specific body conditions and personal characteristics. Indeed, this is precisely what juveniles do in their endless gnaw-play, and when copying parental behaviours.

Managing these numerous Instinctively memorised proximity variations is a complex task. In the large functional repertoire of hominids, it could for example include:

- *rising on tiptoes, leaning* forwards and *stretching* to pick a fruit from a tree by perfectly estimating the right level, angle and distance.
- building an overnight nest in the canopy out of green twigs and branches, in the correct proximity and proportion with a surrounding sphere of free movement to allow rapid escape from danger.
- using a stick of the exact required length to extract termites or other insects and *raising* it to the mouth to *lick* off the living meal.
- *squatting* in shallow water with a wooden spear in the *raised* arm to *stab* a passing fish, based on an exact calculation of its speed and distance.

Species living collectively in herds, packs or tribes naturally evolved rules for appropriate proximity in various functional circumstances in order to maximise their chances of surviving the constant threats from predators and harsh environmental conditions as well as to succeed in joint hunting activities:

- In cold weather, the group instinctively stays together in INTIMATE proximity to keep warm, and far apart to keep cool in high temperatures.
- A pack of wolves or hyenas attacking a larger beast encircle it with each individual approximately the same distance apart, and then gradually close in on the prey.
- By contrast, a herd of buffalo defend their calves with *lowered* heads and *pointing* horns by forming a defensive circle close around their offspring.

- A female elephant keeps her infant safely under her belly, with Intimate proximity between their two different-sized bodies.

Intimate proximity also refers to the space between an individual's own body parts, with or without accessories. There are however many more functional plastic interactions between each body part and the body as a whole, as well as between individuals in direct bodily contact with each other.

Practically all physical conditions of any functioning body rely in one way or another on awareness of Intimate proximity: balance and coordination, inertia and momentum, velocity and amplitude, gravity and kinesis.

- A mother chimp carrying its infant adjusts her usual stance by *widening* the Intimate proximity between her feet for more secure balance.
- The new-born, lying on its back, tries to reach its L toes with its R hand, but repeatedly misses because of its lack of spatial awareness.
- When a gorilla can't reach an itch on its back with its fingers, it uses a stick or twig to extend its Intimate proximity range.
- Young children experience difficulties eating, drinking or washing unaided because they lack the correct **spatial body awareness.**
- Hominids adjusted their own image by using the extra length and weight of accessories or by making themselves look taller or slimmer through body decoration.

The adoption of an upright posture brought with it a confusing realignment of their entire proximity awareness during the hundreds of thousands of years of morphological transition when both quadruped to biped stances were in use. The intimate proximity range of the upright stance, together with deep-seated memories of quadrupedal spatial awareness provided a rich and complex foundation for artistic creation using both body shape facilities for posturing performance (*see Chapter II*).

THE MAIN STAGES OF POSTURING

As we have seen, functional actions have three main stages: the **initial impulse**, the **motion** itself and its **termination**. Hominids had always lived in groups, sharing work and social activities and closely watching each other's emotional states as expressed by the postures, gestures and facial grimaces they learned from members of their family and tribe. They therefore found it easy to comprehend the local body language 'shorthand' for reading the characteristic postures accompanying each of these stages: the predictive impulse, the plastic pattern of the moving body, and its finishing point. The first and last (largely static) stages of each physical action therefore acted as the gestural **beacons** for the action itself.

It used to be claimed that humans are defined by tool use, but modern anthropology proves otherwise. Many insect, reptile, bird and mammalian species use various tools with great virtuosity, including pumping air or water, sticks and branches to reach objects and baits to attract prey. They have been doing so for hundreds of millions years, yet they are no more human now than they were then. Although tool use played a crucial role in the development of hominid plastic body motion facilities, and undoubtedly stimulated the progress of their domestic and sociocultural life, many other factors were also equally important in accelerating their evolution.

The performing conditions for music are based mainly on **time** and **rhythm**, while those of mime/dance include **space** as well as time. If postural gesture is indeed a frozen movement before and after an action, as described above, it should contain some potential rhythm. The plastic rhythm of semantic gestural patterns also often characterises the relationship between acting images; and in ornamental group compositions, the rhythm of successive close proximity sequences plays a significant role in what is being expressed.

By **rhythm**, we do not refer to any physical movement of the motionless posturers, but the visual rhythm of their performance in a joint artistic presentation, and the ever-changing rhythms of the spectators' mental energies as they tried to decode the sequences of symbolic plastic signs they were witnessing.

The posturing choir around a leading personage was choreographed with its own plastic score, as well as each individual chorister, reinforcing the main narrative with their various pose-gestural patterns, **consecutively** or **canonically** around the soloist. The audience therefore had to follow these **contrapuntal** or **syncopated** plastic rhythms in order to comprehend the binary presentation that was unfolding before them.

The circumstances were different with Ornamental performances, especially with accessories, but no less challenging for the spectators, who looked down on the event from a distant vantage point in order to see and enjoy the scattered mixture of different posturing groups - men with sticks, women with domestic objects, boys with masks, girls with garlands and so on. Although each group performed its own attractive pose-gestural composition, seeing them together from a distance gave a very different visual effect. At first, the spectators' eyes darted from one posturing group to another to try and establish some compositional connection between the separate pose-gesturing patterns. But no such artistic unity was there to be deciphered; eventually, the spectators' enthusiasm would fade as they tired and began falling asleep, despite the loud drumming, shouting and whistling.

The same happened when there was a **dissonance** between the plastic rhythm of a performance and the sphere of permitted action. It must be remembered that early pantomimes could last three or four days, with many real and mystic images acting out one dramatic episode after another, while the choristers sat next to one another in the same position on stage during the entire show virtually without moving at all, merely periodically replacing each other. To avoid the danger of boring spectators with such a passive choir presence, the shaman/producer realised that the choir had to *act* and *move* from time to time. Although they had to sit in reasonably close proximity in order to vocalise harmoniously as an ensemble, spatial intervals were introduced for static gestural signs and ornamental plastic patterns.

The most intricate space/rhythm posturing in pantomime can be seen in the same way: the many static pose-gestural signs used to identify a species and its actions, reactions and imminent moves. The succession of these plastic 'beacons' underpinned the mythical narrative on stage, assessing the Totem's action to the very end, and was precisely choreographed for every single episode of the pantomime scenario.

It took performing groups years to establish the right intervals between their stage appearances and to coordinate them with the main narrative of the Totem and its assisting or opposing forces; the postural accompaniment of choristers also had to be composed. Such a complicated syncretic performance could not be achieved without perfecting the rhythm and tempo of all the many pose-gestural patterns performed by the acting personages. Anything less would have been considered a personal insult to the Totem, for which sin the ultimate price would have to be paid.

There also existed a combination of both Semantic and Ornamental types of posture, performed mainly by women. Pantomime choristers were of course semi-professionals, carefully selected by the shaman and his assistants; over a very long period, most of the female population took no part in sacred activities. During secret nocturnal ceremonies, the chosen few would sit around a bonfire with their legs *crossed* in front, deep in the cave, praying for fertility with both arms *stretched up* towards the Goddess Mother, occasionally changing the poses according to the subject of the invocation being sung.

Many surviving Palaeolithic drawings and figurines demonstrate Semantic pose-gestures with Connotative meanings:

- Both arms *stretched* sideways and *angled* upwards or downwards at the elbows like **horns**, to symbolise general abundance in cattle raising and food gathering.
- Both arms above the head, palms together or *open* laterally and *joined* loosely with the palms of the next worshipper in a circle: the figurative sign of a **snake** as a symbol of good health and successful family reproduction.

Anthropomorphic Body Shape

1   2   3   4

5   6   7   8

9   10   11   12

1. Lion headed patron of fertility	5. Amulet with ibis head	9. Votary in bull mask
2. Cow-goddess of puberty	6. Anthropomorphised toad	10. Haida-totempole
3. Ritual vessel	7. Fish-goddess	11. Bear-headed idol
4. Sacred offering	8. Horse-headed god	12. Bird-masked lady

Shaman's Body-Plastic Expressions

1. Dance of reproduction – Africa
2. WU, Shaman or Exorcist – China
3. Magic figurine of the witch – Vinca
4. Performance of puberty rite – Apache
5. Sacred rite ceremony – Denmark
6. Ritual Dance – Africa
7. Cult accessories
8. Dancing Koldun – France
9. Siberian shaman

1. Enjoying her meal
2. Killing a lion in protection of home-base
3. Punishment for stealing the master's food
4. Force-feeding hyena
5. Nursing weaning piglet
6. Chipping a flint weapon
7. (a,b) The bird-catchers and feeders

1. (a,b,c) Duel motion with weapon
2. Double support by spiritual figures
3. Family joint posture
4. (a,b) Plastic motion in a love duet
5. Proximity in a double posture
6. Aggressive motion in a male dialogue
7. Body plasticity in a vocal duet
8. Begging forgiveness in confession

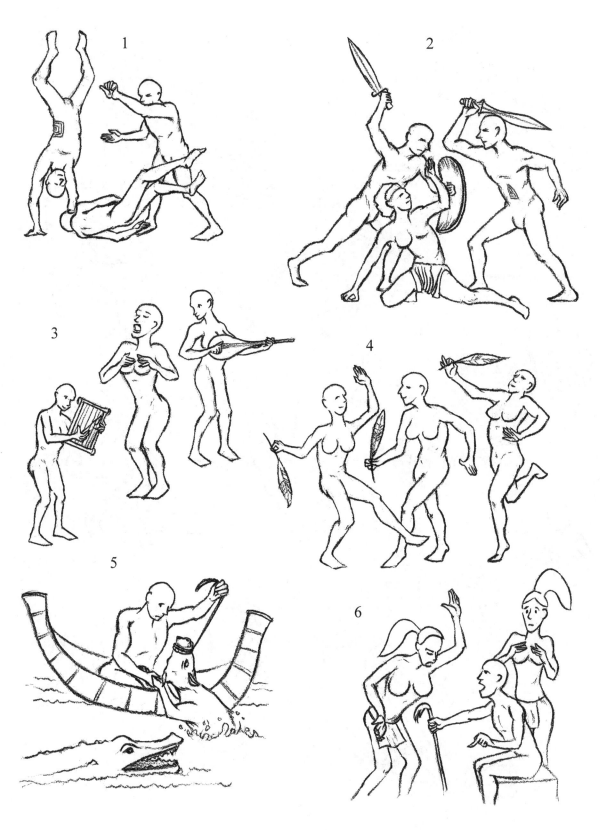

1. The 'Tchaya' fighting group
2. Armed combat with Amazon
3. Single/musicians' trio
4. Triple dance motion with feathers
5. Saving young cattle from the predator
6. Arguing body motion in a family

Plastic Motion in Combat

1
2
3
4
5
6

1. Unison twin-attack by archers
2. Simultaneous counter-attack in a duel
3. Unison trio-march, predicting attack
4. joint defence/attack of two with diverse weapons
5. Acceptance of enemy's surrender by victor
6. Unison attack by two sling throwers

Hunting/Fishing Body Motion

Everyday Survival Routine

Entertaining Contest

1. Initiation of wrestling skills
2. Duel-joint motion
3. Calling for mercy
4. Fighting motion with weapon
5. Salto-mortale from the back of a running bull

Eventually, women came to be included in worshipping and began serving in regular rite ceremonies during full moon. They *sang* facing each other in two parallel lines, either with arms *outstretched* to the moon, or *joined* together in a circle. All female posturing patterns expressed the same sense of personal or environmental fertility. The main plastic motif was a **triangle** formed by *folding* the arms and *placing* the hands on the head, under the breasts, on the belly or on both hips - a gestural pattern was imitating the plastic contours of the female pubis and genitalia, as a symbol of female sexuality and reproduction in the visual arts for sculpture, figurines, rock paintings and decorated domestic objects as well as in the mime and dance repertoire and as a general fetish for luck, success and protection.

The choristers and moonlight worshippers would strike postures between their motion sequences, often performing fascinating static gestural patterns with their joined or free arms, simultaneously expressing the pantomime narrative or the prayer as well as displaying their personal charm and spirituality in a synthesis of both Semantic and Ornamental posturing which made sacred activities more popular by making them more like secular events.

The growing interest in mass celebrations involving local traditions particularly stimulated the art of Ornamental posturing. Children and adults competed for the best group posturing composition, with exaggerated decoration and additional accessories that required accurate calculation of the spatial proximity and plastic rhythms involved for mass public performance (*see repertoire in Chapter II*).

POSTURAL COMPOSITION IN NUMERICAL SETS

The importance of spatial proximity as the key performing condition for posturing is especially true for group performances. In the final paragraph of Chapter I, we briefly summarised the spatial conditions of pose-gestural patterns in functional communication, behaviour and action. The dictionary of mimetic posture is based fundamentally on the same plastic vocabulary and distant, close and intimate spatial conditions. Both the instinctive Functional and volitional Performed repertoires also have the same sets as posturing composition, i.e., **solo, duet, trio** and larger **groups**, represented below in both natural/involuntary and the artificial/conscious forms. All variants are but combinations of individuals, with different body characteristics, emotional expressiveness and so on. Whether performing solo or in a group, each posturer is therefore a unique performing instrument, with his or her own personal plastic skills and spirituality (*see functional facilities in Chapter I*).

Solo performance is unique precisely because of its singularity. Whereas all other postural sets contain within them various individual differences of bodily characteristics, emotional expressions or spatial proportions, the Solo posturer is the purest form of the body as a performing instrument, like a solo flute or drum (*see Functionary facilities in Chapter I*).

As can be seen from the illustrations Intimate proximity under gestural motion, statically 'acting' limbs have clear and consistent patterns of spatial rhythm. The pose-gestural vocabulary developed alongside the body's capacity and agility, from the limited plastic facilities of the neck and torso to the highly sophisticated gesturing of the arms, hands and fingers. Taken together, these forelimb postures and gestures were the foundation of our present coded sign language.

Each arm position – *stretched* upwards or sideways, *hanging* down loosely, and any angle in between – can carry many possible meanings, an equally rich vocabulary of static hand gestures with numerous small plastic nuances of each basic pattern, and an even larger variety of thumb/finger configurations.

The diversity of possible postures within the Intimate proximity range of hominid body parts is almost infinite, and includes such familiar examples as:

Sleeping in a chaotic position with *outspread* limbs

- *Squatting* deep on both legs to reading the footprints of an intruder.
- *Kneeling* with a weapon in one hand and head lowered in prayer.
- *Lunging* on one leg toward the grave, with *lowered* head and hands on the chest.

Performed in pantomime, each of these common pose-gesturing patterns had its own clearly defined fixed spatial limitations, which had to be properly learned within the established mimetic syllabus, and correctly performed for the audience to understand. However, it was ancient hunters and later mime soloist performing animated images in ritual pantomime who were the most accomplished imitators of other being's Intimate proximity.

The posturing repertoire for representing other animals is widely recorded in prehistoric visual arts, and reveals a profound knowledge of the anatomy and behavioural characteristics of different species, which hominids used in elaborating their hunting strategies, and for the pre and post-hunt rites described in Chapter II.

A naked body with tail belted on to the hips and body painted to look like zebra demonstrates various stances and posturing patterns of the Functional repertoire and provides the model for hunters to practice their tactics around the next 'prey'. The solo mime precisely imitates the natural pose-gesturing of a zebra's alert head, or the tension of its *half-squatting* legs. The Intimate proximity of the body parts in question is identical to that of the original model, and when the mime portrayed the way in which the nervous zebra occasionally changes its postural patterns, he does so while always retaining the creature's individual characteristics. The tiniest error in imitating the pose of the zebra's head or limbs would stop the ritual rehearsal, the soloist risking being sacrificed for bringing bad luck to the next hunt.

Solo mimicry of animal and the anthropomorphised images in the intimate spatial proximity range for semi-professional pantomime did not slavishly copy the routines established long before for hunting rituals. As artistic creations, the actions and behaviours of these mythical personages were dramatically motivated by the requirements of the totemythical narrative and the skills of the performer, and the resulting pose-gesturing patterns embodied varying personal and emotional intonations rather than being rigidly stereotypic.

Unlike the tonal uniformity of hunt ritual performances of the universal contest between predator and prey, the totemythic and funerary pantomimes engendered several different dramatic genres, each with its own pose-gestural patterns to express emotional states which hominids could identify in a **generalised** form by body positions:

Epic: *sitting* cross-legged in front, body *leaning* forward;

Dramatic: *standing* with body *leaning* backward, and arms *open* laterally;

Comic: *balancing* on one leg, with arms chaotically *spread out* in an amusing way;

Tragic: *kneeling*, with face downward and *covering* head with forearms;

Romantic: *sitting* on sole/heels, with arms/hands in the lap and *upraised* head;

Grotesque: acrobatic headstand or handstand, with body crouching vertically.

These arbitrary examples and other varieties thereof are described here simply to illustrate the correlation between narrative genres and the corresponding physical and emotional state of the species being imitated, and are based on transferring similar real life reactions to the artificial context of ritual pantomime performance.

Solo performers also had a vast range of Close proximity postures, particularly with accessories. As mentioned earlier, the sphere of possible motion is delineated by the limit of the performer's extremities when fully extended, either by themselves or by means of additional tools. This type of performing repertoire encompassed everyday vital functions such as food gathering and water supply, nursing and grooming, making tools, weapons, domestic objects, shelters and clothing. The reason for focusing on these domestic activities is the search for the primal pose-gestural communication system. To make a call or exchange urgent information, our ancestors had insufficient time for mimicking long motion messages, so they used the **shorthand** of postural signals to indicate the subject, motive and nature of their concern.

The scope of close body proximity motions in both Functional and Performing repertoires was significantly increased by the introduction of **working tools**. Food gathering and housekeeping tasks previously accomplished with bare hands began to be carried out with the help of wood and stone implements, prompting a revolutionary change of the entire plastic motion system and the operating conditions of the hominid body. With all their various sizes, shapes, weights and materials, the new implements affected Close proximity range posturing more than any other, and posed considerable challenges in terms of adjusting posturing balance and coordination, plastic patterns and rhythms, proportional proximity and the entire pose-gestural sensibility. It took many generations to adapt to the ever-growing arsenal of new accessories, recognise their spatial diversity and accommodate the psychological implications of no longer using the limbs directly alone:

- Using **shells** to *drink* from rather than cupped palms.
- *Knocking* fruit down with a **stick** rather than *picking* them by hand.
- *Cutting* flesh from the bone with a flint or bone **knife** rather than *ripping* it away with the teeth or fingers.
- Using a **spear** or **net** to catch fish instead of bare hands
- *Moving* heavy weights on log **rollers** or with **levers** rather than *dragging* or *carrying*.
- *Digging* with a sharp-edged stone or wood **blade** instead of the hands.
- *Holding* a captured creature with a liana **rope** rather than manual *grappling*.

Major differences in proximity range are involved in these and all other Functional examples. Quite apart from the accessories themselves, the performance of each action, before, during and after, requires completely different pose-gestural patterns. And whereas earlier ritual pantomimes could be performed secretly in small enclosed spaces, such venues were now too restrictive for the greater spheres of movement that accompanied tool use, and the shaman had to move out into larger open areas that were better suited to syncretic pantomimes with heavy masks and exaggerated accessories – a move that also gave performers great opportunities to adapt decorative tools and weapons to the correspondingly adjusted Close proximity pose gestural patterns without accessories.

Changing old Functional routines, permanently etched in body and mind, to the new spatial conditions with performing instruments was of course no easy task, even for Homo sapiens; it was like trying to fit a small painting into a large frame, or child trying to *walk* in its father's big boots. It would have been easier to learn new pose-gestures altogether. Nonetheless, our ancestors managed to do so yet again, thereby massively increasing their plastic vocabulary for a more advanced posturing repertoire with musical instruments.

To announce the arrival of musicians from a neighbouring tribe, it was sufficient to mime the most typical gesturing pose with the identifying characteristics of the instrument concerned, as can be seen on many prehistoric rock paintings and art objects:

Drummer: two hands in front of belly, one and up, the other down;
Flautist: two half-open *touching* palms, one behind the other in front of lips;
Bow player: L arm half-*open* laterally with elbow *turned* downward, R arm *crossed* in front of L elbow, with palm '*holding*' bow.

As these static gestural patterns imply, knowledge of intimate spatial proximity is essential for correctly decoding a musician's imaginary profile via the instrument played. Such economical connotative pose-gestures represented another major advance in the art of professional mimicry.

The effect of adding tools and weapons to close proximity gestures with the limbs alone was both positive and negative. The accessories obviously extended the sphere of possible motion to a greater or lesser extent, increasing the amplitude of plastic expression and the skill required to perform it. But at the same time, the new spatial patterns of many small instruments closely resembled existing uncoded gestures with entirely different subjects and motivation, thereby giving rise to potential confusion among spectators, particularly with pose-gestures of the hunting/gathering repertoire. Another negative effect, though minimal, was the limitation on accessorised Semantic posture patterns imposed by the effective absence of the most expressive gestural implement of all: the unencumbered fingers and hands.

Distant proximity between posturer and subject affects the performing conditions of the entire body, and any spatial adjustments in pose-gestural patterns needed accordingly. Whoever the performer – a signaller at the top of a nearby hill, a hunter on a branch, a shaman posturing near a bonfire, or the acting totem in his mythical pantomime – the intended recipient always carefully calculated the distant proximity in order to understand the signaller's meaning correctly in the alternating exchange of plastic messages between both parties.

Over long distances, there are a few specific performance conditions for contact between posturer and perceiver. If the distance between the two was far enough to make plastic signs by the hands and fingers hard to discern, full height limb gestures were usually made, often holding accessories such as sticks or tusks. However, when signalling from the tree canopy, elongated weapons such as spears or machetes were used to stand out from the surrounding greenery.

Over the medium distances of events in open venues, performers also artificially exaggerated their Intimate and Close proximity pose-gesturing patterns to make it easier for spectators to see the coded messages, especially in the comparative darkness of a bonfire or moonlight. For the same reason, both gestural tempo and rhythm were adjusted accordingly, either by slowing down the tempo or sustaining the more intricate hand and finger gestures statically for longer periods.

In some events, like the precursors of modern Voodoo rites, the success of the sacred ceremony depended on actual physical contact between the shaman and his worshippers. This was basically controlled by establishing a suitable distance between the two elements, with the posturing shaman addressing his performance through 360 degrees to the constantly moving throng of worshippers encircling him. Too little distance would diminish his capacity to hypnotise his audience; too far would tend to lessen the perceived spiritual power of his performance. Ingeniously, shamans managed to retain control of the whole ecstatic crowd by maintaining each fixed pose-gestural pattern while *turning* clockwise on the spot in slow motion and replacing it with a new plastic composition on each turn to maintain uninterrupted spiritual connection with his audience.

The proximity conditions for a solo posturer described above, in intimate, close, and distant ranges are also the main performing conditions for any combination of group compositions from Duets upwards. All are closely linked and comprise one or two smaller sets:

Duet: two solos;
Trio: three solos, or one duet and one solo;
Quartet: four solos, or two duets, or one trio and a solo;

Quintet: five solos, two duets and a solo, or one trio and a duet.

All elements of the same set postured simultaneously in these various combinations, but would also perform using the same or different patterns, **in unison** or **contrapuntally**, and with either similar or contrasting expressions. Whatever presentation such groups were performing, they always kept the to the original subject and motivation of their own set and its posturing genre and compositional style in terms of the proximity range of pose-gesturing patterns to avoid confusing the spectators.

These group posturing compositions are analysed below in both functional and performing forms. It was difficult for audiences visually and mentally to follow two or three different pose-gesturing patterns being performed simultaneously on the stage. The imagery rules of joint performance were however just a more advanced version of what already existed, and the subjects of everyday motives, emotions and behaviours as well as their plastic representation were generally familiar to observers, who greatly enjoyed recognising their own characteristics and family problems in the group posturing performance. Occasionally, someone from the crowd would run on stage and try to correct a gesturing pattern with their own version.

The **duet** was the primary unit consisting of two similar solo individuals, although naturally, some of their personal characteristic elements may have been complementary, and some in opposition – positive with negative, creative with destructive, passive with assertive, and so on. The **dialogue** of hominid duets usually reflects the inner feelings and external reactions to the other's behaviours, attitude and manners that underpin the intimate interrelationship between the two. The nature of this interaction would determine the performing genre, compositional style, pose-gestural vocabulary, plastic patterns and spatial proximity.

Posturing Duets encompassed the dualities of much of the functional/performing repertoire: images of mother and infant; gnaw play between youngsters; hunter and prey; man and domestic animal, witch and snake, and so on. There being too many to describe all of them in detail, we focus here on the most significant in terms of the postural dictionaries of courtship and contest as used in the functional behaviours and actions of the mime/dance pose-gestural repertoire.:

Intimate: without accessories, in a limited sphere of limb movement, outstretched and potentially touching another body;

Close: the same space as above, but extended to the limit of the tools used;

Distant: beyond the close range to the limits of visual perception, with or without accessories, over land or water.

As we saw in Chapter I, the duet is the main mechanism for Functional intercommunication between mammals. In a postural dialogue, each semantic pose-gestural pattern must be exaggeratedly clear and expressive, as an artistic rendition of the main plastic motif as performed by the mind and body parts. Some of these pose-gestural patterns express a single intention, while others have two or more possible readings, based on individual motivations, environmental circumstances, the personality of the performer and the genetic background of the species. In order to communicate satisfactorily, great mimetic skill is required to represent all the characteristic elements of the image being performed.

Below is a typical example based on a pose-gesture of the right arm raised outward to the side towards the object of interest, but with different motivations and additional adjustments of hand, head and upper body:

Standing straight up, with L. arm down along the side

1. SALUTATION: a young ape directs his *raised* arm and hand towards the dominant male, greeting him in a submissive fashion with the head and *arched* upper back.

2. INVITATION: the chief *opens* his arm out sideways to invite a great hunter to share his food, with head *turned* R and upper body slightly *inclined*.

3. INTRODUCTION: the shaman presents the image of the Totem to a young man by *pointing* his arm and hand to focus attention towards the god.

4. CELEBRATION: a leader *grasps* a shell containing a celebratory beverage in his R hand to congratulate the victors with his *open* L arm, *expanded* chest and *raised* head.

5. INDICATION: a witch indicates to worshippers the method of sacrifice with her open R arm and *pointed* index finger, her head *turned* L and up.

Sitting on a rock with L hand placed in the lap

1. CALLING: a wounded warrior calls for help with R arm slightly *folded* sagitally upward, half-open palm, body *deviating* L and head *turned* R.

2. QUESTIONING: asking the motivation of new visitor by *twisting* R hand to the R with *half-open* palm upward and *raised* head, *turned* R.

3. PROJECTING: the shaman *twists* R arm/hand to L with *open* palm back to cover someone with R arm *shifted* laterally, upper body *turned* R.

4. REJECTING: a chief refuses an offer by *opening* R arm sideways, *twisting* R hand to the L with *open* palm downwards, and head *turned* to L.

5. WARNING: a chief warns the enemy by *squeezing* R palm, *raising* fist slightly up to his chest and *turning* the *raised* head R.

Kneeling on L knee, with L hand on chest

1. BEGGING: a prisoner implores the victor to spare his life by *raising* his R hand with open palm towards, *leaning* submissively backwards, with head *deviated* R.

2. ADORATION: the groom presents flowers to his bride with R arm forwards, *raised* head and body *deviating* slightly backwards.

3. WORSHIP: *holding* a figurine of Goddess Mother in R hand while *bowing* deeply at the rite ceremony with half-*outstretched* R. arm forward towards the witch.

4. GATHERING: *picking* berries from a bush with fingers of R arm and hand up, *leaning* forward with *lowered* head and *raised* shoulders.

5. SACRIFICE: a prisoner prays before committing suicide with open R arm *holding* a knife in his hand, *twisting* body R with head *raised*.

These fifteen plastic variations of the same gestural motif with a single arm only constitute a small percentage of the full potential range, in order to demonstrate the existence of a complete primate body language of postural sign/signals alone.

The fact that some ape/hominid gestural varieties or nuances are so small as to be virtually invisible to the untrained modern eye does not mean they didn't exist, because since Homo Sapiens' adoption of verbal language, we have lost around 90% of the mimetic plastic vocabulary used by our ancient ancestors. Mature apes communicate with each another in a far more sophisticated body language then most people realise, with amazingly refined tactile inflections executed by the fingertips and lips.

The most important subject for the bodily dialogue between animals has always been, and will always be, **reproduction** – the fundamental precondition for continuing the species. The primordial need of the receptive female to choose the best mate to father her future offspring is the engine which has driven the process of selective evolution in all orders of animals for at least 500 million years.

It must be remembered that the sexually receptive period of our female ancestors gradually changed from being seasonal to regular intervals throughout the year, allowing mating to occur more frequently, but with less productive results. Although hominid males mated under the aegis of Goddess Mother's sacred blessing for beneficial fertility, sex eventually became recreational, involving various attractive postures and tactile gestural endearments, rather than merely a procreative obligation (as evidence by the many primate groups that regularly indulge in sexual orgies, often swapping partners). The sexual dialogue evolved through many generations of Homo Sapiens into a sophisticated syllabus of sexual intercourse, extensively illustrated in the postural sculptures, figurines and paintings of ancient worship sites.

The functional plastic vocabulary of pose-gestural patterns in courtship duets varies according to local custom, the physiological and emotional sexual impulses remain universal. The courtship repertoire of apes is limited to a plastic duet usually consisting of the following pose-gestural sequences:

- The dominant mate periodically checks the receptivity of females by smelling or *touching* their genitals with his hands.
- Sexually frustrated young males publicly display erect penises or masturbate in front of females to entice them into mating.
- Receptive females display their swollen and coloured genitalia to the dominant male to indicate readiness to mate.
- Impatient young males repeatedly attempt to mate with unreceptive females, who *turn* their rump away from these persistent advances and eventually repel the youngsters physically.
- Isolated single-sex groups often include grooming pairs who periodically *mount* each other in imitation of copulation.

Romance and extended foreplay have little or no part to play in the mating activities of apes. By contrast, the simple example below shows the pose-gestural sequences of a standard sexual dialogue between a hominid couple translated verbally to reveal the postural motive along with the body patterns, proximities and display rhythms involved:

1a **Distant** proximity: two individuals *stand* in profile with their heads *turned* to gaze at one another.
M: "I never saw her before."
F: "Do I know him?"

1b M and F *deviate* their bodies slightly towards each other.
M: "What a beauty!"
F: "Why is he staring at me?"

1c M *straightens* his stance, and *turns* to face F at a 90-degree angle – "I must introduce myself."
F also *straightens* her stance to the original position as in 1a, *turning* her head away from M towards the initial direction – "I'd better ignore him for now."

2a **Close** proximity: M *stands* firmly in front of F, *deviating* to the L and slightly *raising* R arm towards F with palm upward – "Please don't go."
F responds by *twisting* upper body to the L to face the stranger – "What do you want?"
M *raises* his *outstretched* R arm higher, now with palm towards F – "Please trust me"
F turns 90 degrees to the L in the direction of the M with *raised* head and arms loose at her sides – "OK, I'm listening."

2b M maintains the same posing gesture with R arm and L hand on his chest – "I really fancy you."

F raises her L arm with palm towards M, and freezes just before touching his L palm – "I like the look of you too."

3a   **Intimate** proximity: F touches the R hand of M with her L fingers and jerks her head in an embarrassed way, raising her folded R arm in front of her chest – "What's happening to me?"

M squeezes the L hand fingers of F with his R hand and lovingly takes her R hand with his L: "You're gorgeous!"

3b   M gently places F's two hands on his shoulders, and his own on her lower back - "I like you."

F moves her hands around his neck and stretches up on her toes towards him – "Me too."

3c   M steps towards F and embraces her with chests touching while kissing and interweaving their bodies.

As we can see, the pose-gestural patterns increase in proportion to the progress of the relationship between the two – but unlike apes, the expressions are more indirect and the sequence more varied, reflecting natural feelings of modesty, uncertainty, mistrust, excitement and so on. These emotional nuances also develop in line with the progressively **decreasing spatial proximity** from distant, via close to intimate tactile contact. The body implements used in this example begin with the head and eyes alone, followed by one, then two, arm/hand/finger units, completed by fully interwoven upper bodies and arms. All elements of such a postural pre-mating duet would of course be controlled and conducted by virtually continuous eye contact.

The repertoire of prehistoric courtship posturing duets was established in three main traditional settings:

A.   During wedding ceremonies, established couples would 'pose-talk' in the local dialect using their highly decorated bodies, illustrating various stages of family life the newlyweds could expect.

B.   Spiritual totemythic pantomime dialogues personifying the union of bride and groom using common symbolic images with masks.

C.   A dance duet by the newlyweds imitating a loving pair of popular local animals – anything from cranes or snakes to rabbits, giraffes or kangaroos.

During such wedding events it was customary for the young guest couples to perform various artistic posturing sequences on the theme of love and sex, while relatives moved around among them with their gifts and decorations.

The postural characteristics of the duets in each of the three courtship/ wedding settings outlined above varied slightly, but shared similar performing conditions in terms of subject, motivation and proximity.

The ironic posturing duets performed by married couples in wedding ceremonies (A) served as a form of marriage guidance, demonstrating the everyday functional repertoire of a busy family: gathering, eating, arguing, sleeping, grooming, mating and so on. Bride and groom immediately copied each of these posturing duets in succession before being given their gifts – a suite of multiple comedic duet performances, in effect, within standard intimate/close proximity ranges for the purposes of entertainment and instruction as well as celebration.

In a highly religious society, the totemythic pantomime dialogues depicting the union of bride and groom through symbolic images (B) were an important device for ensuring subsequent reproduction. A series of ritual personages personifying fertility in harvesting, cattle breeding and creating a family postured around the bride and groom, and the shaman or witch introduced the new couple to the main sacred fertility symbols of the Goddess Mother or a phallic monument in a sequence of pose-gestural duets individually with bride and groom. This ritual event was performed in a symbolic style, and designated by the sacred totemic fable and its personages. The sequence of duets with bride and groom instructed them through a symbolic gestural blessing for fruitful reproduction, presented at various close/distant proximities in a pantomime setting.

By contrast to the first two settings, the newlyweds' themselves led the mimetic dance duet (C), in a graceful secular entertainment accompanied by the other married couples present, all copying their gesturing patterns, tempo and rhythm in canonical sequences. Usually choreographed on the basis of the plastic motifs and spiritual influence of the courtship rituals of the chosen animal, these intricate artistic compositions involved all proximity ranges in a harmonious medley of pose-gestural duets.

CONTEST was second only to reproduction in the struggle for survival, and was no less important to the continuation of the species. As far as pose-gestural duets and their proximity patterns are concerned, contest and courtship are two sides of the same coin, involving similar functional and performing facilities, but contrasting manners and behaviours. Both romantic and dramatic dialogues began by intriguing the **curiosity** of the partners at a distant proximity, followed by a declaration of **intent** at close proximity, with the **sexual act** or **wrestling duel** completed at intimate proximity.

Contests demanded far greater plastic facilities of the body, with more advanced performing techniques, a more strategically focussed mental state, faster reactions and greater sensitivity to spatial limitations. In courtship, both partners usually acted consensually, with similar motivations based on the mutual satisfaction of their desires, with no direct threats to their own interests apart from possible competition from another rival. By contrast, the main functional aim of any fight was as far removed from love, peace, pleasure and creation as possible; it was all about death, destruction, dominance and intimidation. The preconditions for engagement were suspicion, hostility and aggression.

For reasons of survival, most species prefer to avoid unnecessary bloodshed, and often attack preventively very soon in order to pre-empt aggression from the opponent. This makes for rather intricate posturing duets if the performance is to be correctly understood. The two antagonists are complicatedly interwoven, their inner confusion exemplified in the dramatic confrontation. The pose-gestural patterns and proximity ranges of combat images therefore had to be choreographed and performed with great plastic clarity and spatial accuracy in an artistically exaggerated manner.

Opponents usually **alerted** each other for the contest to come at a far distant proximity, either by pheromonal or acoustic signals, at which the defender immediately took all necessary precautions to protect himself and his territory.

At near distant proximity, the aggressor tries to avoid any untimely visual contact with the target while planning the attack, while his adversary desperately looks for his lurking enemy. The limitations of **visual recognition** are the extent of distant proximity in the contest situation. Close proximity is characterised by the attacking ability of the contestants and their potential for **physically reaching** the opponent by *stepping, leaping*, or *striking* with a hand-held weapon. The subsequent Intimate proximity initiates **direct contact** between the two wrestling bodies fighting hand to hand without weapons.

Although the pose-gestural vocabulary of hominids originated from other primates, and earlier, from marsupials, it was mainly developed after the morphological transition from the quadruped to the upright stance. The proximity parameters remained essentially identical to those of the quadruped era, but the liberation of the forelimbs and the upright body allowed contestants to detect each other visually much earlier and at a greater distance. It also massively increased the gestural vocabulary of the arm/hand instrument and created entirely new possibilities for postural duets as well as significantly enlarging the functional performing repertoire of pose-gestural patterns.

Advances in the duet pose-gestural vocabulary proceeded in reverse order of proximity ranges to those in courtship and contest dialogues. As we have seen, Intimate proximity was the **primal tactile contact** of two posturing bodies without accessories, including the contest/duelling repertoire. Later on, these pose-gestural patterns were extended by the adoption of **tools**, which involved the close proximity range. Eventually, new **thrown weapons** like spears and arrows allowed the antagonists to perform at distant proximity.

The main subjects of duelling confrontation at close and intimate proximity ranges, with or without weapons, included:

- Gnaw-playing young to build strong bodies for future combats.
- Ritual practicing of hunting skills by indirect contact with prey/predator.
- Hierarchical duels between two strong males for dominance.
- Initiation of professional warriors.
- Mimetic performance of contest images in pantomime.

Battles involving thrown weapons are not included above because the distant proximity specifications are very different. The warrior/hunter can still reach a target or shield himself over long distances, avoiding the direct contact that would otherwise help them predict the enemy's next move, discover his weak spot or calculate his kinetic power.

The far distant proximity range between hunter and prey or the warrior and his enemy required a proportional adjustment of intimate proximity in their pose gestural patterns:

- For the shorter trajectory of a spear, hunters mainly used the arm/shoulder unit, *twisting* sideways and backward before the throw, with the weapon *raised* above.
- For a higher trajectory towards a far distant target, the warrior *twisted* the body much more and held the tip of the spear higher to gather the kinetic energy to throw the weapon further. In this way, the distant proximity range of the thrower is always in direct relation to his physical power at the Intimate proximity range. Similarly, close proximity pose-gestures with accessories had to **adjust** to the shape, size, weight and substance of the weapon.

Hominid contests usually had three operating stages of postural patterns:

First stage – WARNING SIGNALS
a) Body fully upright, *leaning* towards enemy menacingly, neck *thrust* forward.
b) *Expanded* chest with *arched* back, *outspread* forelimbs and head *raised.*
c) Teeth *bared*, jaws *open*, face *thrust* forward, with *crouched* or *squatting* stance.

Second stage – TESTING
a) *Lunging* forward and *raising* both fists threateningly, head *raised.*
b) *Leaning* toward enemy with R hip, *pushing* with R shoulder.
c) *Pressing* crossed weapons with both hands *raised*, body *lunging* forward.

Third stage – THE FIGHT ITSELF
a) *Grasping* one another with *interlocked* arms/hands and bodies interwoven.
b) *Holding* an opponent above ground and *squeezing* his torso with both arms.

We can see in these posturing sequences a strong mutual influence between the duelling adversaries, in ways common to most mammalian species. They deployed remembered attack signals as well as peaceful ones, having visually recorded the posturing patterns of various predators, **separating** their pre-attack stances from harmless ones, and **memorising** potentially fatal pose-gestures.

The original pose-gestural repertoire of the contest Duet was not artificially created, as it was later in totemythical pantomime, but evolved as a vital **survival mechanism**. To mime a prey or a predator in a hunt, or to scare off an enemy by a warning posture was a regular everyday Functional routine. However, to be sure of a positive result in hunting or in a social dispute, the execution of each posture had to have the desired effect, irrespective of species. This is why the pose-gestural dictionary recorded in ancient sculptures and graphics consists mainly of warning/alarm signals and the plastic identification of intruders.

Duelling postural compositions (excluding the various emotional expressions between partners or opponents in a courtship or contest duets) were basically determined by the strength of motion and its counterforce and artificially counterbalancing the natural equilibrium. However, both opponents were only pretending to fight, feigning the power, plastic patterns and facial expressions of a real contest – as any movie stuntman will tell you, a highly sophisticated but effective technical skill.

A.   When wrestlers *push/pull* one another with *interlocked* arms in an attempt to *knock* each other down, however motionless they may look, there is immense physical and mental tension between both participants, with powerful kinetic forces being deployed until one contestant overbalances the other. Performed in pantomime, the audience may well guess the winner from the dramatic gestural patterns and emotional expressions, without realising the very real difficulties of artificially simulating these tensions and imbalances and maintaining them statically even for just a minute.

B.   When two warriors, one above the other in close proximity clash their weapons, a powerful counterforce accumulates where the weapons cross. The upper combatant, *lunging* forward, *presses* downward on his opponent's weapon with his entire body weight using the maximum available kinetic power to *knock* him down, while the warrior on the ground *struggles* to resist the pressure from his enemy above with his arm *outstretched holding* his machete, *supporting* his slightly *lifted* body with his other arm *placed* on the ground. These two fighting positions are obviously so unequal that they precondition the audience's expectation of the outcome.

C.   A vertical duelling posture composition at the Intimate proximity range with one body *lifted* off the ground, with the ensuing double balance, kinetic potential and interacting patterns. The lower warrior adjusts his balance, depending on potential *shift* in the position of the opponent above his shoulders. He *inclines* laterally or *deviates* his upper back rearwards according to the shape and weight of the enemy he is *lifting*. Though the lower combatant is limited in the use of his fighting skills because his arms are around the adversary's waist, he still controls the action of the warrior above, who has lost his ground support, together with his balance and the ability to use personal fighting techniques. However, the upper wrestler can manage to *grasp* the throat of his opponent with his free hands to try and *strangle* him. Both are *squeezing* each other's neck or waist, relying exclusively on the kinetic power of their own hands and arms and their mental focus and self-control. The spectators can only guess which fighter will eventually win.

Postural duets in a pantomime, like the solo monologues described earlier, are composed and performed according to various different principles. All dialogue genres usually reflect natural feelings, behaviours and actions of the familiar functional repertoire in a basically realistic style. The performances are artificially exaggerated in the limited time and space of the ritual stage to clarify the audience's understanding of the dramatic narrative. All pantomime postures, including duelling, were therefore executed artistically, with connotative pose-gesturing patterns.

It must be remembered that most mythical personages were originally performed in masks, with ornate body decoration. Each new pantomime score was the latest episode of the continuing **saga** of the totem and its search for new sources of food and the protection of his people. The shaman, as the 'son of totem' merely indicated the relevant locations by means of Figurative gestures within the dramatic story line of duelling conflicts involving the Totem's victories in the fight against negative anthropomorphised creatures.

As the single most important medium of primordial intercommunication, the pose-gestural Duet encompassed a far larger plastic vocabulary than could be squeezed into the present study, but this brief summary of the Courtship and Contest Duet repertoire in pantomime will hopefully give some insight into their respective Functional and Performing conditions.

The **trio**, as an uneven number, is inherently unbalanced, and has a sense of irregularity in the animal world. Three-way communication also carries with it an **underlying conflict** in behaviour and Functional relationships. A mother with two infants, a male with two mates, an oestrus female with two rival suitors or a couple with a growing child – all have the potential for conflict, even in a seemingly happy family. There will inevitably be a dominant or selfish parent, a stronger or a weaker mate, a more or less demanding infant, better or worse characters, and the like. One way or another, the trio is an **unsteady foundation** for a functional harmony.

Nevertheless, there are also many gratifying subjects in the trio pose-gestural repertoire, such as romance, loyalty, sanctity, friendship, sibling affection and so on. Some we have already mentioned, and others will be dealt with later. But for the purposes of this analysis, we concentrate on the same three subjects of the functional/performing repertoire: courtship, contest and pantomime. To avoid confusion, bear in mind that we refer here to inner actions of the motionless posturer, and the ways in which each posturer influences the pre- and post-acting state, the interwoven emotions expressed by static pose-gestural patterns and the plastic synthesis of their individual characteristics in a performance based on artistic images.

At distant proximity, it was even more difficult for Neolithic spectators to follow the plastic score of trio performances than duets, as they had to divide their attention in three different directions while simultaneously understanding all three individual messages. The pose-gestural signs would be executed either in **parallel** or in **contrapuntal** patterns, with **canonised** rhythms or **consecutively** syncopated, using a mixture of intimate and close spatial proximities.

A simple and effective method of performing pose-gestural trios was therefore developed to help the audience to follow the drama more easily: two of the three individuals involved usually performed as a harmonious pair, while the third accompanied them in either positive or negative ways and plastically indicated how their duet postural patterns linked semantically to the next, in the same genre and style.

Such trio sequences often opened with a kind of **prelude**, followed by a presentation of **various stages** of the dramatic score and concluding with the **triumphant finale** of the Totem and his entourage. The choreography of the following example is reconstructed from prehistoric mural and ancient sculptural notations of totemythical scores:

This totemythical pantomime is played by five posturing personages: a couple with a baby, and two personified forces – the positive, in the form of the totem, and the negative, in the form of the Demon.

1) Mother *sits* on the ground with legs *crossed* in front, *holding* a baby in her lap. She bids farewell to her husband, who *kneels* and *leans* in towards them. He *pats* the baby with his L hand and *holds* a spear with his R hand ready for an impending hunt.

2) Mother *plays* with her baby as it *lies* on the ground; she *looks out* over her shoulder, prompted by the invisible demon behind her back. The demon imitates a familiar gesture of the absent hunter, who is calling out for her help.

3) The hunter, *crouching* in a pre-attack position with his spear and net, is interfered with by the demon above and behind his head. The invisible demon shows the baby to its father, *holding* it upside down by its ankles, screaming.

4) Both parents come before the totem, entreating their god to find the missing child. *Standing* tall, the totem acknowledges their grief by *raising* his arm above the parents' heads, indicating a promise.

5) The Totem *suspends* his foot over the chest of the demon lying below, who begs for mercy. The confused baby *sits* beside the demon and *sucks* its big toe, *pulling* its foot closer with both hands.

6) The hunter *kneels* to the totem with *raised* head and *leaning* backward, *stretches* both arms towards the god. The totem, in a *lunging* forward position with straight upper back, passes the missing baby to the hunter.

7) The happy mother, again *sitting* with legs crossed in front on the ground, nurses the returned baby. The thankful father stands beside, now guarding the reunited family.

The five dramatic trio interactions in this episode of the totem's exploits – mother and baby, father and hunt, demon and baby, totem and demon, totem and congregation – could run in parallel, or across each other. All seven stages are interconnected in that there is always at least one family member present, and all contain the dramatic plot of the demon and his 'invisible' double actions behind a main personage – an effective naïve pose-gestural production, despite the extended number of individual protagonists.

As we have seen, early totemythical pantomimes were performed under torchlight in confined spaces with a limited cast. There were few transformations by anthropomorphised mythical personages and few changes of scenery. It is reasonable to assume that the dramatic solo of shaman/ totem, the central duet between totem and demon and the trio interaction between totem, demon and hunter represented the beginnings of the pantomime art. Although these ambitious pioneers were amateurs with no theatrical education whatsoever, their ingenuity, spirituality, imagination and physical skill laid the **aesthetic foundation** for the dramatic theatre of the future.

In the process of decoding many hieroglyphic pose-gestural notations from prehistoric murals, we discovered a primitive system for choreographing and recording postural compositions, and this basic example of a trio suite shows that the shaman was able to create and act out with his assistants various solo and small group pose-gestural sequences that combined to form complex narratives intelligible to the audience.

This was of course no overnight phenomenon, but a slow progressive development of mimetic acting technique and in the understanding of **abstract expressions**. When performances moved out from confined spaces into open venues, and gradually began incorporating an entourage of mime/dancers, choristers and musicians, a new era for pantomime dawned. With enough space to use these additional resources to supplement the pose-gestural 'beacons', more exciting, complex and dramatic adventures of the totem could be told, with a correspondingly greater emotional and spiritual impact on the audience. Similar progress was achieved by the shaman in choreographing ritual Funerary ceremonies in the open (*see Chapter II*).

Even in later ritual pantomimes, the number of characters with individual motion scores who were protagonists in the narrative was limited to the totem and his assistants; the others merely accompanied the main plastic score with their pose-gestural patterns. In the following example, the Totem's adventure is presented in two parts of a combat episode concerning the defence of his people. In this particular case, spectators did not see the actual battle, although they understood where, when and how their god fought for them.

Part 1: **Pre-war manifesto**
a) The totem/shaman gives a **commanding** postural signal to attack the enemy by *lunging* on R leg sideways, *raising* R arm *holding* an imposing weapon, and addressing L arm to half a dozen close assistants.
b) These warriors *stand* firmly on both feet with legs *spread* apart, each *holding* a weapon in R hand and a shield in the other, **ready to follow** their god/master.
c) A dozen extras imitate a stone wall with spears as the next **obstacle** for the fighting totem. They stand in line, backs to the audience, legs akimbo *touching* their neighbours' feet, *spreading out* their arms upwards and sideways and *holding* hands with lances sticking up vertically.

Part 2: **The victory**
a) The warriors/assistants *carry* the chief on a large shield, *supporting* it with one arm/hand and shoulder, and the other arm spread upwards and sideways with weapon.
b) The **victorious** Totem *stands* on the shield with feet apart and both arms raised, the R holding a weapon, the L with the mask of some anthropomorphised creature.
c) The extras now *mime* some prisoners of war, with arms behind their backs, all in diverse posing patterns: *prostrated, kneeling, squatting, crouching* to construct a living pyramid below the totem, **celebrating** his success and immortality.

This example contains a potentially rich variety of postural combinations for mass performance: the solo totem with a small group of assistants, or the solo totem counteracting a large group. There was also scope for ancillary combat between small and large groups behind the scenes, in various sets of dual and triple posturing in the pre- and post-battle scenarios described above, depending on the available time and space. However, an important principle of ancient pantomime was to suggest more than was actually shown on stage, forcing the audience to identify with and participate more actively in the event by using their imagination.

Group postural composition also had its own conditions and performing characteristic. As with duets and trios, there were three major types of pose-gestural presentation: communicative, semantic and ornamental. Each could feature different numerical permutations: solo leader with group, two groups with two solo leaders, single group without leader, single or double line or circle in one group, or any amalgam of three or more groups. The pose-gestural patterns were performed on the spot or on the move, as in a procession; in single-sex or mixed sex sequences, with or without accessories, bare-chested or dressed with masks, on flat ground or raised levels.

The COMMUNICATIVE repertoire included various combinations of soloists and groups

Solo leader with Group
a) The shaman summoned desperately needed rain by *raising* his arms skywards while *standing, kneeling* or *lying* flat on the ground with arms *stretched* forward. Male worshippers would accurately follow all the praying shaman's many plastic body patterns as he held each pose-gesture while muttering his invocations in a process that continued until the shaman fell into a trance.

b) Women praying at a lunar fertility rite would surround the posing witch as she supplicated the Goddess Mother to bless their puberty, fertility and parturition. She would sing her call sitting on the ground, periodically moving her upper back sideways and spreading her arms upward or touching her breasts or belly while the worshippers repeated all her pose-gestural patterns in a ceremony that could last until dawn.

Double Group with two solo leaders

a) Two separate groups of relatives are led by the bride and groom during a wedding ceremony, facing each other at distant proximity. The newlyweds salute their guests by *bowing* and holding each pose while both groups of guests repeat the same pattern. When the bride and groom *embraced* each other, the two groups *raised* their arms simultaneously *holding* wedding gifts in a competitive demonstration of their wealth and generosity. Children *holding* hands surround the newlyweds and *raise* their arms towards the couple.

b) Two opposing groups of warriors face each other, with their commanders in front. One group of archers *kneels holding* their bows and arrows in a pre-attack gestural pattern; the second *lunges* forward on R leg towards their opponents *holding* spears in the R hand *arching* upper body back sideways. Both groups, along with their leaders, wait in these poses for the enemy's attack to begin.

Double Group without a leader

a) Two lines of warriors in a pre-attack posture, one behind the other. The first line comprises the *kneeling* archers, as above; the second, behind and above the first, *holds* spears. Both parallel lines of combatants maintain this position, waiting for the signal to strike.

b) Two opposing groups *holding* weapons are placed in six duelling pairs. At the start of the contest they demonstrate their mastery of fight skills by highly developed double-posturing sequences without actual bodily contact during the pre-contest prelude.

One single-sex Group

The ancient annual custom of pairing off new sexual partners continues in some societies to this day. During the **first stage**, hundreds of young men and women display their physique and plastic skills in private session with independent judges, who select about two dozen to prove their beauty, intelligence, practicality, maturity and performing talents.

a) Girl candidates *pose* naked in front of women judges, performing a series of posturing sequences devised by the judges to show off their grace, charm, body harmony, sense of rhythm, femininity and suitability for motherhood.

b) The same process of selection through demonstration applies to male contestants during their private performance in front of the judges, during which they try hard to impress their male judges with their physiques, maturity, flexibility, strength, reaction speeds, balance, coordination and mental/spiritual fortitude. The male pose gestural syllabus was extremely demanding, and the judges particularly severe in view of the young men's future family responsibilities.

At the **second stage**, those selected were free to choose their own partners from the other winners. Both sexes were placed in parallel lines, facing each other, lightly dressed but heavily body painted and otherwise decorated.

a) Trying to attract his chosen beauty, a man would vigorously perform a series of pose-gestural patterns and facial grimaces: *folding* arms to show off his muscles; *squatting*, and *twisting* his upper body; making eyes, *pulling* his lips laterally to display flashing teeth, all with pose intervals in between.

b) The women performed equally effectively, putting on an impressive show by posturing flirtatiously, *offering* their hips or breasts, teasing men by *shrugging* their shoulders coquettishly or *jerking* their heads provocatively, often changing their attractively promising stances.

SEMANTIC performance comprises mimetic initiation, Totemythic and Funerary rituals, Hunting, Combat, Courtship episodes and so on.

Solo leader with Group

a) Children follow their tutor's imitations of the pose-gestural patterns of various animals: *lying, sitting, standing* and *raising* on hind limbs; *kneeling, squatting, crouching, stooping, curled up, twisting, drooping* and so on.

b) A single grazing animal is surrounded by hunters with spears, who hide in a *squatting* position and *crouch* slowly towards the prey, *pausing* after each step and holding weapons *inclined* downwards; then they suddenly *lunge* forwards, *drawing up* their spears and *reclining* backward torsionally.

Two Groups with leaders

a) A ritual battle of the Totem and his assistants against the Demon and his warriors. In the middle, between the two lines of opposing combatants, the leaders attack one another with *kicks, holds* or weapons, using aggressively threatening postures between blows. The watching soldiers enthusiastically cheer on their leaders with vigorous gestural patterns, as a synchronised plastic accompaniment. They *lean* forward with weapons held high when their leader appears to have the upper hand, and backwards with *lowered* weapons when he seems to be losing.

The main element of the Funerary ceremony of senior males usually portrayed the deceased as the hero of his last hunt or battle – fighting off an attacking pride of lions with his sons, for example. The two Groups of performers – the deceased with the lion and his sons with the lionesses – weren't allowed to touch one another even with weapons during this fatal combat. They *stepped* or *jumped* from one Group composition to another, with intricate pose-gestural patterns.

Two Groups without leaders

a) There was always a long prelude to battle. After demonstrating their capacities statically, warriors moved to the next stage of combat. Facing each other on the battlefield, they would try and intimidate their adversaries with warning/threatening postures and insulting pose-gestures to provoke the enemy to attack first, as many mammals do.

b) The same basic scenario might involve a different strategy to demoralise the opponents in the pre-attack stage. Naked young female dancers would perform sexually explicit pose-gestural patterns in front of the enemy, as bait. As soon as any attempt was made to kidnap one of the dancers, she would immediately drop down, exposing the assailants to a cloud of deadly arrows.

Single-sex Groups

a) At the post-initiation graduation ceremony, small Groups of young men would take part in a mass carnival dressed and masked as various animal species, demonstrating their characteristic postures and competing for the best pose-gestural mimicry, presentation style, costume and body ornamentation.

b) The female acting chorus was the main element of Funerary rites, the women's' painted bodies and shaven skulls personifying the mourners' grief. One Group of standing choristers would wail hysterically in various poses with chaotically *stretched/folded* limbs, while others, *holding* hands, moved *crouching* between them in serpentine patterns. Both choruses would then alternately perform the next walking postural sequence.

ORNAMENTAL shows covered many subjects: tribal history celebrations, seasonal festivities, the coronation of leaders, secular exhibitions, inter-tribal contests and traditional processions, or a Solo leader with Group.

a) In a tribal celebration, the chief and his assistants would **symbolically** represent the sun surrounded by a semicircle of heavenly bodies. These **abstractly** choreographed postural images, with extravagantly painted bodies and extra decorations, would each symbolise a male hunter/warrior characteristic: wisdom, bravery, power, patience, agility, and so on, as identified by unique pose gestural patterns, facial expression and individual body decoration.

b) Just as men worshipped the sun in this way, women would take part in lunar rites to celebrate a recent birth, give thanks for an abundant harvest or successful cattle breeding, or pray for a productive hunt or victory in war. The witch would be abstractly decorated as a full moon, her twelve assistants in a semi-circle around her personifying the twelve phases of the annual lunar cycle. Their pose-gestural patterns symbolised the various feelings or states of mind and body that were thought to be influenced by the moon: hope/fear, love/jealousy, happiness/anger, healing/madness, regularity/chaos, creativity/mortality.

Single-sex Groups
During annual inter-tribal festivals, local performing Groups competed in the traditional contest to determine the best talents in a mass posturing composition with accessories.

a) Women, decorated with long **garlands** or small **bouquets**, artistically presented intricate posturing patterns in group plastic compositions, independently or *holding* hands, with colourful, flashing lines displaying their natural body harmony, with frequent changes of rhythm, spatial proximity, group formations and accessory design.

b) Young men with sticks skilfully and artistically *imitated* combat sequences with weapons in groups of three to five participants, using acrobatic tricks and inverted stance/positions before or after conventional sparring with crossed sticks. They periodically changed their fight compositions by differing the number of participants in their groups, and the pose-gestural patterns they performed.

Single Group on multiple levels
The festival repertoire also included a Group posturing pyramid of anything from six to twelve performers in an impressive display of balance, strength and physical agility, with the posturers *standing* on each other's shoulders, *holding* their hands behind the necks of their neighbours. With or without weapons, this highly accomplished and precisely co-ordinated ensemble performance *moved* smoothly from one plastic composition into the next with great artistry.

SUMMARY

There is no doubt that body posturing was a primary communications medium for hominids. Their natural plastic vocabulary of pose-gestural patterns, served and extended the Functional repertoire, and the progressive improvement of posturing techniques also stimulated both mental and physical agility, flexibility, perceptiveness and reactions. Although always inflected by personal style and the local plastic dialect (which varied considerably between the indigenous peoples of each continent), performed postural mimicry was, and remains, understandable to any nationality, race, creed or class. Far from being a language of artificial body signs, it represents the oldest and most universal type of plastic communication among animal species, as the prehistoric record confirms.

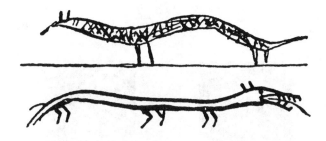

　　　　'KARANAS' Plastic Notation

I. Sign/signals

1. Illuminate!　　　　2. Ankled　　　　3. Retracing own steps

4. Implying humility　　5. Confused　　　6. Recovery　　　7. Optimism

II. Plastic Mimicry

1. Creeping scorpion　　2. Deer's flight　　　3. Mean person

4. Lion's sport　　　5. Pulled by a lion　　　6. Bee　　　Elephant trunk

1. Wrong idea   2. Assault   3. Tripped up

4. Admiration   5. Clapping rhythm   6. Caprice   7. Perpetual motion

IV. Emotional Expression

1. Joy of own superiority   2. Condolence   3. Beguiled

4. Extreme passion   5. Arrogant mood   6. Fugitive   7. Excessive joy

271

fig. III/12

V Description

1. Origin

2. Beauty mark

3. Stiffened side

4. Shy girl

5. Posterity

6. Confusion

7. Grace

VI. Interaction

1. Request

2. Leap in the dark

3. Transit

4. Interruption

5. Split

6. Violence

7. Thrown over

THE SPIRITUAL ROOTS OF EARLY RELIGION

The genesis of the main religions and their effect on primitive societies has long been explained in terms of essentially the same hypothesis.

Our ancestors' minimum requirements were food, water, shelter, and eventually, fire. Preoccupied with the perpetual fight for survival for millions of years, they could find no easy solution to overcoming the dangers they constantly faced and the many losses they experienced in daily life.

Later, when they became expert hunters or gatherers, they still could not rid themselves of deep fears of anything or anybody that appeared to have power over providing these essentials for the individual or the tribe. The only possible conclusion was that such powers could only reside in something stronger, quicker, braver and cleverer than themselves.

But what? If not powerful animals like the mammoth, eagle or crocodile, then the powers that controlled them: the sun, moon or stars, perhaps? Or the elements, like the wind, lightning or storm?

Naturally, hominids sought to contact any such superior forces in order to acquire more control over their lives and the realisation of their hopes and desires – to hunt successfully, for example, or to find a plentiful food source, or to have more children or the means to build a better shelter.

This is how, with the help of their shamans, Palaeolithic communities developed a profound belief in their totems over the generations. This manifested itself in a spiritual sense as well as through body motion. The existence of deities – supreme powers that directed or affected every thought and action of any of his or her hominid 'children' – became an unquestioned part of the fabric of life.

Daily worship rituals therefore came to be seen as the only way to get more strength, or to learn more about an animal, or to obtain blessing for a new adventure. These feelings of awe for superior powers came as naturally as mother's milk, and were so deeply ingrained that they extended as far as accepting the idea of self-sacrifice. Death became an honourable way to become one with the all-powerful totem.

Our ancestors therefore found themselves simultaneously in two manifestly different parallel worlds: **reality** and **fantasy**. When wearing the skin of a totem creature or a mask representing it during a sacred ritual, they believed themselves to be physically **transubstantiated** into the totem itself. If a tribesman accidentally tore his tiger skin in battle, he would expect to turn immediately from a strong and aggressive fighter into a weak and defenceless man.

The same was true of masks. If a participant dropped or damaged his mask during the rite immediately prior to the hunt, the entire mystical performance would be halted. The guilty party could even lose his life, tribal laws often requiring him to be sacrificed to the totem. Although females did not take part in battles or hunting expeditions, women were nevertheless occasionally sacrificed to the totem if they broke accepted tribal customs or the law. With such draconian rules operating in addition to the perils of everyday existence, life was far from easy.

As the most active form of social and cultural development, the importance of sacred rituals to early human history is incalculable. These highly organised tribal activities were directly instrumental in moving primitive man slowly but surely from the status of a clever ape towards the beginning of civilisation as we understand it today. Ritual was not entertainment: it was the university of life and death.

Plastic motion images in creative performance

By the end of the Palaeolithic period, the body motion dictionary that anthropoids had developed was too extensive to be easily memorised. The main plastic vocabulary therefore began to be recorded in petroglyph form.

The most popular totem animal images discussed here correspond to social secular events in specific places and times. However, the fundamental practice was worldwide, with worship by all primeval peoples on all continents evolving in similar ways with only minor local variations.

Each clan had its own totem mammal, reptile, insect or bird. Whether a rabbit, parrot, dragon or something else, this was the creature the tribe was born from and it was therefore their totem, unchanged since time immemorial and present in all personal or sociocultural activities in the clan. The myth, spirit and plastic characteristics of the same animal object passed from generation to generation.

If the totem was a snake, each member of the family would behave mentally and physically like a snake – *walking* noiselessly, *moving* smoothly and gracefully, controlling their emotions and temperament. Killing, even attacking from the back if necessary, to protect their own interests. Parents would encourage their children to play with harmless snakes to get used to their touch and smell.

All juveniles would have to pass a strict test before being allowed to join adult society. In one of the many different forms of initiation practised in ancient times as well as today, boys would be sent out of the home base to sleep overnight in the jungle or savannah; if the child returned the next morning with a catch of some sort, the entire clan would join in celebrating his admission to adulthood. The spirit of the prey having passed into the boy's body via the totem image, the initiate would dance a special pantomime, demonstrating to his family the hunting prowess he had shown the previous night. This example is of course only one of several different types of initiation.

GENETIC INFLUENCES ON PLASTIC MOTION

The process of creating a moving image is not as simple as one may think. Feelings and behaviours are not transmitted genetically like physical characteristics. Each new generation learns its values and the rules of morality and manners from parents and society. Although all these derive ultimately from natural genetic qualities, they are based on the personal characteristics of human images rather than animal ones.

On the other hand, man-made social and cultural circumstances that have existed for generations definitely affect human psychological and physical attitudes, and could perhaps be genetically transmitted. There are echoes of this phenomenon in the analogies we use, such as a person *walking* like a bear or being as big as an elephant; we talk of women being snaky or foxy, or someone *running* like a deer or being as brave as a lion. These animal similes can be traced back to the totemic origins of human spirituality.

There were seven main stages to the process our ancestors used to create images of living creatures: **Observation, Training, Imitation, Spiritual transformation, Body decoration, Rehearsal** and **Performance**.

Even today, children **observe** the actions of any living creature around them from a very early age. They consider its appearance and physiological structure, its age and sex, its behaviour and the way it moves. For early hominids, this was not just for fun or entertainment. Children were eager to remember every detail of the creatures they watched, mimicking how they ran, walked, rolled over or jumped. They experimented with re-enacting what they observed. At first, this was literally child's play – a game. But as the children grew older, they were taken aside by tribal elders for further education.

After their ceremonial initiation, youths would embark on long and arduous **training** involving physical exercises including *stretching, twisting, sudden stops while moving, balancing, gambolling*, contrapuntal co-ordination in *walking* and *running, jumping* backwards, sideways and on the spot, *dropping down* and *rising up* suddenly, *rolling* over and many other *acrobatic tricks*. This was strictly a body workout programme, and only after successfully passing a test would youngsters be admitted to the next stage of training with the shaman and his assistants. Those who failed were required to repeat the course.

After having absorbed the observations and undergone the basic physical preparation, youngsters started to learn the animal plastic dictionary through **imitation** using a syllabus of mimetic expressions based on local species and elaborated through many generations.

Future hunters and warriors had to repeat these routines time and again until their trainers were satisfied that the image they created resembled the creature in question as closely as possible. Anyone who collapsed from exhaustion from this strenuous training régime was considered as having been blessed by direct spiritual contact with the totem. Only during this general training could our ancestors hope to achieve this state.

The next stage was conducted personally by the shaman, having observed and evaluated the student's various performing skills and **spiritual awareness**. He had to be certain that the initiate understood the tribe's mythologies and that he would respect totemic rules and traditional customs. He taught the apprentice how to make his mask and tailor his pelt, how to concentrate his mental imagery while wearing the heavy costume, and how to use all the mimetic techniques he had learned to the best effect in performance.

Unsurprisingly after such prolonged, physically and emotionally intense tutelage, students began to feel and behave like spirits reborn under the leadership of the totem. This transformation was a difficult task for both parties – one can only imagine how many times the master had to repeat his hypnotising sessions before the pupil was able to assimilate enough to be able to achieve the instant and total metamorphosis required.

After making his costume and mask, the newly fledged adult embarked on the fifth stage: learning the art of **body decoration**. This ranged from tattooing and painting to making a masks, robes, bracelets and other performance accessories based on his Totem image, together with hunting accessories such as horns and a complete arsenal of weapons.

Every tribe member would usually have one main mask symbolising his totem and a few other creatures to reflect his personality and his physique. In order for the spirit of the totem to pass through him, each hunter had to make his own masks and costumes. Friends and relatives were however permitted to help with preparing accessories and with body decoration.

Having acquired all the necessary routines, spiritual awareness and outer appearance, the apprentice was allowed to join in with **rehearsals** for hunting and fighting rituals in order to learn the choreography of mythical pantomime and the dance repertoire of various rite ceremonies. We can only guess at the difficulties that even an advanced student had to endure. By this stage however, he was desperate to conclude his studies in the shortest possible time in order to begin life in earnest and take his place in the tribe as a fully-fledged hunter and warrior.

Any hunting expedition usually involved two opposing strategies: firstly, locating and penetrating the herd, and secondly, killing while remaining undetected until the next kill.

As we have seen, hominids had to spend some three to four years just to learn the elementary mimetic techniques needed in order to be spiritually transformed by the totem. One or two more years were required to learn the next three stages for the study and practice of hunting and combat skills. This programme had to be very carefully thought out, as anyone with less than perfect knowledge of his prey would meet with limited success. It is doubtful whether an adult could learn such a large plastic motion vocabulary in as short a period of time as a teenager.

STAGING THE PERFORMANCE

The three traditional phases of any ritual or secular event (and later, shows) were:

i) **Pre-event**. This phase included full dress rehearsals for individuals, partners or groups, either of particular episodes or the entire event from beginning to end. These rehearsals would be watched by shaman, who would interrupt and correct any mistakes he noticed in timing, spacing, imagery, dress, accessories or dramatic and technical points.

ii) **Performance**. This was the highly controlled spiritual and plastic transformation itself, and involved memorising the motion score, concentrating on the opposite object in the individual's line of movement and constantly listening to and watching for any signals, which would require immediate response.

iii) **Post-event demonstration**. The final phase was a matter of analysing and evaluating the event, correcting any weaknesses and reporting back to the Totem via the shaman. Thanks would be given for success and forgiveness sought for failure.

During each of these phases, each participant would demonstrate their own ability to **create** plastic motion images of one or more creatures. Without this prolonged training, they would never have been able to execute these images so compellingly, by simultaneously becoming both player and instrument in a highly detailed symphony of body motion.

INITIATION RITES AND EDUCATING THE YOUNG

Initiation rites contained most of the elements of other sacred ceremonies. The main purpose was to induct male and female adolescents into full membership of the tribe, and introduce them to tribal totems.

THE HISTORY OF THE TRIBE AND ITS TOTEM

In addition to totemic mythology, the history of the tribe, the meaning of puberty and fecundity, hunting and battle skills, food gathering and farming methods, young initiates had to learn the tribe's body language and plastic motion dictionary and basic performance skills including acting, dancing, singing and using sound instruments.

Adolescents were not allowed to attend any rites before being formally invited by the shaman after they reached puberty to take part in the traditional ceremony to initiate new tribe members. These were usually held separately for each sex and performed at night, either as separate events or as a special finale to a routine sacred ceremony.

The shaman would lead worshippers in the performance of an enthralling spectacle of the totem's mystic birth, along with many exciting episodes from the tribe's mythology for the benefit of the young initiates. The audience, mesmerised by the shaman's magic tricks and overwhelmed by the intensely dramatic atmosphere, would gradually lapse into a kind of psycho-physical shock.

In the last part of the ceremony, the initiates were introduced to the tribe's main totem image. As portrayed by the shaman against a background of strange motions, noise and perfumes, this half human, half animal creature with its oversized mask, tail and other sacred accessories made a lasting spiritual impression on the young spectators, who were by now mentally and physically under the shaman's control. The rest of the initiation ritual was conducted by senior worshippers.

276

As well as introducing the initiates to the Goddess Mother, the puberty ritual dealt with sexual matters, and prepared the youngsters for starting a family.

The ceremony for girls was choreographed by the witch, and involved perhaps half a dozen or so initiates circling around a naked man. Other women worshippers *sang* and *clapped* their hands on their sides as the witch joined the youngsters to explain details of the male anatomy, allowing enough time for them to familiarise themselves with it. As the volume of noise, rhythm and temperature of the circling girls gradually increased, the witch brought this merry-go-round to an ecstatic crescendo. When girls began falling down in exhaustion in a trance-like state, women worshippers would take them immediately to the open fire and circumcise them with a small sharp stone.

The equivalent ceremony the shaman conducted for boys was very similar, circulating around a naked woman and culminating in circumcision by the shaman's male assistants.

THE GENERAL EDUCATION CURRICULUM OF EVERYDAY LIFE

Since all rituals were in effect the hominids' complex and highly organised university, the largest part of the initiation ceremony was the educational element. Youngsters initiated into totemism learned the sacred mysteries of various rites. Coached by their elders, boys learned battle and hunting skills; the girls, domestic and farming skills. And adolescents of both sexes acquired all the performance skills needed to take full part in sacred ceremonies.

Every subject in all these educational programmes involved its own plastic motion syllabus for teaching purposes. Elaborated over the generations into a sophisticated motion dictionary, this was eventually condensed into a 'shorthand' system governing virtually all personal interactions. This 'shorthand' was the only way to retain control over the fast growing number of additions to the motion vocabulary over a relatively short period of time. As the tribe grew, so did its rituals and plastic dictionary; inevitably, the time came when the shaman could no longer memorise everything by himself and had to seek help.

Having carefully selected the best prospects from among his older assistants, the shaman instructed them as trainers for each element of the educational programme. Initiates between the ages of twelve and sixteen would study all day under these trainers, and then practise their newly acquired skills at evening rituals.

Given the practical constraints of the time and the lack of educational materials, this highly organised process proved surprisingly sophisticated as an educational method. Shamans also kept in touch (via couriers) with tribes elsewhere, both locally and further afield. These continuing contacts partly explain the great similarity often found between the plastic vocabularies used by tribes living far apart – even on different continents. This phenomenon reflects fundamental similarities of environment and social patterns that allowed shamans to develop a motion language that was globally understood.

All the following examples form part of the continuing traditions of the tribal peoples of Africa.

The initiation of girls (examples):
Female circumcision rituals were often accompanied by public entertainment. At the end of the Dipo initiation programme, girls of the Krobo people in Ghana usually danced to demonstrate their grace and beauty in front of the chieftain and their relatives.

- After the Poro initiation ceremony, **Senufo** girls celebrated their passage into womanhood with impressive dance routines – generally, the subtle and complex Ngoron dance. It often took six months of careful study to master the graceful choreography, with its fascinating *steps* and highly artistic technique.
- The main rite of passage for **Bassari** girls in Senegal is the Ohamana, a name derived originally from the small rattling shells worn at the ankles to enhance the rhythm of

movements. The dancers begin by *moving* in slow motion in a wide circle, and then change the formation into single file, executing tiny *steps* which give the impression of *dancing* on the spot. Long sticks are *held* vertically in the right hand to monotone vocalisations which eventually put the participants into a trance-like state for the circumcision itself.

- According to **Swazi** mythology, humans emerged from a primordial reed, split lengthwise into two parts. This sacred folk myth is the basis for the popular Reed Dance ceremony, in which the Swazi demonstrate their respect for their ancestors. Thousands of girls carrying long reeds gather in a high-spirited marching dance that expresses their feminine and tribal solidarity. With their bodies colourfully decorated, the girls acknowledge their passage into womanhood by chanting and dancing.

The initiation of boys (examples):

Boys celebrated their initiation differently from girls. Instead of dancing, they are expected to demonstrate their masculine qualities such as physical dexterity, discipline and speed of response to danger. **Masai** boys perform a strenuous ritual before circumcision, *running* a kind of marathon in groups of forty to fifty around a monument (the Osingira) specially erected for the purpose. *Holding* a stick in the right hand, they circle the sacred object non-stop for a long time, until, *whirling* convulsively and foaming at the mouth, they eventually go into a rigid trance called emboshona. They start losing control of their actions, and *fall* one by one to the ground. Circumcision takes place immediately after in a secret place, whereupon the youngsters are accepted as real warriors, and receive the sexual rights of manhood.

In **Ethiopia**, one of the most popular sacred events involves young men proving their bravery by *jumping* onto the backs of a line of between twenty to forty bulls. *Leaping* from one leg to another, and *landing* heavily on the animals' backs, the initiates show off their sense of balance, dexterity and coordination in this way. Having passed this arduous test, the participants receive the formal adult name by which they are known for the rest of their lives.

In the final month of the initiation process of the **Teneka** people in Benin, the guardians of the boys to be initiated perform light-hearted sexual slapstick in communal spaces, lampooning the crowd and driving them wild with exaggerated sexual horseplay involving vigorously suggestive body posturing with huge wooden phalluses. After this introductory clowning, the boys begin the circumcision ritual by demonstrating their spiritual readiness for the passage to adulthood with a dance involving heavy *stamping* and powerful *port-de-bras* with *trembling* flywhisks. During the next stage, the boys simulate circumcision on their own necks with sharp hunting knives. The dripping blood symbolises cutting their ties with the past, as if in a spiritual act of rebirth. The actual circumcision is then carried out, after which the boys are accepted as fully-fledged men.

During their rebirth ritual, **Bassari** boys are obliged to withdraw to the forest, where they are prohibited from talking, laughing, smiling, making any noise or looking to the left or right. These constraints are to teach the initiates obedience and self-control. Sequestered together in this way, the boys develop bonds that last a lifetime, and return on the final day to celebrate their passage into manhood. A long line of masked dancers called Odo-Kuta then emerge from the forest to join the celebration. Embodying the spirit of nature, these masks evolved from the Bassari's animistic origins and act as a link between the people and their environment. Since the wisdom of the masks is considered to come from beyond the human realm, their power is deemed to be absolute.

Graduation to warriorhood (example):

The ceremonial initiation of **Bassari** warriors consists of a duel between each graduating male and the Lakuta Mask – a crucial test for youngsters to prove their courage and virility. Every candidate has to battle the opponent ferociously, using all his recently acquired fighting skills to demonstrate his strength and his ability to defend himself effectively. To simulate an actual fight, the Lakuta attacks the young combatant aggressively with a long switch, provoking his opponent to respond equally vigorously.

Masai initiates demonstrate their prowess as warriors in the Red Dance. Glistening in red ochre pigment as they dance and sing together, the boys present the brave attitude and hot temperament required of the warrior. This remarkable performance is dedicated to revered older hunters, who, armed only with their wits, courage and spears, have succeeded in killing a lion. When celebrating their graduation, the warriors launch themselves into a *leaping* dance called Empatia. At the high point of each leap, they *jerk* their shoulders to the rhythm of the guttural *chanting* of the audience and the drumming musicians. The dancers have to *land* close to their chosen mates, *touching* the girl's cheeks vigorously with their long ochre-dyed hair. This seductive and highly competitive performance is characteristic of many ritual events in combining different spiritual functions.

HUNTING AND BATTLE RITUALS

Hunting was of course more important than any other subject – after all, life itself depended on it. And as we have seen, hominids believed that constant practice would help them to be absorbed completely into the image (and therefore the being) of the following day's prey, thereby making the creature itself collude in its own demise.

Naive as this belief may have been, it usually yielded the desired result because practising hunting techniques time and again during these exhaustingly long rituals gave Palaeolithic man a better understanding of his prey, which in turn helped him to improve his hunting technique. It also helped the hunter to reach a better understanding of his own body and increase his own physical abilities in terms of respiration and circulation. The endless repetition increased powers of concentration and helped to hone reaction times. The hunter learned how to avoid mistakes, how to prevent serious injuries and how to turn a counterattack to his advantage.

If a hunt was not successful, Pleistocene man had to perform remedial rituals on returning to the tribe. These could last as long as a week, or until the next full moon. The hunter had to re-enact hunting rites, performing the role of hunter and prey several times, repeatedly proving his technical and physical dexterity. Not everyone could persevere to the end; whenever a particularly exhausted performer fell, he would be replaced so that the ritual could continue without interruption.

This was in effect Darwinian natural selection applied to humans; gruelling as it was, the process selected the strongest and best qualified to contribute to the tribe's survival.

Hunting rituals (example):

In **Kassena** hunting rituals, shamans are extensively consulted by the hunters before each sortie to determine the best time and place for their expedition. The answer depends on the shaman's interpretation of a random pattern created by dropping his sacred fork onto a stone divining board. To protect themselves, the hunters donned garments of pelt adorned with leather talismans for additional protection. The hunt to come is ritually enacted outside and in front of the village, where the spirit of the animal to be hunted is allegorically captured in order to assure success. After the hunt, the men revisit the shaman and ask forgiveness for the animals they have killed, to prevent any misfortune from subsequently afflicting the community. The Kassena, who honour the spirit of the earth for its role in the life of the tribe, reconcile their differences during these ceremonies to ensure continuing harmony within the community.

BATTLE RITES AND FIGHTING SKILLS

The inevitable battles for mating, territory and hierarchical position were powerful spurs to the evolutionary process. Like any other animals, hominids constantly competed for better living conditions, and this was the stimulus for creating the more sophisticated weapons and shelters that eventually gave rise to Stone Age and Iron Age technologies.

Whereas hunting rites were based on direct observation of animals or fellow tribesmen performing sacred rituals, battle rites dealt with unknown characteristics of unknown enemies using unknown weapons and fighting skills. Taking turns to perform each opposing side, participants had to plan defensive and counter offensive manoeuvres against completely unpredictable moves.

The ritual never escalated into a real fight – in fact, the rules forbade any form of physical contact between the antagonists whatsoever (although it involved sneaking up on the 'enemy' as closely as possible, as if in actual combat). Any performer who accidentally touched or hit his opponent or damaged his shield was eliminated from the next real battle, or until he improved his fighting skills.

For a shaman, the public humiliation of defeat was worse than death. He therefore took his duties very seriously, and avoided needless risks. He knew that a minute miscalculation by one of his fighters could jeopardise the chances of winning, and could result in one or more deaths (and perhaps the ultimate horror – being eaten by the enemy).

The plastic dictionary of the battle was very similar to that of hunting but with the addition of a new vocabulary of combat techniques.

The mental and physical stresses our forebears were exposed to during the long process of human evolution are hard for us to imagine. While coping throughout the day with the harsh and often very cruel realities of physical survival, they had to participate at night in exhausting rituals without the benefit of spoken language or illustrative reference. The only source of information about hunting, fishing and fighting was the plastic vocabulary passed down from generation to generation.

COMBAT CEREMONIES WITH ANIMALS

Our ancestors always knew in advance the next animal they were going to hunt. With prey ranging from mammoth or rhinoceros to monkey and ostrich, a vast diversity of plastic motion characteristics, physiologies and defensive weapons had to be learned during pre-hunting rehearsals. It was vital to know how best to repel each attack and how guard against nasty surprises.

Dancing in opposition as hunter and prey, the performers regularly switched roles (and therefore the natural weapons of the animal with the artificial ones of the hunter). These virtually instant **transformations** of fighting motion from defence to attack and back again helped to hone the athleticism and physical flexibility of the male body as well as their facility with different weapons. It also helped to develop their powers of concentration.

Hunting celebrations were always a great success with the audience, which in turn made dancers proud of themselves. The most spectacular combats between hominids and animals in hunt rituals were adapted for use in secular entertainment events. Initially, just dancing duets of man and prey were involved; these later developed into trio performances, then quartets and larger groups. The opposing parties still performed in a realistic style – and when our forebears began domesticating wild animals, they learned even more about them through play.

Whenever an animal was caught alive, it was first used as a combat opponent of the dancing hunter in the hunt celebration ritual. Later, after the sacred performance, the victorious hunters were allowed either to sacrifice the animal to the totem, or to feed it to their families.

To fight a beast in public may have been entertaining, but there were also risks. The personal ambition of the dancer/hunter, along with the stimulus of competition, usually overcame fear of being seriously hurt by a wounded and desperate wild animal.

These hominid/animal combats considerably increased the sophistication of the hunters' performing skills in terms of both presentation and execution. Their experience of fighting in public was often used in funerary and mythical pantomimes – and of course, was the precursor of the gladiatorial spectacles of ancient Rome. In this respect, the bullfights still practised today echo down the distant millennia of our evolutionary story.

Ritual battle contest (example):
A series of wrestling tournaments took place across Africa after each harvest, with large numbers of young men from different tribes demonstrating their personal spiritual power and fighting skills. These tournaments usually began with some twenty-five individual duels, ending eventually with one overall victor through a process of elimination. The rules in these competitions were both strict and pitilessly harsh – they were real fights (although any competitor who actually killed his opponent would be banished from the village, along with his family).

The combatants, armed only with long wooden poles, fought naked without shields or body paint. This gave the audience a better opportunity to appraise each man's fighting skills, masculinity, grace, strength, flexibility, spirit and self-control. These ancient wrestling tournaments were the main form of sport or competitive game all over the continent, and provided the audience with great excitement – a kaleidoscopic panorama of motion.

RITES OF FERTILITY, FOOD GATHERING ANIMAL HUSBANDRY

Performed by and for women, these were held by the female shaman (or witch) either in separate areas outdoors, or in big shelters or caves. The archaeological record confirms women's leading role in the domestic and social lives of Palaeolithic tribes. Matriarchy was widely and deeply established; the Goddess Mother, creator of all life on earth (including totems) was the strongest spiritual power for the entire community during this period.

Not only was she the symbol of home, hearth and prosperity, but also a fetish who brought good luck in hunting or fighting. She was the incarnation of life and death, a sacred personification of totemism and the universe as a whole. This is why images of women engaged in social activities often figure in early paintings and figurines. Some battle or hunt scenes also include silhouettes of women in subordinate roles, praying for a good fortune or blessing their menfolk.

Indeed, at the very beginning of human history, women were also the main shamans. As populations grew, women became more involved in domestic and social activities. In addition to child bearing and rearing, their main responsibilities were farming and food gathering, supplying water and firewood and participating in cultural events, all of which were popular motifs in traditional rituals. These responsibilities consumed most of the women's time and energy, just as hunting did for men.

Fertility rituals focussed on animals (including birds, reptiles, fish and insects) and food (including fruit, vegetables and cereals) as well as the women themselves: sex, fertility, pregnancy, childbirth, health and family. Some programmes of these rites included special processions dedicated to the Goddess Mother and the natural forces thought to influence harvest – the sun, earth, moon and stars, lakes, mountains, wind, fire and so on.

All these elements were reflected in the motion vocabulary of fertility rites. Shamanic monologues or dialogues with totems were based on *mimicry, gestures, postures*, and later, *dance movements*, all of which were easily understood by both performers and audience.

FERTILITY CULTS AND PHALLUS WORSHIP

The purpose of these was to resolve particular female problems, with specific motion routines to ask the Goddess Mother to grant successful conception or safe delivery, for example.

The undoubted efficacy of these ceremonies was based on more than the placebo effect of belief in magic, in that they involved intensive coaching in complex physio-therapeutic exercises designed to remedy the physical problem in question – an ecstatic dance prolonged the point of collapse in the first case, or waist and leg motions while seated in an attempt to prepare the body for an easier delivery.

While these routines were performed, the witch would *run* and *jump* around, *waving* magic cult accessories over the women's bodies, to the accompaniment of loud *claps, vocalisations* and primitive instrumental sounds from the female assistants. The powerfully mystical atmosphere of this type of performance induced cumulative psychological and physiological effects on the participants – a trance-like hypnotic state that in itself delivered beneficial results.

Fertility rites extended far beyond the medical sphere. As the primary symbol of human reproduction, the female image represented the dynamics of family, continuity for the tribe and physical survival. The associated rites depicting feminine beauty, grace and sexuality were therefore vitally important for hominid society. Even imitations of sexual intercourse had a spiritual rather than titillating role.

During these ceremonies, the witch and her female entourage would *parade* naked around a handsome naked couple *standing* motionless in the centre. The worshippers *circled* continuously, *swinging* their breasts and hips, *tossing* their long hair and convulsively *vibrating* their whole bodies to the rhythm of *stamps, claps* and *vocalisations*. Loose *flying* hair evoked the **sowing** of seeds, the *circling* breasts represented **motherhood** and the *swinging* hips, **sex**. *Stamping* feet echoed the sound of *running* bison, and thus symbolised **strength** and **health** for newborns; the *vibrating* body was a stylised figurative depiction of **crops** *quivering* in the wind.

These impressive ceremonies continued over long periods, exhausted participants periodically being replaced by fresh ones. As a primitive dance, this dynamic element of syncretic ritual was not as yet a composition choreographed to provide a show.

Courtship rituals (examples):
In ancient Africa and elsewhere, our forebears used various coded body motions to indicate sexual attraction, including flirtatious *mimicry*, seductive *gestures* and alluring *postures*. The many types of bodily adornment were also used to signal sexual interest and enhance attractiveness. In **Wodaabe** society, for example, a man indicates his interest in the woman of his choice by showing one finger *laid* on top of another; to accept the proposal, the woman replies by *holding* two fingers side by side.

The courtship ritual of the Wodaabe people involves a repertoire of three dances. The first is in two parts:

a) In the morning part (called the Ruume dance) guests were welcomed and local spirits invoked for good fortune. Wodaabe men would show off their looks, charm and physical adroitness and poise through their dancing. As the men *danced* slowly and gracefully in a circle, *chanting* hypnotically long hymns to feminine beauty and grace, the women made their selection; having chosen, each woman would (at the appropriate time in the dance), approach the suitor in question and *run* her fingertip down his back. Still dancing, the man replies with *winks, twitching* the corners of his mouth to indicate where the subsequent tryst was to take place. By the time the dance finished at midnight, such couples would indeed be coupling.

b) In the late afternoon, their body decorations brightly illuminated by the setting sun, the participants would perform the Yaake dance. Shoulder to shoulder, the dancers *shimmer* forwards on tiptoes to enhance their height, and launch into a sequence of facial *grimaces*. Teeth flash, cheeks *pout* in short puffs of breath, lips *part* and *tremble*.

The women judges weigh up the men's magnetism, personality and charm. Those who can *roll* one eye while *holding* the other still are particularly favoured; the Wodaabe belief is that the strength of eyes make the marriage. Older women were by no means immune to the heightened sexual tension surrounding these dances, frequently *dashing* forwards to *yell* at and physically harry their favourite man.

The Geerewol dance expresses male beauty and charm. Three nubile virgins, selected at a previous female ritual dance for their grace and beauty, are appointed to judge the best and best-looking dancers from the fifty or so from whom they will choose a partner.

For a couple of hours, the men *move* in a grand circle, *swinging* their arms gracefully towards the centre, *turning* their heads from side to side, *chanting* mesmerically and *smiling* broadly to show off the whiteness of their eyes and teeth. The winners won the adoration of the women and the respect and admiration of other men, and the rite itself played a key role in the selection of the most promising couples to ensure the successful continuity of the Wodaabe people.

FOOD GATHERING AND HARVEST RITE CEREMONIES

Although they shared the same totemic basis as the cattle breeding ceremonies, food-gathering rites involved no direct *imitation* of living creatures, nor any traditional masks or animal skins.

Neither were there any totemic models of food crops; instead, shamans created plastic motion images with the hands or arms for each botanical species. That this new, symbolic motion vocabulary could nevertheless be easily understood underlines the role of motion as the main language of communication at this stage of hominid evolution. Our ancestors knew these symbols intimately because they used them in their everyday interactions.

Ancient illustrations show arms moving like *waving* branches, women *bending* down like grasses in a strong wind, harvest images of a female figure working with diagonal lines across her body made by two streams of falling grain. The centrepiece of these flora rituals was a tree in blossom, a powerful symbol of fertility and regeneration. Elements of these sacred images have survived through the ages to our times.

Planting and Harvest rites (examples):
The **Bedik** people of Senegal perform a planting ritual to ensure the fertility of their land. During their annual Minymor festival, they call on the spirits to appease the powers of nature, to bless the crops being planted and to drive out evil forces. Those who instruct the Bedik spiritually in the sacred knowledge wear the most ancient masks in Africa, made from the bark and leaves of particular trees growing in the sacred forest. Each mask has a distinctive personality and plays a unique role in maintaining the balance between Bedik life and the spirits.

The first to appear from the forest is the Kankouran, who playfully *chases* and *whips* uncircumcised youngsters. He then visits boys circumcised the previous year, bestowing his blessings on them for their future nuptials. The next arrivals are the bushy Dakota Masks.

Serious and calm, they bring messages of wisdom from the sacred forest, and *dance* with the married women responsible for planting and cultivating crops. Niathoma, the final Mask then emerges and *leaps* around the village, *wielding* sword and switch, *chasing* away evil spirits, and cleansing the area of anything that may bring disharmony. At the close of the ceremony, the Dakota Masks give permission to the Bedik to plant their crops.

Fao is the December millet harvest ceremony of the **Kassena** people of Ghana. Villagers have to behave quietly when the millet begins to flower, because this is the time of pregnancy for the deity's wife. When the flowers mature, the son of the earth priest cuts a stem of millet and makes a flute which he plays as he walks through the village to announce the beginning of the Fao festival. The villagers compose songs for the event, and *dance* to the rhythm of the drums. Guinea fowl, sheep, cows and baskets of millet are brought to the chief's house to be blessed by the priests. Then the women celebrate the harvest by *dancing* to the accompaniment of their calabashes, and honour the earth god with sacred songs.

In Burkina Fasso, the **Bobo** people hold dramatic masquerade rituals to ask permission from the spirits of nature to plant and harvest their crops. The Bobo believe that every act that takes something from their surroundings, from cutting a tree to gathering fruit, has a negative impact on nature. The buffalo Mask (N'sinh) *chases* away the evil the people have brought on themselves by transgressing against nature. The antelope Masks (Kaan) *leap* with explosive energy, *bouncing* through the village on long stilts to *mimic* the animal's long stride until, exhausted by their exertions, they are cared for by ritual guardians, who revive them with a restorative millet drink between each performance.

Using extremely complex *steps* passed down through the generations, the Masks *dance* and *parade* among the crowds all day, removing the negative energy which has accumulated in the community since the last harvest, and entreating Wuro, the creator, to bestow a good harvest, health and prosperity on the tribe. Any mistakes in performing these *steps* was considered a serious ill omen, presaging a calamitous misfortune of some kind.

CATTLE BREEDING RITUALS

Every aspect of prehistoric life was reflected through the prism of the female image. To secure a productive breeding season or an abundance of prey, for example, the witch would lead female tribe members in ceremonies to persuade the Goddess Mother to increase the reproductivity of the species in question.

Like the male hunters, Neolithic females could imitate any living creature to perfection. Although women performed naked most of the time in order to influence the totems with their sexual attractiveness (and therefore fertility), they also sometimes wore animal pelts or tied a snakeskin around their bodies. Their faces, however, would rarely be covered by masks on the basis that better results were often obtained by using the hypnotic power of the eyes.

The main motion themes of these ceremonies were based on imitating the courtship rituals and breeding practices of different types of creature. This was the origin of the images of mating scorpions, snakes, lions and swans found in later rock paintings.

Fulani ceremonies accompanying the annual herding of cattle across the river Niger are among the largest and most joyous celebrations in West Africa. Driven by herders, thousands of animals swim the great river in their migration to greener pastures for six months of the year. Every participating tribe celebrates their animals' survival of this great journey. Masked dancers and singers entertain the herders, showering them with gifts and praise. Fulani girls entice the young men to join them in courtship dances, which usually continue throughout the night, and often result in marriages.

284

The **Hamar, Geleb** and **Karo** people hold similar celebrations with seasonal courtship dances in which the young men imitate the behaviour and characteristic movements of their animals and the spiritual images they represent. To attract the eye of potential partners, they paint themselves in a variety of striking designs depicting birds, lizards, big cats. Singing magicians are tap out rhythmic patterns to accompany the dancing performers.

The sanctity of womanhood

Women worshippers were usually led by a female shaman, or witch, who dealt on a daily basis with most domestic personal, family and social issues involving women or children – especially during the matriarchal period.

All women's dances were usually accompanied by a primitive choir and acoustic 'orchestra' consisting of women *yelling, clapping* and using rudimentary instruments to produce a loud rhythmic noise.

Hunting rituals were even sometimes included in female religious ceremonies, the women *dancing* around a depiction of the intended prey until a hunter entered to dispatch the imagined creature with a spear. Other dances saw the womenfolk *running* and *jumping* around the tribal chief, adorned with full hunting regalia in the centre of the circle.

The function of these dances was of course to assure success in the forthcoming hunt. If it failed, and the hunters returned without a kill, the inevitable consequence was retribution and penance, just as it was in the case of natural disaster, a poor harvest or any other serious setback for the tribe.

To seek the Goddess Mother's forgiveness, the women often had to dance virtually non-stop for a whole week. As each dancer eventually fell from sheer exhaustion, she would be replaced by another. This mysterious dance of atonement later grew into what became known as the Witches' Sabbath.

Unlike later rituals, these dances of atonement had no fixed mimetic composition or choreography in time or space. The women improvised their individual *movements* and patterns, but all to the same beat – single and double *jumps* on one or both legs, *overjumps, balancing* from one leg to the other, *waving* or *shaking* one or both arms chaotically towards the image of the Goddess Mother.

Women performed a ritual ceremony at full moon every month. Moving in two parallel lines facing each other, they beseeched the lunar totem to protect their families, make them fertile, or save their husbands from harm.

Any unusual happening was considered either a positive or negative sign from the deities. Disasters like forest fires or earthquakes were seen as divine punishment for negligence, ignorance or bad deeds; a successful fishing trip or good weather was interpreted as a reward for good behaviour, a worthy deed or divine appreciation of a tribal sacrifice.

Worship ceremonies often continued throughout the night, and sometimes lasted a week. Women usually *sang* and *clapped, walking* or *running*, but always simultaneously and with great spirituality. To create a rhythmical pulse, they would *stamp* their feet heavily, or make percussive sounds with their teeth.

Men usually performed solo or in pairs in the middle of a circle or semicircle of women. They would imitate the totems or deities to whom the ceremony was dedicated, faithfully copying the plastic motions of the totemic creature. Technically and emotionally, it was presented as perfectly as possible in order to please the totem, who in return was expected to bestow good fortune on the tribe. Such rituals were not intended as pleasurable entertainment, but part of the strenuous work of everyday life.

THE EMPOWERMENT OF FEMALE PERFORMERS

Images of animals in hunting rituals were usually performed by male actors; there is no record of women hunting with masked faces, perhaps because of the cult of fecundity and the Goddess Mother.

In Palaeolithic times, they performed mainly in the Realistic style, but only in certain traditional rites: initiation, harvest, fertility and funerary. But in the Neolithic era, women engaged in virtually all aspects of sociocultural activity. Even hunting and battle rituals, formerly the exclusive preserve of male performers, now became legitimate subjects for female worshippers. The sexes were still segregated of course, the women worshipping at separate events and in private, but they retained complete freedom in terms of performing ideas and presentational style.

These new rites were taken very seriously by women, and expressed great spiritual admiration for the Goddess Mother and her son, the Totem. Eventually women also joined mythical and funerary pantomimes; indeed, the female choir soon became a significant part of artistic expression for both subjects.

The female plastic image of mammals was never actually based on direct realistic imitation (with or without mask), as in male hunting pantomimes. The reason was that from the earliest stages the social foundation of a tribe was matriarchal, under the spiritual umbrella of the Goddess Mother as represented by the witch. From the early Palaeolithic era onwards, the sacred image of women personified life, fertility and reproduction in all socio-cultural activities.

The female anatomy is not as physically suited to hunting or combat as a man's. By their very nature (and for sound evolutionary reasons), women have a broader compass than men, a greater awareness of reproduction and survival and therefore more flexibility in both perception and performance. These collective attributes were symbolised in the image of Goddess Mother; fertile women of childbearing age were therefore accorded considerable respect as assets to the tribe.

The image of the omnipotent Goddess Mother never lost its spiritual power, even during the patriarchal period of the late Palaeolithic and early Neolithic eras. The myth of the Totem, son of the Mother Goddess, allowed a logical and seamless progression from one spiritual patron to the other.

THE MOVING FEMALE CHOIR

Although tribes on different continents had various forms of pre-hunting ritual, women played only *static illustrative* roles with very little physical action wherever they took part in these sacred ceremonies. They might, for example, *chant* rudimentary incantations to the Goddess Mother from the sidelines, beseeching her for a successful hunt the next day. They sometimes assisted with props such as horns, tusks or beaks, corresponding to the animals being imitated by the dancing hunters.

Cave murals in Mongolia show nubile women attracting prey in other ways, with groups *walking* and *singing* topless around a hunter masked as a bear. He *stamps* his feet in a heavy balancing notion, from one leg to the other, *turning* slowly on the spot. Women in triangular pelts, holding rattles in both hands, *bend* backwards and forwards, *circling* continuously clockwise.

Many versions of this subject are seen in ancient rock paintings, tattoos and domestic artefacts. They all have a central significance in common: the idea of women worshipping to call for prey, bless their menfolk and plead for abundant fertility. Passive as these motions may seem in practical terms, they acted as a great spiritual support for the hunters.

By contrast, things were very different when women took part in their own private ceremonies mentioned earlier, which were surprisingly sophisticated in terms of complexity and technique. It has to be admitted that Mother Nature (or the Goddess Mother) has perhaps made the female body more physically suited to the motions of dance than the male's.

Hunting rituals were among the main forms of social activity at the dawn of human evolution. As we have seen, women were restricted to providing background accompaniment to the male performers and engaged in virtually no physical motion themselves.

However, female worshippers entirely dominated the subsequent food gathering and harvest rituals. Having been excluded from practising the *mimicry* of living creatures in hunting rituals, women never really approached male standards of mimetic execution. A plausible explanation for this may have been the fear of subsequently giving birth to a child with the face of the animal concerned; in any case, women performers amply compensated for this loss with their very successful *dancing* and *singing*.

Women's plastic vocabulary was quite large and varied. Although it entailed less facial *mimicry* and Realistic *imitation* of animal motions, there were more (and more artistic) plastic expressions for spiritual images and flora. During the matriarchal period, all female socio-cultural activities were led by the local witch who, as the spiritual representative of the Goddess Mother, had total control over women and their children.

As the symbol of puberty, fertility and reproduction, the plastic image of Goddess Mother is always shown in prehistoric artefacts as a mature pregnant woman, with exaggeratedly large breasts and buttocks.

This potent image of fecundity heavily influenced other genres, including mime and dance. Women usually worshipped topless in public rituals, but completely naked in closed ceremonies in order to achieve the closest possible spiritual contact with Goddess.

The main motion motif in practically all ritual performances by women was the *swinging* body: *shaking* shoulders, *swinging* breasts, *twirling* belly, *twisting* hips, *vibrating* buttocks – whichever best demonstrated female attributes and conveyed the magic message about fruitful harvests, successful hunts and the fertility of both people and their herds.

Although symbolic in intent, these motions were presented quite realistically as variations on everyday body motion. This flexible mixture of different styles typified the earliest performances by anthropoids; later on, when the tribal social system became more established, women's cultural activities evolved into a multi-faceted and well organised institution.

MIMETIC CURRICULUM FOR GIRLS

While boys practised their hunting and fighting routines, young girls tried to copy their mothers' progressive motions in dance pantomimes. From the age of seven or eight, they began regular plastic exercises under the tutelage of female instructors; after puberty initiation, they followed an intensive study programme of *dance*, rudimentary *singing* and *playing* rhythmic sequences on acoustic instruments.

This was not of course a fully rounded cultural education, but the necessary foundation for the proper execution of the entire ritual performance repertoire. However, the girls' enthusiasm and natural ambition to compete stimulated their progress.

They had to absorb a considerable amount of information in a relatively short period of time, based on a curriculum that included:

Mimesis – *grimaces, gestures, postures.*

Dance – *steps, passes, turns, jumps, acrobatic tricks.*

- **Physical workout** – *stretching, contracting, rotating, swinging, vibrating, posing upside down.*
- **Arm and hand movements** – *twisting, rotating, vibrating, stretching, flexing, contrapuntal coordination.*
- Use of performance **accessories**, such as horns, tusks, beaks, sticks and branches, torches, vessels, figurines, fruit, garlands, snakes, birds and cats.
- **Head movements**, with free hair: *twisting, shaking, rotating* and *trembling.*
- **Rudimentary song** – solo, duet, trio, in unison or in harmony with other voices.
- *Cries, imitating* animal sounds, solo or in groups, consonantly or dissonantly.
- **Rhythm**: *clapping* accentuated and syncopated beats using one or both hands on thighs, shoulders, knees, forearms or ribs, *slapping* feet against buttocks or *stamping* with the feet, elbows or buttocks while seated.
- **Acoustic instruments**, such as ankle **bangles, rattles**, **dry reeds, sticks, drums** or **shells.**
- **Coordination** and harmony in *singing, dancing, playing* rhythmical backgrounds and *moving* in patterns.
- **Self-adornment**, including body and face *painting, tattooing*, dressing, hairdressing and props.

Before being allowed to take part in the ritual mime repertoire, girls (like boys) had to be initiated by the Goddess Mother or totem. Only after this, at the age of thirteen or fourteen, were they considered fully-fledged members of the tribe.

The Artistic style dominated most female performing events, both sacred and secular, for reasons we have seen.

The legacy of these early anthropoid initiation rituals continues to this day, in the form of modern traditional pantomime. In the later Palaeolithic period, Homo Sapiens' rapid cultural evolution saw a gradual transition from secret closed sacred ceremonies to public events which gradually became appreciated as popular entertainment for adults and children alike. As a result, highly developed syncretic versions of ancient ritual grew into separate performing arts such as dance and pantomime such as we have understood it since the dawn of recorded history.

Female Fertility Rites (example):
The **Yoruba** people of Nigeria believe that women have a dual spiritual force that can be channelled into either motherhood or magic. A traditional Gelede masquerade held every year before the start of the rainy season tries to direct this dual force towards its positive side. Through a series of ritual activities, entertaining as well as educational, Gelede Masks evoke the exalted image of the true role of women. In Africa and elsewhere, the term Mask also refers to a certain role or performed image. Oro-Efe Masks dance to remind the Yoruba to respect senior females and to honour the Goddess Mother. Carved by members of the tribe's secret society, the masks feature a large head composed of various pieces depicting powerful creatures of the bush. Oro-Efe Masks emerge from the sacred forest singing Efe, the traditional prayers. These songs evoke divine blessing on the Gelede festival and they honour both ancestral and living Yoruba mothers.

THE WORSHIP OF NATURAL PHENOMENA

Although hominids gradually learned how to control their immediate environment during the long Palaeolithic era, the speed of population growth created a new set of imperatives. Their intellectual abilities were also gradually evolving, and their minds and lives were still dominated by totemism.

But when, despite endless prayers and worship ceremonies, rain still failed to appear, or a storm destroyed their shelters, or the sun caused their crops to be destroyed by fire, hominids concluded that totems could not after all be omnipotent – there had to be somebody or something even more powerful.

Because of the very nature of the catastrophes which befell them, these powers were increasingly seen as residing in the elements themselves: the sun, moon and stars, and the earth and the natural forces to which it was subject. It was the beginning of a new, post-totemic belief system that eventually evolved into a pantheistic religion in its own right.

Rituals of elements presented the shamans with serious problems in their plastic vocabulary, because there were no longer physical models to work from. How to devise this additional body motion dictionary of invisible or unknown elements like sun, wind, water and fire in all their various forms?

It says a lot for the unlimited human capacity to use motion as a form of expression that they rose so triumphantly to this formidable challenge – a fundamentally aesthetic response whose imaginative vigour is attested by ancient monuments everywhere from Japan to South America.

THERAPEUTIC HEALING

All mammal species have certain ailments in common, but the most widespread is the arthritis that usually accompanies advancing years. It usually originates in the physical pressures on the body earlier in life, when damage to musculoskeletal tissue caused by strenuous and sustained body movement has inadequate time to recover. Long before the body becomes aware of it physically, the early stages of arthritis saps not only physical energy and strength, but also the locomotion mechanism itself.

According to Darwinian principles of natural selection, the weak, the sick and the seriously injured are abandoned when the tribe or herd moves on; only the stronger survive. However, there are exceptions. There are species such as elephants and apes that care for – apparently altruistically – less fortunate groups members, no matter what. An injured elephant is *supported* from both sides by stronger relatives to a watering hole, or assisted to carry out exercises against arthritis that could significantly prolong its useful lifespan.

The efficacy of ancient healing methods nevertheless raises important questions. How did the shaman know what kind of body motion to prescribe as a healing exercise for various afflictions? How were their patients persuaded to use the special routines, and how did they all memorise the complicated plastic motions for each malaise in each individual?

Shamans, witches and medicine men must have been fully conversant with the composition of musculoskeletal tissue and internal organs through carrying out many autopsies, as well as learning from personal experience. Most of these healers were also of course old enough to be familiar with arthritis from their own sufferings. This accumulated **knowledge**, combined in most cases with extraordinary powers of **sensory perception**, gave them the ability tentatively to **diagnose** their patients' internal problems. This talent helped the shamans to experiment with new treatments they devised for their own medical problems. It was not enough to know what remedy to prescribe to a patient. The patient also had to **believe** implicitly that the treatment would work – in other words, the plastic manipulations prescribed also had to be accepted intellectually.

HYPNOSIS

For the shaman/witch therefore, the healing process began with the patient's mind. Treatment was preceded by a session of hypnosis; only when the healer achieved full control of the patient's body would he or she embark on the plastic motion syllabus for the body's physical recovery.

The most problematic issue was to determine exactly what type of treatment was required for each patient, taking into account their sex, age and general condition. With no means of recording or categorising knowledge, the practitioner had to rely on observation, experience and intuition. By examining the patient's manner of walking, listening to their breathing or the cracking of their joints and feeling the hard and soft tissues, a diagnosis and appropriate treatment was decided, involving a therapeutic regime adapted to the patient's own plastic motion capabilities and the qualities of the healer.

Although supernatural powers were (and are) associated with gifted healers, there is no essential mystery about these treatments. The physical condition of a body and its movements always depend directly on each other, but the nature of this interdependence varies with age:

- in **infancy** and youth, the body is in effect 'created' by the *movements* it practices.
- in the **middle years** of adulthood, strenuous work *movements* take their toll, damaging the body.
- in **old age**, the exhausted body recovers physically by means of therapeutic exercise *movements.*

TOTEMIC FUNERAL RITES

Fortunately, many records and illustrations of ancient funerary rites have survived. From time immemorial, every human community has developed ceremonies to bury their dead, and will no doubt continue to do so.

As one of main subjects of the totemic belief system, mourning is the oldest spiritual expression of faith in resurrection. As we know, totemism was much more than a religious institution – it was the foundation of any social or spiritual activity within every tribe. Our hominid ancestors believed the Totem to be living physically inside each creature or element, inside oceans, mountains and the sky and earth themselves. For them, the entire universe was one big family with Goddess Mother its head.

As you might expect, human evolution was not progressing at exactly the same pace all over the world. The earliest prehistoric funerary rites appear long before totemythic rituals. Recent findings from the earliest known hominid burial sites from a million years ago beneath the permafrost, were in fact long preceded by cremations of the deceased. We can therefore deduce that our forefathers initiated a new era in hominid evolution with primitive mourning ceremonies some 1.5 million years ago.

These were originally simple ritual processions around the corpse, ending eventually in the sacrifice of an animal, or in some cases, a child. Although details of the various ancient funerary customs are beyond the scope of this study, it's important to remember that our ancestors believed death to be only a temporary exchange of body, the spirit being eventually reincarnated as a newborn member of the tribe or some other living creature.

TOTEMIC MOURNING PANTOMIME

Mourning rituals focus mainly on the conflict between positive and negative spirits, who fight a battle of plastic motion and sound in a ritual pantomime performance. The primary subject of this pantomime was the story of the tribe, symbolised by totemic images. Wearing an animal mask and pelt, the shaman led mythical characters (played by his assistants) through a labyrinth of conflicts with animals in order to secure new territory with more food and water or a better shelter. The story always had a happy ending.

The mammal, bird and reptile characters were all heavily anthropomorphised, with human characteristics and manners. The two plastic motifs – human and animal – with their respective body motion dictionaries were familiar to the local audience.

Funerary rites provided the second most important subject of totemic pantomime. Then as now, everyone wants to prolong his or her life as long as possible, even after death. Shamans knew how to play on these fundamental human fears and aspirations by creating mythologies of life after death. These could not of course involve the same personifications and circumstances as tribe's own story.

By ascribing supernatural powers to natural phenomena, shamans found a solution that satisfied everybody: themselves, the totem and the worshippers. The eternal conflict between the good and evil, positive and negative, gave shamans enormous possibilities to develop a large variety of unfamiliar mystical images, thereby increasing their power over the tribe.

The simple burial rite procession of earlier times, with a wailing witch and weeping women, developed into more progressive patterns of spirals and labyrinths in the new form of funerary ritual. These slow motion promenades were later complemented by various rhythmical *steps* and *hops* by male dancers, while a female chorus *chanted* rudimentary mourning songs to the accompaniment of a primitive orchestra. These ceremonies went on for some three days and nights, and can still be witnessed today in parts of the developing world, albeit adapted stylistically to tourist tastes.

Once the shaman and his assistants had successfully established regular worship of the new totemythical pantomime, a desire grew in some larger tribes to assume the leadership of funerary rites from the witch and her female followers. To avoid possible social conflict between these two powerful forces, a system of cooperation between witch and shaman developed in which both were endowed with equal creative and spiritual powers.

The fruitful unification of the Goddess Mother and the Totem in this way yielded unexpected results, in that the entire adult community could now take part in mourning rituals in a mass pantomime rite performance composed and staged by both spiritual leaders – a new production from start to finish every time. This activity helped to unite, discipline and strengthen tribal communities.

MODERN MASS FUNERAL CEREMONIES

The performing programme of a burial ceremony was based on a scenario usually played out over three days. The first day saw a series of dances from the local repertoire in honour of the deceased, including any mimes particularly liked and executed by the person in question. *Wailing* and *crying* worshippers continually processed, occasionally presenting the deceased with food, pelts or weapons. At night, a sacrifice to the totem was made to ensure protection and good fortune for the spirit of the deceased.

The second day was devoted to painstaking preparation for the great show to be presented throughout the following night. The shaman, symbolising the spirit of the deceased, *moved* on the ground, as if seeking his totem underground while an array of horrifying monsters tried to stop and to destroy him. After long and exhausting fights, the shaman – by now in a trance state – performed a victory mime to celebrate his eventual reunification with the totem.

During the third and final day, all tribe members danced and sang in a number of social events, as well as taking part in athletic competitions and watching clown shows. The deceased was cremated on the last night, atop the totem tree, a drifting raft, cliff or rocky outcrop, depending on local custom. This model was typical of the more developed societies of the time, rather than the nomadic tribes.

The plastic motion vocabulary of mythical pantomime was enhanced in this way, with new monsters such as eagles with tiger's heads, or winged crocodiles – dragons and demons, in effect.

Shamans and witches clearly faced difficulties in creating models for these images, which differed so radically from what had been depicted before. New, more dramatic styles of plastic motion were required, with **dissonant modulation** for the choir, **syncopated rhythms** for the acoustic accompaniment, **disturbing movem**ent for the mimes, **terrifying** masks, costumes and props and fancy theatrical effects.

Each new **negative imag**e had to have its own body motion text and plastic characteristics to avoid confusing spectators. Shamans did not of course realise the significance of the step they were thereby taking on the road towards the art of performance as we know it today; subject as they were to the irrevocable process of human cultural evolution, they gradually transformed the principle of imitating the natural world into an abstract concept of performance in which movement and design were freed from simple imitation to achieve the infinitely greater complexities of symbolic representation.

It was these ancient rite ceremonies and syncretic pantomimes, executed by highly trained amateurs, that gradually formed the aesthetic foundation of the professional performing arts. Scholars have claimed that some prehistoric murals are of a higher artistic standard than some modern paintings; although we have no physical evidence to prove it, the same is arguably true of the artistry of these ancient dance performances.

Funeral rite ceremonies (modern examples)
Masks appear at the burial of **Bobo** chiefs and at the annual communal funerals in which the souls of all those departed during the previous year are removed from the villages and laid to rest in the ancestral world. The chameleon Mask N'Nan Gui enacts a ritual pantomime in slow motion with reptilian grace. A powerful totemic creature, the Chameleon is traditionally associated with change and the transformation from the mortal to the spirit state. Playing a major role in burial rites, it serves as a messenger of the other world. At Bobo funerals, the Masks confront the lost souls of the dead in a series of ritual dances in order to drive them to the after world. In a surge of explosive energy, they *spin, twirl* and *jump* their way through a set of acrobatic dances. The loud accompaniment is designed literally to wake the dead and to remind them that they have overstayed their welcome in the material world. To underline this, the dancers proceed to tear their masks apart, sometimes disconnecting the head entirely and spinning it independently.

Dogon funerals are performed in three stages. After death, the body is first wrapped in a cloth and hoisted to a burial cave in the face of a cliff. The departed is commemorated the following year in the Nyu Yama ceremony, with songs, dances and an animal sacrifice. The third and most dramatic stage of the ritual occurs every twelve years in the form of a large mass funeral called Dama, which honours all those who died during the preceding period and initiates them into the realm of their ancestors. At the culmination of the burial ceremony, hundreds of Maskers arrive in the village to perform a series of dances to appease the dead and show them the world of the living for the last time, thus easing the spirits out of the village and speeding them on their journey to the ancestral world.

Senufo funerals are directed by a group of **Poro** elders from a sacred grove outside the village. The elders oversee a succession of musicians and maskers, who in the course of two days, preside over the burial of the body and the expulsion of the errant soul from the community. The formal ritual is begun by the Poro musicians, who tell the life story of the deceased in a special musical language.

As the ceremony progresses, the Poro spirit Masks are summoned from

292

the forest. The two most notable members are Varajo, a kind of master of ceremonies, and Kporo, whose sacred duty is to sever the soul from the body and to escort the deceased to a final resting place.

One of the largest masks at a Senufo funeral is the Nafiq, which *charges* at high speed through the forest and into the village. In the image of a gigantic buffalo, with a head made of wart hog, crocodile and antelope elements, the Nafiq symbolises intellectual and physical perfection. Its huge body is constructed on a wooden framework covered with matting. With the head attached to the front, the mask alone is more than two metres high, and can be over five metres long.

TOTEMYTHIC RITE PANTOMIME

THE GENESIS OF PERFORMED DRAMA

As we have seen, the plastic dictionary of hunting and gathering was based on natural movements and motions, learned directly from acting out examples and copying them precisely time after time. By contrast, totemythical rites involved a totally different approach and a new plastic vocabulary which represents a turning point in the social and cultural evolution of hominids.

The unwritten philosophy of totemism is deeply rooted in mythologies, and the need to communicate these mythologies was a primary stimulus to the development of all forms of language. Before the advent of verbal communication, the language of plastic motion was the only medium shamans had at their disposal for creating and collecting narratives about totems of the living world, the elements and the cosmos itself, and passing these stories on from one generation to the next. The scale of the resulting dictionary of motions and sounds they created to convey these complex mythologies was astonishing by any standards.

The archaeological record, notably rock and wall paintings, confirms the immense human capacity for expressive body motion. It is generally accepted that a highly trained and exercised human body is capable of mechanically recording vast amounts of plastic information through muscle memory, and to pass it on through the generations by the continuous repetition involved in the regular ritual ceremonies which were central to communal life.

Pantomime was the main medium of syncretic expression in the first rituals, albeit using a limited plastic vocabulary based on directly imitating creatures, plants (*falling* trees, *trembling* bushes) and human interactions, mimicking their characteristics both in motion and at rest. Hunting or food gathering skills were also presented, using either tools or simple arm motions.

All of these were repeatedly performed by early worshippers before the Palaeolithic era, in the belief that the individual could thereby transubstantiate into the magic image of the totem. All rituals were religious, and represented the single most important aspect of sociocultural life; like work and language, ritual was a vital step on the road to civilisation.

It must be remembered that the first Homo Erectus millions of years ago was not far removed from his primate ancestors, and retained traces of ape-like physical characteristics including a *hobbling* gait, *forward-leaning* upper body and long, unbalanced arms.

These features must have made the body motion style of the very earliest rite-pantomimes appear rather clumsy and inelegant to modern eyes. But as the hominid musculo-skeletal system evolved over the millennia, our forefathers eventually became physically able to perform gestures, grimaces, postures and steps in a far more controlled and realistic way. The archaeological record reflects this gradual process (*see Chapter II*).

To prepare performers and spectators spiritually for ritual ceremonies, shamans therefore chose remote secret locations – underground caves accessible only by crossing water or crawling through a narrow tunnel, for example. These hardships were willingly endured for the privilege of being admitted to the home of the sacred totem, as a form of cleansing penance before participating in the ritual itself.

The interior of the space was elaborately decorated to inspire awe in those who entered, and to maximise the sense of mystery, myth and magic. Impressive phantasmagorical effects were achieved using a combination of colourful murals, stone sculptures of unknown creatures and burning torches. With natural and manufactured sounds echoing within this strange and intimidating space, worshippers were soon in the heightened emotional state of fear and excitement that the shaman required for the hypnotic ritual to take place.

RITE-PANTOMIME COMPOSITION AND PRODUCTION

The totemythical repertoire included not only everyday tales of birth, childhood, social life and the totems' battles for existence, but also the genesis of the tribe itself from the totem. The opening performance was usually followed by the blessings or punishments the shaman wished to bestow on individual tribe members. As the shaman's leadership of the tribe was believed to be directly sanctioned by the totem, he and he alone had the right to communicate with the totem on the tribe's behalf to pray for victory, rain, fertility or whatever.

In performance, the images of the totem were created with artistically exaggerated features and a good measure of theatrical tricks and effects. But something else was needed if the already excited spectators were to feel able to participate in the ritual, so a special pantomime evolved using a plastic vocabulary that combined both the performers' stylised motions and those of everyday secular communication.

Half human/half animal characters would communicate with each other using a mixture of fauna and flora vocabularies, but when addressing the audience, the shaman would use the domestic plastic dictionary exclusively. This distinction served to emphasise the difference between ordinary tribe members and the cast, as representatives of the divine totem.

The shaman led the *jumping, yelling* performers on stage until they *collapsed* in a state of trance, *writhing* convulsively on the ground. This was the point at which the worshippers became spiritually united with the totem. The ceremony usually ended with a special event, such as an initiation rite.

As we have seen, the only way to communicate totemic myths in the absence of spoken language was by the plastic dictionary developed by the shamans. How did this come about?

As a natural artist/composer, the shaman worked initially on the basis of studying every last visual and aural detail of his surroundings, accurately imitating and then memorising the poses and movements of the chosen creature in every circumstance – courting, feeding, hunting, fighting, listening, sniffing and so on. The shaman then chose the most effective and easily readable motions to express the subject in question, and exhaustively rehearsed them before performing to the rest of the tribe.

Finally, the most expressive motion 'snapshot' of the creature was selected and fixed through constant repetition as a memory of the body as well as the mind, for passing on to future generations.

This was the essential process by which body motion dictionaries developed as the primordial language of hominid communication, and this quasi-artistic endeavour was sustained over a very long period of time by generations of shamans, each one refining and developing the body of plastic knowledge inherited from their predecessors.

This body motion vocabulary evolved substantially during the Mesolithic and Neolithic periods, acquiring the sophistication it would require to act as a primary building block of human civilisation, forming the basis of the later pantomime theatre of ethnic groups in Africa, Asia, Australasia and the Americas. Even in group performances, individual participants had their own distinctive actions and character, plastic score, costume, mask, props and so on, making it possible to relate more complex mythological narratives involving familiar totems, tribal heroes and half human/half animal creatures.

Evidence to support this model has been found in anthropological discoveries all over the world; in two particular instances – sculptures of a bear and two bison respectively – traces of innumerable footprints circling the objects survive, together with primitive wall paintings of the same animals and their body parts.

The origin of performing arts

Mythological pantomime was the social origin of the performing arts because it was the first to involve something more than directly copying natural motion and movement – an essentially artistic stylisation of the natural plastic vocabulary.

Shamans were now acting in three different capacities:

- as *auteur/dramatists*, insofar as they were selecting episodes from the totemic narrative that could be learned through a plastic score.
- as *composers, choreographing* the entire show to have maximum impact on the audience.
- as *artistic directors* of a **syncretic** performance encompassing mime, dance, vocals, acoustic instruments, masks, costumes, scenery and special effects.

Rite pantomime, however, was only the acting part of the ritual; the other elements remained sacred worship, with a didactic purpose for the audience, rather than mere entertainment. The archaeological record reveals many recurrent motifs in the acting out of mythological characters – sometimes even intonations of plastic expression. One clearly shows the familiar natural domestic and sexual motion dictionaries; others present mythical creatures with strikingly artificial gestures and postures, with a human lower body grafted on to the head of a bison, the upper extremities of a kangaroo and the tail of a horse, for example.

The purely mimetic vocabulary was gradually enhanced by abbreviated and stylised symbolic gestures, grimaces and postures, which were progressively filtered through the generations to form a motion dictionary capable of communicating **abstract** concepts as well as physical surroundings.

Hominids extended their plastic vocabulary in this way during the Mesolithic and Neolithic eras, and in the process laid the foundations of all pantomime theatres of tribal societies all over the world. An important characteristic of totemythical rite-pantomime was the **individualised** presentation of a particular personage in the drama, with each actor having their own plastic score, actions, costume, mask and props. This individualised personification helped audiences to follow the mythical narrative and to recognise the roles played therein by various familiar totems and tribal heroes.

The secret of acting and mime

The terms acting and mime have different meanings in different contexts. Here, they are used to describe the performances in pantomime or prehistoric shows in front of audiences.

The survival imperative was, as we have seen, the main stimulus for mimetic adaptation in the evolution of animals. Species that for whatever reason were unable to adapt their functional facilities for the purposes of protecting themselves through artificial camouflage or mimicry eventually died out. The roots of mimetic performance in insects and amphibians are so ancient (some 500 million years) that these artificial behaviours have become deeply entrenched as stereotypical natural characteristics of the species in question. Later, more advanced orders of birds and reptiles developed their mimetic skills to high standards of performance for bodily communication, especially in courtship/mating, hunting/fighting and the ritualised initiation of juveniles.

The history of mammalian mimesis begins with marsupials, because of their soft muzzle tissue and flexible limbs and tail. However, as we have seen, the main body language tools of nearly all mammals, humans included, are the eyes. Eyes not only record and transmit external information about plastic signals and gestural expressions to the brain, but they also send out crucial messages and warning signs. An animal's inner feelings and even its intent to act and can be read in its gaze.

Mimetic facial expressions are performed by other parts of the head in addition to the eye, eyebrows and lashes, such as the antennae, whiskers, tongue/lips, teeth/fangs, chin, cheeks, nose/proboscis, ears, horns and hair/skin, whose functional repertoire and motion dictionaries are described in the section on head/facial motion in Chapter II. Humans have developed their facial miming vocabulary using these parts in both social activities and in the performing arts, and head and facial signs and gestures play a major role in the mimetic culture of hominids right up to the present day.

The next stage in the evolution of mimicry was in postural performance, as described in the sections on body parts and limbs motions in Chapter II. Our thesis about the origin and evolution of mimetic motion tools can be summarised as follows:

Stage 1:   **Eyes** – the primary perceiving/signalling tool for mimetic expression and covert action.
Stage 2:   **Head/face** parts as interpretative instruments.
Stage 3:   **Body posturing** – the motionless imitation of the natural plastic patterns of others.
Stage 4:   **Limb motions**, the main tools for mimetic actions and deliberately misleading behaviours.
Stage 5:   **Psychological** and **spiritual** elements of mimetic study and performance.

PREHISTORIC MIME/ACTING AS A PERFORMING ART

The study of prehistoric depictions of sacred images being performed and surviving film of mime/actors in indigenous societies untouched by the modern world raises many fundamental questions about mimesis in hominids:

Were the performers full-time mime/actors? What led to the creation of plastic texts for dramatic, epic, comic, lyric and other genres? What kind of communication existed between performer and spectator? And what makes a mime effective for the audience?

Although miming is often thought of as a silent language of symbolic signs and gestures, we are dealing here with mime in its original form, where the performers express feelings, reactions and thoughts nonverbally in a basically realistic but artificially exaggerated way.

Controversial as it may sound, the main compositional principles of the plastic score for ancient pantomime were:

- to predetermine the most common natural characteristics of certain species of animals.
- to select animal species for the playing totemythical personages.

- to stylise them artistically and combine them into coherent mimetic motion sequences.
- to use these plastic rhythms and patterns of the face and other body parts to achieve whatever effect the dramatic genre required.
- to convey this message in mime as clearly as possible in order to engage the audience as co-agents in the mystical narrative transaction taking place.

Individual performers would usually combine their own interpretations of all the main performing elements – narrative score, emotional expression, plastic text, tempo, rhythm and spatial proximities. Although the narrative and staging of the pantomime was dictated by the shaman, there was creative licence for individual inflection of the mimed image, even in group presentations.

THE MIME/ACTOR AS PRODUCER/COMPOSER

Whoever produced the pantomime, the compositional process always began with a clear idea of exactly what was to be conveyed, to whom, in which style, at what type of venue (open or closed), and whether with or without rhythmic acoustic accompaniment.

With these conditions in mind, the full-time mime/actor would choose the main artistic profile of the image to be performed in terms of its general silhouette, shape, size, age, limb proportions and other plastic details and physical contours. The search would then begin for the stereotypical motion characteristics of the chosen model, and its defining individual body stances and motions when *standing, sitting, walking, leaning, crawling, squatting, smiling, crying, yawning, calling, saluting*, and so on.

After collecting enough of these physical identifiers for the subject, the mime/actor would carefully select those that best reflected the intended inner characteristics of the plastic portrait. Like the choice of colour palette for a painter or material and technique for a sculptor, it was a long and painstaking preparatory process.

Over the millennia, shamans discovered the most effective ways to impress their worshippers and to lead them in the desired direction. It was not enough to compose elegant plastic monologues; the motion text had to be unambiguously clear, with neither unnecessary detail nor repetition, and based on the quintessence of common everyday body motions in order to be instantly and easily understood by the audience, on the basis of their own personal education and experiences.

So, to enact the social, moral and spiritual theme successfully, several basic conditions had to be fulfilled:
- finding a **specific narrative** for **artistic** body language performance.
- creating the sequence of dramatic episodes to tell the story and its emotional subtext through **exaggerated** mime interpretation.
- clearly defining and choreographing the opposing forces whose conflict provided the **dramatic** tension.
- planning a scenario of episodes suitable for **nonverbal** interaction.
- thinking in terms of **plastic** images and their characteristic behaviours on stage.
- devising a chain of dramatic '**beacons**', as the main compositional focus for the plastic motion patterns of the interacting mime personages and spectators.
- framing all elements of the pantomime in a *unique* style.

THE BODY AS MIME INSTRUMENT

Like a Stradivarius violin, the body of the shaman or experienced mime/actor was capable of reproducing a vast range of expressive nuances. Remember, we are not talking here about slavishly copying natural behaviours, but artistically stylised intonations of a plastic theme by the unique personal facilities of the individual performer. The face alone, like a small stereo

TV screen, could convey a minor natural emotion in an exaggerated way, transforming a hardly perceptible feeling into a powerful character motivation on which the entire drama could hinge.

And like the violinist, the full-time mime actor used his body motion in any number of variations in **tempo, rhythm** and **dynamics**. By plastically entering into the very spirit of an animal, the performer's trembling arms would become locust wings, or his swinging legs a lashing crocodile tail in a magical evocation of the mood and nature of these sacred creatures. Such a powerful illusion of **physical re-embodiment** and **spiritual incarnation** was predicated on having highly trained bodies, extreme sensitivity to nuance and incredible feats of self-control and mental focus.

But how could so-called 'primitive' man have been such a sophisticated performer, so many hundreds of generations before Stanislavski?

A reasonable enough question – until you consider the evolutionary context. If a caterpillar makes itself resemble bird droppings to avoid being eaten, hunting fish act as plants to attract their prey and early hominids *acted* the part of various imaginary anthropomorphic creatures in funerary rites, it is easier to understand how their descendants could achieve such high standards of mimetic performance in totemythic pantomime.

The fact is, mime-acting was a landmark of hominid cultural evolution, initially prompted by the **survival imperative** and facilitated by the **accelerated development** of the species' conceptual intelligence.

The ingrained habit of constantly focusing on the next meal, reproduction and potential threats made our ancestors infinitely more sensitive to the slightest changes in their environment than we are today. The consequent abilities of *intense observation* and *instant evaluation* and *reaction* are what enabled prehistoric mime/actors to perfect their art. Gradually honing their miming skills in terms of both perception and performance by hard experience, the best exponents developed their acting talents to the point of being able to foresee the intentions of their partner/opponent before any action was executed.

Regular training of muscle memory and locomotion mechanics in a limited space increased their control over the mind and emotions as well as improving their physical abilities to create and portray imaginary subjects; their anatomical flexibility and refined sense of balance and coordination even allowed full-time performers to incorporate dazzling acrobatic tricks in their motion sequences.

The syllabus of exercises for solo or group performance included:

- **regular practice** with imaginary accessories and physical powers, and miming elements such as water, sand and fire as well as the invisible bodies of animals.
- **mimetic expression** of mass, size, momentum, elevation and so on.
- spatial **body proximity** in functional motions, expressions and posturing.

Naturally, the manner in which these routines were performed was strongly inflected by the distinctive personal characteristics of the individual mime-actor, especially in terms of his tempo and rhythm, his physical shape, size and abilities and his fixed point technique for accurately conveying the illusion of *inner* feelings and *outwardly expressed* emotions. All these facilities and performing conditions were harmoniously combined for artistic pantomime presentations.

DRAMATIC INTERACTIONS IN MYTHICAL PANTOMIME

As an artificial performing art, pantomime had its own rules for composition, acting and perception. In the same was as any modern theatrical play orchestral performance, five main elements were involved:

- a narrative or **plot-line** in nonverbal **plastic** text.

- body motion instruments, spatial patterns and proximity.
- interaction with audience.

Prehistoric theatrical shows were always performed to spectators. The totem with its acting entourage would lead semi-hypnotised worshippers into a purified state, or occasionally a revolt for their liberation. Spectators would do more than simple follow the pantomime narrative or watch the mime-actors perform on stage; they also actively encouraged them (or in the case of unsatisfactory portrayals, pelted with rotten eggs). The audience was and remains the barometer for accepted standards of professional mime-acting and its plastic technique, communicative effectiveness and emotional truth.

There are two basic types of interaction in any mime-acting: between the performers, and with the audience. Both usually reinforce one another, even in negative dramatic circumstances, for the sake of maximum clarity to the observer. For the same reason, mime-actors also used their best possible body motion 'shorthand' to portray the chosen image; and in dialogues, the two protagonists would mime one after the other rather than simultaneously, with the still partner providing a passive accompaniment to the active one until their roles were reversed.

In recreating his acting monologue, the mime-actor would lead the audience from one dramatic episode to the next without stopping, since even a short unexpected pause or interruption would instantly and inevitably destroy their suspension of disbelief, bringing the spectators' consciousness back down to banal reality.

As with harmonic modulation in music or the tempo and rhythmic proximity patterns of locomotion and dance, the mime-actor's main spiritual objective was to achieve a new mental state through his **fixed point** the plastic expression of highly concentrated inner feelings – a kind of mimetic stamp, memorised by the performer in accordance with the shape and state of his body, partnering circumstances and personal emotions. Achieving his state naturally required frequent regular practice, and like all professional skills, would eventually disappear without.

Sustaining successful interaction with an audience simply by means of silent plastic motion and posturing is a considerable performance challenge. It required more than comprehension of the mime-actor's body language to earn the spectators' trust and engage them emotionally – they had to fall completely under his **spiritual influence**. To achieve this, the performer had to work masterfully and imaginatively with his subject matter, and compose a clear sequence of plastic 'beacons' based on carefully chosen familiar motion and gestural patterns.

SUMMARY

The magic of this interaction between mime/actor and audience was based on:
- reproducing **easily understood** actions and behaviours and delivering them with skill to create effective dramatic episodes.
- clearly articulating the performer's plastic vocabulary, using concise **exaggeration**, in a meaningful sequential motion text.
- selecting characteristic natural motions for artistic **stylisation.**
- carefully **planning** the body language of these plastic images during performance.
- conveying **intention** as well as action through postural signs and gestural motion.
- high standards of physical agility and flexibility, with complete **mental control** over all body tools.
- exhaustively **practicing** both technical and mental exercises.
- a highly developed sense of how to create **spatial illusions** at all proximities.
- the **muscle memory** and **fixed-point skills** to sustain imaginary plastic portrayals.
- the ability and performing **charisma** to lead and engage an audience.

- a distinctive personal '**signature**' in terms of mental and plastic facilities.
- the ability to express **inner** states through outer plastic motions.

The anthropological preconditions of pantomime can be summarised as follows:
- **mimesis** and pretence as a survival necessity for animals.
- the vital need for constant **vigilance** and mental concentration.
- the **conditioning** of instinct natural selection and individual experience.
- the essential role of **pretence** in juvenile play.
- the **ritualisation** of syncretic performance in early funeral ceremony.
- the shamanic introduction of **mimetic art** in a dramatic context.
- gradual **refinement** into artistic totemythical pantomime.

MIME AND DANCE IN SYNCRETIC PERFORMANCE

IMAGERY DANCE AND MIMETIC EXPRESSIONS

The many correlations between archaeological evidence from ancient sites and recordings of the practices and customs of modern tribal peoples reveal the same principles of composition and presentation at work.

A particularly popular image in the religious pantomimes of the Australian Bushmen, for example, is the 'praying mantis', which is also extensively depicted in rock paintings. Its plastic characteristics are clearly recognisable: big, strong lower extremities as if tensed for a high forward *jump*, an exaggeratedly long torso and thin upper extremities. The physical similarities with the creature's small pointed head, long thin neck and antennae are instantly recognisable. A sequence of characteristic arm motions is followed by allusion to the *waving* of wings as if preparing for a flying *leap*.

Researchers have remarked on the close resemblance between the Bushmen's praying mantis performance and the primeval pantomime rites of aeons ago: sharp *turns* of the head indicating the creature's constant vigilance against predators, short nervous *twitches* of the antennae, various *jumps* on one leg or the other, while *turning* or still, but always with *shaking* head and *waving* arms. Bushmen believe that the mantis *rotating* its head augurs well for the hunt and fortunes of the tribe.

In 1956, Dean and Carell documented the totemythical image of the crocodile performed in an elaborate hunting dance pantomime by an aboriginal chief in the same style as that elaborated thousands of years ago. The actor *lay down* and *shook* his whole body to imitate the creature *diving* and *swimming*. Then, *rising* suddenly, he *jumped* up high from one leg to the other as if catching an imagined prey; rapidly and repeatedly *twisting* and *turning* his body, he *threw* himself forwards in a low somersault and displayed at the end the agonising death throes of the prey.

Other images from early pantomime rites survive in aboriginal dances representing fights between totem-kangaroo and totem-dog, a prolonged fight to the death choreographed for both parties using a complicated plastic vocabulary including sneaking *steps,* attack and defence *mimicry*, aggressive *poses*, intriguing *movements*, tricky *jumps, lifts* and so on. This represents an important step towards harmonising two distinct motion scores in a pantomime duet, and modern audiences were duly impressed by these paradoxically primitive yet highly professional performances.

The plastic vocabularies of Mime and Dance have fundamentally different approaches to performance and presentation. Although both are based on the same body language, mime describes an object more **naturalistically** on the principle of precise imitation, whereas as we shall see, ritual dance expresses the same emotion or action using more **abstract** and generalised plastic motions.

300

A mime, for example, uses *stamping, pawing, walking* or *running* motions in an exact plastic copy of the movements of an elephant or a zebra; by contrast, a dancer creates the animal's image by using only one or two of the main plastic elements of these movements in an exaggerated and stylised way. Both are conscious, artificial performances based on careful studies of natural life, and require a well-trained body, quick reactions and well-developed intelligence and muscle memory.

PLASTIC IMPLEMENTS AND MOTION VOCABULARIES

- With no actual animal on stage the mime creates the *impression* of *pulling* a stubborn mule with a rope, or *pushing* it from behind.
- Wearing a long-eared half-mask of a hare, with a symbolic short tail attached to a belt, the dancer *taps* out warning messages the way hares do, *pawing* and *jumping* around in **characteristic manner**.
- Two fortunate hunters bring home their prey. A young masked performer **naturally** mimes the dead animal by *hanging* from the horizontally held pole, *grasping* it with his hands at one end and feet at the other.
- A high pole is erected in the middle of the home base area, as the main venue for performing rite ceremonies and secular festivities. During funeral pantomimes, the pole represents a tree or a hill, and is decorated accordingly with twigs or grass. The mimes imitate various creatures when *climbing* the pole, lingering at the top, then *descending* to continue the action.
- A crocodile fights with a bear in an astonishingly choreographed duet. A merry-go-round of *stomping* and *pawing, crawling/ swimming, pushing/pulling, leaping/diving* ensues – most of the main functional motions, in effect, attesting to highly developed **plastic performance** skills. Exacting fight moves were also included, like *lifting* and then *throwing* an opponent over the head, *leaps, splits, somersaults, dives, jumps, twists, turns* and *rolling* onto the ground.

The seemingly primitive movements of apes in fact had great emotional and spiritual power. When warfare or some natural disaster was expected, such as flood, storm, fire or earthquake, the crowd of warriors would start *stamping* the ground in unison with the females to the rhythm of drumming, to the point of literally *digging* their feet into the ground.

Mime/dance performance was of course based on the vocabulary of gestural communications so that the audience could easily follow the narrative by reading the plastic motion signs and signals being performed.

As the apogee of the entire mimetic culture of apes, hominid mime/dance performances stimulated the abstract visual presentation (and therefore perception) of both the natural and spiritual worlds – and as such, they are major landmarks in the cultural and intellectual evolution of our species (*see Chapters III and IV*).

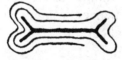

THE SYNTHESIS OF RITUAL MIME AND DANCE

Mime and dance share so many physical, emotional and aesthetic characteristics that it can be difficult to separate the two for critical purposes.

It was this very closeness of the two intertwined genres that gave rise to their eventual **synthesis** in early pantomime rituals.

The totemythical text of these syncretic performances included mimetic *grimaces*, *gestures* and *posturing*, dance *steps* and *jumps*, expressive *shouting* and *noise* and the manipulation of *masks* and other accessories.

As we have seen, shamans and witches improvised many dance sequences for various sacred images, based on the tribe's traditions and culture as well as their own personal vision and spirituality. These eventually separated dance from pantomime into a genre of its own – and one of the most popular social activities of our species, right up to the present day.

However, mime (pantomime) was and remains, after countless generations, the easiest and most natural form of plastic communication between human beings all over the world.

After the two genres split into distinctively different performing arts, mime nevertheless retained some progressive dance motions in its plastic vocabulary, and vice versa. Understandably so; after all, both are played on the same 'instrument' – the human body – and relate similar narratives under similar conditions of time and space.

There are also significant differences between the two:

In **mime**, the plastic language and 'portrait' were initially based on a direct realistic imitation of the natural external characteristics of the object being presented. More advanced plastic reflections of natural objects evolved later, which focused the audience's attention on selected emotional details to arouse the spectator's imagination.

In **dance**, more dynamic and progressive motions of the same object could be developed, the key physical characteristics being presented selectively and in an exaggerated, stylised form. Unlike mime, dance was not restricted exclusively to familiar objects - an unlimited range of artistic motifs allowed dance to acquire a multi-faceted variety of highly creative plastic sequences based on a growing body motion vocabulary for articulating myth and legend, ethnic characteristics and new abstract images and choreographies.

As well as being based on a fundamentally different approach to theatrical composition, **mime** also followed a totally different method of studying performance technique and presentation. Mime generally did not require musical accompaniment and could very well be played in silence, except for the inner rhythms of the performer. However, it can equally take place in response to, and simultaneously with, background sounds, mechanical or otherwise.

By contrast, music provides not only the metrical base for **dance**, but the creative idea, the structure of the composition, the choreographic style, performing image and dramatic action. Musical concepts such a melody, dynamics and intonation apply equally well to the interpretation of plastic body motion.

Mime is essentially presented by a single protagonist – even when a group is involved, the audience could only follow the narrative by concentrating on one personage at a time; any more starts to become confusing. Generally speaking, the untrained human eye can only comfortably follow the grimaces, gestures and other expressions in one place at a time – and only one moving object at a time.

Paradoxically, these perceptual limitations of the spectator give the choreographer of mime a unique opportunity to lead the audience through a labyrinth of dramatic intrigues by a chain of motion signals right up to the final curtain.

Dance has always been able to accommodate both solo and group performances. Witches and shamans choreographed multiple animal characters just as effectively as their solos for the Totem or Goddess Mother, reflecting the relevant plastic characteristics of each subject accordingly. But unlike with mime, a witch or shaman from another tribe could present the same narrative in a different choreography that accorded with local customs, environmental circumstances and abilities. Because dance does not depend on **naturalistic** imitation in the way that mime does, it can affect the audience through **abstract** choreographies designed to resonate with the individual or a group in question.

The use of props and stage design is also very different between mime and dance. In **mime**, performers usually work with non-existent articles whose form they evoke by body movements – even sets and decorations can be conjured in this way. But the audience still believes that they are watching a girl *sitting* at a table writing a love letter, or a boy *climbing* an invisible rope ladder.

In **dance**, props and stage architecture are more than decorations – they are intrinsic parts of the choreography itself. They extend natural plastic abilities and enhance the artistic effect of progressive motions, enlarging the possibilities of the space, the performance and the body motion text.

Unlike mime, **dance** has a different form of costume design for each composition. And as dancers play only one role at a time, for which the costume is specifically designed, they can change their costumes any time during the performance (behind the scenes, naturally).

In **mime**, the performer chooses a single neutral uniform and 'mask' to reflect his or her personal plastic characteristics. Thus dressed, the mime. can change his appearance at will, transforming himself from human to animal, for example, before an audience not fully aware of this transformation. The conventions of each are fundamentally different.

The main instrument for a **mime** is the face. Inner feelings and external phenomena can be expressed solely by the performer's eyes and face muscles, without moving the rest of the body at all. By contrast, the dancer can perform with the face completely concealed by a mask.

Legs are the main instrument for the **dancer** – the feet, to be more precise. A seated dancer could evoke images of *fighting* mammoths or *stampeding* bison using the feet alone.

Mime and **dance** are related to each other like brother and sister, with the same parents, similar faces and body shapes. But their mentality, characters, tastes and behaviour are very different.

Motion arrangements for ancient choirs

What prompted our ancestors to begin singing in groups as a social activity, to the accompaniment of acoustic instruments? How were the instruments created? And how did they manage to sing before the development of spoken language?

Naturally, these new sociocultural manifestations evolved over many thousands of years, and in many different ways in various parts of the planet.

THE GENESIS OF CHORAL SINGING

As we have seen, ritual ceremonies began during the period of Homo Erectus some three million years ago, and were originally conducted by the witch or shaman alone.

The next step in the development of ritual was to consecrate a small group of worshippers as assistants, who the shaman coached in a broad programme of magic routines, including a wide repertoire of posing motions and vocal utterances. This exclusive group both produced and performed the mythical pantomimes, using mime, dance, song and other acoustic accompaniment. The remaining tribe members were not as yet allowed to witness these sacred proceedings by the shaman and his chosen followers.

Women also had their own secret ritual ceremonies, in which they prayed for a rich harvest, fertility and so on. The religious activities for each sex played a similar role in their socio-cultural evolution while gradually developing their performing skills – particularly in *singing* for the females, and in the use of *noise-making* implements for males.

As time went by, tribal populations increased to the point that these sexually segregated nocturnal ceremonies became so large that they could no longer be held secretly in caves, so they began to be conducted in open-air venues – a welcome move that soon made these ceremonies the most popular public entertainment events.

As more and more youngsters became involved, new production techniques had to be developed to suit these wide-open spaces for the performances to engage the attention. The performing repertoire grew, and with it the requirement for more rehearsal time.

The singing part of female ritual events became separated from the dancing part some million or so years ago, at which time the male acoustic accompaniment turned into a primitive orchestra – a significant step in the early evolution of music.

This meant that both the choir and the orchestra could now practice independently from the dancers, bringing the standard of performance to a higher level by introducing more sophisticated harmonies and vocal modulations in ensemble singing. Both technique and presentation improved.

PLASTIC AND ACOUSTIC MOTION OF SEDENTARY CHOIRS

The earliest choirs performed in a *sitting* position, in a semicircle around the youngsters *dancing* in the middle of the venue. They sang local rudimentary tunes, in different rhythms according to the choreography.

Singers were never allowed to change their sitting position during the performance, as they were expected to concentrate their entire vocal and plastic motion performance on the mythical personages being enacted or the danced images of fauna and flora.

Sedentary choirs were not, however, completely motionless. As they sang their rudimentary songs in unison, performers often *moved* their heads and waists, *bending* or *twisting* from side to side. They would even *rotate* the whole upper body in both directions while *sitting* cross-legged in the same spot, their buttocks resting on both feet. While singing they also used a large variety of 'port de bras (arm motions) symbolically to imitate the ritual objects in the middle – *flying* birds, *crawling* snakes, *swimming* fish, *posing* antelopes, *bending* grass, *trembling* bushes, trees and so on. This plastic vocabulary always functioned in the same semantic framework as that of the dancers, as an echo of the main dramatic composition, the two different elements being combined in a genuinely syncretic performance. Both elements could be performed smoothly in unison or contrapuntally with the moving dancers and playing instruments, using syncopated rhythms and motion dynamics.

The main noise-making implements of hominids were the arms and legs. Different methods of *clapping, slapping* the thighs with open hands or the ribs with elbows, *snapping* the fingers, *gnashing* and *snapping* the teeth and so on. All these acoustic motions helped dancers to maintain the right tempo, and were instrumental in creating the atmosphere essential for performing ritual ceremonies. Before these acoustic motions became generally adopted, singers used to make noise by moving their arms freely around their own body or each other's, and or towards the dancers or acting cast.

The singing repertoire usually included several local tunes that every tribe member knew by heart. It was not particularly difficult for the choir and the dancers to follow each other, because the same vocal and plastic sequences were constantly repeated. However, the tempo, rhythm, dynamic and body motion characteristics of this repertoire was constantly changing, and worshippers had to learn all these nuances carefully in order to be able to switch from one subject to another in the correct time and without interruption.

The main problem was to coordinate the vocal technique with the acoustic motions of the arms, and this required prolonged practice. Each new member of the choir had to pass a test in vocal and body motion technique in order to be accepted by the shaman or by his assistants. The stimulus of competition and the personal determination to excel were powerful incentives, and produced miraculous results. It should also be remembered that any false move or sound could upset the entire ceremony, and thereby expose the community to serious future problems; guilty parties could pay for such a grave offence with their lives. Cruel as such performing conditions appear today, they were certainly highly productive.

STANDING CHOIRS ON TWO SIDES OF THE VENUE

As we have seen, the syncretic form of ceremonial rites required serious preparation of each element, including a freely *moving* choir. The shaman and his assistants had to create a score for each group according to the main idea and the general scenario of the performance. The singers had to learn and practice new versions of old rudimentary tunes, dramatic *cries* and voice modulations, together with new variations on traditional plastic sequences – *mimicking*, arm *motions* and body postures (while still remaining more or less in the same initial position).

It was no easy task to create such complex and highly coordinated combinations of singing, acting and specially choreographed arm motions, body *twists* and *bends* with the right timing, rhythm and spatial patterns, and represented a significant milestone halfway along the road of our cultural evolution.

MOVING CHOIRS IN MYTHOLOGICAL PANTOMIME

The next step towards more professional performing standards involved the singers *moving* as they *sang*. When discussing initiation, we outlined the aesthetic education of youngsters after the circumcision ceremony. At the age of thirteen or fourteen, girls continued to study singing and dancing with closed groups of women ritual club; they already knew all major skills of voice modulation, the basic repertoire of songs and dance movements, the complete alphabet

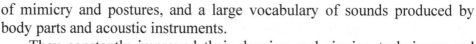 of mimicry and postures, and a large vocabulary of sounds produced by body parts and acoustic instruments.

They constantly improved their dancing and singing techniques and presentation, now using more advanced choreographies whose main objective was to attract males sexually. Formerly closed, such religious ceremonies now became, thanks to their dramatically improved qualities of musicality, vocalisation and overall grace, open to the general public as joyfully received entertainments.

These two performance genres – the original midnight rituals of female worshippers singing and dancing around a Fertility Tree or phallic sculpture, and the later ritual performances celebrating beauty and joy, are still in evidence today.

The more complex compositional patterns of mythical pantomime demanded better preparation in both technique and presentation. Boys, after the circumcision rite, became charges of shaman's assistants. They had to follow a very intensive course of studies: hunting and battle routines as well as a large curriculum of mime, dance and music. Although the extent of their vocal routines was limited, they practiced extensively with sound instruments, especially drums. Until then, only a few drummers had *accompanied* performances, *interjecting* characteristic cries and hisses from time to time.

At this time too, we see a promising new element enhancing the pantomimes and other ritual events: the female choir. The shaman was intent instilling in the whole community a strong belief in totemism to assure his own total power and control over the tribe. This is why shamans emerged from the caves into open areas, to attract everybody with the colourful and exciting repertoire of mystical presentations of the totem's life and actions.

The choir *sang* rudimentary songs, using a variety of body motion postures, *moving* in and through the acting area, focussing on the totem's position, filling in gaps in scores and so on. Although the singers never lead the shows or played any dramatic parts, they significantly improved general standards of pantomime by creating a better atmosphere for the performance and adding more intensive action to form a multi-layered presentation. This was the precursor of the much later dramatic chorus of Classical Rome and Greece.

SINGING DANCERS IN SECULAR EVENTS

The youngsters of the tribe, full of energy and enthusiasm, and after many years of learning and practicing how to sing, dance, mime, play acoustic instruments and make decorative accessories, were now eager for new social activities. The most talented youths were selected to participate in sacred events, but the rest also wanted to involve themselves in the cultural life of their community. They took matters in their own hands, and organised – initially on a small scale – daytime events, which were gradually enlarged and refined to the point where they became performances and eventually, popular social events based around everyday activities. Their foundation remained strongly religious, but they allowed all adolescents to enjoy a new form of cultural activity, and they sang and danced for pleasure nearly every evening.

At first, girls *sang* and *clapped* their hands while boys *danced*, and boys *played* acoustic accompaniment. They basically copied adult routines, but with less emphasis on religious aspects and with much freer choreography. Over time they created the new mixed-sex repertoire, singing and dancing together, occasionally *holding* hands or each other's' shoulders.

Time and again, successive young generations proved themselves capable of developing the old traditions, and built up new performing skills by changing the melodic patterns of vocal tunes and ornamental plastic motions with *joined* arms. They also introduced a completely new form of ritual singing – the hymn – in which the usual image of the Mother

Goddess was replaced by a singing soloist or dancing couple. The lyrical tunes of rudimentary songs were now followed by a cheerful allegro, thereby also transforming the choreography and dancing style. The youngsters pushed their communities into accepting more exciting rhythms, melodies and dynamic *movements*. Eventually, the acoustic accompaniment was also refined by the use of syncopated *clapping, snapping* fingers and *slapping* their behinds by *kicking* the feet back while *dancing*.

They also divided the vocalisation between the male and female singers – not only by phraseology, but in their harmonies as well. Dancers *moved* and *postured* at the same time as *singing* in unison with other voices in duets, trios quartets and small ensembles.

It is hard now to appreciate what an enormous leap these innovations represent in socio-cultural life of hominids. In the evolutionary scheme of things, the 'leap' took place over hundreds of thousands of years, but it opened up a much broader artistic canvas for future performers, and as such, is of cardinal importance.

Primitive orchestra and noise-making instruments

The number of instruments and opportunities for making sound progressively increased. The group of percussion instruments grew to include tusks, bones and hoofs as well as sticks of different woods, shapes and sizes.

Right from the start, the most important and practical instrument was the **drum**, of which innumerable different types existed. Drummers, and all later instrumentalists, had to study long and hard before being allowed to perform in public. The shaman would only consecrate those who passed with flying colours to serve in the ceremonial rites – even the drum would sometimes be consecrated as a holy instrument in itself.

The next great musical advance was the **pipe**, initially as a simple instrument made from a bone or reed, which later evolved into variants with two or more pipes (such as pan pipes). Much later still came the instrument derived from the **bow**; when our ancestors first heard the sound produced by a bowstring, they equated it with the voice of the totem.

Practitioners soon found that the sound the bowstring produced varied in pitch according to its tension, and soon this erstwhile weapon was also consecrated as a divine symbol for success in hunting or battle. Some tribes only ever used the bow for this purpose, and not as a weapon at all. All these discoveries represented an important turning point in the evolution of music.

THE PROGRESSION FROM SOLO TO ORCHESTRAL PERFORMANCE

Although scholars had assumed that these instruments originated thousands of years ago, the latest archaeological discoveries indicate that some 700,000 years is more likely. The primitive sounds they made gradually evolved into a wide range of acoustic motions based on the rhythmic beat of drums, continuous flute melodies and the tremolo of bowstrings, giving the choir and primitive orchestra the option to perform either separately or together, in true syncretic fashion.

The noise part could be exclusively mechanical, without any particular rhythmic pattern. This can be termed **decorative noise**, as opposed to a **sound composition**, which involved the same sounds played according to a deliberate rhythmic structure. Performers wearing noise-making bracelets of seashells or bone on their wrists or ankles could equally well perform either type of noise accompaniment.

When the choir worshipped whilst singing, *holding* hands and *moving* in a circle, the singers concentrated on producing rudimentary tunes in time with the rhythm and tempo of the dance steps and patterns. Although metrical, the mechanical sound of the bracelets only created a decorative background noise; if the same worshippers performed livelier rudimentary songs with *stamps* and *claps* to some prearranged rhythm and tempo, the result can only be described as a sound composition. As a rule, improvisation was not permitted in group performances except in the case of dances deliberately choreographed to be chaotic, such as the 'witches' Sabbath'.

Sound compositions could be either **stationary**, with all choristers and orchestra members producing the noise accompaniment while standing on the spot, or **travelling**, with the performers following simple steps to make dance patterns.

All noise-making (and later, the instruments themselves) were consecrated by the shaman as his mystical accessories, which he selected and classified. Instruments in each category – **percussion, woodwind** or **strings** – were subdivided according to timbre, pitch and dynamic range (just as we categorise the human voice from bass to soprano today), and eventually, all this vocal/noise information was systemised into an acoustic motion 'dictionary'. The shaman knew exactly which instruments to use for the next episode of his pantomime or ceremony. Both choir and orchestra parts were carefully composed, rehearsed and presented under the shaman's direct control.

Orchestra members needed much more time to study and rehearse their technique for group performance than the choristers did, which is why the earliest archaeological illustrations only show small ensembles – never more than a sextet.

Many wall paintings show men *playing* such accompaniments while also *juggling* and performing other tricks with their instruments. Such mixed noise/motion entertainments, still a favourite in street shows and circuses today, represent a genre of folk entertainment that stretches right back to before the Palaeolithic era.

Fond as they were of showing themselves off in public, our ancestors doubtless achieved great results with these syncretic presentations of simultaneous *dance, juggling* and *noise-making*, and all the shaman's assistants could accomplish these motions while also miming, singing and acting.

When senior drummers performed with the Totem or Goddess Mother, they shadowed the sacred image while *tapping out* an accompaniment with their hands on the drum held between their knees as they *danced*; when the image of the deity paused, the drummers made rhythmic sound sequences accordingly, as if reflecting the deity's state of mind.

Singers in sedentary choirs always had a complete range of noise-making implements nearby when they performed – small wooden sticks, gazelle ears, antelope hoofs and so on – which the choristers periodically used while singing, or during vocal intervals. They also used many different types of rattle, hanging from the belt around their waists. Later, in the post-Palaeolithic times, dancers often played **lyres, tambourines** and **flutes** while they sang.

EARLY DECORATIVE ARTS AND BODY GRAPHICS

The earliest forms of decorative art cover all forms of personal adornment, domestic crafts and naive representations of ritual totemic subjects rather than art in the sense of aesthetic creations by an individual expressing his or her personal beliefs and emotions to others.

What has it to do with plastic motion, you may ask? A woman *lifts* her brow as she thinks about something special; a soldier *stands* to attention when seeing an officer; a child suddenly *stops playing* when it senses danger; a woman *sits motionless*, but her eyes *turn* straight at you; a musician slips into the next key; a sculptor *observing* an expanse of rock suddenly sees the outlines of his future monument as if embedded in the stone; a painter *applies* the final brush stroke. All these are examples of 'outgoing' body motions, consciously reproduced expressions of inner emotion, which remain within for as long as it takes until a physical or mental trigger forces it out. In performance, however, the motion's realisation of this inner emotion doesn't have to be delivered by the same person – it could be executed just as well by some other expressive facility, such as **tattooing.**

The entire prehistoric period abounds with rock paintings, from the most primitive drawings to intricate artistic compositions, and we are naturally fascinated by their origins and the role they played in human cultural evolution.

Our present focus in on the aesthetic nature of these arts as a manifestation of plastic motion. When our forebears found pleasure and excitement in observing the impressively colourful world around them, they wanted to find ways of making themselves part of their polychromatic surroundings. A long process of trial and error ensued, of obsessive experimentation fuelled by a burning curiosity and thirst for knowledge. The emotional driving force guided their efforts towards the artifice of **body painting**, and later, **tattooing**.

These aesthetically and technically different decorative styles were the two main forms of artistic expressions executed on the human body – the precursors of all other art forms including the decoration of clothing, tools and other domestic objects, and eventually rock paintings, sculptures and much more. What is generally termed 'Primitive Art' today represents more of an intellectual and technical advance over what went before than the Renaissance in the modern context. Although only a tiny fraction of what was created by anthropoids in prehistoric times has survived, its artistic potency, beauty and depth is indisputable.

BODY PAINTING AS AN EXPRESSION OF IDENTITY WITH NATURE

The superior intellect of hominids allowed them to understand the multitude of ways in which colouring helps animals to assure their own survival. Used to gleaning useful information from their surroundings, they eventually deduced why tigers and zebras are striped, why giraffes and leopards are spotted, why monkeys or bears are brown and black or some insects multi-coloured. With this understanding, they naturally wanted to acquire similar survival advantages by colouring themselves.

They knew from experience which plants left blue, green, yellow or red marks on the bodies of children when they *brushed* against them. Shamans observed how some minerals or rocks made the hands white or ochre red, or how charcoal blackened the feet. This led to the production of primitive paint, initially based on plant oils, and first used secretly to adorn magic accessories of their trade. Over the generations, shamans began using these paints to decorate male bodies before hunting, battle or other rituals.

The results were so positive that this type of decoration soon became very important for the entire community, including the children. Our forebears believed that these **mystical patterns** in body paint originated from the totem, and when applied by the shaman and his assistants, provided real protection against any danger the wearer may be exposed to. Hunters decorated as tigers, pythons or eagles during a rite ceremony **were spiritually transformed** into the creature concerned, and hunted or fought accordingly – a miraculous reincarnation that testified to the shaman's mystical power of over the community.

The tradition of **body painting** ran deep and strong, and lasted a long time. Each community had Symbolic patterns for its own totem, shaman, chief hunter and elders. The shaman *marked* all infants with a specific totem sign at birth, just as every clan and each ritual event had its own visual symbol, all of which helped to cement social hierarchies.

In addition to *painting* or *tattooing* (which sometimes covered the entire body), each tribe also developed its own clothing styles based on scraps of pelts, feathers or other embellishments. These were different for males and females, children and adults and seniors or junior tribe members. Decorative patterns for everyday activities were for obvious practical reasons far simpler than those adopted for ritual ceremonies, where the decoration procedure was a sacred rite in itself, and could last for days.

The most sophisticated decorations were reserved for the witch or shaman, so that they would stand out among other tribe or clan members. The horns fixed to the shaman's head, or the witch's hair lifted high for the occasion allowed them to be more visible to the crowd as the focus of audience attention. Participants at the earliest ritual events or family celebrations usually performed naked, or with minimal genital covering. This gave them complete freedom to *jump* and *move* around, as well as providing the best opportunity to display their body paint or tattooing in the constantly competitive atmosphere among clan members.

Recent archaeological discoveries reveal evidence of cosmetic pigments as early as Palaeolithic times, a million years ago. Hominids originally produced these creams and colouring materials for medicinal rather than aesthetic purposes. After finding that the oils of certain fruit and vegetables made the skin feel soft and healthy, they began *applying* them to the entire body.

Our ancestors learned about different colouring materials, mainly mineral in origin: dark blue manganese dioxide, red iron oxide, various clays and copper-based pigments and so on. These pleasingly attractive bright colours were increasingly used for body decoration from the period of Homo Erectus onwards.

The custom gradually pervaded all aspects of social activity, *decorating* home bases, domestic objects and body coverings as well as for ritual purposes. Certain colours acquired special Symbolic significance, although the specific meanings varied from place to place. White could signify virginity for one tribe, happiness and beauty for another, and the devil elsewhere.

For Aztecs, red signified the east, blue the west, yellow the north and green, the south – but in China, the equivalent directions were blue, white, black and red respectively. Papuans warriors painted their bodies in red and white, Amerindians in red and black, while ancient Britons painted themselves in dark blue woad. The elements or certain minerals also had their special colours: red for fire, yellow for earth, white for iron, blue for water, and so on.

More complicated designs required more sophisticated decorating methods, for which hominids developed a new technology using **stamps** of clay and oil (known as pintaderas) to print repeated patterns on body surfaces. Although this was faster and more efficient than painting by hand, the pigment also faded more quickly; real permanence only became possible with the advent of **tattooing**, as we shall see later.

For males, body paint was used mainly to create the visual impression of great size, strength and bravery. Biceps were *emphasised*, aggressive beaks or fangs *painted on*, and menacing red and white circles *applied* around the eyes. There main motivations for such exaggerated styles were:

- to **assure** the closest possible union with the totem.
- to **frighten** the enemy in battle.
- to **confuse** predators or prey.

For females, body paint was used mainly to accentuate sexual attractiveness, with white or blue lines running along the arms and legs, around the nipples and navel, and so on. Females wore colourful necklaces, belts and bracelets around the elbows, wrists, ankles and knees. The main decorative emphasis was however reserved for the face and hair. Although the decorating resources were the same for all, the patterns and designs differed between girls and mature women, and between each individual. The main focus of every **design composition** was nevertheless the symbolic sign of the totem, which would usually be placed as a sacred charm in the middle of the forehead or on the hair just above the forehead.

RELIGIOUS, SOCIAL AND SEXUAL BODY DECORATION

Body decoration was not something to be taken lightly, but a serious religious and secular custom, often awkward and painful, but also paradoxically enjoyable. Clan members had to learn these complicated skills from a very young age, locating the required materials, learning how to prepare the exact mix of colours and studying tattooing techniques to find out the correlation of lines and dots with the anatomy. They also had to learn the many traditional semantic patterns for different ritual occasions, the limits of each design with regard to the totem and the drying time of each different pigment.

The body painting alphabet built up over a period of one to two million years, gradually refined by generations of shamans and preserved in a catalogue of **rock paintings** which have subsequently been misinterpreted. Petroglyphs of male and female silhouettes surrounded by various black zigzag lines, double circles and spirals (*fig. III/14*) in fact correlate to decorative designs *tattooed* or *painted* on bodies in black and white figures.

The study of early tattooing compositions on the human anatomy reveals that some of the pattern lines correspond to the shape of the body, while others project something else. Early rock graphics show circles and triangles underlining the muscles of a male or the main physical attributes of females. Most often, however, the body is painted with abstract totemic signs of, confirming the spiritual as well as aesthetic significance of these activities.

A line *spiralling* down around the legs or arms makes them look long and sinewy. Circular lines around a woman's breasts and buttocks draw attention to these features and emphasise their roundness. The triangular line on the face of a male, connecting the ears with the jawbone, has a hypnotic effect on an observer, automatically focussing the attention on the totem's amulet fixed between the eyes above the nose.

These body decorations obviously weren't just for fun – as well as making the body look attractive, the carefully wrought patterns clearly had a deeper religious or domestic meaning. But they also taught early humans the basics of painting techniques, composing with colour, and a greater aesthetic appreciation of the beauty of the human body. Stimulated by the ever-increasing competitiveness between individuals, families and tribes, there was a constant stream of new decorative inventions designed to make the wearer look stronger or better than others. Some mixed pigment with birdlime glue to attach further decorations (such as moss or down) to the painted design; others used small flowers or grains to similar effect.

Tattooing and scarring
It would be easy to assume that the idea for self-decoration initially arose from observing the striking visual effect of the red or white medicinal substances *applied* to scars acquired naturally in battle or hunts. In the absence of such scars, it was decided to inflict them deliberately by *cutting* with sharpened stones or bones along previously marked patterns, which they then *painted* with medicinal pigments to dry. Before long, this new affectation spread throughout the community.

Like the *painted* designs, the *tattooed* patterns had specific Symbolic meanings, indicating social status, spiritual closeness to the Totem, loyalty to the clan, wealth, bravery, special accomplishments and so on (*see fig. III/14*).

As tattooing designs and methods improved over hundreds of generations, the *cutting* technique was eventually replaced by *pricking* (although scarification remains unchanged to this day in some societies). Bone needles were replaced by a more efficient new tattooing tool – the toothed comb, which could make several skin perforations with one *movement*. Males were *tattooed* on the head, thighs and buttocks; women, on the neck, breasts and bellies. Some tribes combined both cutting and pricking methods to increase the variety of decorative effects. In some cases, the design covered the entire body, in which case body hair was first completely removed.

The original inhabitants of Japan used a variety of geometric patterns for tattooing as well as depictions of gods, birds, humans, animals, mythological personages and even entire scenes. Some of these plastic images were highly artistic, and executed as immaculately as any modern tattoo artist.

Conclusion

Researchers have concluded that caves recently discovered in different parts of the world were used for ritual worship and mythical performance by primates very much earlier than was previously thought. Despite the gap of millions of years, comparisons between what we can deduce about such activities and the rituals performed by unmodernised tribal groups in Africa and Australia reveal many fundamental plastic similarities between the two – the evidence of a progressive sociocultural continuum is incontrovertible.

The ancient sacred rites of the African Bushmen took the form of very long two or three-act mass pantomimes in which each participant played the role of a different totem-animal. The rock paintings that seem at first to suggest that many figures are randomly placed are in fact a visual shorthand for representing such scenarios of many interacting totem images, with various creatures in postures of aggression or acquiescence, as a form of dance notation for future generations. In our chapter on the visual arts, we explore these extraordinary cultural landmarks in more detail.

There is no doubt that the ritual pantomimes in the Neolithic period were indeed fully syncretic performances. motion symphonies involving almost independent theatrical genres being performed alongside each other in the service of the same idea: veneration of the totem. Over time, each genre developed its own performing skills, with shamans and worshippers learning their respective plastic vocabularies by heart and in some cases, recoding them graphically.

The language of mime was divided into *direct imitation* of nature and the same motions in stylised or symbolic form to create more abstract motifs. the same kind of **artistic stylisation** was simultaneously extended to other means of expression including costumes, masks and props.

This method of analysis will be applied later to the anthropology of ritual dance since Homo Erectus, about a million years ago – by which time it had finally evolved away from syncretic rite pantomime into a separate genre of its own. The totemythical pantomime tradition that was already in evidence over two million years ago continues of course to survive in many different forms, right down to the modern British Christmas 'panto' enjoyed by so many to this day.

fig. III/13   Primal Sacred Dolls for Rite-Ceremonies

Acting Puppets in Theatre-Marionette   Source: Internal. Auction Catalogues

Tattooing and Scarring Patterns

Source: Barber-Mueller Museum, 'Arts and Culture'. Geneva 1999

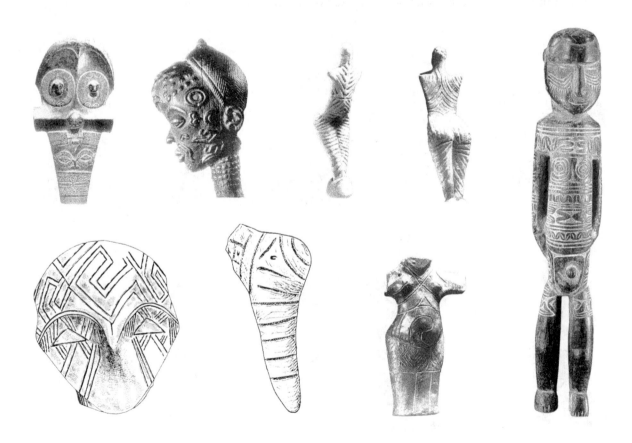

Earlier Masks for the Rite Ceremonies

Source: Ethnographic Museum of Palermo

Scenario/Notation of a Totemythic Pantomime
Source: Editors – *Native Americans* - 1995

Chapter IV: RITUAL DANCE AS A KEY SOCIAL ACTIVITY

Historians, philosophers, archaeologists and anthropologists have all attempted to determine the origins and meaning of dance. However, most of these abstract academic approaches have succeeded only in confusing matters with misleading and often contradictory analyses, and the useful insights they contain are often coloured by the author's subjectivity or area of professional expertise.

With its long and complex history and the infinitely varied roles it has played in human evolution, dance cannot be pigeonholed by any reductive label like 'an art' or 'a sociocultural activity'. My own conclusions on certain aspects of the subject are based on more than fifty years as a dancer, choreographer, dance teacher, researcher and author (including a number of works on folk and social dance ethnography).

Before discussing dance *per se*, it is important to establish what type of dance we mean. Dance as part of a syncretic ritual ceremony? The cultural expression of a tribe's socialisation? Dance as public entertainment? Or more modern forms, like ballet, contemporary dance, art gymnastics, figure skating, fitness dance, aquatic dance and so on?

Although all of these have their own distinctive vocabularies and artistic and anthropological features, they are united by being based on:

- **the same instrument**: the human body.
- **a common language** of plastic body motion.
- **a single code** of compositional rules.
- **a shared belief system** regarding the significance of the natural environment, and the aesthetic that this gave rise to.

Ritual dance can be traced back to the beginnings of human evolution, and can be subdivided into different categories, each with its own particular genres and styles for performance by one, two, three or more individuals or mass presentation.

The general characteristics of the main sacred dance genres and their physical, psychological and socio-cultural origins are described earlier in relation to Oldowan rituals employing a plastic motion vocabulary based on direct physical imitation of natural objects.

317

This vocabulary was committed to memory and gradually developed into a nonverbal communication system with its own hunting, labour and domestic 'dictionaries'.

As this mimetic library continued to expand in the course of being handed down from generation to tribal generation, shamans eventually had to 'edit' the huge number of natural gestures and postures into a shorthand of symbolic body motion to signify each sphere of activity: hunting, food gathering, domestic family functions and so on. These ritual dances were performed by mature members of the tribe, the hunting scenes mostly (but not exclusively) by men, and harvest scenes usually by women.

The main difference between these first rituals and the religious events of the Acheulean period lies in the changing role of the shaman. Before, the shaman had acted either alone or as leader of the tribe; thereafter, he conducted the ceremony from the sidelines. The role of female worshippers also changed; instead of merely *sitting* in a circle around the witch, they now participated in the ceremony directly by *moving* in circles or towards the centre and back again.

HUNT/FAUNA DANCE AND TOTEMISM

Whereas the tribesmen in earlier rituals performed various hunting motions individually, they now danced in unison, demonstrating their bravery, skill, strength and dexterity as a group.

The element of competition that this involved introduced a powerful new incentive for each dancer to improve and refine his performance. Performing for a live audience rather than for a deity generated a different type of emotional response in the dancers. In evolutionary terms, it was the first step on the road that led eventually to modern forms designed solely for public entertainment.

The hunting repertoire was the most popular ritual dance in the tribe. Even millions of years later in our own prehistory, young men continued to learn the hunting skills of their elders through ritual dance as a religious ceremony. However, in later periods these dances acquired a more complicated choreography.

The hominid physique and its kinetic abilities gradually improved from generation to generation. The arms and legs became extremely flexible, to the point that it grew difficult to distinguish between the *movements* of the hunt dancers and those of the prey they were imitating.

The art of mimesis – the apparent plastic transformation into an animal, bird or reptile – was no sudden overnight phenomenon, but emerged gradually as an integral part of the evolutionary process. Our ancestors found it by no means easy to rehearse the various routines day in, day out, to achieve the perfection required to guarantee their own survival.

Mentally and socially, this process was based on totemism. The pleasures of self-perfection, the belief in divine blessing for all performers, the aesthetic, psychological and physical effect of ritual hunt dancing on the tribal audience were all important factors in the development of ritual dance. Hunt/ fauna dance evolved into an artistic show with its own characteristics, and as such became a favourite for inclusion in all secular performance events in tribal society.

The animal dance repertoire contains representations of literally all the world's creatures. There are three major categories: **Masked, Totemic** and **Imagistic**. Some mixed forms were also included in ancient ritual ceremonies and traditional secular events. The subjects included every type of mammal, bird, fish, reptile and insect, as well as supernatural mythical creatures.

MASKED DANCE

As described earlier in the ritual dance section, see Chapter III this primitive pantomime dates from the very earliest days of organised hunting and hunt training, and was based on directly imitating animal characteristics and behaviour.

The range of possible motion was restricted by the weight of the mask (made from an actual head of the intended prey) and the stiffness of the pelt being worn. No mimetic facial expressions could be used, and no gestures, as both hands *held* a baton, spear or sharp bone under the pelt. Dance vocabulary was therefore limited to natural *movements* of the torso, very rudimentary *steps, hops* and some *running*, all of which were memorised as a plastic fauna 'dictionary'. Dance was involved because our ancestors prepared for the hunt, carried it out and demonstrated it to the shaman afterwards in the form of a carefully presented mime-dance performance.

The essence of masked dance was to create, through endless rehearsals, a perfect *moving* copy of the intended prey. Dressed in the mask and pelt of the hunted object, the hunter had to sneak as near as possible to the herd, mingle with the grazing cattle and kill as many of them as possible by spear or a sharp bone. The tribe was then saved from starvation for another week or so. In the meantime, the hunters may already be practising the next dance pantomime, having discovered prey of another species passing close by.

For Palaeolithic man, masked dance was life's university. Through studying natural fauna, he discovered ways of using his own physical abilities. It was a popular form of social activity, and an intensive way of developing human communication – and the best school of survival.

Masked dance remained for a long time a strictly Functional part of the hunter's strategy, or a way of celebrating success on returning to home base. Though the plastic vocabulary of animal motion – *moving* the head, arms, torso and legs – was still rather primitive, it nevertheless broadened and rapidly improved, as did the standard of imitation and hunting techniques.

Dancers alternated between the opposing roles of hunter and prey, learning how to transform instantly from one to the other, not only in outward appearance, but also emotionally and spiritually.

To dance under these conditions wearing a heavy mask and/or pelt required good co-ordination and special training to avoid any miscalculation in time or space. This was particularly important for groups of mime-dancers performing a complicated score of contrapuntal motions and rapidly changing episodes, sequences and tricks. Masked dance was at this point merely a realistic representation of the hunt, as yet without any signs of totemism.

It would be a mistake to think that totemism was invented or introduced by, or in the name of, a single individual. It was present from the very beginnings of human evolution, as an intrinsic element of anthropology. It took millennia for it to be established as a religion in the hearts and minds of hominids, when our ancestors eventually became mentally and physically ready for such a belief system. As an indicator, this will help us better to understand their spiritual attitudes and social communications later on.

Our hypothesis as to the origins of totemism as the prototype of human religion is that the performer spending often long periods under a bison's head-mask and pelt gradually began to feel and behave like the animal itself in the trance-like atmosphere and agitated circumstances of the rite itself, with the moonlight, blazing flames, beating drums and so on.

Eventually our ancestors reasoned that if performers could assume the being of a real bird, reptile or a mammal, such a metamorphosis could also happen the other way round. It was therefore logical to see mankind and the rest of the animate world as indissolubly linked, with equal functional and reproductive needs. It follows that hominids should know every characteristic of their fellow species (including wild predators) in order to respect them and to thank them for their willingness to be prey.

But who controls who wins or loses all these games? An agent of some kind must surely be conducting these mysterious metamorphoses? Who organises the reproduction of gazelles and delivers them to the tribe?

It could be only an entity that exists permanently within the community, who is part of our life, our body and soul from birth to death and even beyond. These endless questions and anxieties eventually led our forefathers into elaborating the theology and philosophy that underlies the development of mankind's first social and moral constitution: totemism, which brings us to the next form of hunt/fauna dance.

TOTEMIC DANCE

Because of its diverse ideological and compositional background, totemic dance is divided into three themes: hunting, mythical and animal. We know this from the detailed descriptions of mythic rituals by scholars of the past, and see it depicted in the ancient stone carvings. It is however difficult for us today to fully understand and appreciate the essence of totemism and its basis in the spirituality of all living creatures.

Totemic dance is primarily a **theological** and **aesthetic** expression of human spirituality, and secondly of the flesh. From this perspective, it is easier to grasp the motives and sensuality of the behaviour involved, both individually and socially. The Mesolithic/Neolithic hunt-dancing ritual became a major focus of a tribal interest and activity, offering the potential for spiritual and practical gratification.

The same type of hunters as during the Palaeolithic era continued to demonstrate the same performing and fighting skills, but with more refined mimetic techniques using a larger body motion vocabulary. The greater physical flexibility and agility of the hominid body shape allowed more plastic variety to be introduced to the fauna dance repertoire in **mythical pantomime**.

The most important development in mime-dancing was the new spiritual representation of hunters by themselves and images of their prey. After the long and confusing process of social and spiritual evolution discussed earlier, our forefathers were constantly worshipping while they *danced* the animal repertoire, instead of just imitating as before.

After this great theological turning point, dancers wore light, open masks and scraps of pelt instead of full hides. This modernisation of costume liberated the performers, and allowed spectators to see all their facial expressions clearly and to follow the motion text of the performer's body. Being physically more free and flexible in the execution of complicated *movements*, the performer could represent agile creatures more accurately, thereby increasing the plastic facility for more advanced choreography and *acrobatic tricks*.

In addition to performing some fascinating choreography while dressed as the animal, the dancer was completely transformed by the shaman's voice and spiritual influence into a physical incarnation of the object being represented. Each performance was specially prepared as a psycho-spiritual hypnotising session. It was initiated, conducted and concluded by the shaman, usually in an **ecstatic trance**.

Totemic fauna dancers had far more possibilities for expressing themselves through body motion than masked dancers. From now on, actions depicting inner feelings such as happiness, fear or curiosity could be reflected by facial *grimaces* and *gestures* of the head, arms or legs, followed by natural body *movements*.

Obviously, these rites were not as yet dramatic performances, but undoubtedly they eventually became so, containing as they did the main ingredients of theatre as we know it today. The pre-programmed score and primitive choreography, both formally recorded in petroglyphic notations, are archaeological evidence of the human artistic mentality and its symbolic vision of the environment. Various new weapons (bow and arrows, shields and spears) greatly enlarged the sphere of motion for the arms, increasing the vocabulary of postures for depicting different attacking and defensive skills.

The spiritual side of our species has always been receptive to new *stylised steps* and *body expressions*, often through studying the courtship dances of other animals. The technical and emotional standards of totemic dance in pre-hunting rites had reached such a pitch that audiences were horrified to witness their relatives spiritually and plastically metamorphosing. In these frequently performed representations, the protagonists seemed to be reincarnated into the spirits of the prey they wanted to catch the following day. Our ancestors had no doubt that antelopes could hear them and would sooner or later present themselves as willing victims.

The new dance lexicon now included rather complicated additional *manipulations* with weapons including some partnering *lifts*, many *stamps* and more advanced *steps* and *travelling movements*. There was also the mimicry of facial expressions, and dramatic interactions within the group with highly intensive patterns of fighting skills.

The characteristic performing conditions of these dances are evident in all other acts of worship such as totemic-mythical and harvest rituals, fertility and initiation rites, funerary and secular ceremonies, though each was distinguished by its own particular approach.

In totemythic pantomime, there could for example be a herd of buffalo helping their totem to fight his enemies; in a harvest ritual, the worshipping women would implore the totem to grant abundant fertility to the local species hunted, impersonated by male dancers. Wedding ceremonies usually included a pair of birds depicted in courtship; a group of females might execute a snake dance based on *zig-zag* patterns as a symbol of a successful puberty.

To avoid any confusion, we shall reconsider Totemic dance as a choreographic performance which either directly or symbolically portrays the Totem's icon by *dancing animal images*.

IMAGISTIC DANCE

The choreographic principles of *imagistic* mime-dance were the opposite of those in totemic dance. Dancers believed that they continued spiritually to embody the human part of the anthropomorphised totem; they would never have the audacity or disrespect to take down the patron's animal symbol from its high perch on their dwelling. In contrast to mythical rituals about the image or the story of the totem, Imagistic mime-dance represented only images of living creatures, their dreams, their love, families, birth, battles and death. Performances sometimes included the use of live snakes, birds or insects, either in the dancers' hands or on their bodies.

As the aim was to represent the individual animals as closely as possible, dancers had to learn the characteristic plastic structure and motion of other creatures much different from us. This required constantly practising many routines imitating the typical cries, postures and actions of the animal in question.

No wonder, then, that many of the mammalian images that remain in dance today echo human feelings, attitudes, problems and actions; no wonder we often symbolically refer to our children and loved ones as animals of various kinds.

The choreography of imagistic dance took many forms. Performing solo, for example, the dancer perhaps represented a lone gazelle searching for her lost calf as it howls in panic for its mother. The mother eventually finds its offspring and the reunited pair once again graze happily together. The same dancer acts both parts throughout, ranging emotionally from loss and fear to hope and happiness, combining contrary plastic characteristics simultaneously: maturity and immaturity, insecurity and protectiveness, and so on. It involves two images of a single species with the same survival instinct, but with opposite motion intonations: fighting for life on the one hand, waiting for death on the other. The single dancer performs a multiple drama.

With two protagonists, the duet allowed a greater variety of subjects for the imagistic dance repertoire. Take the mating of leopards, for example, or a territorial fight between a bear and a python. In the first case, two individuals of the same species dance the same subject with equal plastic facility, but with sexually opposite motion intonations. The grace of the female leopard *rolling* on her back or tenderly *biting* her partner contrast with the male, *lying motionless*, exuding latent power, ready for instant action to defend his position in the pride hierarchy or to mate.

The image of a pair of big cats that the dancers create is infused with their own personal characteristics, experience and humanity; the same subject in another execution might look completely different. In this way, the aesthetic value of the image being danced is determined by the personal qualities inherent in the individuals' performance.

In the second example, two males of different species with very dissimilar external images engage in territorial conflict. As mammal and reptile, their plastic motion characteristics differ completely; although both creatures were much admired by our ancestors as spiritual models for the totem, their paths seldom cross, apart from in the occasional cave.

The imagistic dance duel between bear and python could last for days, and involved two physically and technically strong dancers to demonstrate the full range of their fighting capabilities in a stylistically sophisticated choreography. As with the previous example, the performers perfectly captured the plastic image of the creatures they were playing in an accomplished demonstration of their individual fighting and mimetic motion skills.

Imagistic dances involving three of more performers followed essentially similar principles of performance and composition, varying only in terms of the animal subject, number of dancers, dramatic theme and so on (*see section on female dance*).

Totemism is mankind's primary religious and philosophical belief system and is based on the inter-relationship between human beings and everything else in the universe: the planets, the elements, flora and fauna. Indeed, it is still practised by remote communities in some parts of the world.

Amazingly, in petroglyphs carved hundreds of thousands of years ago, we find silhouettes of dancers demonstrating different *jumps* and *postures* in imitation of animals. Our ancestors never hated the predators that endangered them; on the contrary, to be named a tiger, eagle or python was deemed as great honour. This is why imagistic dance was such a popular subject for the initiation of children, and much appreciated by adults as a performance.

SACRED WAR DANCE

Hunting and battle dances have the same basic vocabulary of fight skills, strategy and plastic motion. As we saw in the previous chapter, very different opponents are involved. In hunting, men chase or fight animals, while in war dances they fight each other. Even though humans and animals are from both mammals, their psychological and physical behaviour and range of body motion are distinctively different (quite apart from other factors such as self-consciousness, spirituality and powers of judgement and analysis).

The following examples are only a fraction of the many worship routines practised during the later Palaeolithic era. The new metal weapons of the later Bronze and Iron Ages brought with them new combat techniques and coaching methods. Amazingly, the strict

322

humane rules that prevented injury during these combat performances remained in force until the Roman Empire. Many tribes nevertheless did not observe these civilised rules; even today, head-hunting and cannibalistic rites are still practised in remote corners of the world.

COMBAT MODES

The choreographic interpretation of the adversarial action of battle falls into three main categories: **Intimate, Close range** and **Distant**.

Intimate combat

These wrestling matches are generally conducted in hand-to-hand combat without weapons, with the strength and power of the entire body being deployed in **direct contact** with the opponent. The motion of both fighters is in constant opposition to each other: attack is warded off before counterattack, and so on.

Such intimate physical contact does not give the combatants much opportunity to see each other in their entirety, making it difficult to anticipate the adversary's next move. This is therefore sensed through *body contact* and the opponent's *balancing positions*, or by intuitively predicting the counteraction. The hypnotising effect of eye-to-eye contact is also used.

This mimetic duel was suitable for the mythical or funerary pantomimes, but not for independent choreographic compositions. For these, though the dancers work under basically similar mental and physical conditions, more breaks and a larger performance area were required for preparing and executing *stretched out* poses, body *lifts, jumps* and *turns*.

Though these *exaggerated steps* and *fighting motions* would look unnatural in a mime, they enhanced the dance performance. In the same *wrestling* subject, the dancers would have solos to demonstrate their physicality and courage by individual *jumping* or *turning tricks*, circling aggressively around each other for psycho-spiritual destruction, impressing their opponents by using complex *movements* and displays of unexpected attack and defence skills.

The kinetic power of these adversarial motions in combat duels is often based on leverage – when a dancer *rolls* his opponent over the hip, for example, or tries to *throw* him over the shoulder. The combatants' balance is the weak point in intimate combat – once the opponent loses his equilibrium, he can easily be knocked down. When this happens, as it often does, everything depends on how quickly the overpowered combatant can muster the strength and momentum needed to reverse the situation.

Though these basic rules are well known, the audience remains largely unaware of the timing and techniques required, or which group of muscles to use; neither are all observers are familiar with standard fighting techniques or special wrestling *tricks*, such as how to get out of a *double lock* or how to end such a fight.

Genetically speaking, human beings' natural fighting instinct is older than the impulsion to dance. All mammalian offspring begin their daily routine with fights for the best position to suckle. As they grow, fighting forms the basis of most play. Mature animals constantly fight each other to get prey or to escape from predators; males fight for females, mothers fight to protect their young, and so on.

Our ancestors developed the skills and techniques of intimate combat through the millennia, incorporating these motions into ritual pantomimes. These became progressively more stylised and were eventually artistically transformed for secular dance performances.

Close-range combat

This is a form of combat in which the fighters' reach is increased by **weapons** – either natural materials such as horns, beaks, tusks, jawbones, claws or talons, shells or stones, or a man-made fighting instruments like cudgels, bone knives, sharpened branches, bundle of reeds or nets.

Our forefathers originally used thick pelts to protect the body, but later constructed shields made from woven reeds, bark or clay. Although masks were worn in ritual pantomimes to make the sacred images easier to recognise, these were not required for secular events or open competitions.

As we saw in the previous chapter, the anthropology of combat began at the earliest stage of human evolution in close correlation with mime and dance, in syncretic ritual pantomime. As with dance in the past, combat initiation in both hunting and battle forms was developed to such an extent that the shaman had to separate wrestling studies from pantomime into a different training programme.

However, ritual war dance and sacred combat had so much in common that they continued to be taught together. Hence, the dancing wrestlers and the fighting dancers were the same performers, but with different ritual functions. They had the same kinetic force and plastic facility, the same powerful control of balance and co-ordination and identical partnering skills in adversarial communication. The only real difference was in the amount of force applied by either the upper or lower extremities during the performance.

It must also be remembered that performing combatants were never allowed to *touch* each other in close range fighting with weapons (*see Chapter III*). Whether acting out a duel or in a group, the *dancing* wrestler therefore had performed a different type of motion which simultaneously proved the quality of his actual combat skills and demonstrated perfect psycho-spiritual control of his mimetic abilities. The demanding fighting techniques and the dramatic atmosphere required so much concentration that the wrestlers had to strain every nerve to the limit, the smallest error being penalised.

The new conditions and motion capabilities for close-range combat included:

- **No direct contact** between opponents' bodies.
- **Space between combatants** to allow appraisal of the situation before action.
- Unlimited opportunities to perform the **Battle dance syllabus.**
- **Kinetic amplitude extended** by weapons.
- **Increased spatial potential** to use the additional fighting skills of the legs.
- **Aesthetic premium** on the simultaneous demonstration of combined wrestling and dance performance skills.

FIGHTING SKILLS FOR BOTH **INITIMATE** AND **CLOSE** RANGE

Arm motion with weapons

Attack
- *Striking* with a cudgel or *slashing* with a bundle of reeds with one arm, vertically, diagonally or horizontally, *shifting* downwards or sideways.
- *Stabbing* (with beak, tusk, bone-knife, claws or shell) with one arm, *pushing* upwards, diagonally, horizontally or downwards towards the object of attack.
- *Whipping* and *pulling* down by lianas, using one arm in a *rotating* and *slashing* forwards movement, followed by *pulling* the whip back while it remains *coiled* around the opponent's body.

- *Striking* or *stabbing* with a spear or talon, with one arm; striking and *pushing* in any direction.

Defence
- Protecting any part of the body with a small shield by quick *shifting* motions for instant defence.
- Camouflage: *falling* and *covering* oneself with a large shield made of reeds; by both arms; *lying still* on the ground.

Simultaneous attack and defence
- *Stabbing* and *beating* by double horns or spear (with both arms) and *repelling* the attacker by standard defence routines, all in a mixed fighting motion combining kinetic action with presentation.

Leg motion repertoire

Attack
- *Kicking* with one leg while maintaining one's stance on the ground; in any direction, perhaps *turning* on the spot; in *striking, pushing* or *pulling* with the foot, *knocking down* the opponent by *catching* him under his knee or ankle, and then *pulling* horizontally. *Kicking* simultaneously with both legs, or one after the other in succession while *jumping* in the air; in any direction and/or aerial *turns, landing* on the ground with both legs.

Defence
- *Lifting* up one *bent* and *turned-in* leg in front to protect the middle of the body, ready to repulse the attacker; *crouching* simultaneously on the supporting leg; *bending* the body towards and down to the defending leg.
- *Kicking* chaotically with both legs while *laying on the back* to confuse the attacker; *kicking* with both legs; looking for the opportunity to *hook* him in a 'dead lock' and *knock* him over by *rolling* on the ground using leverage as mentioned earlier.

Distant combat

Distant fighting had a different aim, approach and execution. Its main purpose was to destroy the enemy physically – a real fight for life or death.

Like all other creatures, men are born with an innate instinct for survival. However, with their superior intelligence, this instinct was, through the millennia, partly channelled into developing new and more effective weapons of destruction. Boys learned from early childhood how to use various weapons for attack or defence, how to scalp or how to behead their enemies.

As with close-range fighting, weapons are also involved, the motions depending largely on the type of weapon used. Combatants had to consider not only their own physical strength and will to win, but also had to estimate quickly and accurately the **distance** to the target, the anticipated **speed** and **trajectory**, and the likely **position** of a moving target, taking into account wind speed and direction, timing and any other obstacles that may arise. Novices would have to practise these skills for a very long time until they were sufficiently developed to achieve the desired result.

Distant combatants never had close contact with the enemy, at least not at the start of a battle. Their success depended on their individual skills. Warriors could not afford to make mistakes, either individually or from the point of view of the communal strategy. There was only one question: whether to live or die. Even if the combatant was not killed by the enemy through a mistake he made, he could be punished or sacrificed by his own clan on returning to home base.

KINETIC POWER

Distant battle skills are based on the kinetic forces of *pushing, pulling, throwing, rotating* and *spinning*. Whether *hurling* sharp stones or *pulling* bows; *slinging* projectiles or *throwing* a spear, discus or boomerang, the kinetic input must correspond to the release that follows. The missiles had to follow exactly the right trajectory, with the height, speed and curvature required to hit target. Distant warriors were also constantly aware of the threat of incoming missiles from similar weapons sent from the same distance and with the same force by the enemy. These are the movements for right-handed combatants for both close and distant ranges:

The *pushing* kinetic force for *punching* or *stabbing*

Preparation
- Large *step back* with the R foot, *balancing* on the bent R leg.
- R arm *draws back* with *bent* elbow, *squeezing* weapon with R hand.
- L arm *rises, covering* the chest and torso by a medium size shield.
- Upper body *leans* back, *swinging* a little to the right and *bending* laterally.
- Head faces L shoulder, *shifting* back to the upper body accordingly.
- The eyes *concentrate* on the target, recharging the spiritual power.
- A deep breath is drawn after calculating defence/counterattack motions.

Strike
- The *balance changes* powerfully from back R leg to L front leg.
- The upper body *shifts* forcefully forward towards the enemy.
- R arm *punches* or *stabs, pushing* with body and fist or weapon forward.
- L arm with the shield *balances* to the left/back, *twisting* the upper body.
- Short final impact, *exhaling* simultaneously and *releasing* a short cry.

Release
- Head *jerks* upwards, *adjusting* the balance after the attack.
- Quick *move back* to balanced position while taking defensive precautions.

The *pulling* kinetic force of the kneeling archer

Preparation
- *Balanced* placement on R knee, with body in profile to the enemy.
- *Raising* up L arm, with the bow, in front of L shoulder.
- *Picking* the arrow from the quiver with R arm, and placing it into the bow.

Accumulation
- *Pulling* the bowstring to its limit with R arm.
- *Flexing* the upper body to the right back, for maximum power.
- *Raising* and *turning* the head to L shoulder to take careful aim.

Strike
- The arm *unleashes* the arrow.

Release
- the body returns to a neutral position.

The *throwing* kinetic force for the angled trajectory of a spear

Preparation
- Raising R arm with spear above the head.

Accumulation
- *Running* steps, while *holding* the spear with R hand on R shoulder
- Small *hop* on R leg, inhaling, *lifting* spear upwards and back with R arm.
- *Contracting* the whole body by *arching* to R back, *balancing* L arm in front.
- *Stepping* L leg forward to increase momentum.

Strike
- Upper body and R arm *push* spear forward, *balancing* laterally with L arm.
- Complete exhalation during the *throw*, simultaneously *releasing* a short cry.

Release
- *Return* to neutral position and *preparation* for the next attack.

The *throwing* kinetic force for the horizontal trajectory of a boomerang

Preparation
- Pre-start position *balanced* on R leg, with L leg *crossed* behind.
- R arm *raised* laterally *holding* boomerang, while L arm *lifts* shield up/ forwards.
- Upper body *swings* to R, simultaneously *flexing* backwards laterally.
- Head *turns* to L shoulder, calculating weapon trajectory.

Strike
- *Large step* forward onto bent L leg, *leaning* forward and *shifting* balance towards front.
- The boomerang is *thrown* with R arm from the side around to the front, the L arm *balancing* laterally.

Release
- Position *maintained* while following boomerang trajectory visually.
- Returning boomerang *caught* with L hand, and starting stance resumed.

The *throwing* kinetic force for the vertical trajectory of a sling

Preparation
- Body *balances* on spread legs, in a profile position to R.
- Missile *loaded* by the L hand into the sling, *fixed* at the R wrist.

Accumulation
- Anti-clockwise *rotating* motion begun by straight R arm with sling.
- L arm *rises* up L, balancing centrifugal force and *pointing* to target.
- Head *turns* to L shoulder, calculating the force and speed required.

Strike
- The upper body *bends* to L, and the stone *thrown* in a vertical trajectory.

Release
- After a pause to *check* the result, neutral starting position *resumed.*

The *throwing* kinetic force of a discus thrower

Preparation
- Both legs *held* together in a *crouched* position, with discus in R hand facing front.
- Upper body *swings* R, *bending* L and down in a *twisting* contraction.

- R arm *holding* the discus *opens* out laterally, L arm *raised* in front
- Head *turns* to L and upwards, *looking* over L shoulder to take aim

Accumulation
- *Holding* the same posture, *spins* anti-clockwise with both feet.

Strike
- Large *step* forwards with *bent* L leg, *pushing* upper body by *leaning* towards front.
- *Throwing* discus up and forward with R arm, *balancing* L arm laterally.

Release
- *Returning* to neutral position after visually *checking* the discus trajectory.

These examples show that irrespective of circumstances and personal physical abilities, every fighting motion contains a **predictive** element prior to the action itself, both of which vary according to the weapon used.

All Combats and War dances involved three main stages: preparation, execution and post-evaluation.

Preparation contained the reason for, and potential energy of the action itself. Whatever the form, genre or style of performance, it involved:
- Balanced position and settled rhythm of breathing.
- Mental concentration and appraisal of the opponent's fighting ability.
- Sacred blessing and preparatory placement with weapons.

Execution is the kinetic realisation of the dramatic scenario and the choreographic text, combining fighting actions and the trajectory of the weapon used:
- Psychological and physical predictive motion.
- Performing the action, with or without weapons.
- Relaxation after releasing the fighting motion.

Post-evaluation, in which the dancers analyse the dramatic and technical result of the last combat in terms of its composition and emotional impact on the audience. This is followed by a reconstruction of the sequences performed, either in the mind or physically, for the correction of any errors or miscalculations:
- Visualisation or physical reconstruction of the last episode.
- Spiritual, technical and dramatic analysis of the composition.
- Practical post-action corrections to the performance.

This creative cycle is the basic formula for the spiritual and aesthetic evolution of the performing arts in both wrestling and dancing.

THE ANATOMY OF WAR DANCE

OPERATIONAL CONDITIONS

Like hunting and totemic dances, war dance was the basis of many other ritual ceremonies. We know that patriarchy became dominant during Palaeolithic times, gradually taking most of the leading social positions away from the women. The performance of previously exclusive female dances by males became more and more popular in many tribes. Men were now also performing war dances in fertility and healing rituals and in phallic and initiation rites in addition to the old totemythic and funerary sacred pantomimes.

As tribal populations grew, the availability of prey diminished. With tribal territorial boundaries fixed long ago, the ever increasing demand for more space for new generations inevitably gave rise to greater inter-tribal tension and aggression. The conflicts that occurred more and more frequently cost much time and energy, not to mention innumerable lives. Each tribe had no choice but to create its own guard units for attack or defence.

The chief or a shaman always invoked the totem's blessing to kill the enemy. This spiritual support stimulated the development of weapons and fighting skills, and domestic areas gradually became converted into virtual armed camps.

Battle initiation

One of our ancestors' main concerns was the need to instruct future warriors in the techniques of warfare. The basic training of boys for hunting and battle rituals in the Palaeolithic era is described in the previous chapter; over the next million years or so, circumstances changed in terms of religion, environment, economics and culture.

Warfare instructors developed advanced new systems for coaching young men and boys. In addition to the old battle routines, they were taught new ones with more sophisticated weapons and new wrestling skills.

Future warriors had to learn a new syllabus of dancing *steps, jumps, turns, lifts, acrobatic tricks*, the latest techniques of intimate-range combat without weapons, either against one opponent, two, or a group. They had to study close range combat with all the weapons available at the time: how to use them from any combat position, how to take a weapon away from the opponent; and how to fight with bare hands against an armed enemy.

In distant combat, they were taught how to use *throwing* weapons individually; by contrast, all strategic manoeuvres were taught in groups. Instruction was also given in the use of signals, administering to the wounded and so on. Regular competitions and special games were held to stimulate personal motivation and to increase concentration. Reactions were honed by catch a moving spear or boomerang and sending it back. They were taught how to scalp or behead an enemy.

With each tribe devoting much time and energy to strengthening its warfare capabilities by acquiring the most advanced weapons and deploying the best warriors in this way, the potential for war thus progressively grew.

Plastic motion syllabus

It is unfortunately impossible to separate the dancing sequences from wrestling ones because the combat skills of the time were a plastic synthesis of both. When dancers had to overcome some dramatic obstacle when performing a totemythic pantomime, their choreography encompassed real fighting skills, whose motions were seamlessly woven into the dance. In real battles, the reverse was true.

Naturally, the combatants of whichever continent performed their own local style of **wrestling dance**. However, the basic syllabus and standard war dance techniques were the same, and can be seen in many frescoes and figurines:

- *crawling* or *rolling* over; *moving* while *squatting* or with the *knees bent*; *sneaking* towards the enemy to gather intelligence, *diving* or *falling* to the ground, face up; *striking, kicking* repeatedly with one or both legs in succession; *rotating* legs on the ground or in the air, in any direction, and *turning* the upper back.

- *bending, swinging* and *rotating* the torso in any direction; various *'port-de-bras'* with or without a weapon; *punching, stabbing, blowing, slapping, cutting, slinging, pushing, striking, throwing, catching, pulling, squeezing.*
- *posing, marching* or *running* steps, in any direction and in circles; *stamping* repeatedly with one foot or both; complex sequences of *'pas de basque', 'pas balancé', 'pas suivi', 'pas coupé', 'pas ballonné'* and *'temps lié'* – all in a rustic manner.
- repeated *small jumps* on one or both legs in succession, or on both legs at once; *medium jumps* from one leg to the other in any direction and *turning; grand jumps* on the spot, with the legs together or apart, *striking, kicking* or *rotating* legs, with or without turns; *grand jumps* moving in any direction, and *turning;* acrobatic tricks on the ground (such as break dance elements) and in the air (*somersaults, 'pas cabriole', 'flic-flacs'*) – all in a rustic manner.

This syllabus is only the basis of the larger war dance programme used in Palaeolithic combat training as part of spiritual as well as physical education. Shamans and teachers already knew how to control the body through meditation and divination, and all *steps* or *movements* were founded on religious practice and belief.

War preparation

Although declaring war was easy, by drum-beat, voice, or beacons, much time and stress was involved in preparing any invasion campaign. It only takes a few warmongers to find a pretext to stir up sentiments against neighbours, and the instigators rallied the rest of the tribe to battle by performing the aggressive motions of combat dances.

Seeing these performances, all the other men of the tribe would join in one by one until all those capable of fighting entered into an emotional understanding of attack and defence. The procession of *dancing* warriors *stamped* the ground heavily, *rattling* their weapons, *screaming* and *drumming* loudly. When the agitation reached its climax, the shaman took over.

The next stage was the performance of an intriguing choreography portraying the neighbours' alleged offences. This ritual dance was dedicated to the totem, both as a report and as thanks for giving for his blessing on the enemy's destruction. The spectacle would end with an animal sacrifice.

After securing the necessary spiritual support, the war proper began. All combatants and young women rehearsed the choreographed battle parade and pre-attack preparations. The rest of the tribe prepared ammunition, camouflage, and protective fences.

Female worshippers served in ritual ceremonies at night, dancing for the goddesses and asking for their blessing. In the meantime, the shaman sent out scouts to collect information about the enemy's strength, position, spiritual fortitude and fighting capabilities in terms of battle formations, ammunition, and so on.

This was followed by setting out the attack strategy and tactics based on the information gathered. At the end, all the combatants and young females performed the war dance parade to demonstrate their resilience, martial spirit and readiness for battle.

War dance repertoire

This differs from the functional combat dances of totemic ritual pantomimes representing mythical subjects mentioned in the previous chapter. The choreography of battle rites was usually (but not exclusively) a group composition, perhaps with solos, duets or trios of leading combatants performing for both sides. However, the War dance was always strongly rooted in the sacred, and had a clear purpose which governed its preparation and performance.

DANCE PARADES FOR PERSONAL DEMONSTRATION

The day or a week before the battle, all men and young women marched singing in the open, demonstrating their fighting strength and spirit, their willingness to die for their tribe, their territory and their gods. Drums and flutes created loud, threatening rhythms that were meant to be heard by the distant foe. Old women also sent clear messages by *rudimentary cries* intended to intimidate the enemy. While *marching,* young females would *manipulate* various weapons around the body using both arms in succession; the men would do likewise with heavier accessories. Suddenly they started *stamping* the ground in unison, following the rhythm of the drums in a tremendously loud crescendo, and *digging* the feet into the ground. All this, the enemy was designed to hear.

Men and women usually *paraded* in separate groups, and not always in unison. One group would do *manipulation routines* with weapons, while the other would continue *changing formation* during the march. They could be lining up in front of each other, making canonical '*port-de-bras*' or *contrapuntal motions* with weapons.

After this choreographic dialogue, the women broke into '*footwork*' on the spot, or slightly shifting the line to the front, back or side; the men *banged* lances and shields to the beat of the drums, while *jumping* in a line, *crouching*, *striking* with weapons, and so on.

This was nevertheless a real demonstration of combat skills and manoeuvring, in a well-choreographed presentation of warfare. Above all, these exercises made the warriors mentally and physically more confident for the battle to come, giving them spiritual faith in their victory the following day.

PRE-ATTACK DANCE

War is about killing, and many would never return from battle. Warriors did not therefore rush to engage in combat, preferring instead to draw out the time and wait for the enemy to initiate hostilities. Men often began with the traditional introductory dance, lining up in front of each other. They would then try to impress the enemy with their bellicose attitude and physical condition by using unknown *steps* and *movements*, their bodies and weapons adorned with colourful stripes. The warriors would dance the first fight sequence in unison to the right. After observing the effect on the enemy, they would follow up with a more aggressive dance to the left, before repeating the same *zig-zag pattern* with increasing ferocity until the two opposing lines faced each other at close-range distance.

Finally, the accompanying cries and the drumming would stop. This was the signal for the fighting to begin; if it did not, the chief or his deputy would start to yell and make faces at the enemy, along with insulting *gestures* and *poses* in an attempt to provoke an attack. One of the opposing sides would eventually lose their composure, and the battle began.

VICTORY DANCE

Victory was the most joyous subject of sacred and secular events for the entire community. After the dead were buried and the wounded had been tended, the victors began a triumphal ceremony that could last a week or more.

This ritual was usually opened by a parade of warriors showing off their trophies, such as scalps or heads, ammunition, or the enemy's personal possessions. The women would sometimes *hold* the heads or scalps in the middle of the battle site, *standing* in a circle facing outwards, while the triumphant dancers *encircled* them, demonstrating their bravery, strength and martial spirit in a warlike way.

In a kind of action replay, the combatants would then illustrate the most exciting events of the battle. These reconstructions for the victory ritual involved series of duets, trios and group presentations in intimate and close combat ranges, to show the dramatic highlights of the operation and the final rout of the enemy to the shaman and other tribe members.

The sacred programme was followed by the symbolic female snake dance, and the heroic male eagle dance, as a thanks to the totem and to the Goddess Mother. Young warriors performed unusual war dance compositions with two shields per performer. Female singers also participated in the thanksgiving by *moving around* the victors with impressive 'port-de-bras' – a phallic ritual in which all adult women glorified the victors as vigorous specimens of manhood fit to father future generations. The finale was a mass improvisation celebrating happiness and honour to those who had once more saved the tribal home.

BURIAL WAR DANCE

This is described under holy funerary rites and ceremonies in the previous chapter. In the present context, it is however worth pointing out the difference between death in a hunting or domestic accident and death on the battlefield. Unlike the former, the funerary ritual for dead warriors was a most sacred ceremony performed on a much larger scale.

THE FEMALE ROLE IN WAR DANCES

It was important for any tribe to be respected as warriors. To demonstrate their military prowess, our ancestors put on show as many combatants as possible in the parades that preceded hostilities. Unfortunately, men able to fight accounted for only around a quarter of the tribe's population, so young women also played a significant role.

Women did not generally participate in fighting on the front line, with one exception: the naked female dancers who performed to distract the enemy sexually before battle was joined. For this purpose, they moved forward from defensive positions up to the front line. In effect, they were used as live shields and camouflage for the warriors crowding behind them. At the right moment, the warriors would *surge* forward through the line of suggestively dancing women to attack the surprised enemy.

Although women almost never fought physically (except perhaps at a distance, as archers or a spear throwers), they did however *wrestle* between themselves in pre-battle parades or post-battle celebrations.

The main role of older women in war was to worship in various ritual ceremonies every night to mourn the battle dead, to beg the deities to save husbands or sons from harm, or to invoke death on the enemy. During the day, women had to look after the warriors and the wounded, supplying water, food and medicine.

Otherwise, women's main spiritual support was by choral singing. Their simple evening chants and melodic vocal modulations helped to restore the combatants' physical and spiritual fighting forces that had been depleted during the day's hostilities; it recharged their spiritual power for the next battle. The sounds of flute or voice wrought miracles for these highly sensitised warriors. Like a drug, it stimulated the strength of will, and belief in victory.

As war raged, teenagers and older men played their part in helping the combatants by making boomerangs, preparing stones for slings, sharpening arrows and spears, braiding shields and so on. Practically the whole tribe was involved in the war effort, which could go on for weeks or even months.

1. Marching soldiers with weapon
2. Reconnaissance squatting locomotion of scouts
3. Running locomotion
  a) contestants   b) Warriors with shield
4. Wagging motion on riding camel in a saddle
  a) trotting   b) galloping

1. Unison sequences of dancing motion
2. Harvest patterns in ritual dance
3. Fertile body motion of scattering seeds
4. Unison steps in puberty rite-ceremony
5. Secular dance with fan
   b, c, d in solo   a, e in duet

fig. IV/3

Khmer Dance Notation
One of the earliest practical systems in graphic description for dancing syllabus

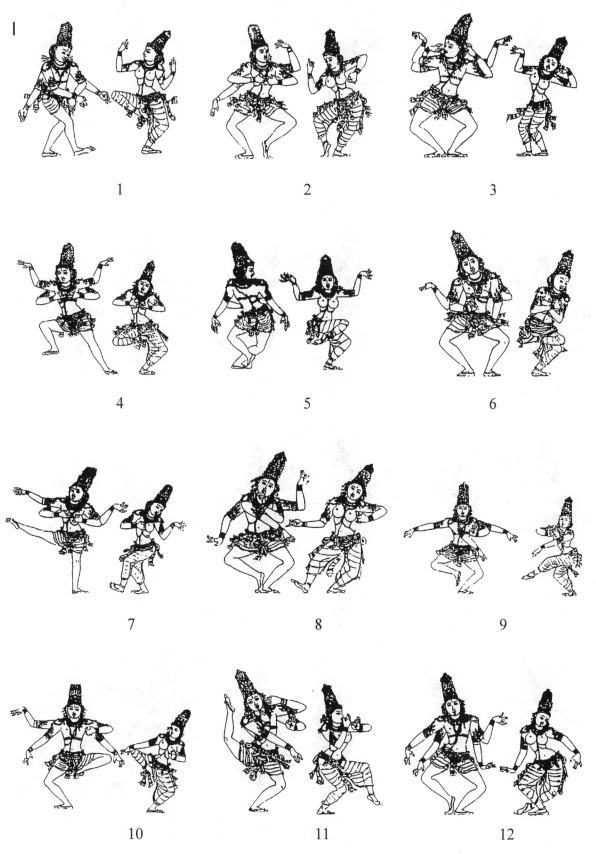

fig. IV/4

Source: R Hugs, *Gesture Language of Hindu Dance*, 1941

II

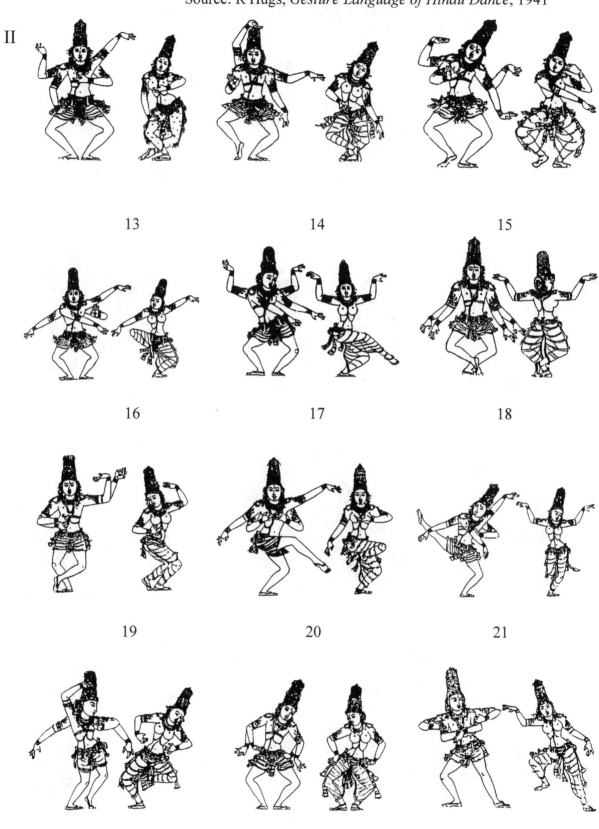

13   14   15

16   17   18

19   20   21

22   23   24

fig. IV/5

III

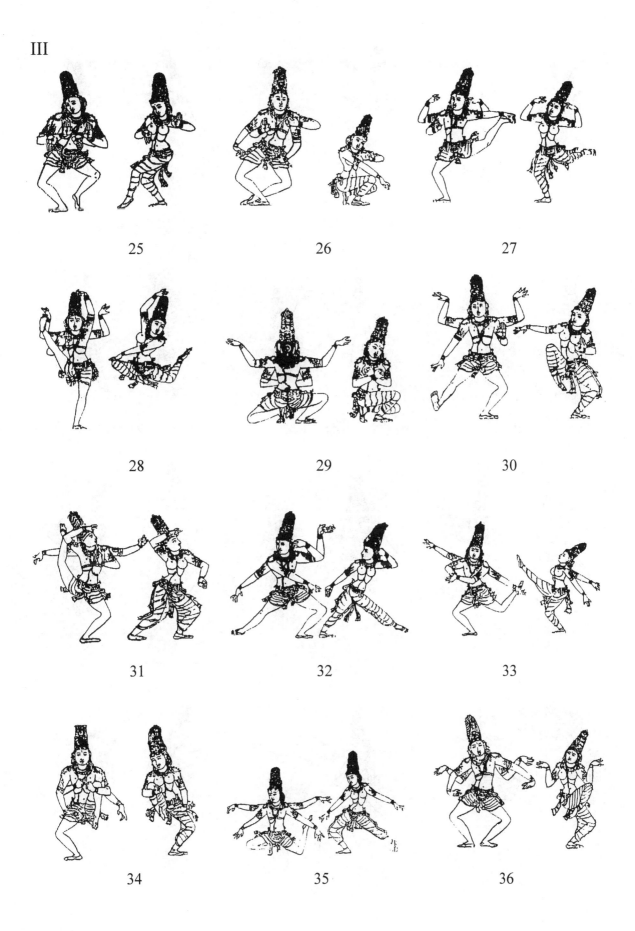

25   26   27

28   29   30

31   32   33

34   35   36

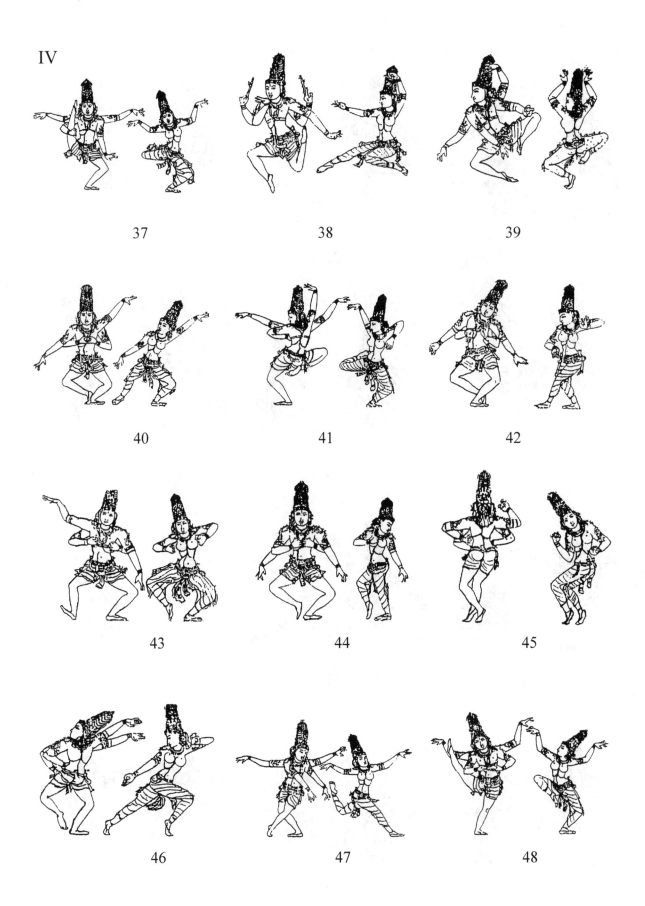

IV

37

38

39

40

41

42

43

44

45

46

47

48

Male's Spiritual Choreography

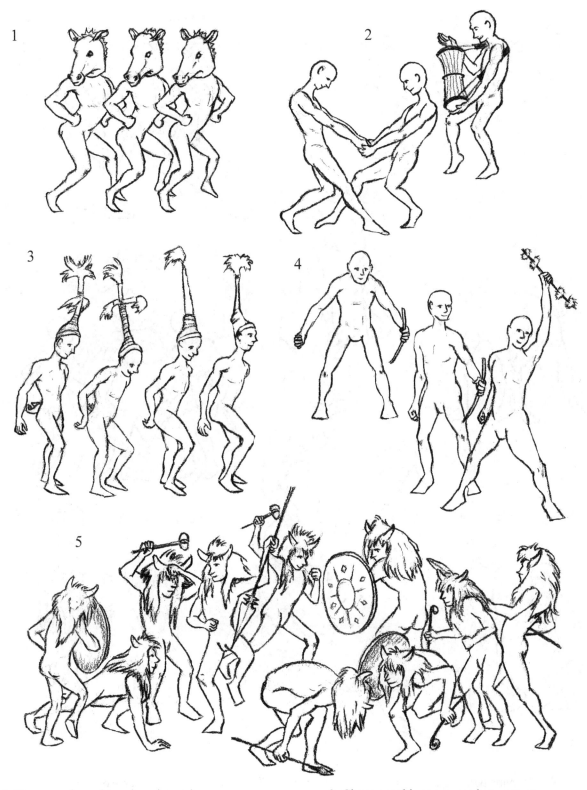

1. Horse-maskery dance in unison trio
2. (a, b) Partnering motion and drum accompaniment
3. Choreographic sequences in a contest
4. Pre-war dancing warm-up
5. Hunt ritual dance of Amerindians

Pantomime Skills in Performance

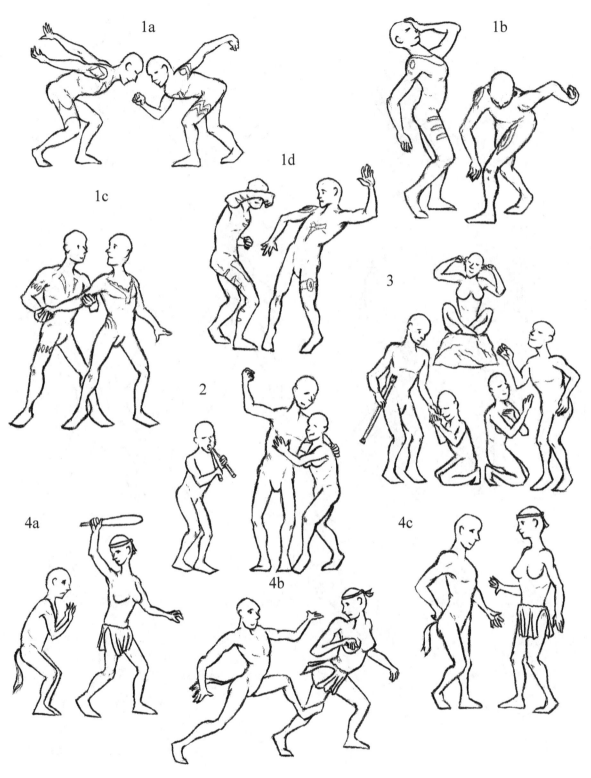

1. (a, b, c, d) Mime postures of frozen
   wrestling motion
2. Drunk couple and flutist

3. Performing again the same old scenes
4. (a, b, c) Pantomime episodes of satyr
   following the annoyed nymph

War dance strategy

As we have already seen, the main strategic tool in prehistoric battles was ritual dance, as opposed to dance as entertainment, or for fitness or therapy. We are not talking here about tactics and manoeuvres, combat techniques or any other characteristic of a real wars, but dance as a spiritual weapon which in some respects had a much stronger effect on the enemy than the physical pain of being clubbed or stabbed. It was also not a matter of affecting the individual, but the wholesale destruction of the enemy's fighting abilities in terms of concentration, aggression, self-control, the will to fight, the sense of self-preservation, precautionary measures and so on

This was precisely the effect of naked young female dancers appearing suddenly in the front of the enemy. And that is why some front line combatants approached their opponents by *zig-zag dance sequences*. The more these dancers closed in on the enemy, the stronger the hypnotising effect on the adversary, for whom it became increasingly difficult to escape this powerful spiritual influence. Nor could the defenders avert their eyes, since they had to be aware of what their opponents were doing. They became mesmerised by the female dancers, like rabbits transfixed by a python.

This explains why some petroglyphs depicting battle scenes show strange naked female silhouettes dancing among male warriors. With the supernatural power vested in the worshipping dancer in Palaeolithic times, they were sacrosanct; killing them would have been like murdering a priest today. Inexplicable as this may seem to modern eyes, human history has always been shaped by beliefs in superstition, the supernatural and the spiritual. These have been, and remain powerful forces; ignoring them does not make them disappear.

FERTILITY RITE DANCE

Fertility rituals performed by women in the open air figured prominently in the programme of any early Palaeolithic tribe. Usually led by the witch, the women danced almost every night to pray for the fecundity of the tribe and its animals and harvests.

The compositions were basically similar, involving primitive movements with the upper and lower extremities. *Holding* hands, the dancers *promenaded* in slow motion, either in circles or in lines *moving* towards each other and away again, sometimes *bending* their bodies in opposite directions, *stamping* their feet heavily or *lifting* one leg in front. Whatever was being prayed for, the women always *danced* the same sequences together while *singing* primitive prayer chants.

THE ROLE OF THE MOTHER GODDESS IN TOTEMISM

Women held powerfully influential positions in tribal society. Crises in the tribe or clan were solved by the intercession of the Mother Goddess' image, played by the witch. If an angry totem had to be appeased for some misfortune, a beautiful young virgin was sacrificed. The female image symbolised birth, the life force and reproduction in all its forms.

The witch's impersonation of the Mother Goddess was believed to have enormous power: to increase the tribe's population, to protect women during pregnancy, to give medical help, to bring rain, to bless a battle or dwelling. Like the shaman, the witch was assumed to have magic for virtually anything the tribe required; like the shaman also, the witch/leader was the most intelligent person in the tribe, and therefore the best equipped to teach life and survival skills.

The main purpose of female rites was of course to pray for better harvest, fruitful puberty, successful hunting, healthy children and so on. As they evolved over the millennia,

341

these ritual dances and the contemporary male hunting rituals gradually became more advanced in their choreographic composition and decorative design, although still based on the same simple pattern: *moving* together clockwise in a circle around the central Symbolic object (moving in the opposite direction of the sun's trajectory being forbidden by ancient custom).

As the *chanting* dancers often worshipped naked, they preferred to hold their rites at night, in secluded moonlit places hidden from prying eyes. The main reason for dancing naked with their hair *falling* loose around the shoulders was to please the totem, son of the Mother Goddess, in whose power it was to grant whatever was being prayed for. Any new-born child or calf, victory in battle or communal good fortune was reason enough for celebration, in which female dancers would thank the totem for its generosity, sometimes by sacrificing an animal or a young girl.

Each of the ritual dances was specially choreographed for the subject being celebrated. The *dance steps* were no longer as primitive as they had been a million years earlier, and the instrumental accompaniment was richer and to a more complicated beat. The *screaming voices* of the choir were more emotionally charged.

The dancers kept pace with these developments by elaborating various combinations of *walking steps*. Instead of using one *simple step* at a time, as they had hitherto, they would now perhaps make *one long step* followed by *two short ones*, or *two long* followed by *three short,* then *pose,* and so on. The arms had more freedom of movement, to – instead of always *holding hands*, dancers now *circulated* with free arms, which were used to portray many subjects in symbolic form, such as agricultural activities, harvest products, the *flapping* wings of a bird, an ostrich's neck, a mammoth's trunk or a snake.

The gathering rites performed by women also gradually evolved over this million-year period, and all these originally very primitive ceremonies were considerably enhanced by the introduction of such quasi-artistic performing skills.

PHALLIC CULTS AND REPRODUCTIVE UNCERTAINTY

Fertility ritual dances were designed to secure the tribe's future by enlarging its population as much as possible, and many phallic sculptures and depictions have been found in caves and open areas. As mentioned earlier, tribal worship of the middle Palaeolithic era gradually began to focus on the sun (during patriarchy) rather than the moon (during the matriarchal period).

We have also established why females typically outnumbered males by almost two to one. This increasing problem forced new solutions to be sought. No matter how numerous or healthy the women, a lack of male providers and sexual partners put at risk the future of the family, the clan and indeed of the whole tribe.

This need for survival brought about radical social, religious and cultural changes. The main focus of fertility rites became the phallus in the centre of a hidden worship place. Naked women and girls danced and around this symbol of fecundity in the moonlight. The dancers *shook* their hips, *twirled* their breasts, *fell* down on their knees and imitated copulation by *rotating* their heads with free *flowing* hair, and *twisting* the whole body, in order to increase the sexual excitement of the males. Such groups of females *swinging* their bodies in phallic ritual dances are seen in petroglyphs and other graphics of the time. These same *movements* of *shaking* hips and shoulders later became the choreographic basis for belly dancing, one of the oldest examples of female plastic harmony.

Initiation Dance

SOCIAL AND SEXUAL EDUCATION

Initiation rites were by far the largest category of human socio-cultural activity. As countless tribes – entire races, even – had lost the struggle for survival during the first two to three million years of human evolution, healthy population growth was the major preoccupation of all social groups.

Each new generation was taught the rudiments of everyday life by Initiation rituals, whose most important object was the sexual introduction of youngsters to each other. For thousands of generations, these rituals were practically the sole means of educating the young in the local body motion vocabulary for mime and dance routines, choral performance and the use of primitive instruments. Children were accepted into these secret spiritual clubs from around ten years of age. Youngsters were expected first to watch adults perform and then practise what they observed.

From the early Palaeolithic era through the Stone Age, our ancestors gradually evolved larger, more complex motion vocabularies that provided the wider range of expression required for more sophisticated communication within and between clans and tribes. Over time, these new ways of using body motion turned into new forms of education and communication.

THE FIRST FEMALE DANCERS

At first, mainly women were involved, but eventually dance became accepted as the centrepiece of social, cultural and religious life by men, too. Dancing became as natural as eating, breathing or sleeping. Each tribe developed its own distinctive choreographic repertoire of ritual and secular dances – in effect, their own body **motion dialect**, which in itself formed the basis of later **ethnic styles.**

The dance vocabulary for initiation and domestic motion 'dictionaries' were very limited at first. Popular enthusiasm, however, combined with women's' natural spirituality, wrought a miracle of sorts. While husbands, sons and brothers were away hunting or practising with the shaman, the women worshipped through dance every night, developing new choreographies, working with the chorus or primitive orchestra to create a new repertoire. Unlikely as this non-stop activity may sound, sufficient pictorial evidence exists to corroborate women's' total involvement in this process.

PLASTIC MOTION INITITATION FOR JUVENILES

Like a primitive finishing school, aspiring teenage initiates were taught how to *stretch out* the stances, how to *walk* softly and smoothly, how to *balance* props on their heads, how to co-ordinate the *movements* of different parts of the body, how to read the plastic motion score, how to communicate with others, how to keep mental and physical self-control, how to respect their elders, and all the other 'hows' of the tribal life and custom.

Only after this exhaustively broad-ranging preparation (which could last anything up to a year) would the children be ready for initiation proper. The first subject was of course hunting, and girls as well as boys were taught the characteristics of the flora and fauna around them. They had the elements explained, and were coached how to imitate these characteristics mentally and physically. Although these activities may have been perceived on one level as amusing games by the initiates, they were in fact a quick and effective method of non-verbal physical, intellectual and spiritual education.

THE BODY COMMUNICATION SYLLABUS

The dictionaries of motion and behaviour for different living species were carefully systemised in separate programmes of performance courses, to be memorised by heart and passed on to the next generation. It was in the initiates' own interest to study and observe the natural subjects they were learning about in order to refine the quality of the imitations they were asked to perform. In this way, and by practising bodily communication within their families from an early age, they often succeeded in acquiring very large plastic vocabularies.

Because of the real physical dangers involved, actual hunting skills were not taught until the age of thirteen or fourteen. Easier methods of trapping and catching small prey were introduced earlier, and the youngsters would practice play-acting both sides of the hunt with imitation weapons. Being solo performances, these involved instant transformations from hunter to prey, thereby developing their acting and movement skills. The more they practised, the better they became, earning encouragement from their teachers and a belief in becoming spiritually closer to the totem.

While boys studied fishing and hunting, girls worked on their mimetic skills of *zigzagging* snakes, *flying* birds, *swimming* fish, and so on. The general competitive spirit eclipsed any resentment of the rigours and sheer hard work of the initiation process.

The curriculum of the first two years of initiation included a general mental and physical preparation in which the initiate learned basic tools for interpreting the plastic motion characteristics of the world around them, together with the history and customs of their tribe, totemic mythology and their local environment.

On reaching sexual maturity, male and female initiates embarked on a final year of lessons together, during which they were prepared for the intimate and important puberty initiation ritual described at the start of the previous chapter.

Secular Domestic Dance

Tribal populations were increasing from millennium to millennium, and so was the quality of their social and cultural life. Eventually, our ancestors developed an agricultural economy, and started domesticating and breeding cattle. They were constantly improving their techniques for hunting, fishing and food gathering. Tribal numbers grew so much that additional venues had to be found for their social activities.

The modern tool and masonry technologies industries of the later Pleistocene brought more secure shelters and progressive new techniques in hunting, fishing, arable cultivation and animal husbandry, providing tribe members with more food, shelters, weapons, clothing, tools and domestic accessories.

PUBLIC CELEBRATIONS AND FESTIVITIES

Any successful event, whether a hunt, a rich harvest, a birth or a wedding was grounds for celebration. These festivities were mainly based on secular dances, which eventually became public events run in the daytime in front of the entire tribe. This was another turning point in the cultural evolution of mankind – another giant step towards performing arts as we know them today.

As time went by, the central object of these rites became a big flowering tree as a symbol of the fertility of everything surrounding the community: its people, flora and fauna. More than that, the customary profile of ritual dances was revolutionised. Worshippers now faced the audience in a semi-circle, or with three to four *moving* circles of dancers *holding* hands, with the tree in the middle. Although staging the show mainly for the audience, the performers also did so for their own enjoyment.

NEW SPATIAL PATTERNS IN OPEN VENUES

The patterns from which these secular ceremonies were composed were rather limited: one or two **frontal lines, diagonal, semi-circle** and **zigzag**. However, being visible from three sides, the open performance space encouraged more varied choreography that allowed more scope for movement and more personal interpretations of myth, legend and artistic images.

The increasing prosperity of the clan brought with it a growing capacity for spiritual, emotional and physical experience, which somehow had to be expressed. The preferred way of doing so was through dance, as the most popular medium for social interaction.

As we have seen, this was no longer simply a matter of presenting imitations of living creatures. To perform ritual ceremonies dedicated to the new gods of water, fire and wind, the shaman had to develop more abstract plastic motions to indicate the natural characteristics of these elements to the audience.

From ancient graphics on stone, one can decipher the perpetual *waves* of storms at sea, or see strong winds *bending* and *shaking* grasses and bushes, or the flames of a forest fire *jumping* in every direction, all expressed artistically by *dancing* females, supported by the rhythms of primitive instruments and natural implements.

NUPTIAL CEREMONIES

The most popular subject of all for secular dancing was the wedding ceremony. From earliest childhood, human beings were fascinated by the courtship dances of the fauna that surrounded them – birds in particular, but also animals and insects. For this reason, many Wedding ceremonies began with imitations of these creatures by dancing couples. Dressed as ostriches, crocodiles, scorpions or whatever, these performing pairs demonstrated an idealised introduction to mating (sometimes even simulating copulation to propitiate the gods), using **abstract symbolic** body motions.

During the performance, the gods would be asked for their blessing on the fertility of the newlyweds. The tribal choir and acoustic ensemble would provide a musical background to supplement the performance.

After the courtship presentation, the bride and groom would appear, dressed specially for the occasionally to portray a pair of lovebirds, *dancing* in slow motion with their chests *pushed out* and *open* arms, *sliding* smoothly with small *steps* along a spiral path clockwise towards the centre of the circle, facing but not touching each other. At the very end, they put one cheek on the partner's shoulder, and *wave* their arms like wings, *opened* towards the back. This type of ceremony can still be seen today in Mexico, Sicily and Mongolia.

Following this lyrical introductory ceremony, the entire tribe joined in the festivities and showed their respect to the new family by bestowing various favours. One group of female dancers *balances* large plates or baskets full of fruit on their heads. Another group of male dancers *jumps* around with different items of food in their hands, such as chicken, rabbit or fish, making everybody laugh.

This would be followed by a group of flower children *running* with garlands in a zig-zag fashion, *holding* the floral tribute high above their heads. The purpose of this snake-like motion was to symbolise happiness for the newlyweds. At the end of their respective greeting dances, each group would place their gifts at the feet of the bride and the groom, each group and individual competing to show their wealth and generosity. Once the official part of the ceremony was over, everybody joined in the dancing around an open fire. These were the origins of the folk/social dance genres we know today.

The motion styles and lexicon of these dances differed from clan to clan. To establish which clan an individual belonged to, it was customary to ask what they were dancing; in other words, dance had become a recognised way of expressing personal and social identity to other communities.

Functional Mimetic Dance

CULTURAL ANTHROPOLOGY

As any modern cultural anthropologists will admit, the evolution of the performing and visual arts still presents us with many unknowns. There remain unexplained gaps and unanswered questions relating to prehistoric systems of communication, education and cultural continuity.

How did our ancestors, millions of years ago, communicate and perform totemic ritual pantomimes without spoken language? Who taught them such advanced mime and dancing routines and techniques of artistic presentation? By which secret methods and technologies have ancient visual and performing arts been preserved so as to survive the ages?

In answer, we can at least deduce that the communication codes of early hominids were similar to those of any other animal species: expressive motion, rudimentary cries, rhythmic sounds produced by using parts of the body and artificial tools, and the use of colour, light and smell. And that early hominids learned everything they knew from careful observation of other species and the world around them.

The only secret in preserving aspects of visual and performing arts was through cultural heredity based on the body language which was passed on from generation to generation.

In other words, the development of the entire animal world from insects to humans follows the same evolutionary principles inherent in all nature. Cultural anthropology is therefore based on our forebears' adaptation instinct.

The main subjects of the earliest spiritual and cultural activity were the totemic rituals and mythologies already described, and much research has been devoted to mythology as the historical and philosophical foundation of humanity.

The major themes of ritual mythical pantomime on any sacred subject were hunting, fighting, mourning and totemic worship. All these **syncretic** performances were produced by the shaman using mimicry, dance, song and percussion performed by semi-professional amateurs.

THE FUNCTIONAL DANCE GENRE

This multi-syllabus genre is the oldest of all ritual dance forms. At the beginning of this chapter we described primitive dance as having a functional role in **syncretic** mythical pantomimes, along with *singing* and *playing* instruments. It was a passive function in that it was used by the shaman only to set the scene or to demonstrate various characteristics of the lead roles, which were performed as solos, duets or trios. As the **active** elements, these individuals use the same expressive tools of movement, voice and instruments, but perform together in a way that involves the mind, spirit and body of the performer.

Functional dance carries the underlying dramatic narrative of the myth, in support of the leading performers who bring the drama to its climax or conclusion. Any deviation from the accepted standards by the dancer could easily mislead the audience into losing the thread of the fable, in contravention of the sacred rules governing performance.

In functional dance, any participant or group scene was designed by the shaman for the particular mythical subject as an integral element of the syncretic performance. It was absolutely forbidden to change or to delete anything, for any reason, without the shaman's permission. He was the only one who could make corrections or improvements, perhaps by inserting a more advanced solo or a more complicated duet. To understand the full dramatic and multilingual characteristics of the functional genre, it helps first to consider the anatomy of the performers concerned.

PLASTIC ANATOMY

Any study of ancient anthropological illustrations reveals the astonishing extent to which our anatomy has changed – it is easy to forget the massive physiological and neural transformation that has taken place over the last 30 million years. From the advent of Homo Erectus 3 million years ago, the body gradually developed its unique musculo-skeletal structure, with four *balanced* and *coordinated* extremities, flexible vertebrae and complex movement capabilities. Eventually, it evolved into the versatile instrument for plastic communication and cultural performance of modern Homo Sapiens.

Our ancestors' tough way of life obviously made them physically very strong and hardy, but it was the use of the body as language which did the rest. To communicate using plastic capabilities requires more than physical strength and flexibility. All meaningful gestures and postures must be clear and emphatic if they are to be read and responded to correctly. Any mistake in this respect could have disastrous consequences for the whole tribe. Like the voice or a drum, the plastic anatomy of our ancestors had to be perfected as an instrument for the language of physical motion and movement.

These complex plastic capabilities did not of course appear overnight, but over millions of years. Though many of the incredible cultural monuments of our prehistory all over the world may date back perhaps 70,000 years, they are in fact the end product of some 700,000 years or more of previous evolution.

Palaeolithic man increased his plastic motion capabilities because the physically developed body allows high standards of performance in both technique and presentation. To take part in totemic pantomime dance, with its large syllabus of *high jumps, turns, lifts* and *acrobatic tricks*, a strong and flexible body was required, dexterous, athletic in form, well balanced and possessed of considerable stamina. There can be no doubt that these performers were called upon to display remarkable control of muscular tension, physical power and co-ordination. Without these facilities, they would never had been able to dance the long hunting and fighting sequences of mythical pantomime. Only an endless regime of regular practice and constant self-control kept their bodies in perfect condition for both communication and ritual performance.

TOTEMYTHIC SCENARIO

By 'scenario', we mean a pre-prepared, set programme for performing a story or a fable for theatrical presentation. Although it may seem an over-ambitious term to use of the time before spoken language, the shamans of the Palaeolithic era did indeed imprint mythical fables (and therefore the pantomime 'scores') on murals or petroglyphs. The fact that the code for precisely deciphering these 'scores' has yet to be discovered reflects more on our own ignorance than that of our ancestors who inscribed them there.

Totemythic scenarios were composed and designed as syncretic performances for five media: song, dance, mime, instrumental accompaniment and design. Creatively speaking, those preparing such scenarios had to bear certain rules and conditions in mind. Each scenario had to focus on one clear idea or theme – about the history of the tribe, for example, or the conflict between two opposing totems, or the journey of the deceased into the underworld, or the war between sacred birds and reptiles.

The success or failure of a rite pantomime depended on how well the shaman visualised its scenario. What kind of a moral message does he want to pass on to the audience? Which interacting images convey this **message**, and which dancers represent these functional **images**? What part of the syncretic performance is presented by the female chorus? Which dramatic background sounds are played by the **instrumentalists**? What **costumes**, masks and props are produced, and how are they used to greatest effect?

Generally speaking, after assessing the central theme and the resources available for its performance, the shaman began to visualise the dramatic part of the scenario – the oppositions between the various characters and groups. Although both counterparts had to be more or less equally balanced, the conflict between darkness and light always had a **positive outcome**. As the backbone of the creative process, the **central** sacred theme held the entire dramatic composition in constant focus by means of the functional images being acted out. Every component of mythical rite pantomime functioned either in support of or in opposition to the main moral idea, as embodied in the superior forces at its heart.

The shaman knew how to impress his audience – he could read their minds as well as the minds of his performers. He used the dramatic score to lead them in the spiritual and psychological direction required. He could accurately predict the precise audience reaction to any turn in the scenario, and such intriguing patterns and tricks were often used.

The mythical scenario being acted out under the aegis of higher forces could drive the audience into a hysterical trance states – it could even result in violently aggressive mass behaviour of the type we have witnessed in recent history.

Because of the individual circumstances of each occasion, funerary pantomime was only a small part of a long and mostly improvised ceremony which, as we saw earlier, included mourning of the deceased and celebrating his or her entry into the spirit world. The ritual pantomime itself was usually performed during the last night of the ceremony as a whole.

The improvisation had no scenario prepared in advance, except for certain dramatic actions specially devised during a week of rehearsals in the form of variations on a basic religious template. Instead of a composed scenario, there was a programme of various combats and *peripetias* depicting ways for the deceased/shaman to see his totem by heroically overcoming a series of monsters, demons and other obstacles. By the late Palaeolithic, funerary pantomime had developed into a mass syncretic performance.

POLYVALENT PLASTIC IMAGERY

The basic dictionaries of body motion were more or less established by Palaeolithic times, having been gradually built up over millennia of observation and practice. The resulting system can be divided into three main categories:

a) The motion **vocabulary** for basic everyday domestic communication.
b) Miming natural **characteristics.**
c) **Plastic instrument**s for performance.

Each of these contained several parts according to the subject:
Vocabulary: motion signs for hunt, battle, funeral; food-gathering, cattle-breeding, harvest; puberty, fecundity, birth; domestic, family, initiation – all social activities.
Characteristics: body gestures for fauna, flora, the elements, natural phenomena, and facial expressions of grief, anger, disdain, guilt, surprise, disgust, fear, shame, horror, happiness and so on.
Plastic instruments: head, face, neck, shoulders, arms, hands, fingers, torso, belly, breasts, hips, legs and feet.

In turn, these can be subdivided into smaller elements:

Hunt: masks, costumes, weapons; battle skills; tracking, catching and killing; skinning, butchering and preserving.

Fauna: mammals, birds, reptiles, fish, amphibians, insects, spiders.

Head: eyes, nose, ears; mouth, lips, teeth; cheek, forehead, chin, hair, beard, moustache, eyelashes and eyebrows.

Right from the start, the shaman cast mature dancers to perform the main dramatic narrative of the scenario using the plastic motion dictionaries of mimetic *gestures, postures* and leg *movements* based on the elements listed above.

All other solo and group performers supported this narrative by using the dance *steps* and *sequences* of the 'score' to illustrate the conflicts and intrigues of the drama as it unfolded. They also represented anthropomorphised creatures and other spiritual images using a mixture of natural body motion and mimetic dance vocabularies.

Arm motions and gestures

Apart from minor variations, the techniques for realistically imitating living creatures were similar for all tribes. The spiritual image of an eagle or a snake was conveyed using similar motions corresponding to the nature of the animal. As mentioned in the previous chapter, each tribe had its own style of dance execution, determined by local customs and environment and the tribal totem.

Functional dance vocabulary included a large variety of *port de bras,* both with and without props – a mixture of traditional *gestures* and mimetic *motion* personifying the snake, the bird or a flame. However, the equally functionally important *port de bras* of a female chorus was expressed by motion patterns of the arms and hands, choreographed especially to underline the plastic score of the leading mime-dancers, or to add expressiveness at moments of heightened drama. The hands and arms were the main plastic tools in these fragments, for presenting the fable and for leading performers and audience through the twists and turns of the drama.

Leg movements and steps

Legs are the dancer's main motion instruments. In functional dance, each and every motion has a meaning and plays a part, directly or indirectly, in the dramatic narrative. Through many generations, shamans carefully selected certain *steps* and *movements* to characterise each protagonist, and dramatic sequences were also composed for duets, trios and groups.

In time, the plastic image of each lead performer or acting group evolved into a fixed **choreographic portrait** of traditional mythical images. Audiences had no problem in immediately recognising familiar motion sequences, even when presented by unfamiliar performers. In other words, the totem and his followers always had a major **motion leitmotif** in the same choreographic style, with various personal intonations and manners. Its dramatic counterpart naturally had a contrary plastic portrait, with contrasting *steps* and *movements*. With such straightforward and clearly different characteristics, audience confusion between the two was almost impossible.

Early anthropologists and missionaries describe the ritual performances of African bushmen, Australian aborigines or the Tunguses of Eastern Siberia as being rather advanced in their execution. To the great surprise of these travellers, these 'primitive' peoples had ensembles that demonstrated exceptional acting and singing abilities, along with sophisticated techniques of mime and of dance whereby extremely difficult sequences were faultlessly executed. Such high standards of plastic body motion, mimesis and rhythmic discipline could only be the result of systematic dance education, regular rehearsals, long practical experience, complete self-control and profound spirituality.

As with the mimetic plastic dictionary mentioned above, the shaman and his assistants used their observations of other creatures to select and systemise all *steps* and *movements* according to their kinaesthetic characteristics, scope of body motion, pattern, amplitude, and so on.

KINETIC DICTIONARY OF DANCE LOCOMOTION

Main elements
Steps: regular, on the toes, *crouched, kneeling, posing, stamping ...*
Running: regular, on the toes, *kicking; hopping, jumping* forward ...
Dancing: elements and sequences; by one leg, two legs together and in succession.
Jumps: on one leg, on both, from one to the other, from one to both from both to one.
Turns: on one leg, on both in succession; straight up, on the toes, *crouching, squatting, hopping*, etc.

Spatial and motion conditions for each *movement*:
Regular step: short, medium, long, slow, semi-fast, forwards, backwards, sideways; *sliding, kicking, marching, dragging.*
Running step: short-long, high-low, quick-slow, light-heavy, forwards-backwards, with *turns*
Dancing elements: on the spot/straight up, on the toes, crouching; towards, back, sideways; travelling – forwards, backwards, from side to side, with *turns*; petit/ grand, heavy/light; quick/slow, 'a terre en l'air'.
Hops on one leg: low, medium, high; on a spot, travelling in any direction, with *turns*; on the same leg or in succession; with arms, props or special patterns.
Turns on one leg: clockwise, counter clockwise; straight up, *crouching*; flat footed, on the toes, on the heel; on the spot or *travelling* forward, sideways, in a circle; outside or inside of the working leg; with or without props.

Each movement could have mixed elements and a variety of tempos and rhythmical patterns, kinaesthetic potential, personal interpretation and performing styles.

Dance *movements* and *sequences* are the second major choreographic text of mythical pantomime after mimetic plastic motion. Both of these expressions of the functional genre complement each other in the presentation of the mythical subject and its sacred images.

DANCING IN TIME AND SPACE

Like any other performing art, the dance of mythical pantomime is constrained by time and space. However, mime-dancers could to some extent control these conditions in ways that the creatures they imitated could not. The meaning of *grimaces, gestures* and other motions can vary according to tempo. The same applies to *travelling* motion; the shape, size and height of the space being used naturally dictated certain choreographic patterns to the shaman. It is difficult to analyse constraints of time and space separately, as they are so closely interrelated in performance.

- With a march in tempo andante, long *steps* are preferable (unless executed on the spot).
- With the tempo moderate waltz measure, lower levels of rustic style are usually used – 'pas de balancé', 'pas de basque'. But tempo allegro allows big *jumps* and *turns*, crossing large spaces (in a rustic manner).
- With tempo allegro vivace, *short pulsing beats, tiny steps* or *small jumps* are used, depending on the time signature – and in more limited space, the same step on the spot.

- Slow tempos usually require less space for interaction than the fast. In any repetitive motion, increasing the tempo always reduces the amplitude of legs and arm *movements* (and therefore the amount of space used).

With other motions, however, any increase in tempo can create a stronger momentum that has to be calculated against the available space. Constant *fast running* in a circle requires extra space to accommodate the centrifugal force that pushes the dancers outwards from the centre.

The characteristics of movement and music have a lot in common. The mystical sound of **bowstrings** can lead worshipping females in slow motion to the somatic agony of the trance that follows.

The lyrical voice of the **flute** makes dancers *move* slowly and smoothly, with motions in legato, with graceful '*port de bras*' in tempo adagio or largo.

Drumming patterns in staccato rhythm can have a powerful effect, and induce trance states which in War dances could end in death. Rhythm plays a vital part in dance, and drum patterns provided the dramatic score for solo monologues. Sequences of various rhythmic patterns and changes of tempo provided the acoustic framework for the spiritual and plastic image.

The dialogue between **pan pipe** and **drum** provides an impressive soundtrack for the wedding duet of *dancing* and *miming* pigeons, for example. Women's 'snake' *port-de-bras* and the men's 'bison' *stamping* feet created a polyphonic effect, either *canonical* or **contrapuntal,** with *crescendo* or *diminuendo* dynamics.

The sound of primitive instruments was the spiritual and dramatic foundation of mythical pantomimes, particularly the functional mime-dances. Syncretic performance stimulated the development of each performer in all artistic directions: mime, dance, spirituality, singing, playing instruments, making costumes, masks and props. All of these were involved in the creation of the artistic image.

More than any other genre, functional dance requires a proper costume for each character of the mythical pantomime. In effect, costume was the spiritual and artistic completion of the image and fable being performed.

THE SPIRITUAL FOUNDATION OF DANCE

Mythology is based on human experience. In any part of the world, whatever the different totems, customs or environment, our ancestors created similar spiritual representations of living creatures, plants and the elements in their ritual performances.

The mythical repertoire therefore contains **standard subjects** illustrated by almost identical imaginary monsters with human characteristics: in different masks, costumes and sets; with various vocal and instrumental accompaniments; in diverse personal performing styles; and using contrasting choreographic texts featuring dramatised conflicts between anthropomorphised creatures.

The **acting abilities** dancers all over the world were honed in this way over many generations using similar principles and methods of performance and training. The psycho-physical foundation of mind and body was the same, with identical compositional styles, morality, self-awareness and artistic imagination.

If the performers of ritual pantomimes were indeed as good as the first western observers purported them to be, they must have had proper training and widespread experience. A good actor has to know much more than the basics which can be studied as a youth; the mind and his body has to be honed into a performing instrument sophisticated enough to express two or more themes simultaneously.

Early performers had the advantage of being able to transform themselves instantly into the image concerned, both spiritually and psychologically. For us today, this remarkable ability borders on miraculous; it allowed the mime-dancer to feel and play his dramatic role better, and it gave the audience the immense satisfaction of experiencing a complete, in-depth portrayal. This is exactly what happened to the pioneer anthropologists centuries ago when they saw these sacred ceremonies before the advent of mass tourism.

DRAMATIC INTERACTION

The dramatic **scenario** of any mythic pantomime was based on a central conflict. The pattern of interaction between individual or group counterparts was increased by progressive zigzags and up-down-ups to the climax of the drama. The shaman/ choreographer usually presented each opposing pair or group in a gradually escalating intensification by progressively introducing more complicated dance sequences and demonstrations of fighting skill. The performers' counter-moves were executed as a highly sophisticated double-motion action, with as yet primitive weapons or props. Opponents were not allowed to *touch* each other with weapons – touching was only permitted in hand-to-hand wrestling. No women danced in pantomimes at this time.

The mythical confrontation usually happened between a man and an anthropomorphised creature, or between two opposing totems. These conflicts were traditionally executed as **dancing duels** in three main phases:

a) **Self introduction**, in which the opponents individually demonstrate their physical abilities, fighting skills, bravery and spiritual power.

b) **Battle routines** and dance sequences using intimate or close combat, *moving* around each other. Also *lifts, mimetic counter-strikes, counter-offensive motions,* and so on.

c) **Celebrating victory** on defeating the opponent – a triumphal dance variation, with elements of combat motion.

Group fights normally featured opposing pairs of combatants fighting/ dancing under basically the same conditions as a single pair, as described above. There were also various combinations of one against two, two against three and so on, with corresponding adjusted double or triple combat motions and dance routines.

As with mime-acting performances (*see Chapter III*), dance duels in mythic rituals also required special abilities:

- a **synthesis** of dance and fight techniques with mimetic motion.
- complete **self-control** and constant awareness of the opponent's possible moves (based on reading his mind-set).
- strategic **changes of tempo** and rhythm to confuse the enemy.
- close combat attacks in **slow motion** for the benefit of the audience.
- **fast reactions** for defence and immediate counter-offence.
- exaggerated **amplitude** of presentation for better visual clarity.

The conditions of group combat differ from those for single opponents:
- everyone involved has to follow the overall action and adjust their *moves* to the requirements of the group.

- small Groups of three to four fighters execute the same dance sequences in unison, with cumulative spiritual power, but in individually varied **personal** ways.
- group members have to feel permanently in spiritual and emotional **contact** with each other.
- concentration has to be divided in both directions (towards the opponent as well as their own group).

Our ancestors developed their performing abilities mainly through mythical pantomimes. Mythology was their university, the crucible in which the human qualities and characteristics we possess today were first forged.

200,00–300,000 years ago, there was of course no Stanislavski or Noverr to give instruction in dance-mime or acting-dance, just as there was no-one 300–400 million years ago to teach mammals, birds, reptiles and insects how to conduct courtship dances. The development of body motion as a language was the result of the natural process of selective evolution.

The same thing happened to primates, who first learned primitive courtship *moves* and *mimes* from surrounding creatures. As the millennia passed, they gradually refined their mimetic and dancing techniques during their daily rituals. The genetic heritage of our ancestors kept developing, and they empirically formalised their rudimentary motions without the need for verbal text.

Hominids continuously selected and systemised motions suitable and for their plastic facility, committing them at first to memory, then to physical inscriptions on stone. Any newly discovered motion was tried out exhaustively by incorporating it into their everyday plastic motion vocabulary. Their creative process was one of **selection, testing** and **adjustment** – the experimental method that stimulated the development of *mimicking, gestures, poses* and *movements* into a common body motion vocabulary for the future Homo Sapiens.

On the evidence available today, it is hard to imagine a different genesis and developmental path for mime and dance.

Abstraction in ritual choreography

SPIRITUALITY

The late Palaeolithic saw the beginning of a new era in socio-cultural evolution. As we mentioned in the previous chapter, the development of hunting and animal husbandry skills gradually persuaded our ancestors to change their spiritual outlook on their totemic connection with the animal world.

Even subconsciously, a degree of uncertainty and confusion arose in the mind of early hominids about their totemic beliefs, respected and powerful though these still were. However, everyday dealings with domestic and wild animals gradually led our forefathers to the common sense conclusion that they were mentally and physically superior to other living creatures, rather than their equals.

While they still depended religiously on the totem's patronage, increasing knowledge of cosmology and a new belief in a universal deity were slowly and irreversibly influencing the tribes' social and spiritual life. They turned their hopes and prayers towards the elements and the planets, and the old religious institutions and customs gradually came under review.

Visual and vocal depictions of domestic objects, local animals and natural phenomena inevitably led our ancestors to a new philosophical conclusion. If everything and everybody is but a fraction of an infinitely vast universe, all its component parts must somehow be cosmically interconnected. Simplistic as this may sound, it must be remembered that we are talking about nonverbal languages here.

BODY MOVEMENTS

The shaman had once more to find a new plastic and sonic alphabet which could be built into a motion vocabulary of progressive *sequences, cries* and *chants* that would be flexible enough for the sociocultural activities of the time. There seemed to be no better solution than to create an entirely new lexicon for the *mimes, gestures, postures* and *onomatopoeic sounds* already in use for everyday spiritual and social activities.

To demonstrate the new cosmology, shamans created new plastic and sonic signs to indicate each part of the universe. Constellations were designated by visual images from the living environment; new sounds were developed to represent comets, fire, thunder and other natural phenomena.

Learning to communicate with these new plastic and sonic vocabularies was no easy task. However, the major expressive tool for any choreography remained the *rotation* of the buttocks and hips. The female body became a **fetish**, a universal symbol, in sacred or domestic, lyrical or dramatic performances, as well as demonstration of luck and success in other subjects. During the long Palaeolithic era, the image of woman dominated practically every aspect of secular and spiritual life.

Obviously, this spiritual development also affected cultural life. On many Palaeolithic murals and petroglyphs, strange signs such as goat horns, snake's heads, scorpion claws, raven's beaks, bull's eyes, branches, twigs, flowers and leaves are seen around the main object. Masks, amulets and body decorations also bear similar designs.

ABSTRACT COMPOSITION

By **abstract** choreography, we mean a dance composition in which most of the body motions and decorations have a **quintessential** semantic significance. Early hominids found it confusing and difficult to personify the elements, planets and other natural phenomena in abstract ways. Developing sufficiently impressive techniques of spatial communication to embody spiritual contact with these new forces was an enormous imaginative feat for the shamans and witches of the time.

The abstract spiritual vision of cosmic subjects and their representation through movement required a hitherto unique creative approach, and no doubt took hundred millennia to evolve the suitable plastic motions of the kind seen on frescoes of groups of female worshippers performing a rainbow dance or allegorical combats between Jupiter and Mars.

Performers of abstract dance had no physical models to follow, such as images on rock, masks or sacred objects. The only tools available to them for spiritual communication were their minds and bodies – plastic motion, spatial patterns and inner substance. Only by their own personal character and physical abilities could these dancers express actions and feelings. The beauty of the human body and its *harmony of movement, rhythm and expression*, was enough to make any deity feel proud of the most superb creation of all.

Representing the **multiple** imagery of their natural surroundings in abstract ways was a major challenge for our ancestors. After the hard daily struggle to survival, they studied the heavens during the long evenings, contemplating their connection to the mysteries of the cosmos. With the limited intelligence at their disposal, they tried to work out all these strange phenomena and the ways in which these new gods could help them survive and protect their environment.

FEMALE DANCERS

Women doing high *jumps* are never shown in the paintings or petroglyphs of the time. They are often shown *walking* and, very occasionally, *running* during rituals. A soft, sliding *'pas-allé'* predominates, when *carrying* sacred objects or executing various *'port-de-bras'* in harmony with what has been termed **eukinetics**.

There are several possible reasons for this:

a) During nocturnal ceremonies, we know that female worshippers usually performed naked in order to be more sexually attractive to the totem, and now also the new gods. The naked body, with loosely falling hair, gave dancers more **freedom of movement** and opened more opportunities to impress the deities in whatever form with new plastic capabilities in order to solicit special consideration and favours.

b) The new **symbolic abstract** gestures and postures became the origin of the unique aesthetic culture that appeared much later. The spirituality inherent in woman's reproductive role because of the very nature of her body gave our ancestors enormous psychological and physical support in all their fights for survival. Bearing in mind the infinite symbolic significance of the Mother Goddess image for the tribe, this idealisation may also have stimulated the creation female figurines and portraits by tribal craftsmen.

c) Although female dancers still executed hard *stamps* and small *jumps*, there was a clear predisposition towards grace, sentiment, spirituality and motherhood. Symbolising peace, reproduction and stability, the image of the Mother Goddess in body motion gradually crystallised during the millennia of anatomical evolution. This was in contrast to the males, with the totem 'above', who for most of the time was involved in conflict and wars. Although an apparently natural balance, the woman's role in socio-cultural evolution during these earlier stages is arguably more positive and productive for future generations.

d) Worshipping mothers could not physically do big *jumps*, as their hands were occupied in supporting their *swinging* breasts. They therefore preferred to *walk* in a dance, *bending their knees smoothly* in a *sliding/swimming* motion in order to keep their arms free and to minimise any discomfort to the breast. An exception to this was the *rotation* of the breasts sometimes used as a plastic expression of femininity and reproduction.

e) Physiologically too, women were often incapable of *jumping high* or executing *sharp contractions* because of menstruation and during pregnancy or nursing. Such parts in ritual dance were usually performed by unmarried women or teenage girls.

Port-de-bras

From careful observation of prehistoric miniatures on decorated domestic objects, it is possible to approximate body motions, gestures and posturing patterns – right from the most primitive forms to the relatively advanced abstract choreography of sacred pantomime.

Time and again, a leitmotif emerges of female arms in various *'port de bras'* addressed to the stars, either individually or in a chain of *joined hands*, mostly in an upward motion that expresses the spiritual dialogue with higher forces. Ritual accessories symbolising animal, plant or domestic subjects are sometimes *held* in the hands.

Petroglyphic notation also shows women dancing with vessels on their shoulders, imploring the gods to send much-needed water, or *walking heavily holding* a tusk in front, praying for a successful hunt, and so on.

In earlier pictures, dancers are seen *moving* their arms in unison, in mono-kinaesthetic mode; later on, approaching the Neolithic era, female worshippers are seen at night rituals individually performing much more sophisticated *'port-de-bras'*, with or without props, in a poly-kinaesthetic and contrapuntal choreography involving the entire body: *diving* in front, *arching* back, *bending* laterally, *swinging* and *rotating*.

SPATIAL PATTERNS AND PROXIMITY

According to some scholars, most mimetic dances looked similar apart from the number of performers involved and their body decorations. This is not so. This confusion is understandable, when most archaeological illustrations show worshippers moving clockwise in circles.

The **circle** was then and remains now the primary and most popular spatial pattern for performance. When our ancestors first socialised around an open fire or a carcass, they naturally placed themselves around the centre facing inwards. Human beings have retained this preference ever since, whether worshipping, celebrating or entertaining. Clockwise, as we know, follows the sun's apparent trajectory, indicating continuity with the universe. Being essentially circular by nature, the cycles of day and night, climate, harvest, reproduction, love, life and death are all manifestations of the cosmic circle of existence.

The spiritual power of the circle had no limitations. A security circle would be drawn, built or grown around an object to be protected: the family dwelling, source of drinking water, herds, food stores, sacred places or whatever.

The sun also personified successful hunting. Predators circle their prey. Eagle circle above before they attack. Herds of several grazing species often defend their offspring by forming a protective circle. The symbolism also extends to the lunar cycle, with nocturnal rituals using the circle as a sacred symbol of hope and fortune. The moon was considered the patron of puberty, marriage, fecundity, pregnancy, birth and the new-born, as well as the family and the tribe. The circle had a magic influence on the lives of our distant ancestors in many ways.

The **zigzag** or **labyrinth** other important and spiritually popular spatial pattern. Unlike the smooth and peaceful form of the circle, the labyrinth or maze has sudden twists and turns, surprises, dead ends and other intriguing and dramatic characteristics. The geometrically sharp and convoluted patterns of the Labyrinth usually represent **negative** forces. Spiritually, they counteract the mystic circle, balancing the perpetual conflict between light and dark.

The **positive** meaning of a zigzag line lies in is its personification of the snake image, as described earlier. labyrinth patterns were also used by the shaman during mythic and funerary pantomimes to illustrate the twisted path of the life being mourned.

Finally, the confusing intricacy of labyrinthine passages is analogous to the restless human mind, ever striking out into new and unknown directions. Dissatisfied with the status quo, it perpetually searches for something different – and often ends in a blind alley.

The **straight** line of dancers is the **neutral** spatial pattern. Falling between the spiritual functions of the circle and the labyrinth, it was used less frequently than these two in performance – an open line of worshippers easily loses the performing focus of a magic action, and with it, the power of a sacred ceremony.

This comparative lack of focus would reduce ritual dance to secular domestic performance, except in the case of war ceremonies involving two lines confronting each other (as in the duels already mentioned between the goddesses of water and fire). In these cases, however, both lines of dancers are placed **sagittally**, moving forwards and backwards. All their physical and spiritual attention is concentrated towards opposition.

A vast range of **spatial patterns** exists in infinite combinations, such as *double* or *multiple* separate circles, zigzagging in circles or straight lines, big diagonals, two angled small diagonals, semi-circles or small attached arches, and moving around the central axis, in line or across.

The expressive use of pattern in abstract choreography developed to a very high level between the Palaeolithic to Neolithic eras. Populations were growing very fast, and therefore the need for large spaces in which to perform sacred ceremonies and accommodate hundreds of worshippers.

New spatial proximities were therefore required for **mass** ritual performance. A simple *promenade* with free or *joined* hands using an advanced pattern was clearly more effective than complicated *steps* in one gigantic circle. The beat and plastic score were easier to follow, the performers' attention better focussed in the direction of the idol or leading shaman, and the choreographic accuracy of each performer was easier to control.

Representing these complex proximity patterns of simultaneously moving circles and zigzags with chorus lines and multiple motions was beyond the pictorial powers of the muralists, painters and carvers of the time. All attempts made to draw such ceremonies that have reached us through the ages seem to us beautiful but deeply enigmatic. Nevertheless, we have sufficient archaeological evidence to prove the existence of mass religious rites held in large plains during the later Neolithic period.

Inter-tribal communication

Neighbouring tribes occasionally gathered for social and cultural events, and to trade young females, tools, calves and decorated objects. Competitions were also held in *singing, dancing, combat* and other skills. During these week-long annual festivals, thanks would be given for the harvest, newly born cattle, peace, health and other blessings.

These were friendly competitions designed to consolidate an often fragile peace and to develop inter-tribal links. All tribe members performed simultaneously within their own prescribed zones. With the musicians, singers and dancers all taking turns, the performance was continuous – a colourful **kaleidoscope** of sound and movement. Dozens of circles were probably involved, all moving clockwise at different speeds in a magnificent mass spiritual celebration of the universe.

Each participating group performed its own local repertoire of mimetic dances based on their traditional choreographic vocabulary, rhythmic patterns and dialect of rudimentary cries. Performers wore masks with symbolic designs of the sacred images familiar to all tribes.

When performed consecutively, these group ritual performances with their multitude of characters and spiritual plastic images formed part of spectacularly impressive mass secular events. Performed simultaneously, however, with no common theme, style or semantic connection, the result was inevitably chaotic and confusing.

Inter-tribal communication nevertheless stimulated our ancestors' general social evolution. Not only did these regular cultural exchanges gradually give rise to a more aesthetically-driven approach to performing and visual arts, but they also led to the creation of larger united communities. In this way, these friendly and peaceful events laid the foundations of the highly developed civilisations of the future.

SUMMARY

There can be no doubt that our ancestors began to experience **aesthetic** pleasure in the enjoyment of nature in motion while watching the beauty of *moving* dancers, *running* antelopes and *flying* birds – not just in terms of the physiology of their everyday behaviour, but in a harmonised vision of spirit, plasticity and grace. The philosophical understanding of multi-faceted images of the universe as personified in dance was also the foundation of the prehistoric visual arts aesthetic.

Although it can be argued that abstraction has no material subject, this is not exactly the case with the performing arts, where presentations are based on constant physical *movement* rather than a fixed image. Abstraction in audio-visual performance stimulated human evolution by introducing complex new sonic and plastic vocabularies for communication, education, recreation and worship. In terms of cultural anthropology, abstract syncretic mime-dance was in some ways the true forerunner of modern orchestral opera-ballet theatre productions.

Composition styles of ancient dance

'Composition' has two main meanings in the visual and performing arts: the creative process of an artistic production, or the final result of this process, i.e., "the composition of this music took months" (process) as opposed to "this mural is a well-balanced composition" (result).

The visual arts are ruled by **spatial** factors; the vocal and instrumental arts, by **timing**. By contrast, mime, dance and the other arts of body motion are subject to both temporal and spatial factors.

All creative compositions fall into various distinctive categories (such as forms, genres and styles), which are the foundation of any dramatic, musical, pictorial or plastic expression.

During the earliest stage of cultural evolution there was only the primitive form of a **round** ritual dance in a **group**. Later came hunting **solos** and **duets**. Then new formations of acting choristers, warriors, dancers in syncretic presentations or in holy **procession** emerged in improvised compositions for funerary ceremonies.

In dance composition, the **form** determines the **scope of action** (extract or miniature, for example) and the arrangement of performers (solo, duet, trio, quartet and so on). **Genre** characteristics appeared mainly in totemic rite pantomimes, together with the first mythological fables and characters.

The traditional genres of mythical pantomime were: **epic, dramatic, lyrical, comic, tragic, mystical** and **grotesque**. Each performing art acquired its own genre characteristics in addition to its timing and spatial considerations. For mime and dance, these included **masked, hunting, totemic, imagistic, wrestling, functional** and so on.

The relentless progress of cultural evolution eventually forced the shaman to look for new expressive possibilities in mythical pantomime, in which the early **realistic** style of all ritual performances was at least in part gradually replaced by **artistic** styles of creation and presentation. The later Palaeolithic era brought even more progressive spiritual thinking and a more abstract perception of the surrounding environment, thereby heralding the introduction of **symbolism** in the performing and visual arts.

REALISTIC STYLE

This includes performances based on:
- Exact mimicry of **instinctive** mental and physiological reactions.
- Characteristics of **natural** behaviours and expressions.
- **Premeditated** action and its preparation.

A: Exact mimicry
Consider the following scene: animals are *grazing* peacefully, with no sign of any predators. Suddenly, the noise of a falling coconut hitting the ground *freezes* all action. The animals respond by the following motions: they *stop chewing, glance* in the direction of the noise, *prick up* their ears, move their eyes in all directions in search of danger, *flex* their leg muscles and *bend* their knees ready to flee. Discovering no threat, the animals return to their former peaceful state.

In terms of plastic motion, this translates into three phases of expression. First, the animals *walk* around looking for food, head and shoulders *twisting*, both eyes *moving* simultaneously in the same directions, *chewing* mechanically while at the same time smelling by *moving* their nostrils and listening by *pricking up* their ears. In addition, they occasionally *move* their head and tail to chase away biting flies, or to get rid of other annoying insect parasites by *kicking* their legs or *shuddering* their skin. While this is going on, they are constantly *turning* to all sides to check on the whereabouts of a calf or the rest of the herd. Anything up to a dozen of these natural motion sequences is included in this first part of the episode.

The reactions to the sudden **distracting** noise in the *second* part of this episode are described above. In the *third* phase, upon establishing the false alarm, the animals *return* to the peaceful condition in which they began, with possible adjustments reflecting inner psychological and physiological tension rather than any outward expression of being on guard and ready for self-defence – a state of mental and physical readiness for immediate self-preservation.

This realistic style replicates the physical characteristics of individuals of the same species, but of different sex, age and social rank, as these factors correspond to different types of reaction and instinctive behaviour.

Although the natural body motion of mammals is often aggressively opposed by others of the same sex within the herd hierarchy, this nevertheless represents typical normal behaviour for the species in question. Aside from occasional natural conflicts, the members of any group always act in unison with a common attitude when grazing, travelling, looking after their young or defending themselves against predators.

B: **Natural behaviours**

Of special interest in this category is the courtship motion vocabulary. Though much speculation has been published on this subject, it appears that some authors did not have sufficient time or information with which to conduct detailed research.

The subject of this dancing duet is sexual foreplay, as instinctive *as eating, sleeping, hunting* and so on. The continuation of the species is of course the main stimulus of sexual activity. What follows are actual examples, as can be seen in wildlife films and TV programmes as well as in formal scientific accounts.

- A cock bird woos his chosen female by first demonstrating his physical abilities, thereby implying the promise of healthy offspring as well as support during and beyond the hatching period. The female merely *watches* as the suitor begins performing short, *accentuated sideways steps, bowing* and *moving* his head and neck back and forth. He continues with small wing beats in time with his legs, until the female yields. At first she *shakes* her feathers, then *twists* her neck a few times with a proudly *raised* head, showing herself off. The mimetic duet is on. *Lifting* her legs one by one, *flapping* her wings, either simultaneously or one at a time, she *runs* around the male with slightly *bent* legs, uttering short *cries*.

- All the while the male *turns* with *tiny hops* on the spot so as always to face his chosen one. However much this may look like a dance, it is not. It is not some kind of a ballet when calves *play* and *frolic* on the grass, *jumping, rolling over, rubbing* against each other, *kicking* and *pushing*. These natural, pre-mating motions based on the plastic capabilities of the species, rather than any choreography that can be learned and executed for public display by individuals or groups, and passed on to future generations. Courtship display is the natural physiological preparation for the sexual intercourse to follow. However, most mammals do not use plastic preparation for the act of mating.

- There are other very different examples. A pack of monkeys in the jungle is engaged for most of the day, except for breaks for eating and sleeping, in group copulation with no concern for the identity of their partners. In complete contrast to the pair-bonding model, this behaviour is as natural to them as it is for a human to quench his thirst.

- This demonstrates unusual and apparently unnatural behaviour for a female animal. A strong young lion challenges the leadership of the dominant male, who has grown weak and is no longer as physically and sexually vigorous as he used to be. A long and dramatic duel follows, by the end of which the old lion is obliged to go. The victor takes over the pride, and immediately tries to mate with a young female with cubs, but is rejected. This happens several times until the young lion realises that he first has to kill the offspring of his predecessor. The lion does so in front of the entire pride, which appears to observe the spectacle in a temporary state of shock.

C: <u>Instinctive</u> action

This category contains models of the plastic behaviour of various species, based on instinctive motions in opposition to each other. In the food chain that underlies our global ecology, most species are predatory. The instinct to kill for food is a basic natural behaviour, and all predators display distinctively different profiles of plastic motion from the species they prey upon.

- A heron *swallows* a frog without *blinking*, but keeps a respectful distance from a hungry wolf. A tiger *creeps* as close as possible to a grazing gazelle, chasing it to exhaustion and eventually catching and killing it. The gazelle tries to escape as soon as it becomes aware of the danger, using its standard technique of *zigzagging leaps*.
- Birds of prey hunt differently because of their unique way of life and flight. When searching out prey from on high, an eagle places itself directly above any prey it spots before *swooping* down with *folded* wings to makes its catch. The prey on the ground has little chance to escape.
- A different situation is when two leopards try to hunt down a bison. In self-defence, the prey at once counter attacks both predators so aggressively that the leopards give up immediately, having learned from experience that a fighting bison will always kill at least one of its attackers before the second can strike.

There are too many different methods of catching prey to describe in detail here. However, hunting scenes always consist of two opposing creatures fighting each other for life or death.

Note also that in a group, whether attacking or defending, the same species can use different approaches, a pack of wolves, for example, pursues a single deer, first surrounding it, then attacking together from all sides. The deer saves itself by *leaping* over the tightening circle of aggressors if it spots the predators early enough.

- When a grizzly bear tries to catch an antelope calf, the entire herd at once surrounds the calf in a protective circle, every second antelope facing the centre while the others face outwards to the attacker. For defence they can now *kick* their hind legs at the predator, and the others can fend it off with their saw-like horns – a well organised defence that often saves the herd from losses.
- A flock of *flying* cranes aggressively counterattacks a hawk bent on snatching a young crane from the air.

The last three examples, unlike the earlier ones, demonstrate the same survival instinct inherent in both the impulse to attack and defend. Such premeditated action by the predator involves sophisticated strategies and techniques by both opposing parties. The spider *spins* its web and waits for a fly to become trapped. The python *hypnotises* a rat, which then *moves* as if voluntarily towards the *open* jaws of the predator. The fox, when *running* away from *pursuing* wild dogs, produces *tricky patterns* with its footprints to confuse predators into giving up the chase.

The examples of individual predators in the 'C' category reveal the difference in impulsive actions between species. While the 'A' and 'B' categories of the Realistic style demonstrate the plastic motion characteristics of only one type of animal, the 'C' category is characterised by deliberate, pre-planned strategies involving preparation prior to attack or defence.

All three categories of the Realistic style of presentation are accurate, direct imitations of the natural motion characteristics of the creature in question.

The above examples of animal behaviour only represent a small fraction of the 'zoo-plastic dictionary' used daily by all anthropoids, humans included. The question is, how did hominids manage to preserve such a vast amount of information?

The answer seems to lie in a combination of five factors:
1. The **vocabulary of body motions** memorised by successive generations of representing the same animal Totem. This single-species plastic dictionary would be easy to remember if constantly practised.
2. The **unique memorising abilities** of the shaman and his assistants, refined by repeated performance of various animal subjects in Funerary and Mythical pantomimes.
3. **Regular studies** by youngsters during initiation rites, alongside their own observation and imitation of anything *moving*, fixed in the memory by a child's great capacity for learning and remembering.
4. **Visual notations** including tattoos, decorated objects, petroglyphs, murals, sculptures, figurines and other media.
5. **Practical use** in everyday social and personal communication.

Taken together, these factors allowed a large plastic vocabulary to be accumulated from one generation to the next, and preserved in the communal memory.

To ensure accuracy, the following examples of episodes in which the plastic image closely replicates the original action are based mainly on petroglyphic illustrations, supplemented by photographic material from literary and scientific sources. The mimetic score of *gestures, postures, steps* and *body movements* reconstructed in this way has to be re-choreographed for practical application.

Finally, these models of plastic motion are compared against vocabularies personally observed by the author while watching ancient rituals in Asia, America and in the Far East during the last fifty years. In addition, evidence has been drawn from a wide range of studies on anthropology and prehistoric art. The examples of animalistic images discussed below are presented in order of their practical importance and popularity.

According to prehistoric graphics, the most significant animal for our ancestors was the bison. Easy to imitate, with no upper extremities, no *leaps* or special movements – simply *walking* or *galloping* steps, with a degree of active movement in *head butting, stamping,* and *whipping* the tail. In the 'A' category of the Realistic style, the direct imitation of a bison was no problem, as we have seen in chapter I. The main distinguishing plastic characteristic of the species is its horns, which at the primitive early stage of mimetic presentation were still physically present as part of the head being worn as a mask. They remained attached to the animal's skull, and hunt dance performers wore the entire pelt, complete with legs and tail.

The characteristic motions of terrestrial mammals like the zebra, are basically similar to cattle. The only real difference is that they use their hoofs and teeth for self-defence instead of horns. These various natural defence strategies (including those of the canine and feline families previously mentioned) provided models to add to our ancestors' complex fight vocabulary in the form of *kicking* legs and *clashing* teeth.

The motion profiles of burrowing or amphibious animals (such as beavers, weasels or rabbits) and tree-climbers (such as genets, koalas and squirrels) are somewhat different.

- The realistic presentation of a beaver quoted earlier involved the performers clad in beaver pelts building dams in a purely imitative way – *scurrying* around by little steps, *stretching, diving, carrying* armfuls of earth and twigs and *placing* them at the imaginary dam site. Everybody suddenly *stops* when predators are discovered, disappearing quickly on all fours.
- A rabbit brings vegetables in its mouth to the warren. Naturally gregarious, the rabbit *gambols* around. Suddenly *spotting* a fox in front of the burrow, the rabbit *throws* the vegetables at the fox's head and beats a hasty retreat, *zigzagging* with great *leaps* to escape the predator. Meanwhile, the fox desperately tries to catch its prey. The rabbit *runs, jumps, postures* and tries to hide, in a complex contrapuntal sequence of movements. Eventually the rabbit manages to *dive* into its burrow after this prolonged confrontation.

Here, the performers superbly demonstrate the plastic characteristics of two opposite mammalian species with contrasting motion vocabularies. Apart from the mimetic illustration of food gathering, the rabbit's is limited to short or long *leaps* involving both front and rear legs. But the dancer playing the fox has a rich variety of *slow-motion steps* and *running combinations* to choose from, all combined into complex patterns of movement with challenging *postures* and *turns* executed in totally unpredictable ways. Though in the Realistic style, this genre is in effect more of a dramatic duelling **humoresque**.

Arboreal creatures have two separate vocabularies according to whether they're *climbing* or on the ground, giving performers a much wider range of different expressive motions using two aspects of the same plastic dictionary.

- Our ancestors on all continents sooner or later developed hunting techniques using weapons to reach distant prey, including those in trees. Painted in green and white, the senior hunter *crawls* in the grass, *climbs* the tree, and hides in the branches. He waits for panda to return, *shoots* an arrow and comes down from the tree to collect his prey and celebrate his success.
- Young hunters, masked by boars' heads and pelts, imitate feeding animals as realistically as possible, *moving* around on all fours. *Chomping* and *grumbling*, they gradually *approach* the prey. Suddenly they all *rise* and surround the busy panda, *stamping* noisily, *clapping* and *screaming* to distract the animal's attention. The young hunters continue until the prey reaches its den high in the tree. After the panda *falls* from the tree, the youngsters *hail* the chief and join in celebrating his success. The second soloist, dressed in panda outfit, imitates the *movements* of a *grazing* mammal. He keeps an eye on the boars *grazing* around him. Eventually, scared by the noisy attackers, the panda *runs* in panic to the top of the tree. Hit by the hunter's arrow, the animal *falls* down in agony. The happy hunters *carry* the prey away, *suspended* on two poles borne on the shoulders.

This is a carefully planned dramatic scenario using two very different motion vocabularies and involving complex sequences of multiple actions by two hunting forces – the senior hunter *crawling, climbing, waiting motionless* and *hitting* the prey with an arrow, the youngsters *feeding, rising up, stomping* and *clapping*. Both forces on the hunting side are driven by the same objective – to kill. By contrast, the panda *roams* peacefully on the ground, *feeds, runs* in panic, *climbs* the tree, then *crashes* to the ground – the opposite side of the action. Though very different, the mimetic motions of all three dramatic roles exemplify the realistic style.

New **artistic** elements now enter into the equation, in the form of scenery and costume. To make this fable more realistic, the shaman brought poles, rocks and branches to represent the tree, hill and bush. Moreover, he painted the body of the main hunter, who obviously could not climb the tree/pole clad in mask and pelt. This need to camouflage the hunter's body is what prompted the parallel advance in representing the hunt in performance.

ARTISTIC STYLE

Premeditated behaviour and action

This style of representing animals was a major step in human cultural evolution. As discussed earlier, shamans came to realise the difficulties and discomfort of using heavy bison or alligator heads as masks. After the discovery of clay and pigments in the mid-Palaeolithic era, they created an alternative in the form of artificial mask. Thereafter, all shamanic and hunting decorations became lighter and more stylised. In practical terms, the light and colourful demi-mask with stylised costume opened up unforeseen possibilities for using a vastly expanded plastic motion vocabulary for animal images.

The traditional choreography of all ritual ceremonies was established and jealously protected by generations of shamans and their assistants, who were the only people allowed to change, improve or modernise them. In order to retain their leadership and spiritual control over the community in the face of the rise of paganism, shamans were forced to consider a modern repertoire using more sophisticated techniques and presentation. Another factor was the constant competition for socio-cultural status between neighbouring tribes. Taken together, these circumstances pushed the shamans into reforming traditional and improving standards of performance.

'Artistic' in this context means more than mere artifice; it covers the entire process including the creative concept, the personality of those executing the piece, the use of professional materials, spacing, timing and many other aspects (discussed later in the chapter on visual arts).

The stylisation of images and play

For now, our subject is how natural motion vocabularies were stylised into artistic pantomime dance presentations. Mimicking adult activities was always a favourite game for the children of any tribe. After watching regular rituals and playing with domestic animals like dogs, rabbits, chicken and cattle, they tried to follow their parents' way of imitating animals. With no education or experience, the little ones enjoyed acting out images of these creatures in naive, purely mimetic presentations.

Nature saw to it that these primitive play performances had other positive effects. The children's fertile imaginations and natural talent for mimicry compensated for the lack of masks, costumes or instruments (apart from sticks to create basic rhythms). A dry twisted branch could represent buffalo's horns, a braided liana belt hanging behind could be the tail, a few feathers attached to the head indicated a chicken, a dry grass skirt was a rabbit's fur, and so on.

Children selected one main characteristic motion of a creature and adapted it in various **stylised intonations** to construct an improvised fable, without any preparation and without having worked out the narrative first. Though choreographed by the **personal interpretation** of the performers, these amateurish improvised Realistic imitations of the natural world were only Artistic insofar as they were performed for the sake of personal enjoyment rather than that of an audience.

The fact that many petroglyphs show children playing and domestic animals beside the main theme suggests that it may have been the sight of these children's games that inspired shamans to add new elements to the traditional animal motion vocabulary and to elaborate more modern ideas for their performances.

Competition and status as stimuli

The *first* stage of artistic development was the **spiritual image** of the totem, which was mainly reflected in anthropomorphic decorations (head coverings, face make-up, body paint, adornments, props and so on). Almost the entire body of the hunter or warrior was tattooed (except for the pelvic area) or painted according to the action to follow (see fig. III/14).

The second stage involved revising all plastic dictionaries to bring their vocabularies into line with more modern criteria for evaluating fables and performers' abilities. The decorative design and the motion text of traditional dance/pantomime could now be extended by adding more advanced and more effective mimicry and dance techniques (*grimaces, gestures, postures, steps, jumps* and so on). This in turn meant that the soloist could, according to his abilities as a performer, be encouraged by the shaman to incorporate his own personal tricks into traditional mythical or funerary rites.

In his new role as producer/choreographer, the shaman's creative attitude also changed. He now had more flexibility within the traditional totemythic framework, and this wider artistic scope to include new mimes and motions opened up tremendous new opportunities. Instead of demanding a mechanically identical imitation of animals, the shaman could now offer performers the freedom of a more artistic approach.

Unimportant details of everyday body motion in both human and animal performing vocabularies could be omitted. From then on, incidental episodes or fragments could be cut from ritual mimetic performances. Performers were required to concentrate solely on the leitmotif of the myth being presented. In traditional choreographies, the shaman would nevertheless make adjustments in exceptional cases.

The main subject thus became dramatically clearer and more effective as a performance. Each scene became crystallised, as did the entire performance. These **modernisations** gave the shaman great opportunities to create a new repertoire of mythical rites. Images of animals could be **stylised** in artistic ways. Instead of dancing with heavy buffalo horns attached with a demi-mask to the performer's head, or dancing with huge mammoth tusks on the shoulders, performers could now hold props before them with both hands. All living creatures could now be replaced with **artificial representations** during dramatic clashes in mythical pantomime. The live python around the hunter's neck was replaced by snakeskin stuffed with dried seeds; real eagle's wings were replaced by sticks covered with eagle feathers, and so on.

The liberating effect of decoration and mask

While realistic styles of action and decoration were still used in social rituals, the same performers were already executing the new Artistic dance/mime sequences in mythical and funerary pantomimes. After moving out from the limited space of a cave into large open areas, visibility problems arose because of the audience being further away from the action. In their attempts to bring the performance closer to the spectators, the shamans and their assistants found another ingenious Artistic solution by extending the amplitude of *steps* and *movements* to **exaggerate** the actions being mimed. This discovery was a very significant turning point in the evolution of the performing (and later, visual) arts.

Analysing these petroglyphs in more depth reveals masked hunters in antelope costume with their arms extended by long sticks. This was almost certainly to allow the performers to imitate the animal's enormous *leaps* by *pushing* both sticks to the ground ahead in order to *lift* themselves high into the air and *leap* forwards two or three metres.

The aboriginal people of Australia used the same technique to express the image of kangaroos in ritual dance. African Bushmen even learned to *walk* and *jump* on two long poles or stilts, while wearing a demi-mask and the skin of a giraffe's neck. Other rock drawings show two performers painted with zebra stripes; the front one *raised* up, with two protruding ears on the top of zebra demi-mask, while the back one *leans* forward with the left arm on his partner's shoulder and the right arm *holding* a rope/tail behind. Both are *hopping* and *kicking* in a comic style of presentation, like modern pantomime cows.

These examples all demonstrate the first experiments with the new artistic style. Even taking into account a time span of some five hundred thousand years, the fundamental stylistic difference between Realistic imitation and Artistic creation remains clear in both production and presentation.

SYMBOLIC STYLE

The development of the symbolic style in the performing and visual arts was a long and confused process. The sacred rituals of hunting, war, fertility and initiation continued in their original realistic style. By contrast, both the funerary and mythical rite pantomimes gradually evolved in the artistic manner – pantheistic and elemental cults began timidly incorporating modern new plastic motions in their worship, using magic symbols for the first time. Young secular dancers embraced the new trend with some success at all domestic Floral dance events.

It is important to understand why and how such a fundamental aesthetic volte-face affected the entire Neolithic culture that followed, including pantomime rituals and dance education. Tracing the convoluted evolution of performing arts from its Realistic roots through the artistic phase to the symbolic, we will examine the influences that led sacred and secular choreography in the direction of modern perceptions and performance methods.

Summary of characteristics

In terms of composition, the symbolic style of ritual dance differed greatly from traditional rite-pantomime performance – not only because of the animal/totem subject matter, or the leading role of males, but in the degree of realism in its production and presentation.

All male performers were familiar with the living creatures that surrounded them, the totemic background and mimetic skills. With minor spiritual and practical adjustments, basically the same motion routines were used for both funerary and totemic pantomimes for a million years or so.

However, food gathering and primitive agriculture involved a different approach, despite their origins in the same spiritual background. As far as the animal world is concerned, it was clear that all creatures including humans were created and controlled by the totem. But in the Flora's sacred field of the Mother Goddess, things were rather more confused.

Why did the same fruit or vegetables grow well in one place but not in another? Who and how was regulating the vital water supply? What caused sudden storms, fire and lightning? Who sent clouds of flying insects to destroy a rich harvest or food stores?

There had to reasons. The answer the shamans proposed was that if the Mother Goddess created the land, then everything on it was under her control. Any success or failure therefore depended on her. It follows that she must therefore be the symbol of reproduction and destruction, of good luck and misfortune, of victory and loss and ultimately of life and death.

It was the same three-tiered hierarchy – only this time, Mother Goddess/witch/ tribeswoman instead of totem/shaman/tribesman. Except that now it was a question of a more advanced female, who (we repeat) is naturally a stronger survivor and a better custodian of the family: inherently more patient, wiser, more practical and socially more active than male.

Naturally, these same qualities also stimulated the development of women's intellect and adaptability. As a result, led by the witch, women eventually established the new polytheistic religion of paganism. The Mother Goddess still controlled the lives of all creatures, as well as the earthly environment. However, the elements and other natural phenomena acquired new spiritual symbols.

'Shorthand' communication

The symbolic style involves basically similar plastic motion vocabularies, spatial patterns and decorative design as other styles, but in quintessential forms that summarise characteristics and spirituality. As we have seen, the realistic style of ritual pantomime was based on the **direct imitation** of animals using actual heads as masks and pelts as costumes; the Artistic style involved **mimetic imagery** of the same creatures using stylised decoration, masks, costumes and props along with distinctive details such as horns, beaks or tusks. In the symbolic style, these accessories were transformed into symbols with **multiple layers** of meaning, and used with entirely different motions.

These ritual attributes would have spiritual and metaphorical significance extending far beyond their literal sense, and in performance would communicate much more than merely the physical recognition of some animal. A goat's horn, for example, might symbolise cattle breeding, domestic utility, human fecundity (phallus), declaration of war or a zodiac sign according to the subject matter and context. The same principle applied to Floral rites in which the worshippers addressed their praise and prayers to the Mother Goddess and the new goddesses.

The same happened to all non-verbal dictionaries. Hominids gradually adopted a symbolic system of communication based on *gestures* and *postures*, from simple illustrative indications (*pointing*) to signals that contain within them multiple meanings in **abbreviated** form – a massive plastic vocabulary of unspoken communication. The symbolic motion dictionary was no longer based on *imitating* natural objects, but on crystallising their essential being, indicating the same subject through pure **artifice**; it had more to do with perception than mere vision, with the subtext rather than the text.

Coded motions and mimicry

Symbolic choreography was the inevitable anthropological result of social, cultural and spiritual evolution. To communicate spiritually with many gods rather than a single totem, while at the same time interacting personally with each other, required a more complex performance language. Carefully selecting the most expressive elements from the old vocabularies, our ancestors filtered them in everyday use over several generations until their quintessence became incorporated into the body motion lexicon of tribal communication and ritual pantomime.

The multiplicity of small, highly detailed motions for each subject became too confusing to incorporate into coherent dance performance. The shaman/ choreographer therefore once again had to develop symbolic signs which could visually summarise an archetypal subject or subjects in a single *movement* of the hands, arms, legs or feet.

Worshippers depicted in ancient frescoes dancing with arms *held motionless* in an angular position above the head, for example – the usual symbol of a bull's horns – are not in fact mimicking the beast. The intended meaning is far more broad-ranging; depending on context, the significance could include praying for a rich harvest or the successful breeding of cattle, praying for a good marriage, or a healthy new-born child, or begging the moon to save her husband from mortal danger on the battlefield.

Snake images

Early man was fascinated by the mystique of serpents. In different ways, aboriginals of all continents feared the magic power of the snake and its image.

All the goddesses of harvest, fire, wind, forest and earth and the sacred mistresses of life, death, war, love, health and fortune symbolically personify aspects of human life in one spiritual way or another. Once again, the main plastic instruments were the arms – only this time, not in a fixed position as for the bull's horns, but in sinuously powerful, multifarious '*port-de-bras*', supported by similar body motions.

The most popular form of snake dance was a sedentary composition whose choreography was based on the expressive motion of the hands, arms, head and torso. *Sitting cross-legged* on the ground, female worshippers performed in unison, their arms in their laps in a snake-like pattern, as if *waking slowly* to a background beat of drums and a rudimentary voice-modulation. At the beginning, the snake image is simply introduced by appropriately *painted* arms; the hands then *mimic* the familiar motions of the reptile's head and tail. This is followed by an impressive quasi-magical moment when the arms *rise up* like the snake's entire body, capturing the creature's dramatic beauty. Suddenly, the posture then *freezes* in the familiar traditional 'snake portrait'. The opening scene is usually completed at this stage, and the Symbolic ritual dance begins.

Murals depicted the chorus of *singing* dancers *seated* in front of or around a spiritual symbol such as a wooden pole or stone column, a tree (sometimes sculpted), an idol or a sacrificial object. According to the subject of worship, the focus of the composition could be the witch, who sometimes took part in the performance, as one of the goddesses mentioned above. The plastic vocabulary of the sedentary dancers would in any case have included a large variety of rhythmic and dramatic motions of the arms and torso.

Group figurines of the Palaeolithic era show performers' hands *joined* in front, or behind the back, or on each other's shoulders. Many painted domestic objects (plates, vases and boxes) depict the ornamentation on dancers' arms in clear geometric lines and other symbolic configurations. There can be no doubt that the shaman/choreographer already knew at this stage how to use performance techniques based on sophisticated kinaesthetics (in unison, contrapuntally and canonised) to create complex multiple-motion presentations.

The advent of symbolic styles opened the door for fertile imaginations, particularly on the subject of the elements and planets. The main plastic tools for standard ritual dance were of course the legs. The snake image was usually represented symbolically by females, and only rarely by males. The Earth Goddess could be seen performing **solo**; the Mistresses of Fire and Water in **duet**; the sacred patrons of life, death and love in **trio**, the spiritual representatives of the four compass points in **quartet**, and so on. No matter how many female idols a choreography contained, almost all of them danced the stereotypical symbolic vocabulary of *snake motions*.

As if by magic, these sacred images provided the spiritual link between worshippers and superior powers Although this in itself was nothing new, the apparent plastic and psychological transformation from human to goddess resonated far more powerfully when performed in the newly sophisticated symbolic style.

The monologue of a goddess, dialogues or group interactions were all based not on natural motions as before, but on a new symbolic vocabulary of **coded** motions, rudimentary cries and bodily adornment and decoration.

SNAKE DANCE – A

The Rain Goddess appears in front of seated dancers, her naked body painted and her long braids of hair *falling* down her shoulders like thin snakes. A larger 'snake-belt' is around her hips, the head and tail falling between her knees. The goddess *poses* with her legs *held together* and feet parallel, her arms *stretched upwards* and *turned out*, coming together where hands *joined* to look like the head of a snake. Her eyes *hypnotise* the worshippers to prepare them spiritually for the ritual ceremony to follow. The praying women open the introductory phase with a sinuous *'port-de-bras'*, accompanied by rudimentary chants. The pianissimo sound of the pan pipe and drums follows the tranquillo dynamics until all *return* to the starting position.

The Rain Goddess begins by *vibrating* her hands, *transferring* this tremolo gradually into both arms, torso and hips, both legs *held* tight, until her entire *outstretched* body *trembles* convulsively, while *ringing* the bangles on her wrists and ankles. Finally, she *drops down* on both knees, *placing* her buttocks on her heels, with her head, arms and chest down in front on her thighs. Once the goddess has been introduced in this way, the seated dancers remain in the same *motionless* position. After a *pause*, the Rain Goddess (still accompanied by the chorus and instrumentalists) performs a fertility rite in the form of a plastic motion dialogue with her worshippers. The structure is traditional, but presented in a modern symbolic style.

From inscriptions on bracelets and wedding rings of the same era, other possible dance compositions on the same subject can be reconstructed – not with any guarantee of absolute accuracy, but supported by evidence of other archaeological sources and published studies. These artefacts act as summaries of prehistoric human communication through dance.

Let us return to the Rain Goddess reconstruction. After the two introductions, the symbolic choreography of the worshippers split into different semantic directions to develop a dialogue, sometimes performed harmoniously in parallel and in unison, but more often in contrapuntal or cross-related modes to work through the resolution of **conflicting** intentions or circumstances.

Examples of the latter might involve the Rain Goddess beginning by blessing the season's breeding of cattle by *galloping* in a circle, arms above her head in imitation of a bull's horns, in time with *pulsing* drum beats. The seated dancers *echo* her symbolic message with onomatopoeic cattle chants, following the goddess' rhythmic patterns to the end of each motion phrase. The goddess dances on the spot, *rotating* her pelvis – an archetypal symbol of fertility and abundance. Sustaining their chants, the choristers echo the goddess' dance sequence using only their arms and torso. The ritual is brought to a close with both the soloist and surrounding sedentary chorus performing canonically in a *harmonious* synthesis of plastic patterns, grace and voice.

SNAKE DANCE – B

The symbolic ritual dance of the elements represents the two popular goddesses of water and fire – two deities with similar dramatic power, whose opposite characters are reflected by contrasting plastic motion scores.

The dancing chorus, now no longer seated, is divided into two conflicting groups representing the opposing spiritual forces. Wearing appropriate symbolic costumes, the main antagonists (both soloists) act out a dramatic conflict using similar snake-like motions, but with opposing plastic motifs choreographed in *tempo rubato* and contrapuntal rhythmic patterns or dissonant harmonies.

Many illustrations of ancient dance from different continents show the element of fire being expressed by the arms, which depict flames with a sinuous upward motion while remaining on the spot. Running water, on the other hand, involves the dancers *skimming in zigzag patterns*, with snake-like arms in a *waving motion*. In both cases, similar *port de bras* can be seen, but using different spatial patterns, rhythms, intensity, kinaesthetics and dramatic effect.

BIRD IMAGES

Birds were a much admired and popular spiritual subject, and are often seen on prehistoric monuments and in primitive art: humans with wings, or birds with human heads and so on. As one of the first species to be bred domestically by our ancestors, birds had become an important part of all domestic and ritual activities; sacrificing a family bird to the totem was therefore a great loss as well as a real honour. Gradually the bird's image developed into multi-dimensional spirit of dreams, love, success, youth, energy, sexual potency, bravery, intelligence and beauty. All tribes everywhere used the symbolic image of the bird in one way or another, both in communication and mythical performances.

Although the spiritual characteristics of the snake and the bird had much in common, their anatomy and body motions are quite different. Unlike the snake's, the sacred image of the bird was symbolised choreographically by the large amplitude *flapping* of *outstretched* arms like wings, *arching* the neck and back, and by *flying jumps*. Our forebears knew all the characteristics of the birds around them by heart, of course. It was therefore easy for them to evoke the plastic portrait of a bird's image for symbolic ritual dance.

There were three types of composition for such choreography, depending on the age and physical condition of the dancers.

Middle-aged worshippers would represent the bird image while seated, using the torso and arms, *singing* while *moving* their winged arms in *slow motion*, with various symbolic *postures*. Accented according to the rhythm of drums, their body motions were in unison, in harmony or contrapuntal, with or without soloists performing in front, but always with one or more instrumentalists playing.

Young female dancers usually used the same symbolic motion of *port-de-bras*, but in a group composition representing birds in flight. One fresco shows *light, quick walking steps*; another, *small flying jumps* forward. Often these were in a circling pattern, using *flapping motions* by *stretching* the arms upwards and back, and gracefully *arching* their necks and backs, with free *flowing* long hair or decorative lianas. Some drawings show *flying* anthropomorphised creatures with the head and wings of a bird, but on the body of a naked woman, *moving in a zigzag* pattern imitating *flying* flocks of storks, geese, swans, or cranes.

Having discussed symbolic postures in some detail in the previous chapter on mimetic culture, it is interesting to see how these were used as the motion text of ritual choreography. This is the third version of the bird image:
- Solo eagle dances, or **duels** between a hawk and a kite in rite pantomime were purely mimetic presentations of bird predators in action. romantic, intriguing and impressive – but not all of these qualities were stylistically suitable for symbolic ritual choreography. Dance *movements* could not be integrated with motionless pantomime *postures*, either dynamically or spiritually.

Even though their plastic background was identical, the compositional principles of each were inherently contradictory. Aesthetic considerations obliged the shaman/ choreographer to symbolise the bird's plastic characteristics, demonstrating the essence of this sacred image through motion – not the bird itself, but its spiritual power as expressed by the human body.

THE PHYLOGENESIS OF DANCE: FROM INSECTS TO HUMANS

Whenever the earliest socio-cultural activities of our ancestors are discussed, dance is presented as a primal form of psycho-physical expression and bodily communication. Views of dance in this evolutionary context take into account the limitations of hominids' plastic facilities and motion vocabulary, their powerful spiritual dimension and the ever-present exposure to danger – after all, prehistoric life was by no means easy.

INTER-SPECIES INFLUENCES

After observing a sheldrake, kagu or flamingo seeming to perform a type of dance before feeding, an ape mechanically imitates the *movements* in the expectation of also obtaining food. Our ancestors had no way of knowing that these birds were *stamping* the sandy ground to coax out the worms beneath.

A similar principle is inherent in the development of war dance. It was from seeing species like elephant, rhino and hippo *paw* the ground when preparing for an attack that hominids learned to begin their own sacred war dances with *heavy stamps*, digging their feet into the ground.

The social behaviour of chimpanzees *promenading* in groups around a central object such as a tree, rock or pole is a phenomenon worth examining closely. Beginning as a quiet, slow performance, it gradually turns into a frenzied, boisterous event. But what exactly is it? A dance? A physical exercise? A functional ceremony? A precursor to the human round dance? These are big and controversial questions to which there are as yet no satisfactory answers.

ANIMAL COURTSHIP RITUALS

In Chapter II, we discussed courtship displays and the pre-mating 'pantomime' of nearly all animal species. Here are more examples of such self-representation by different birds:
- **Bearded Bellbird**. The male demonstrates his tricks to watching males and females, *jumping* some four feet into the air from his perch and landing in a *crouched* position on another branch, showing off his proudly *raised* head and *outspread* tail plumage.
- **Victoria Crowned Pigeons** perform an amorous 'pas-de-deux' in which the male *dances* and *bows* in a clearing and the female *runs* around him with slightly *bent* knees or *straight* legs, simultaneously *spreading* her wings. Both utter soft *hissing cries*.
- **Blue-backed Manakin**. The male challenges a subordinate male to a contest by performing a certain choreography which his rival tries to follow with a fraction of a second's delay. When a female eventually appears, she watches the developing contest. The tempo and complexity of the dominant male's motions increase until the subordinate male can no longer follow, and he quits. The winner continues his (by now, Solo) variation until the female joins him in a celebratory duet.

As these examples confirm, animal Courtship rituals are mainly performed as **solos, duets**, or **trios**, and are all based on the strictly functional imperative to reproduce. The major body motion patterns and expressions are motivated by the desire to attract a sexual partner through self-exhibition. The contests between males are designed to ensure the strongest possible gene pool for the continuation of the species.

SYNCHRONISED PROGRESSIVE MOTION

Synchronised swimming or flying motions – the sudden simultaneous changes in direction by a shoal of fish, a swarm of flying insects or a flock of birds, for example – are highly sophisticated group motions involving an immense ensemble of individuals moving as one, with rapid and co-ordinated changes in tempo and spatial patterns. Whether fish, insects or birds, these creatures usually follow an invisible 'leader', more by inner reflexive power than by external physical recognition.

Instinctive by nature, these motions are motivated by the twin imperatives to feed without becoming food for others. All things being equal, it can be easier to find food as part of a group than as a small individual. And whereas lone individuals have little chance of escaping a determined predator, small creatures feel much more secure in large groups (sometimes even scaring off much larger predators). These mass synchronised motions (often with luminous effects at night) are therefore not dances, as they have been described by some commentators, but strictly functional instinctive behaviours.

The *playing* and *jumping* of juvenile mammals, with their many *gestures, postures, turns, tricks* and pretended *bites* are often considered as a type of dance. Not so – these improvised body motions are stimulated by an inherent need to develop various physical survival skills. However, this play-wrestling and nipping differs fundamentally from the merely impulsive unconscious actions of functional behaviour in the three previous examples.

Social play and pretence signal a new and more advanced relationship in the family or group, and imply a more sophisticated neuro-physical structure. As such, these motions point the way forward to the complex evolutionary bridge from low mammals to primates.

THE CHIMPANZEE ROUND DANCE

Compare the chimps' 'round dance' in the example above with the apparently similar progressive *movements* of various species in the other examples. When considering the phylogeny of plastic facilities – that is, the sequence of evolutionary events involved – our attention focusses on crucial changes that appear in the functional background and emotional motivation of the chimp ceremony.

According to several descriptions of this phenomenon, the chimps begin by *walking* one by one behind each other after the dominant male, initially on all fours, at a *tempo andante*. At a certain point, the leader gives some (as yet undeciphered) signals with his voice and his right arm to get the pack to *march* in a more orderly fashion.

Stage I: Preparation
Infants *hang* on their mothers' back with a secure *grasp*, gazing around apprehensively. Juveniles become over-excited and disorganised, and frequently lose the hierarchical order. All *move* clockwise in a circle, in the direction of the sun. After a while, the whole pack get themselves organised in the correct hierarchical positions, and *move in unison* to the same tempo. This signals the end of first preparatory stage – a kind of warm-up that introduces what follows.

Species as diverse as hunter-ants, chicks and elephants also *walk in a chain*, following their leader in either *zigzagging* or *labyrinthine* patterns. Although the same hierarchical principles apply across all classification orders of insects, birds and mammals, these are merely functional locomotion activities that facilitate communication when on the move, and as such, are driven by the search for food or the need for self-protection – **instinctive**, unconditioned survival reflexes rather than **premeditated actions**.

Such are the as yet unanswered paradoxes of evolutionary theory. However, these instances do provide yet more proof that the real origin of volitional progressive movement lies hundreds of millions of years ago in the creatures of prehistory.

The main hunger and security motivation of diverse species in these natural functional behaviours and bodily communications is self-evident:

- Hunter-ants destroy anything living they encounter by *killing, devouring* and *trash-cleaning* in a highly organised and impeccably disciplined group action.
- Newborn chicks blindly *follow* their parent, learning everything mechanically by directly mimicking parental plastic motion and behaviour.
- Thirsty elephants pass along common tracks, carefully protecting their calves from predators along the way.

By contrast, the chimps' Round dance has no equivalent in the functional or behavioural activities of any other non-primate species under similar circumstances, except insofar as it teaches juvenile chimpanzees the skills of marching together. The question therefore arises again – what kind of progressive motion are we dealing with? A ritual, a dance, or an exercise?

Stage II: Manifestation

Consider what happens next. In the second part of the circling procession, the dominant male chimp continues *walking, leaning forwards* on slightly *bent* knees. At a given moment, having made a number of *steps*, he *raises* himself up on tiptoe and *lifts* his head. The whole pack then tries to follow this sequence of movements. Some inevitably make mistakes, but eventually they manage to act bipedally in unison.

One of the middle-aged subordinate males gets bored with the proceedings and decides to have some fun. Suddenly, he *turns* and starts *marching backwards*, now on all fours, still maintaining the clockwise direction. His companions scream their displeasure and confusion, and order is restored when the leader again makes a signal by *drawing* his right arm laterally.

Stage III: Initiation

The dominant chimp initiates the third part of the 'round dance' with heavy arhythmical *stamps* and *jumps* on all fours in the same direction and tempo. The excitement rises as the march continues. The *stamping jumps* get heavier, the *shouting* louder. As the tempo gradually increases, so does the emotional pitch. The circular marching eventually stops, when the euphoria reaches its climax.

Stage IIII: Improvisation

The chimps execute more *heavy stamping* on the ground at a faster tempo, *turning* simultaneously towards the centre to face each other. This final part of the ceremony progresses into a kind of bacchanalia, with the dominant male placing himself in the middle along with his closest family members. They begin *jumping* even higher on the spot, *slapping* various parts of their bodies, *throwing* themselves to the ground in between, *squealing* and *yelling*; females *wave* their arms chaotically or *roll* on the ground. Males *drum* their chests with fists, or *somersault*. Suddenly, the leader *drops* to the ground in a state of trance, and the whole pack follows to the ground him one by one. The event is over.

The big question remains: what is it? The most probable answer is that this extraordinary phenomenon is both a prototype of performance and a social entertainment. A prototype of performance because it involves a routinely repeated choreography consciously known in advance, even if in a very primitive form. And social because the motivation is behavioural rather than functional: to help each other in gathering, hunting, nursing, grooming, protecting – and entertaining.

DISPARITIES BETWEEN SECULAR AND SACRED PERFORMANCE

As we have seen, the main difference between ritual performance and secular/social events lies in the different physical and psychological approach of the participants. In a show, dancers perform primarily for an audience; when **entertaining,** the participants dance mainly for their own pleasure. In the case of the chimps, both categories coexist – a semi-instinctive ritual performance during which they show off to each other or for the benefit of other species, together with **improvisational acting** for their own enjoyment.

For these reasons, the progressive motion of chimpanzees can legitimately be described as a precursor to dance in its most primitive form, but with clear indications of a show or event. Obviously, it has no spiritual background; rather, it is a manifestation of the mature apes' desire to bond with the younger members of the pack in order to strengthen the troop as a whole for the purposes of group activities such as gathering, hunting and nursing. All these activities require disciplined behaviour subject to communal rules regarding hierarchy, grooming, play and intercommunication.

Given that chimps are an intelligent, social and highly developed species (and genetically close to humans), it is hardly surprising to see them *mimicking, dancing, gesturing, posturing* and *moving* impressively in a smooth and consciously controlled manner; it is after all logical that our nearest species should show similar phylogenetic roots in their behaviour, non-verbal communication and socio-cultural activities. Yes, great apes do have a flair for dance!

They are also able to ritualise some social activities and personal behaviour, although in simpler and more naive ways than hominids. Although lacking spoken language, the evidence suggests that all anthropoids have similar sensitivities and emotions to our own. Chimps could probably learn the polka more quickly than some humans!

PLASTIC MOTION ANTHROPOLOGY

The roots of dance evidently arise from a much deeper anthropology of motion, originating in the plasticity of early species such as insects and spiders. From these deep roots, it took some 300 million years of physiological and musculo-skeletal evolution to arrive at the complex multi-dimensional aesthetic of dance as we understand it today.

As dance evolved, body motion became progressively linked to the major vital functions, like hunting, feeding and mating. During the early ape/ hominid stage, it also became a natural plastic expression of a happiness and contentment. More complex emotional (and later, spiritual) dimensions followed until dance had become a primary expressive instrument for defining the species' relationships with the rest of the animal kingdom. The main conditions and characteristics of both dance and dancer are:

Dance performance	Mime dancer
Traditional or improvised	Physical growth and education
Functional or premeditated	Childish, mature or superior
Processional or in limited space	Native talent or experience
Male, female or mixed	Sexuality and reproduction
Solo, duet, trio or ensemble	Plasticity and musicality
Round, labyrinthine or free pattern	Balance and coordination
Masked, imagistic or mimetic	Motion technique and presentation
Plain or with singing, clapping	Partnering or random
With/without sound accompaniment	Performing passion or commitment

Unison, canonised, contrapuntal	Magic image or natural behaviour
Ritual: hunt, totemythic, funerary,	Accordant or discordant attitude
Initiation, fertility, healing...	Premeditated or improvised
Secular entertainment repertoire	Performing contact with audience
Shamanism and witchcraft	Dialogue with deity through trance
War strategy and wrestling contests	Plastic motion and spirituality
Comic, lyrical, dramatic, tragic	Mood or body expression
Realistic, artistic, symbolic, abstract	Dramatisation and artistry
Potency of creativity or destruction	Mimicry, concentration,
Professional or amateur	Re-embodiment

This demonstrates that dance is not just about **movement** in time and space, as some scholars contend. As a powerful sexual stimulus for the reproduction of a species, dance genes are already present in the unborn ape through the long process of selective evolution.

Think of a tiny baby, a few weeks old, resting on its back after feeding and *waving* its arms and legs. *Smiling* and *giggling*, it unconsciously expresses its contentment by as yet uncoordinated plastic motions. Within a few months, on hearing a drumming sound, this same baby reacts instantly with various body *movements*, impulsively trying to follow the beat of the drum. At a year old, it *bends its knees* (*demi-plié*), *shakes* its body, *nods* its head and *waves* both arms, sometimes *clapping*, in chaotic *port de bras*.

This potency of bodily movement and **innate impulse to dance** remains hominids' richest and strongest motion expression, and lasts all their lives. In old age and no longer able to walk, our ancestors sat and watched tribal festivities. By *clapping, shaking* their frail bodies and *nodding* their grey heads, they expressed their excitement through dancing motions, just as they had done as infants.

Conclusion

Ritual dance was for our ancestors a sophisticated and complex form of communication because it unlocked the language of the body – the most sensitive instrument for expressing human feelings and emotions. In answer to the question "How are you?", human beings would reply "I am still dancing" in their local plastic motion dialect to indicate their sound mental and physical state.

It was through dance images that our forefathers dreamed, learned, loved, hunted, fought, mourned, celebrated, worshipped, entertained and healed. There was no part of human life that was not expressed through dance, and the loss of a person's ability to dance was tantamount to death.

Dance is the main expressive body motion, projecting in one way or another almost all of our ancestors' personal or social functions.

Hominids' primal dance motions are undoubtedly the oldest and most effective form of self-expression, communication, healing, entertainment, devotion and education. Dance enshrines custom and the promotion of social manners. Dance is our history, anthropology and mythology; it is also our drama, music, sport, games and celebration of physical beauty.

The dancer is the most popular image in all forms of visual art. Aesthetically, mime-dance is the quintessence of syncretic perception and performance. Dance is the universal nonverbal language, a symphony of plastic motion and a transcultural instrument for psycho-physical healing.

Dance is a moving representation and spiritual image of the mysteries of the animate world and the perpetual motion of the universe. According to ancient mythologies, the

Creator wrought human kind in a dance. Dance is life, and our existence on this planet is but a short episode in the all-embracing choreography of the infinite cosmic dance.

EPILOGUE

Today, with functional motion modernised by innumerable highly sophisticated tools and weapons, the physical and mimicking facilities of our species have suffered a long period of continuous decline. With each advance in the never ending march of technology came a corresponding diminution in the need to appreciate and express the natural skills that had been refined over millions of years through mime, dance and sport.

Paradoxically, the cerebral development that makes us human has, after some 50,000 years of incredible 'progress' and the establishment of what we like to call 'civilisation', led us inexorably in the direction of self-destruction, mainly by substituting natural physical motion and action by various mechanical 'improvements'. This process has reached the point whereby modern children are increasingly losing interest in performing any bodily activities, preferring to sit passively and practically motionless in front of a computer or TV screen, and getting progressively fatter and stiff-jointed as a result. Over time, this is a worrying prospect, unless countermeasures are urgently considered.

Nobody is of course to blame for this gradual demise of our body's plastic motion facilities. Nature designed and developed the human body in response to specific environmental conditions over the ages, and as we have repeatedly seen, the body shape and structure of animals either adapts to any change in these conditions, or the species disappears. The principles of natural selection that Darwin set out the fundamental conflict between genetic inheritance and progressive survival-oriented mutation within whatever the prevailing environmental conditions may be.

Human intelligence is today capable of creating machines that could eventually perform all human work, as well as engineering our genes and reproduction. Machines could put us in charge of every planet in the solar system. But the body can only carry out its functional life if it moves regularly, in one way or another. Over the last thirty years, the industrialised world has seen an alarming increase in obesity in children as well as adults, and a corresponding decline in body motion facilities. If the present trend continues, about half the Earth's population will suffer from the diseases of stasis by the end of the 21st century. In these terms at least, the decline of regular body motion is quite simply the beginning of the end.

375

Dancing Motion of Birds in Courtship

1. Nightjar courtship
2. Stork displays
3. Dance of pugnacious lorikeet
4. The ostrich displays
5. The crane dance

Enjoying Dancing Together

Modern composition by Bonobos   Source: *My Family Album*

Lyrical adagio in classical duet

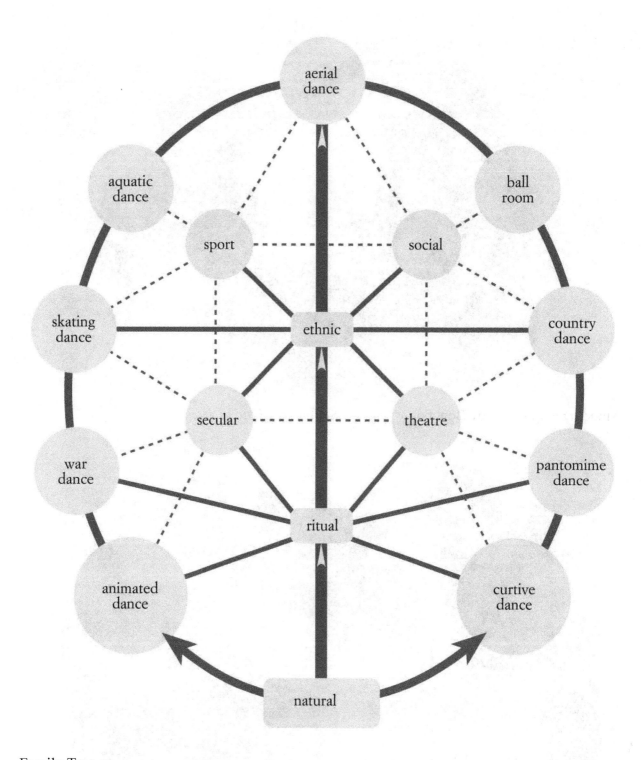

Family Tree

BIBLIOGRAPHY

GENESIS OF MAN

1. Attenborough, D.	*Life of Mammals*	BBC	2002	London.
1a. Attenborough, D.	*Trials of Life*	Little Brown & Co.		Canada.
2. Bleek, W.	*Bushmen Folklore*	Africa	1929	London.
3. Boaz, N.	*Eco Homo*	Basic Books	1997	New York.
4. Brinson, P.	*Anthropology & Study of Dance*	University Press	1985	Cambridge
5. Bronowski, J.	*The Ascent of Man,*	BBC	1976	London.
6. Capps, B.	*Native Americans*	Time Life Books	1995	USA.
6a. Catlln, G.	*Illus. of the Manners of N. Amerindians*		1876	London
7. Castleden, R.	*World History*	JG Press	1996	USA.
7a. Fage, J.	*History of Africa*	A. Knopf Publ.	1978	New York.
8. Choney, D., & Seyfarth, R. M.	*How Monkeys See the World*	Univ. Press	1990	Chicago
9. Darwin, C.	*Origin of Species the Descent of Man*	Univ. Press	1859	Oxford.
10. Greenwood, J/. Stini, W. A.	*Nature, Culture & Human History*	Harper/Row Publ.	1977	New York
10a. Hahn, C.	*The Native Tribes of S/W Africa*	Harper/Row Publ.	1966	New York
11. Hanna, J.	*Dance is Human (non-verbal comm).*			
12. Johanson, D/ Shreeve, J.	*Lusy-Child*	W. Morrow & Co.	1989	New York.
13. Johanson, D/ Edgar B.	*From Lusy to Language*	Cassel & Co.		London
14. Johanson, D./ Ligabue C	*Ecce Homo*	Electa	1999	Milan,
15. Jolly, A.	*The Evolution of Primate Behavior*	McMillan	1972	New York.
16. Kenedy, M.	*The History of Archaeology*	Prospero Books	2001	U.K.
17. King, J.	*First Peoples: First Contacts*	British Museum	1991	London.
18. Könemann, D.	*Gwion Gwion* (Aust)	Mond Media	2000	Köln.
19. Kosinowski, Z.	*The Clock of Centuries*	Osmojbe	1997	Moscow.
20. Kunen, M.	*The Ancestors and the Sacred Mountain*	Heineman	1982	London.
21. Leakey, R.	*The Making of Mankind*	Rainbird Publishers	1981	New York.
22. Loy, J./ Campbell, B	*Humankind Emerging*	Harper C. College	1996	New York.
23. Murdock, G.	*Africa: Its Peoples & Their Culture History*	McGraw Hill	1959	New York
24. O'Neill, R.	*Early No Drama*	Lund Humphries	1958	London.
25. Skoyel, J./ Sagon, D.	*Up From Dragons*	McGraw-Hill	2002	USA.
26. Smirnizki, E.	*Genesis of Things*	HHH	1995	Moscow.
27. Spenser, B./ Gillen, F.	*The Native Tribes of Central Australia*		1938	London.
28. Stchechner, R.	*Between Theatre & Anthropology*	Univ.of Penn. Press	1985	USA.
29. Stow, G.	*The Native Races of South Africa*		1905	London.
30. Wendt, H.	*From Ape to Adam*	Bobbs Merrrill Co.	1972	New York.
31. Wormington, H.	*Prehistoric Indians of the South West*		1947	Denver

BODY MOTION and its FACILITIES

1. Adrian, M./ Cooper, J.	*Biomechanics of Human Movement*	Benchmark Press	1994	Indianapolis.
2. Basmajian, J./ C.Deluca	*Muscles Alive*	Williams & Wilkins	1985	Baltimore.
3. Birdwhistell, R.	*Kinesics and Context*	Univ. Press	1970	Phil, Penns.
4. Blacking, J.	*Anthropology of the Body*	Academia Press	1977	London.
5. Broer, M.	*Efficiency of Human Movement*	W. Saunders	1979	Philadelphia.
6. Counsilman, J.	*The Science of Swimming*	Prentice Hall	1968	Englewood Cliffs, N.J.
7. Diamond, J.	*Behavioral Kinesiology*	Harper & Row	1979	New York.
8. Duvall, E.	*Kinesiology: The Anatomy of Motion*	Prentice Hall	1959	Englewood Cliffs, N.J.
9. Fit, S.	*Dance Kinesiology*	Shirmer Books	1996	New York.
10. Flint, T.	*Dynamics of the Human Form*	Arcturus	2003	Toronto.
11. Forster, E.	*Movement of Animals*		1968	Cambridge, Ila.
12. Frankel, V.	*Basic Biomechanics of the Skeletal System*	Lea & Febiger	1980	Philadelphia
13. Germain, B.	*Anatomy of Movement*	Eastland Press	1993	Seattle.
14. Gowitzke, B.	*Scientific Bases of Human Movement*	Williams & Wilkins	1988	Baltimore.
15. Granit, R.	*The Basis of Motor Control*	Academic Press	1979	New York.
16. Granit, R.	*Reflexive Control of Postures & Movement*	Holland Biomed Press	1979	New York
17. Hollinshead, W.	*Functional Anatomy of Limbs & Back*	Saunders	1976	Philadelphia.
18. Huber, E.	*Evolution of Facial Musculature & Expression*	Hopkins Press	1931	Baltimore
19. Ivamtzki, M.	*Plastic Anatomy Arts of Man*		1955	Moscow.
20. Kennedy, P.	*The Moving Body*	Faber & Faber	1985	London.
21. Kern, S.	*Anatomy & Destiny of the Human Body*	Bobbs Merrill	1975	New York.
22. Luce, G.	*Body Time: The Natural Rhythm of the Body*	Paladin	1973	
23. Luttgens, K./ Hamilton, N.	*Kinesiology*	Brown Banchmark	1997	USA.
24. Morton, D. /. Fuller, *D*	*Human Locomotion & Body Form*	Williams & Wilkins	1952	Baltimore.
25. Nordin, M.	*Basic Biomechanics & Musculoskeletal System*	Lea & Febiger	1989	Philadelphia.
26. Norkin, C.	*Joint Structure & Function*	A. Devis Co.	1986	Philadelphia.
27. Rose, J. / Gamble, J.	*Human Walking*	Williams & Wilkins	1994	Baltimore.
28. Ruch, T.	*Physiology & Biophysics*	W. Saunders	1979	Philadelphia.
29. Smidt, R.	*Motor Learning Human Kinetics*		1991	USA.

30. Steindler, A.	*Kinesiology of the Human Body*	C. Thomas	1970	Springfield, Illinois
31. Todd, M.	*The Thinking Body*	Dance Horizons	1968	New York.
32. Wirhead, R.	*Athletic Ability & Anatomy of Motion*	Harpoon	1982	Sweden.
33. Woolacott, M.	*Development of Posture & Gait*	Univ. of S. Car. Press	1989	Columbia, SC.

COMMUNICATION

1. Argyle, M.	*Bodily Communication*	Methuen & Co.	1975	Guildford.
1a. Bauml, B.	*Dictionary of Gestures*	Scarecrow Press	1975	New Jersey.
2. Brown, C.	*Art of Sign-Language*	PRC Publishers	2002	London.
3. Brun, T.	*The International Wolfe Dictionary of Sign Language*		1969	London.
4. Buck, R.	*The Communication of Emotion*		1984	New York.
5. Bull, P.	*Bodily Movement. & Interpersonal Comm*	Witley	1983	Chichester.
5 a. Bull, P.	*Posture and Gesture*	Pergamon	1987	Oxford.
5b. Burgoon, J/. Sain, T	*The Unspoken Dialogue*	Houghton	1978	Boston.
6. Cooper, J.	*Encyclopedia of Symbols.*	Thames & Hudson	1978	London
7. Darwin, C.	*The Expression of Emotions in Man & Animals*	Univ. Press	1965	Chicago
8. Dupbar, F.	*Emotion & Bodily Changes*	Col. Univ.Press	1954	New York.
9. Efron, D.	*Gesture & Environment*	King's Crown	1941	New York.
10. Ekman, P.	*Emotion in the Human Face*	Pergamon	1972	New York.
11. Fast, J.	*Body Language*	M. Evans	1970	New York.
12. Guedj, D.	*Universal Hieroglyphy*	Callimard	1996	NewYork.
13. Hinde, R.	*Non-Verbal Communication*	Universal Press	1972	Cambridge.
14. Hann, J.	*The Performer /Audience Connection*	Univ. Tex. Press.	1983	Austin.
14a. Hugs, R.	*Gesture Language of the Hindu Dance*	Univ.Tex. Press	1941	New York.
15. Jorio, A.	*Gesture in Napales*	A. Kendon	2000	Indiana
16. Jung, C.	*Man & His Symbols*	Jupiter Books	1974	London.
17. Lamb, W.	*Body Code*	Princeton Book	1979	New Jersey.
18. Mallery, G.	*Sign Language Amerindian*	Dover Publishers	2001	USA.
18a. Morris, D.	*The Naked Ape*	Cape	1967	London.
19. Morris., D.	*Intimate Behavior*	Cape	1971	London.
20. Narayanaswani, B.	*The Fundamentals of Ancient Hindu Dancing*	Munshiraw	1980	New Delhi
20a. North, M.	*Personality Assessment Through Movement*		1972	London.
21. Kao, R.	*Dictionary of Bharata Natya*	Oneut Longman	1988	USA.
22. Towkins, W.	*Indian Sign Language*	Dover Publishing	1969	Toronto.
22a. Vansina, J.	*Body, the Ultimate Symbol*	Lippincot	1979	New York.
23. Von-Cranach, M.	*The Perception of Looking Behavior*	Academic Press	1973	London.

24. Von-Frisch, K.	*Dance Language & Orientation of Bees*	Harvard Univ. Press	1967	Cambridge, Mass.
25. Wainwright, G.	*Body Language*	Hodder Headline	1985	London.
26. Watson, O.	*Proxemic Behavior*	Hague Mouton	1970	London.
27. Wund, W.	*The Language of. Gestures*	Mouton	1973	Paris. Mass.USA.
28. Wolf, C.	*"A Psychology of Gesture"*	Arno Press	1972	New York.

SPIRITUAL CULTS

1. Beckwith, C./ Fisher, A.	*African Ceremonies*	H. Abrams	2002	New York.
1a. Blacker, C.	*The Catalpa Bow (Japan Shamanism)*	Allen & Unwin	1975	London.
2. Castaneda, C.	*Magical Passes*	Lavgan Productions	1997	Mexico.
2a. Cristie, A.	*Chinese Mythology*	Chanceller Press	1968	London.
3. Drury, N.	*Dictionary of Mysticism and the Occult*	Harper & Roul	1985	San Francisco.
4. Drury, N.	*Shamanism*	Element Books	1989	Boston.
5. Drury, N./ Tillet, G	*Occult*	Barnes & Nobel .	1997	New York
6. Folley, T.	*The Book of the Sun*	Quarto	1997	London.
7. Folley, T.	*The Book of the Moon*	Quarto	1997	London.
7a. Frazer, J.	*Totemism and Exogamy*		1910	London.
8. Germand, P.	*An Egyptian Bestiary*	Thawes & Hudson	2001	London.
9. Gimbutas, M.	*The Goddesses & Codes of Old Europe*	Thawse&Hudson	1996	London
10. Greenbell, B.	*The Transformation Energy*	Sophie	1996	Kiev.
10a. Harrison, P.	*Totem Voices*	Grove Press	1990	New York.
11. Harnet, M.	*The Way of the Shaman*	Bautom Books	1982	New York.
11a. Jong, E.	*Witches*	Abradale Press	1999	New York.
12. Kunen, M.	*The Ancestors & Sacred Mountain*	Heineman	1982	London
12a. Lanier, G.	Goddesses in Art	Abbevill Publishers	1997	New York.
13. La Fonteine	*The Interpretation* of Ritual	Tavistock Publishing	1972	London.
14. Scott, G	*Phallic Worhsip*	Luxor Press	1966	London.
14.a Mbiti, J.	*Introduction to African Religion* Books	Heineman Edue	1975	Portsmouth
15. McKenzie	*Mythologies of the World*	Prod. R. Johnson	2001	New York.
16. Merleau-Ponti, M.	*Phenomenology of Perception*	Routeledge & Kegan	1962	London.
17. Scott, G.	*Phallic Worship*	Luxor Press	1966	London.
18. Smith, G	*Secret Museums of Mankind*	Gibbs Smith Publ.	1999	USA.
19. Spoucer, J.A.	*Mystical & Sacred Sites*	Headline Book Publ.	2002	London.
20. Tinbergen, N.	*The Study of Instinct*	Oxford Univ. Press	1951	London.
21. Tomkins, S.	*Alter Imagery & Consciousness 2 vols.*	Springer	1962	New York
22. Wallis Budge, E.	*Egyptian Magic*	Dover Publishing	1971	New York.
23. Wosien, M.G.	*Sacred Dance*	Thames & Hudson	1992	New York.
24. Zahan, D.	*Religion, Spirituality in Africa*	Univ. Press	1979	Chicago.

382

MIME AND DRAMA

1. Alardyce, N.	*Masks, Mimes & Miracles*	Coope Square	1963	New York.
2. Basso, E.	*Ralapalo Myth & Ritual Performance*	Univ. Press	1985	Philadelphia.
3. Beckerman, B.	*Dynamics of Drama*	A. Knopf	1970	New York.
4. Broadbent, R.	*A History of Pantomime*	B. Blom	1901	New York.
5. Bowers, F.	*Japanese Theatre*	Rutland, Charlar	1977	Tokyo.
6. Chauawe, R.	*Histoire des Marionettes*		1972	Paris.
7. Cormford, McDonald	*The Origin of Attic Comedy*	Doubleday	1961	New York.
8. Dorcy, J.	*The Mime*	Speller & Sons	1961	New York.
9 Epstein, A.	*Mime Theatre of E. Decroux*	Cristalis	1958	Paris.
10. Fekner, M.	*Apostols of Silence*	Univ. Press	1985	Rutherford, N.J.
11. Fabre, G.	*Drumbeats, Masks & Metaphor*	Mass. Univ. Press	1983	Cambridge.
12. Gippi, S.	*Emotion Exercises Psychotechnics*	Art	1967	Moscow
13. Goran, S.	*Mimesis and Art*	Univ. Press	1966	Stockholm.
14. Hawblin, K.	*Mime*	Headlands Press	1978	San Francisco.
14a. Karp, P.	*Ballet and Drama*	Art	1980	Leningrad.
15. Kipnis, C.	*The Mime Book*	Harper & Row	1974	New York.
16. Lecod, J.	*La Pedagogie du Mouvement (gest, mimes, acteurs)*		1987	Paris.
16a. Lorelle, Y.	*L'Expression Corporelle du Mime Sacre au Mime du Theatre*	Collections Dionysos	1974	Paris.
17. Lowler, L.	*Mime, Movement, Theatre*	St. Martin Press	1989	New York.
17a. Lowson, J.	*Mime Pitman and Sons*		1957	London.
18. O'Neill, R.	*Early Nodrama: background, character*	L. Hamphries	1958	London.
19. Pechnold, A.	*Mime, the Step Beyond Words*	NC Press	1989	Toronto.
20. Piaget, J.	*Plays, Dreams & Imitation in Children*		1973	London.
21. Rutberg, I.	*Pantomime, the First Experiments*	Soviet Russia	1972	Moscow.
22. Ridoway, W.	*Dramas & Dramatic Dances Tragedy*	Origin of Greek	1964	New York.
23. Shepard, R.	*Mime, the Technique of Silence*	Drama Books	1971	New York.
23a. Slawski, R.	*The Art of Pantomime Arts*		1962	Moscow.
24. Spolin, V.	*Improvisation for the Theatre*	Univ. Press	1963	Illinois,
24a. Taylor, D.	*The Greek & Roman Stage* Classical Press		1999	Bristol.
25. Towsen, J.	*Clowns*	Hawthorn Books	1976	New York
26. Wylie, K.	*Satiric & Heroic Mimes*	Univ. Press	1948	N. Caro.
27. Zoete, B.	*de Dance & Magic Drama in Ceylon*		*1975*	*London.*

DANCE AND MARTIAL ARTS

1. Acogny, G .	*African Dance*	Nourelles Ed. African	1980	Dakar, Senegal.
2. Blum, O.	*Dance in Ghana*	Dance Perspective 56	1973	New York.
3. Boas, F.	*Function of Dance in Society*	Horis.	1972	Brooklyn
4. Bonnet, J.	*Histoire General*	Chez d'Houry	1974	Paris.

de La Dance

5. Chujoy, A.	*Dance Encyclopedia*	Barns & Co.	1949	New York.
6. Darbois, D.	*African Dance*		1972	Prague.
7. D'Aronco, G	*Storia della Danza Popolare e d'Arte*	S. Olschki	1962	Firenze
8. Dean, B./Carell, V	*Dust for the Dancers*		1950	Sydney
9. Dean, B.	*The Many Worlds of Dance*		1966	Sydney
10. Dobrovolski, G.	*Dance, Pantomime, Ballet*	*Art*	1975	Leningrad.
11. Dunham, K.	*Dances in Haiti*	Univ. Cal. Press	1983	Los Angeles.
12. Fergusson, E.	*Dancing Gods* Univ. Press		1931	New Mexico.
13. Gdyle, A	*The Black Aesthetic*	Ancor Books	1972	New York.
14. Gorer, G.	*Africa Dances*	W. Norton& Co.	1962	New York.
15. Huet, M.	*Dance, Art & Ritual of Africa*	Pantheon Books	1978	New York.
16. Kinney, T.	*The Dance its Place in Art and Life*	Stocks	1924	New York.
17. Korolyova, E.	*Earlier Forms of Dance*	Shtinza	1977	Kishineu, Moldova.
18. Kubic, G.	*Dance, Art & Ritual of Africa.*	Random House	1978	New York
19. Kurath, G.P.	*Dance, Folk and Primitive*	Funk & Wagnalls	1949	New York.
20. Kurath, G./ S. Maiti,	*Dance of Anahuac.*	Aldine	1964	Chicago
21. La Meri	*Total Education in Ethnic Dance*	Marcel Dekker Books	1977	New York.
22. Laubin, R & G.	*Indian Dances of N. America*	Univ. Oklah. Press	1977	USA.
23. Longdale, S.	*Animals & Origin of Dance*	Thawes & Hudson	1981	London.
24. Louis, M.	*Le Foklore et La Danse*	G.P. Maisonneuve & Larose	1963	Paris.
25. Lawler, L	*The Dance in Ancient Greece*	Univ. Wash. Press	1964	Seattle.
26. Laws, K.	*The Physics of Dance*	Schirmer Books	1984	New York.
27. Mensah, A.	*Music and Dance in Zambia*	Ministry of Culture	1971	Lusaka.
28. Mooney, J.	*The Ghost –Dance Religion*	Univ. Press	1965	Chicago.
29. Pern, S.	*Masked Dancers of W. Africa: the*	Time Life Books Dogon	1982	Amsterdam.
30. Pantchenco, G.	*History of Martial Arts-2 volumes*		1997	Moscow.
31. Peterson, A.	*The Anthropology of Dance*	Indiana Univ. Press	1977	USA.
32. Rust, F.	*Dance in Society*	Routledge & Kegan	1969	London.
33. Sachs, C.	*The World History of Dance*	Norton	1937	New York
34. Smith, J.	*Dance Composition*	Lepus Books	1976	London.
35. Thowson, R.F.	*African Art in Motion*	Univ. Ca. Press	1986	Berkley.
36. Warren, L.	*The Dance of Africa*	Prentice Hall	1972	New York.
37. Welsh Asante, K.	*African Dance*	Africa World Press	1994	Trenton N.J.
38. Welsh Asante, K.	*Zimbabwe Dance*	Africa World Press	2000	Trenton, N.J.

MUSIC AND INSTRUMENTS

1. Basso, E.	*Musical View of the Universe*	Univ. Penn. Press	1985	Philadelphia.
2. Blackwood, A.	*Music of the World*	Quatro Publ.	1991	New Jersey.
3. Chernoff, J.	*African Rhythm & Sensibility*	Univ. Press	1979	Chicago.
4. Council	*Musical Instruments*	Horniman Museum	1977	London.
5. Dealling, R.	*Ultimate Encyclopedia Musical Instruments*	Carlton Books	1996	London.
6. Dean & Carroll	*Softly Wild Drums*		1958	Sydney.
7. Dutoit, C.L.	Music, Movement, Therapy	Daleroze Books	1971	London.
8. Holst, I.	*An ABC of Music*	Univ. Press Oxford	1963	London

9. Jackson, I.	*More than Drumming*	Greenwood Press	1985	Westport.
10. Oxford	*Concise Dictionary of Music*	Univ. Press	1975	London.
11. Paklen, K.	*Music of the World History*	Crown Publ.		New York.
12. Rouget, G.	*La Music de La Trause*	Gallimard	1980	Paris.

VISUAL ARTS

1. Bacon, F.	*Body Art*	Autback Print	2000	Australia.
2. Bahn, P.	*Images of the Ice Age*	Weidenfeld & Nicolson	1997	London.
3. Bahn. P.	*Prehistoric Art*	Univ. Press	1998	Cambridge.
4. Biebuyck, D.	*Tradition & Creativity in Tribal Art*	Univ. Press	1969	Berkeley
5. Brodrich, A.	*Prehistoric Painting*		1948	London.
6. Coulson, D.	*African Rock Art*	H.N. Abrams Inc.	2000	New York.
7. Gimbutas, M.	*Civilisation of the Goddess*	H. Collins	1991	San Francisco.
8. Gröning, K.	*Decorated Skin*	Thawes & Hudson	1997	London.
9. Kozlowski, J.	*L'Art de la Prehistoire*	Jaca Books	1992	Milano.
10. Layton, R.	*Australian Rock Art*	Univ. Press	1992	Cambridge.
11. Leakey, M.	*Africa's Vanishing Art*	Doubleday	1983	New York.
12. Meyer, A.	*Oceanic Art*	Könemann	1995	Köln
13. Mountford, C.	*The Artist in Tribal Society*		1961	London.
14. Mountford, C.	*Paintures Aboigienes d'Australie*		1964	Unesco.
15. Reed, H.	*Artist in the Tribal Society*		1961	London.
16. Singh, M.	*Himalayan Art*	MacMillan	1971	London.
17. Tilley, C.	*Material Culture as Test.*	Routledge	1991	London.
18. Turpin, S.	*Shamanism & Rock Art in Rock Art*	Fndn. Inc.	1994	San Antonio.
19. Walsh, C.	*Australia's Greatest Rock Art*	Brill & Co.	1988	Batharst.
20. White, R.	*Prehistoire*	Sud Ouest	1993	Bordeaux.
21. Willcox, A.	*The Rock Art of Africa*	Holms & Meier	1984	New York.

Index

CPSIA information can be obtained
at www.ICGtesting.com
Printed in the USA
BVHW010152110122
625973BV00013B/588